From Buckets To Billionaires
Volume 2

A journey through the life and times of Queens Park Rangers FC from 1996 to 2001, as seen through the pages of In The Loft fanzine.

Edited by Howard Prosser
With additional selected material from hundreds of readers

First published in 2010

© IN THE LOFT

For further details on ordering further copies of this book and information on Volumes 1 & 3, please visit www.intheloft.net or e-mail editor@intheloft.net.

Printed and bound in the UK by the MPG Books Group, Bodmin and King's Lynn.

ISBN 978-0-95606-13-1-7
British Library Cataloguing-in-Publication Data
A catalogue record for this book is available from the British Library

Acknowledgements
To everyone who has bought, written for and sold In The Loft, this book would not have been possible.

Cover story
Iain Dowie and Gerry Francis celebrate the 6-0 thrashing of Crystal Palace in May 1999, ensuring QPR remained in Division 1.

For dad

Contents

Foreword

My first contribution for In the Loft was not even published under my name. Instead I chose to hide behind a cunning alter ego – Tonni Sandy (an ingenious anagram of our own Andy Sinton), forced upon me after an article published by my old man received a fair bit of stick. The editor did eventually suss me out after my hand writing (a dying art) in later articles — in my own name — gave the game away. He once asked if I realised it was an anagram of Andy Sinton, or was it a fluke? Come on Howard here we are now many years on – what so you think? (Fluke! – Ed).

I was once what you may call an obsessive. From January 1987 through to the end of the 2005/6 season (when my season ticket jumped up 30%) I missed only one QPR home game and went to countless away matches. Examples of this include my parents arranging their respective marriages after seeing the fixtures so as not to clash with a home match, turning down Kate Moss for a date because QPR were at home to Stockport in the evening and myself and the Ed leaving a night club in Amsterdam at 5am on a Saturday morning because we had to get back to see the R's at home to Grimsby. Obsessive? Some may argue insufferable prick.

As an aside only two out of those three examples are actually true — I'll leave you to decide which one is a fabrication.

As well as reminiscing over the days in the top flight, a look through the first volume also bought back a lot of my own personal memories that I had chronicled in the fanzine that have become clouded over the years. Examples include the giraffe that I first spotted in Corfu that proceeded to follow me and stalk me back in England, raising my hopes of a great season ahead following a vivid dream sequence on the hallowed turf; the evil spirit who terrorised me in my own bedroom the night after we trashed Liverpool away and put a curse on me that made me miss every great away game; and I also remembered how I survived an attack by a vicious pack of piranhas in the river Thames — I had a shirt on saying 'QPR for Europe' and nobody could swallow that. It was also me who exposed certain clubs looking to introduce genetic engineering to clone players and save on transfer fees.

Andy Ward wrote the last forward and his articles were on the whole always positive. So here I am writing this — arguably the complete opposite. The First Division gave miserable gits like me the opportunity to vent our frustrations on paper and looking through this volume will confirm this but I think I came into my own as a fanzine journalist in those miserable years, although I did go a bit quoting crazy. However that was the great thing about fanzines back in the day. They gave a voice to anyone who cared to bother.

This volume, as the last, ends with a relegation season, sob. 2001 saw the arrival of Ian Holloway as manager and the despair that we all felt dropping another division would be blown away over the following three campaigns. Many fans, me included, who have seen Rangers play in the top flight, will remember these seasons as some of their happiest ever but that is for another chapter altogether...

Matthew Holley

Introduction

It's not ideal to kick off a new book with some apologies, but unfortunately there is a need for a couple. Having put hundreds of hours into producing Volume 1, when I received the book back from the printers I was aghast at the finished product. Firstly, the cover looked nothing like it should. The fonts had reverted to default as I did not embed them in the saved pdf file — my fault but something I was disappointed the printers did not pick up on as the proof copy was printed exactly as it should have been. The insides of that final proof copy contained many errors that I corrected, and finally it was ready to go to print.

After first being horrified at the basic look of the cover, I then discovered the original proof copy had been the one used to print from, not the final updated copy. Ideally the volume should have been reprinted, but with deadlines to meet from stockists, I accepted a discount on the print bill and decided to go with it. If you were disappointed with your purchase, there are valid reasons — my editorial skills have improved with age, honest!

The discount in the print bill has been passed onto this volume, and understandably new printers have been sought to make sure the same mistakes won't be repeated.

My second apology comes with the late arrival of this, Volume 2. 2009 just flew by and I simply did not have the time to devote to it. Having finally started worked on it earlier this year, I soon realised the amount of material available compared to Volume 1 yielded further issues. Whereas contributors used to pen articles by hand, the speed of using word processors and e-mail now meant issues were containing longer articles. To have crammed everything from 1996 up until the present would have meant a 600-700 page volume, anything smaller would not have done justice to each passing season, and to those contributors regularly chipping in with 2,000 to 3,000 word articles every issue. So, gulp... there will be a third volume — *hopefully* to appear in 2011 — continuing from where this leaves off in 2001.

With In The Loft entering the computer generation in the mid-1990s, many issues remain on disk so the need to scan and re-type stuff has lessened, helping speed up the production of Volume 2. In the case of front covers and original graphics, reproductions have been done direct from PC to the print read file, and so are brought to you with greater clarity than originally presented in issue form — digitally enhanced as

The original cover of issue # 130

8

they say in the movie industry. I also came across material that never made it to print, and the odd front cover that never materialised.

Unfortunately, the boxes of hard-copy that made up the first 125 issues or so, and every single hand-written letter and article received, were purged when I moved house a few years ago. This included a couple of hand-drawn cartoons by a young Pete Doherty, which would probably be worth a few bob these days!

I'm often asked if I would ever bring back In The Loft. It's very doubtful, I think I stopped at just about the right time. The last five years would have been quite hellish to write about, and sales would probably not made it worthwhile anyway. The internet has consigned most fanzines to the history books, indeed all printed matter are fighting against the giant. At least 'A Kick Up The R's' is still going, and I hope it will for a long time yet.

As editor, I always tried to find some middle ground each issue, balancing fact from fiction, truth from reality. Sometimes I felt I got it spot on, other times not so much. Examples being my prediction the likes of Les Ferdinand, David Bardsley, Trevor Sinclair and Peter Crouch would play for England. I said the same about Kevin Gallen, Nigel Quashie and Paul Murray, and I couldn't have been wider of the mark! Indeed, only last season I thought QPR would get promoted after the 4-2 win at Derby, only for the season to capitulate thereafter. Glad I wasn't able to put that one in print…

So, onto Volume 2. Whereas Volume 1 of 'From Buckets To Billionaires' concentrated on happier times for QPR, Volume 2 covers some much darker days for the club. In truth, 'Buckets' and 'Billionaires' had very little relevance in Volume 1, but it laid the foundations for what was to come following relegation from the Premiership in 1996. The following 300+ pages paint the bigger picture, but to start with I thought I would try to analyse how and where things started to go wrong before the billionaires came to the 'rescue'.

Hindsight is a great thing. Fans often reflect on the Thompson era as one of selling off our best players, seemingly lining his own pocket at the expense of the team. It's difficult to accept this was the case. Thompson claimed to have never taken a penny out of the club, saying that the books needed to be balanced as revenue from all other aspects was not enough to cover expenditure.

The club often reported losses of approximately £1m per year before transfer money could be taken into consideration. During Thompson's reign transfer fees show a £7.2m profit — £21.9m worth of players sold, £14.7m bought. Calculate the profit over the number of years Thompson was in control and you begin to understand how the club remained a profitable outfit. Perhaps we should have been grateful that we had so many profitable assets as without them the grim financial days of the late 1990s and 2000s may have been with us much earlier.

Whether or not Thompson had access to his family's millions to invest in the club is open to debate, but the fact remains Thompson took over in 1989 with the club in profit, and left it that way in 1996. Investment in the side would have been great in 1993 to push on from 5th place in the Premiership, though any hope of actually competing for the title was never a realistic proposition — 21 points short in 1992/93 showed the enormous gulf in quality that was simply beyond a club like QPR to bridge. Perhaps a salient point, in 1983/84 when QPR ended 5th, the club were only 7 points off the champions Liverpool yet I don't recall criticism of Jim Gregory's failure to invest further in the side. Instead he sold our top scorer to Tottenham.

I'm not necessarily trying to defend Richard Thompson, just trying to put down how the club was run financially under him. It's a pity that so many fans were unable to fully enjoy the days of the early 1990s, and I'm not exempt from that. It's only when you look at how far the club has fallen since then, that you can fully appreciate what we once had. The stats show QPR were run very efficiently under Thompson — hardly any club can claim that in this day and age, and something Chris Wright failed to maintain when he bought the club in 1996. Despite relegation — which was all to do with Ray Wilkins and not Thompson — it was a time to see how a new man at the helm would do things differently.

Everyone was happy enough when Wright took over. A QPR fan and fairly rich, investment in the side soon arrived. Millions were spent — most of which came from his own pocket in an attempt to get the club back in the Premiership. Under the right management it could have worked as the quality on the pitch was there. Those first two seasons in Division 1 really put us on the road to ruin; had promotion been achieved who knows how the future would have unfolded. Two disastrous years into Wright's reign and the pot was dry.

Whether Wright was unable or unwilling to invest further, who knows, but it was time to recoup. In the twelve months between January 1998 and January 1999, £8m worth of players were sold, but it still wasn't enough. The sale of Wasps' training ground for £8.5m was soon swallowed up. By the turn of the century the club was losing half a million pounds a month and debts totalled over £10m — the majority of which was to Wright, and administration was to follow a year later. The squad was high on numbers but low on quality, relegation could not be avoided. The only sellable assets were Peter Crouch and Jermaine Darlington — it would be another three years before the club raised a single penny in transfer fees. Amazingly, until the takeover by the 'billionaires' in September 2007, QPR spent just £2.7m on transfers in the whole of the 2000s — less than the £3.25m spent in the 1970s, three decades earlier.

In his five years as chairman, Wright spent just short of £10m on players, and raised £11.2m in outgoing transfers. Compare this small profit to that of the Thompson era and it's little wonder the club were on the road to going out of business. Matters weren't helped with the lack of Premiership money and ITV Sport going bust —

everything was going against Wright, but had he picked the right manager when Wilkins departed things could have been very different.

Wright eventually had to write off some of his debts, and with the aid of a crippling £10m loan, QPR finally came out of administration in May 2002 with Nick Blackburn appointed chairman. Some stability had been established, but financially the club was still on its knees until Briatore & Co arrived.

It's easy to blame chairmen for the demise of QPR, but if I were to pinpoint a defining moment to set things in motion it would have to be the sale of Les Ferdinand. Had he been effectively replaced and QPR remained in the Premiership, we could still be there to this very day — probably still moaning about Richard Thompson. ...but then I'd have been needing a different title for these books. You need no reminding how Wilkins wasted Ferdinand's transfer fee — if only we could turn back time.

In the two years since Volume 1 of From Buckets To Billionaires was published you'd have told me the club would be in a worse position on the pitch by the end of the 2009/10 season, my jaw would have dropped. The 2009/10 season was simply the most embarrassing in our history, quite how we have managed to retain our fan base is a credit to those that kept the faith. I guess as QPR fans we've learned to expect the unexpected but what we shouldn't expect to lose is our identity. Hopefully under Ishan Saksena and Neil Warnock that will start to come back after Flavio Briatore tried his best to tear it all apart.

The 2010/11 season really does feel like a 'make or break' season in many aspects. There's only so much a fan can take. By no means is that a demand for promotion — just some positive signs that we're heading in the right direction and stability is returning at all levels. As long as we have a real football club to support — not one that alienates its fans and messes with its heritage — trips to Loftus Road should always be looked forward to. The Premiership will always be there when we're good and ready for it.

Judging by the opening weeks of the 2010/11 season, maybe, just maybe, the time may soon be with us when the top flight is represented by QPR again. This is our 11th season at this level since departing the Premiership, and not once have we ever maintained a push for promotion — half the time we've been battling against relegation. Even the law of averages would suggest QPR should have made the play-offs at least once. It's been fifteen years since QPR stood side-by-side the best teams in the land, the majority of which have been highly forgettable. A resurrection under Ian Holloway for three or four years has been all we've had to rave about in recent times. You can read all about that and more in Volume 3, and until then, enjoy the read.

Howard Prosser
Editor, In The Loft – 1988 - 2006

Chapter 1

1996/97

Chris Wright – our saviour?

Despite relegation from the Premiership, there was a feeling of great optimism on the opening day of the 1996/97 season as Oxford United rode into town. Lifelong fan Chris Wright was on the verge on a £14m takeover of the club, and with all key players retained, coupled with the expected investment into the squad that Richard Thompson was unable to produce, a return to the top flight at the first time of asking appeared a sure thing. Fourteen years later and we still haven't come close. You wouldn't have found a single QPR fan back then that would have predicted such a future, yet within three weeks of the season starting the seeds had been sown that would help map out our fate.

Kevin Gallen was crocked just two games in and would miss the rest of the season, then Ray Wilkins departed by mutual consent — the real reasons behind are still shrouded in mystery. Looking back at events in that first week of September, I can only conclude that, at his first board meeting with Chris Wright, Wilkins was told to bring his playing days to an end, but nothing more sinister. This is something Wilkins was probably picking up vibes from throughout the pre-season. Having had a couple of days to ponder his fate, Wilkins allegedly received a call from a member of the board telling him in no uncertain terms to quit playing or resign, and so his hand was forced. Maybe one day we'll know the truth.

Wilkins had started all of QPR's opening four games, and despite 7 points from 12, he along with the rest of the team hadn't been convincing. The board felt something had to give, and it had to be Wilkins. The whole matter should have been dealt with more professionally, but I guess that's something we've had to get used to. Wilkins couldn't get the playing bug out of his system and went on to play for a number of lower league clubs, whilst Chris Wright eventually decided that Stewart Houston was the man to take QPR back to the promised land. Oddly, Houston soon brought in Bruce Ricoh as his assistant, thus reversing their roles once held at Arsenal.

Houston was given millions to spend and how badly we needed it, pity it took so long before he finally added to a depleted and inexperienced squad. It was three months before replacements for Wilkins and — more importantly — Gallen, were signed. Gavin Peacock and John Spencer proved to be immediate hits and had the pair arrived a great deal earlier, the play-offs at the very least would have been a formality. 5 wins from 19 matches prior to their arrival meant the season could not be rescued.

December and January were great months, producing some memorable victories, stunning goals and extraordinary comebacks (well, just the one). That point at Port Vale proved to be just one of four from the next 24 available. A revival late on pushed us to touching distance of the play-offs but in the end we run out of games. A typical no-show at Bradford brought the season to a close, one of a number of simply unacceptable performances throughout a season of contrasting highs and lows. Whilst the Bantams celebrated staying up, the jury was still out on Houston & Co. ❑

Que Sera Sera

So against West Ham, the inevitable finally happened. After 13 seasons, Queens Park Rangers were no longer a top-flight football club.

Conclusive proof that QPR employs certain individuals with warped minds came at the end of the game. After the team left the pitch following a lap of honour (or shame, if you're cynical), some idiot decided to play 'Que Sera Sera' over the PA system, as sung by Doris Day. Now bearing in mind we had to put up with West Ham fans chanting 'You're going to End-ers-leigh' to the same tune, the choice of record was poor to say the least.

Now I'm sure many Rangers supporters will look back at various matches, and recall wasted opportunities and points that were thrown away. I can certainly think of a few games like that. But if I had to point an accusing finger at where things went wrong, I'd do so with the woeful performance that saw QPR lose 2-0 at Southampton. Personally, I believe that a lot of team spirit went out of the window that day, never to be recovered all season. I know I wasn't the only Rangers supporter who left the Dell that day thinking this side would be in trouble if it didn't buck up its ideas. But that's just my opinion.

Trying to be positive, it has to be pointed out that its important that Rangers respond well to what has happened and get a good start when the new season begins. Otherwise, like 95/96, a rot could set in. And in the Nationwide League First Division, excuses won't be so acceptable.
(Raymond Eaton – issue # 100)

Relegation Blues

If you know your history, an interesting, some even may say worrying trend is beginning to emerge. The following seasons — 1975/76, 1985/86 and 1995/96 — all seasons ending in a 6 (in case you didn't notice) and seasons which promised much but ultimately failed to deliver and ended in disappointment. A heartbreaking and cruel end to a Championship challenge in 1975/76. Complete humiliation and abject misery at Wembley in 1986 (even though I was there I still maintain that I've yet to see the R's play at Wembley) and now this miserable piss poor excuse for a campaign that I've just had the misfortune to witness. What delights, I wonder, will season 2005/6 have in store for us?

It was a season that started badly and got worse. The soppy optimism and childish outlook on view in the excruciatingly crap programme however continued all season and, just like the teams' form, got beyond a joke. 'What a season we've had' the editorial in the West Ham programme read. Hmmm.

Anyhow one thing that the programme — which surely no-one buys for any reason other than to add to the collection — did achieve, apart from make us a bigger laughing stock than we already were, was to seemingly rub its ridiculously sad and optimistic outlook onto a fair percentage of QPR fans.

Take the night that Mark Hateley was paraded in front of us before the Spurs match for instance. You would seriously have thought that Rangers had signed a superstar judging by the rapturous and enthusiastic reception he received. That's when you know you're in the shit when a 34-year-old has-been, well past his sell by date and not yet fit enough to play for a good few weeks, is seen as a saviour.

However, when talking about sequences, in many ways the latest campaign could be viewed as not being typical, i.e. relegation was promised and delivered. Nuff respect (you can tell I'm from sarf London) to Ray and the boys. What with his intelligent inspiring transfer dealings and the teams' wonderful fighting qualities forever epitomising a never-say-die attitude, at least now, unlike the aforementioned seasons, Queens Park Rangers FC can no longer be referred to as a 'nearly team'.

Regular readers of my columns (hello mum) will probably now be expecting an article littered with abuse and criticism of the team. You will however be a trifle disappointed. In fact yours truly is not in the slightest bit bitter or angry. In fact I firmly believe that the spineless, useless, overpaid tosspots deserved every minute of the standing ovation that they were afforded at the end of the West Ham match.

Not that I participated of course, or even stayed behind. I've always been told that it's disrespectful to make a noise at a funeral so I didn't. The journey home could not go quick enough for me but I did end up having a discussion with West Ham fans on the Central Line. I politely enquired of them how it's possible that a second rate 'mickey mouse' outfit such as West Ham can still be in the Premiership whereas our second rate 'mickey mouse' outfit is looking forward to entertaining the likes of Barnsley and Grimsby next season. The conversation remained constructive, albeit slightly heated at times but we did however conclude, before I alighted at Bond Street that it's probably mainly down to good management (hello Ray).

With Rangers lamentable form last season, I've taken to playing football on a friend's Playstation. Normally I find the prospect of playing video games as exciting as a night indoors listening to Leonard Cohen reading tourist guides to Manhattan and Berlin. However, I'm desperate following our relegation season. It may sound sad but when the real dramas played out at Loftus Road – 'The Theatre Of Dreams', have done so little to uplift you it can provide a certain amount of pleasure to select QPR on a computer game and steer them to victory.

The game itself is superb, featuring state of the art graphics, great gameplay and superb sound with John Motson providing the commentary. When selecting QPR you're given the 94/95 season's squad of players. Strangely enough Les Ferdinand is your star man and stands out head and shoulders above the rest. With his lightning pace, superb control and shooting power you've always got half a chance — even against better sides, if he's in the starting line up. In fact remove Les from the equation and you're left with a completely average squad... sob, these computer games get more realistic all the time.

Certain events have helped to lift the gloom and provide a chink of light in the dark curtain currently closed over Loftus Road. The Sunday following the West Ham match saw me retreat to a well-known watering hole in Greenwich. I didn't want to be with people who knew everything about football and considering this pub is frequented by a sizeable number of Millwall fans I feel I made a very good choice. Incidentally, I'm known in this pub as the 'Lone Ranger', not I hasten to add because I'm such a badass macho desperado but because I happen to be the only QPR fan they know.

"The Lone Ranger," a voice sounded upon entering the pub, "We'll be playing you next season ho ho ho." My reply — not as quick as Sinclair but definitely quick even by my sharp tongued standards – "Well my good man I wasn't aware that when we got relegated yesterday we dropped two divisions." The following Sunday, defeat at Ipswich saw Millwall plummet through the First Division trap door. Laugh? I thought I'd never stop.

So what of the R's chances of making a quick return to the Premiership this season? I suppose it largely depends on whether we can keep the same squad of players together and whether or not the rich promise displayed by the younger players, Quashie in particular, turns out to be not just promise. All eyes will undoubtedly be on Sinclair — will he stay or will he go? Apparently he's happy to stay and who can blame him, after all he'll have an opportunity to play at his true level this season.

Many Rangers fans, probably the same ones that actually read the programme, seem to think that promotion next season is as good as certain. My view? I've heard that you can get odds of 9-1 on the R's winning the title next season. Tempted? Well I was but I was however slightly under the influence at the time of seeing the odds and was seeing treble. 999-1 on Rangers to win the title seems like very fair and realistic odds to me.

There will be people who will find my attitude ever so slightly pessimistic but try to remember that this is QPR. Can anyone really imagine this team going to Grimsby for example, on a wet windy night and battling for important points?

I do of course seriously hope that I'm wrong. If come next May when we descend on Bradford as Nationwide League champions I will be perfectly happy not only to have

egg in my face but to be covered in the stuff, and believe you me if there's on thing that I can't stand in this world, it's smegging eggs.
(Matthew Holley – issue # 100)

It could have been oh so different...

Someone has said this before but it's the best way I can find of expressing this situation. It's like in the film 'Clockwise' where John Cleese is trying desperately to make an appointment. "It's not the despair," he gasps at one point. "It's the hope." I swear I was happier before the Sheffield Wednesday game when I just thought OK, we're going down. The same with the Man Utd game, no-one would have been anywhere near as upset if the second half had gone the way of the first and they'd stuck one or two chances in to win the game.

What actually happened was the biggest kick in the teeth I've experienced in eight seasons with QPR, people have said "these things happen in football," which they do, but very rarely on that scale. It was simply a nightmare and it doesn't surprise me at all that people were in tears, they must have been the few who could actually comprehend what was happening as everyone else was in shock. To put it slightly less philosophically, it didn't just suck. It really sucked.

And it had to be the most despised player in the most hated team in front of the most undeserving fans probably in history who applied the killing stroke. It could have been worse if it had been a dodgy penalty — but that's the only way. I thought I had said all that needed to be said a while back about Liverpool fans, and I have tried hard ever since to stay off the subject, but this lot bring the whole thing to new depths.

Man Utd are very quick to sing a little, not much but a little, in the middle of 10 straight wins, and very keen to give David Mellor and the world in general the benefit of their sophisticated 'United good, everything else bad' football analysis. But 1-0 down away from home when, just for once, their team needed something back off them, what do they produce? Nothing. I heard them twice in between the two goals, once to cry for a penalty and once to berate David May for not meeting their standards.

Still, it is worth considering what happened when they did score, with the benefit of TV of course as it was impossible to take anything in at the time. 200 miles from home, needing a point to go top, and getting it in the last attack right in front of their travelling(?) support, what would any other team have done — run over to the fans to share the moment, that's what. But United clearly just run back to the centre circle to high-five Cantona and applaud the ref. Their players aren't stupid, they know they can't diss the fans publicly (with the exception of Schmeichel who clearly is a bit thick), but they also know how bloody useless their 'supporters' are, and they showed it. Anyway, it would be nice to just dismiss this lot as the sad cases that they are, but it can't be done anymore.

The three squads of Manchester United, Liverpool and Newcastle cost an unbelievable 96 million pounds (documented fact, from 'The Times', 4/3/96). Naturally, these three dominate the league — and where did this money come from? I needn't go on, you can fill in the rest for yourselves. Football is being shaped by the self-interested thanks to backing from the kind of people who think it's funny to wave 'Cantona – it's someone else's turn to suffer' posters in your face in South Africa Road after the game. Then when you express the opinion that, putting it mildly, you don't like them very much, the first reaction is disbelief ("Us? What did we do?") and the second is "A-ha, you're just jealous." If they think I would swap lives with them they're even more stupid than I thought — which is saying something.

QPR may have gone down but we will keep, even increase, our self-respect and our standing amongst genuine supporters on occasions like that game where the home players and supporters were first class throughout, and our dignity where the number of incidents after the game were unbelievably few considering the immense provocation. Remember, that which does not kill me, only makes me stronger. Keep the faith.
(Andy Ward – issue # 100)

Hateley, are you gonna be the one to save me?

Finding Rangers supporters, who think Mark Hateley has been a good signing for QPR, is harder than finding ones who thought the Thompsons had done a good job as owners of the club. After Wilkins signed him, we had to wait over two months before he made his debut for the club, but we didn't have to wait a further two months to realise that Wilkins had made a terrible mistake in signing his old pal.

I'm amazed the same player made such a big impression in Scotland. A ratio of better than a goal every other game, SFA Player Of The Year, an England recall, and five Championship medals make a pretty impressive list. But you can't help but wonder if Mark Hateley is the best advertisement for just how bad Scottish football really is.

He has however given a few of us supporters something to laugh about. One of the lads who regularly supports our youth team, referred to Hateley by a name you would normally associate with a famous old comedian. And he wasn't the only one. After I came back from that fateful day at Coventry, I heard that Radio Five's Pat Murphy, who was reporting at the game, described Hateley's performance by saying "He looked like he was polishing up his Max Wall impersonation." This probably owed as much to his movement (what a funny walk), as it did his appearance.

I wish I could have written about how inspiring Hateley was for us last season, sadly the only inspiration here concerns the rather large cheque that made its way into a Glasgow bank account last September. I bet Walter Smith must have felt like he'd won the National Lottery.

Should Hateley's form turn around this season in much the same way Steve Yates form did last season I will gladly admit I was wrong and eat my words. But personally I reckon there's more chance of him getting a decent haircut.
(Raymond Eaton – issue # 100)

The Wright man for the job?

'Who wants QPR' the headline read on the back of the Evening Standard on 10th May, a day after Richard Thompson agreed to sell his family's holding interest with the club. Speculation and rumours have been rife since, although one man — Chris Wright — appears head and shoulders above anyone else in the race to buy QPR.

This summer has certainly seen a lot of activity going on behind the scenes at QPR. Richard Thompson's decision to put QPR up for sale provided at least some good news at the end of a dreadful season in which QPR lost their Premiership status. Thompson's decision to sell has seen mass re-organisation at QPR, which includes;

- Clive Berlin taking over as Chairman, with Alan Hedges taking over as Managing Director. The new owner/s of QPR will have to incorporate both Berlin and Hedges in these management roles as part of the package.

- Peter Ellis stepping down to the board as Honorary Director, but without voting rights.

- Ray Wilkins' future with QPR should be unaffected.

In many ways, QPR fans should be thankful to both Clive Berlin and Alan Hedges for initiating the move to force Thompson to sell QPR. Both had formulated a plan whereas they would, for a fixed sum, take over the complete running of the club, selling it on behalf of Thompson who would then be able to further his interest in Leeds United. When approached, Thompson agreed to the deal on the grounds that a buyer for the club to be found as quickly as possible, in the £8-£10 million mark. Simple but effective. Had QPR still been a Premiership club, Thompson's attitude to the proposal could have been different, but Berlin and Hedges had an inkling that Thompson had been looking for a 'way out' for some time, and their timing on the face of it was perfect.

So, just who will be QPR's new owner/s? There have been several interested parties, with the front-runner being Chris Wright. He is certainly the man most QPR fans would want to see take over from Richard Thompson, but just who is Chris Wright?

A soccer fanatic all his life and season ticket holder at QPR for the last 20 years, 51-year-old Chris Wright is the multimillionaire owner of Chrysalis and Sheffield Sharks basketball team. He describes himself as an "entrepreneur and eccentric", and taking control of QPR would fulfil a lifetime ambition. It's quite a contrast to 30 years ago when Wright graduated from Manchester Business School in 1966. He had lost his place on a Marks & Spencer management training course, and his mother was adamant that he got "a proper job". Like most 21-year-olds in the sixties, Wright had little interest in anything other than music, and started booking bands on the university circuit. 30 years and countless 'rock discoveries' later — from Jethro Tull through to Wet Wet Wet and Sinead O'Conner — Wright is now one of Britain's richest men having sold his Chrysalis record label four years ago for £85million. Today, the new Chrysalis Group has been transformed into one of the most successful TV and radio companies in England. Nowadays, he leaves it to others to spot the talent and takes time to indulge his other great passions in life — horse racing and football.

Subsidiary Chrysalis Sport 'discovered' Italian football for Channel 4, his Heart 106.2 radio station is already making waves in London with over a million listeners, and his drama company Red Rooster has had a string of hits including The Sculptress — the murder mystery starring an over-sized Pauline Quirke.

Wright's prize possessions include a royal blue turbo Bentley — normally driven by his chauffeur Annie; a £1million yacht anchored outside his holiday home in Cap d'Antibes in the south of France, and a 450-acre stud farm in Gloucestershire, where his wife Chelle and three children live.

Wright has been in intense talks with QPR and is certainly the fans' favourite to buy the controlling stake owned by the Thompson family. Wright would be unlikely to continue the trend of selling the clubs' best players, he is QPR through and through and understands exactly what it takes to run a successful business.

If Chris Wright does take control of QPR, it seems likely that Wasps Rugby Club will ground share Loftus Road under one 'Umbrella' club. Apart from the obvious wear and tear the pitch will suffer, it's hard to say just how this would otherwise effect QPR. It would benefit Wasps far more than us, and it would be a shame to see various parts of Loftus Road decked out in the colours of yellow and black in accommodating our new tenants. However, if this is the only way Wright sees himself being a part of QPR's future, so be it.

(Ed – issue # 100)

Penalty claws

It had been 86 league games since we last scored a penalty — we didn't know how lucky we were. How many other games might have gone like Leeds; a goal down, piling on the pressure and then the bleeding ref gives us a penalty. That's all we need. Lukic saves with ease and all the momentum slips away. Funnily enough, Rangers missed a pen on my first ever visit to Loftus Road, Trevor Francis taking aim and slotting the ball into the Loft against West Ham. Then we were spoilt for a while, Wegerle and Wilson being excellent penalty takers. Now we're almost praying not to get one. The worst thing about the Leeds games was that still no-one seemed to know who was going to take it. Anyway, who's taking them this season? Here are some suggestions...

Trevor Sinclair

Would almost certainly blast it over the bar but if Trev should be emotionally scarred for the rest of his career, at least 99% of this future career will probably not be with Queens Park Rangers, so someone else can suffer for it.

Mark Hateley

Like in Father Ted when they set Father Jack's wheelchair to automatic using a big stick and a bottle of whisky, suspending a huge wad of cash four feet in front of Mark's head and then pointing him towards the spot might lead to him cannoning into the ball in his rush to get the beer vouchers and propelling it in the general direction of the goal. Then he could be pointed in the direction of back to Glasgow that would be well worth at least one missed penalty.

Karl Ready

Bear with me on this one. A West Ham fanzine once memorably commented on Justin Fashanu that his attempts to control the ball were more powerful than his shots. Similarly the ball could be placed on the spot and someone could shout "Make that Karl, get it under." Power if not accuracy could well be the result. Or, we could bring in a specialist to sit on the bench and be brought on at the appropriate time...

Kevin Pressman

Taker of the finest penalty I've ever seen, in a shootout against Wolves two seasons ago. Pressman tore up and leathered the ball into the top corner at Mach 3. This could also enable QPR to further test the club theory that a number of inadequate goalkeepers is better than one good one.

Me – I rule

My penalty philosophy is that Kevin Gallen hit it too hard against Leeds, more precision is required in sliding the ball along the ground to 'get it on target son'. Maybe not.

Jackie Chan

On the grounds that perhaps there is some link between karate-kicking skills and on-the-spot expertise.

Jean-Paul Gaultier

On the grounds that, in case anyone didn't get the last one, there may be a link between on-the-spot expertise and being a French tosser.

Sylvester Stallone in Escape to Victory

Oh no, hang on, he was the 'keeper who saved a pen. It's coming back to me now, Stallone was the American who despite knowing nothing about football, mixed blinding saves with schoolboy errors in equal amounts. Films eh, what are they like.

Michael Jackson

With one touch of his Rhinestone glove the ball would become a floating orb of pure light. Peace and angelic delight would suffuse all present, especially the goalkeeper who would weep with pure joy as the beautific vision glided by into the net. Then Jarvis Cocker would run on, grab the referee's whistle and disallow the goal for handball.

What the hack, whoever takes it is bound to miss anyway. So my vote definitely goes to Homer Simpson. At least he would say "Dow!" when he missed it.
(Andy Ward – issue # 100)

Welcome to the Premiership – QPR 2-1 Oxford United

If anybody thought life in the First Division would be a breeze, think again. There are many better teams in this division than Oxford, yet they came to Loftus Road, dominated the first half, and no doubt left feeling they deserved at least a point. All this from a team who less than a year ago were two divisions lower than QPR when the teams met in the League Cup.

After an indifferent pre-season, QPR played for the most part as complete strangers to one another. It was no surprise when Oxford took the lead through Jemson, and it could so easily have been more. Maybe it was a good thing. If the players thought they could walk through games in this division to earn victory, they were quickly proved wrong and responded with a second half performance that at best was reasonable, but was enough to gain an important victory. Sinclair was the architect, laying on well taken goals for Gallen and Dichio, the latter's celebrations earning him a booking.

Dichio had replaced Hateley with 15 minutes remaining, and although Hateley didn't do a great deal wrong, just about everyone in the ground expressed how they felt about him as he trotted off. "It's all your fault we're in this division," shouted one, yeah right.

Wilkins asked for patience with Hateley from the fans, which for his benefit and ours, he should have at least got.

(Ed – issue # 101)

Ray Wilkins – Did he jump or was he pushed?

I was particularly saddened to hear the news that Ray Wilkins and QPR had parted company. Ray made us believe that he was perfectly happy at QPR, despite relegation last season. He came across as someone who loved QPR, having been associated with the club for seven years. He always looked to possess the qualities required to become a manager, and when he was appointed in November 1994 I don't think there was one QPR fan who wasn't relishing his 'second coming'.

After a great start, it all turned sour last season, but I believe Ray was working along the right lines to get QPR back into the Premiership at the first time of trying. He accepted the blame for relegation, but was determined to put things right. The next thing we knew, he was gone, by 'mutual agreement' following the first board meeting of the season. The full events that initiated his departure may never be known.

Ray played a good game and talked a good game. His enthusiasm towards QPR was always evident, even in the darker days of last season. Not many managers would survive the sack following relegation, but Ray's position as manager never looked in doubt. That makes the timing of his departure so hard to understand. 7 points out of 12 was hardly a poor start to the season, but maybe not enough to keep everyone on the board at QPR happy.

I wonder just how hard new Chairman Chris Wright attempted to keep Ray as manager, presuming of course it was Ray who first offered his hand. One minute Wright is one of us, paying to watch the games from the stands. The next minute he's chairman. Had Wright been in charge for a few months longer, perhaps the whole situation could have been averted. Just how well did Wright get to know Wilkins as a person and a manager in the short time they were together at the club? Not well enough apparently.

Ray has since signed for Hibernian, but his heart is still very much with QPR I'm sure. You only have to look at the reception he received when taking a corner down the Loft end to see how well liked he was amongst QPR fans, and even with relegation looming last season, never once did I hear any "Wilkins Out" chants.

There are many fans glad to see the back of Ray, but I, along with the majority I believe, share the view that his leaving comes as a great disappointment. Like Trevor Francis seven years ago, we've lost a manager, a player — and a whole lot more.

Quote ... Unquote ...

"I'm off to meet the board members on Monday, it's my first time – and it could be my last." – Ray Wilkins, 1st September.

"Ray Wilkins' contract as manager of QPR has been terminated by mutual consent." – Official club statement, 4th September.

"I have been involved in professional football for more than twenty years and this is the hardest situation I have ever had to deal with. It's an extremely difficult time for me and it would be fair to say that I have been left a little stunned by the events." – Ray Wilkins, 4th September.

"I've only been in this job for a couple of weeks and already I've lost my star striker and my manager. Perhaps I should have stuck to music. I have nothing but respect for Ray as a professional and as a man. But now we have arrived at this point, we must all look to the future." – Chris Wright, 4th September.

"I just cannot get the playing bug out of me and at the moment I want to stay in the game not as a manager, only a player. So if there are any clubs out there who would like a 39-year-old midfielder, I would love to hear from you." – Ray Wilkins, 5th September.

"We had promised Ray a substantial amount of money and we even targeted players for him to sign. He went away from our Board meeting delighted, but something happened overnight. It was a big surprise to me as anyone else when he decided to leave because he was set to stay." – Chris Wright, 5th September.

"It's been a traumatic week for me and my family – nothing short of horrendous. The statement released by the club was 100 percent accurate, not has been portrayed. It was not a resignation – I've never walked away from any challenge in my life. My leaving had nothing to do with me playing for the team. I want QPR fans to know I wouldn't walk out on them." – Ray Wilkins, 6th September.

"There was money on the table for me, so my leaving had nothing to do with that. I just got bad vibes from the Board meeting." – Ray Wilkins, 7th September.

"Loftus Road was alive with rumours last night that Ray Wilkins decided to leave after receiving a telephone call only a few hours after being given a 'substantial amount of money' to buy new players. The call, believed to have come from a senior source at the club, was enough to make Wilkins suddenly leave a job he had seemed excited about only a few hours earlier." – Mail On Sunday, 8th September

"I've heard rumours about the phone call. I can't say there will be a witch-hunt but if I find out this has happened, I shall be absolutely furious. Ray left our meeting very happy, then a few hours later he rang and said he's changed his mind." – Chris Wright, 8th September.

"Maybe Ray Wilkins felt too much pressure to succeed after the take-over, and decided to go. Saying things like 'I'm going to my first board meeting, it might be my last' showed that. Ray is a nice guy, and it's sad, but maybe it's best for him and QPR we start afresh." – Chris Wright, 9th September.

"I've had a pretty traumatic week. I've lost my job, lost against Luton (for Wycombe) and when I heard QPR were beaten by West Brom I felt even worse." – Ray Wilkins, 9th September.

"It's crucial we get the right man to replace Ray. I don't want a good loser – show me one and I'll show you a loser. At the moment I feel a bit like a wounded animal. But I aim to strike back. I'm not used to being beaten – football is all about winning." – Chris Wright, 9th September.
(Ed – issue # 101)

Strike a blow

When I heard the news that Kevin Gallen looks set to miss the rest of the season, I was absolutely gutted. He started the season so well, not only scoring goals but looking the perfect striker all-round. Just how we're going to replace him remains to be seen. I had high hopes for Steve Slade although after his diabolical performance against West Brom, I think QPR should waste no more time in finding a replacement for Gallen. I had hoped Mark Hateley had played his last game for the club, maybe not now. What happens if Dichio gets injured? The season started so well, but is just going from bad to worse. No manager, no star striker, no wins for four games (up to Barnsley) and the probability that we haven't seen the last of Hateley. Now I hear we've been linked with Alan Curbishley to take over from Ray. Alan who?
(Alan Smithfield – issue # 101)

No problems for Houston... hopefully

And so to the new man, the first manager of QPR since Jim Smith to have no previous connections with the club. That will make his job harder, but getting QPR promoted to the Premiership this season will help his cause no end. Houston gained one full Scottish cap in a playing career that saw him play for Chelsea, Brentford, Manchester United, Sheffield United and Colchester United. He brings with him ten years worth of experience as coach at Arsenal, for whom he has also managed briefly on two occasions in the last eighteen months.

Hopefully, Houston can instil some of the defensive qualities into QPR that have been Arsenal's trademark for many years. Needless to say, I wish him well with QPR but if promotion isn't achieved this season, how long will he get with the club?

Houston inherits a team currently lying 6th in the league, but the signs are he will have to make two or three raids in the transfer market if we hope to gain promotion this season. The need for a striker to replace Kevin Gallen is most urgent. Steve Slade will hopefully come good in time, but his non-appearance in the last few games suggests his day is still some time off.

The team also needs some cover down the wings, as well as a central midfielder, especially now Wilkins is gone. The likes of Brazier, Quashie, Challis and Murray have been filling in OK, but to rely on such inexperience is asking for trouble.

One player Houston would do well to buy is Matt Jackson. Matt has been excellent during his loan spell, showing good defensive attributes as well as an eye to get forward. He wouldn't cost more than half a million, and will add some much-needed competition in defence.

(Ed – issue # 101)

So much so soon

Wow. It's difficult to know where to start. No sooner have we dipped a toe into the choppy waters of the Nationwide League than we've been catapulted into the deep in the clutches of one of those cool squid things with lots of tentacles and suckers and stuff. Ray Wilkins' departure appeared to take everyone by surprise, more in the timing than anything else. Last January I would have understood, May would have made sense and in the summer on Chris Wright's arrival would have been easily explained. Four games into the new season was a bit of a shock though, certainty in the light of Ray's previous assertions that he was not one to walk away from a challenge. Still, however much the tabloid press wanted to read between the lines, it would seem that nothing more sinister than a change of heart was Ray's motivation to leave. It appeared that Ray was finding being a player/manager more and more difficult — remember that his best spell as manager was when he was injured in his first few months.

There may be more to it than that — I can believe that Ray was not pushed but there is no evidence that Chris Wright was pulling very hard to keep hold of him, but I wouldn't know, and not having to sell newspapers for a living there is no point in idle speculation on my part. Enough for me to pay respect to Ray Wilkins as a great player and an absolutely first-class ambassador for the club, and to wish him the very best for the future. Likewise Frank Sibley, whatever his merits 30 years with the same club is not to be scoffed at nowadays and he is also due some respect.

So now we have Stewart Houston and we should probably think ourselves lucky to have got someone so well respected within the game, particularly in view of Manchester City's increasingly desperate efforts to find a manager. I'm still available by the way Frannie, I've got 8 days holiday left and I reckon in that time I could sell Kinkladze to QPR for 50p, play a couple of games up front myself and rake in a few bob compensation when I get sacked — and still have plenty of time to get back to my real job. Who says no one wants to be a manager?

On the pitch, with some moisture coming back into the wickets I've been slightly more effective of late as well as contributing some handy runs down the order (and dropping everything in sight to be honest). All of which meaning I only made it to one game in the opening month, West Brom—picked a good one didn't I? Confidence was sadly lacking, not helped by the 'men v boys' scenario in midfield with Sneekers rampaging over, around and through QPR's hapless kids.

The return of Barker and Impey would appear to have helped matters though — Impey in particular popping in a couple of goals in three useful, and excellent, away results at Norwich, Barnsley and Swindon. The standard of performance has dropped dramatically since then and time and patience will be required until Houston settles in and the injury situation clears up — I hope that most of us will be adult enough to supply it.
(Andy Ward – issue # 102)

Be positive!

Well first of all well done to Chris Wright for giving us all some piece of mind by finally buying the club (at least he's an R's fan), however it'll be interesting to know why Ray left. Ray will be sadly missed now he's gone but I reckon he was probably better hanging up his boots at the end of last season and not to continue playing like he did. There are those who'll probably argue that we didn't have anyone good enough to keep Ray out of the side, well who's fault is that?

As for Stewart Houston and Bruce Rioch, I for one think it's positive. The football might not be brilliant but playing good football is secondary this year to results, we must get out of the Nationwide League at the first attempt and when we've done that we can all re-group and start again.
(Jason Archer – issue # 102)

The comedy season so far

Hasn't the season been a great laugh so far?! What do you mean "no"! OK, we've lost our manager, our best striker is out for the season, and the injury list takes longer to read than 'War and Peace', but let me set out the argument as to why you should have enjoyed the season so far more than most. I bet I can convince you!

Let's start at the beginning — well, near enough. Fratton Park, and the best dive since Alan Shearer fell like a one-legged man in an arse kicking competition at Blackburn last season. I am of course referring to the young lady who braved the fresh sea air (which obviously had quite an effect on her) to show off her charms in the Rangers goalmouth. Some bright spark commented that the experience had been the "best sex he'd had in ages," but I hadn't stopped laughing by the time Martin Allen tried to put the matchball into the next day's game at Southampton with one of the worst attempts on goal I've ever seen!

Next was the Wolves match — one of the best grounds I've ever been to and a wonder goal celebrated long and hard by the sizeable Rangers following. What really made the game from our car load of R's fans was the sight of yours truly providing half-time entertainment by looking very gormless on the Wolves video screens...

Unfortunately we couldn't get to the Bolton game as several months ago I'd purchased tickets for the England v Pakistan game at Trent Bridge. However, this lead to witnessing another spectacular 'dive'. As we watched the Sky coverage at a nearby pub and Rangers desperately searching for an equaliser, up popped Macca to prompt another R's fan (who had earlier claimed to be a steward) to run full pelt at the giant screen in the pub and belly flop to the floor, prostrate in adoration to the 'big Irish idol' (© Tony Incenzo).

Other highlights include the superb chants at Norwich (B.S.E., B.S.E., B.S.E...) and after Ade Akinbiyi's attempt to outdo Martin Allen for worst shot of the year — "Are you Hateley in disguise." Let's also not forget the classic "Sing when you're farming."

Finally came the events at Barnsley. The attendance for this game was 13,003, but surely by the end of the game it was more like 12,000 as more and more northerners got thrown out as their team was torn to bits by Rangers. Add to that Dichio's 'we shafted them' salutes, and more top songs – "Can we play you every week", and surely by now you can see why it has been such an amusing start to the season. Now watch it get even funnier if we sign Ade Akinbiyi to solve our problems up front...
(Paul Maynard-Mason – issue # 102)

Not the best of starts

Although Stewart Houston has only been in charge of QPR for six matches, unfortunately the need has arisen already to constructively criticise his ideas and motives as manager of QPR. The appointment of Bruce Rioch as coach only adds to the confusion, and concern. The last few QPR performances have been absolutely terrible to watch. I accept we have a lot of players out with injuries, but what players Houston has had fit and available, he has used in an appalling fashion. In the last 12 months, QPR have given debuts to nine players aged 20 or under — Brazier, Challis, Quashie, Murray, Plummer, Slade, Perry, Graham and Mahoney-Johnson. Add to that Gallen and Dichio, and we have a full team of players with little or no experience. All 11 have featured this season, and at times QPR have fielded a team that wouldn't be good enough to grace a reserve team fixture.

To make matters worse, Houston has come in, changed the playing formation from 4-4-2 to 3-5-2 from his first game in charge, and is actually playing players out of position to accommodate these changes. Drafting in youngsters can be a tricky business. Half a dozen at a time is asking for trouble. Playing them out of position leads to the sort of performances and results QPR have had in the last couple of weeks. Unless Houston has a rethink over his formation and tactics, QPR will be heading towards the Second Division faster than you can say "Bring back Hateley."

QPR IN CRISIS -
HOUSTON CALLS FOR EXTRA TRAINING

The continental 3-5-2 system is very hard to put into practice successfully. Liverpool, Aston Villa and Chelsea are the only teams to have succeeded with the system because they have the players to suit. If Houston believes Brazier and Graham can rampage up and down the flanks, defending and attacking at ease when they're barely out of nappies, then it makes you wonder what he learned under George Graham in all those years at Arsenal. Just what is Brevett doing at centre-back? Why hasn't Dichio got a proper strike partner? And just who is our sweeper? Houston should scrap the system immediately and revert back to 4-4-2, which everyone is much more familiar with, playing his most experienced team whenever he can.

Whilst it's not my wish to condone the players that represent the future of the club, surely it's up to Houston to make an urgent raid in the transfer market to make sure the kids are brought in at the right time. QPR have sold/released six midfielders in the last

year — Osborn, Zelic, Hodge, Holloway, Goodridge, Wilkins, and have brought in just Murray in return. Is it any wonder we're so short of experience through the middle? God only knows what we'd be like if Barker got injured, it's bad enough losing Impey every now and then. If new faces aren't brought in immediately, QPR can kiss goodbye of making one of the two automatic promotion places this season. The money is there, it's up to Houston to spend it. A defender, a couple of midfielders and a centre-forward would do for starters. Following the Port Vale match, patience is thin on the ground with all supporters. Stewart, it's down to you to make sure things don't get any worse.
(Ed – issue # 102)

Relegation Blues – Part 2

(A continuation from issue 100 but this time with a slight touch of the hump).
Two rabbits who have spent their whole lives in a laboratory, are set free by animal activists. For the next three days they eat as many carrots and cabbages as they can and even indulge in a bit of fun with some lady bunnies. On the morning of the fourth day the old rabbit decides he wanted to return to the lab. "What the hell for," asks his pal. "In the past few days we've had carrots, cabbages, lettuce and best of all those ladies last night. What's your problem?" "Life is good, I agree," says the older rabbit, "but the thing is, I'm gasping for a fag!"

That was one joke doing the rounds over the summer break. The other completely preposterous joke was the one that QPR had a squad capable of making an instant return to the top flight. Even more laughable was the one that QPR would not just return but would walk it!

On what possible basis for Christ's sake? Anyone stupid enough to take the ridiculously low 9-1 odds on the R's winning the First Division may as well have thrown their money straight down the drain. Those who seriously expected the R's to be a force in this league either;

a) Overate this current QPR side — without doubt the worst I've seen in years and believe you me I've seen some shit.
b) Underate and have a total lack of respect for the Nationwide League. Or,
c) Still hang their stockings up at Christmas.

The look of shock, horror and anguish on fans' faces as Port Vale scored their second goal, following on from successive desperate home displays, tells its own story (things must be bad when 11 games have gone and words like desperate are being used). Even yours truly, winner of pessimist of the year in the south east for the past five years, didn't expect it to be this bad though. I felt that Rangers had a squad that may flirt with the top six but ultimately would be nothing more than a mid-table side. However, after the Port Vale shambles who would bet against us being in the bottom three come Xmas? Tell you what, there's more chance of that than being in the top three.

Against Port Vale new boss Stewart Houston and his team experienced the sort of abuse that was never reserved for Ray Wilkins and his clueless team of last season. Good old super Ray, without doubt the worst manager to manage the R's for a long while, but nevertheless still talked in good stead amongst the Loftus Road faithful. How the hell did he get away with it?

At Wimbledon last season me and several others started to call for Wilkins to resign. The looks we got! I was even told off by a tosspot sitting in front of me who claimed that it wasn't Wilkins' fault and that he hadn't wasted the transfer money. Okay, it's conceivably possible that the guy in question had just been labotomised but what excuse do the other Rangers fans have who not only worshipped Wilkins but persisted in chanting the cringe worthy "Super Ray" chant week in, week out.

Wilkins may have gone but his legacy remains. We're left with a toothless side lacking not only bite but any semblance of organisation and drive. We have a defence still looking more likely to concede goals than keep them out. A midfield which, although showing occasional glimpses of promise, seems incapable of imposing itself on a game and an attack which rarely threatens, lacks pace and, minus Gallen, CLASS.

The news of the full extent and seriousness of Gallon's tragic injury didn't just ruin my weekend when I heard about it, but also dashed any hopes that I held for the season ahead. Towards the end of last season I felt that Kevin was looking a better player than he ever had done for QPR. Not only was he scoring more regularly but also his whole game had improved. I had predicted great things from him this season but alas the season is only two games old and it's all over, not just for him but also, I fear, the team. In fact, I feel sorry for Houston. There's little that any man can do to halt the alarming decline of the club which has progressed from just beginning to rot to a state of almost total decay. Chris Wright appointed the wrong man, the only man who could have stood half a chance of turning things around died a long time ago. His name? Jesus Christ!
(Matthew Holley – issue # 102)

Anyone but Arsenal

When the candidates to replace Ray Wilkins as manager were banging about, I can't say that I was over-joyed with the names the press were coming up with. Alan Curbishley was certainly one name I didn't want to see at Loftus Road, mainly because I was unfortunate to watch a couple of Charlton games at the Valley last season. Stewart Houston I thought was a much better although I did have many fears about his style of football. The day after the 2-1 away win at Swindon in the League Cup, Houston was quoted to have said "We went out and we did a job." He then went on to make several references to being 'just like Arsenal'. These comments shocked and saddened me considerably. I can't think of anything (and I really tried you know) worse then being like Arsenal! I have always believed that the way we play is more important than winning cups (although this may also be an excuse for us winning bugger all for the last 29 years) and I hope it will stay that way. Rangers are renowned for playing good passing football and having flair and creative players with character. This is our tradition and we are proud of it. Is this tradition all going to go down the pan in an attempt to be 'More like bet Arsenal'?

THE first thing QPR players had to learn when new boss Stewart Houston took over was how to behave like sheepdogs.

Houston likes to control his players from the touchline by a series of whistles. In the style of One Man and His Dog, Houston gives them One Man and His Dug-out.

He perfected his act at Highbury where his coded warblings were intended to have the opposition running round like sheep, but usually left his men penned in their own half.

His usual code at Highbury, the *Daily Star* can reveal, was:

● **One short blast: Prepare to spring offside trap.**

● **One long blast: Get behind the ball.**

● **Two short blasts: Everybody behind the ball.**

● **Two long blasts: Pack the penalty area.**

● **Three long blasts: Intended to fool the opposition into thinking it was** full time, a signal for Merse to knock the ball 40 yards for Wrighty to snatch a late winner.

At Loftus Road, a senior QPR player, who didn't want to be named, said: "It's very confusing. At first we thought Stewart was merely trying to find his teeth. Some players took to it. Simon Barker was a natural. And Rufus Brevett responded well.

"Next I suppose we'll be getting Spillers biscuits to dip in our tea at half-time. Still, if it is successful, Winalot might be an appropriate sponsor."

(The Daily Star – Issue # 102)

The recent games against Swindon didn't suggest that our defence was going to be like Arsenal's and up-front we looked decidedly short of ideas. Away games will be the biggest test of what Houston proposes to do tactically. Will he go to Port Vale and Oldham with five men at the back and hope to pinch a goal and then sit on it for the rest of the game? Will our main attacking option be our full-backs sending long balls down the line? I know it's wrong to judge Houston this early but by saying that he wants us to be more like Arsenal he is giving me serious worries. I don't want to have to watch long-ball football this season (of course against Crystal Palace it will be impossible not to). We have always tried to pass the ball along the floor — I really do hope it stays that way.

(Chris Wildey – issue # 102)

Five million to spend?

Reports that Stewart Houston has £5million to spend, may, if spent correctly, save QPR from a season of mid-table mediocrity, but just when will Houston make his first raid into the transfer market? I find it quite unbelievable that Houston is not finding it an easy task to recruit new players, stating that even Premiership teams are having problems — with so much money in the game, surely it's never been easier?

Houston appears to have aged so much since joining QPR that he's starting to look like Tom Hanks at the end of Philadelphia. So hurry up Stew, put us out of our misery and take advantage of Chris Wright's generosity before he uses it for other causes. Gavin Peacock will do nicely for starters.

(Ed – issue # 103)

A season of consolidation?

Writing some 24 hours after the 1-1 draw with Sheffield United, it is hard to imagine what the solution to our problems consist of. Despite 8 points from the last 4 games, at the moment points still appear hard to come by. Presently most of the players are trying hard individually, but as a unit, we're looking second best in most of the matches at the moment. How I wish Ray Wilkins of a few years ago was out there playing now, offering guidance and vision to the much younger players.

Part of the answer would be to go out and buy new players. It's all quiet (bar speculation) on the transfer scene at present, but that's not necessarily a bad thing. With the odd exception, Rangers seem to have made a succession of bad buys. Given the choice, it is better to wait for a good signing to come along than for another Zelic or Hateley to be on our books immediately. And in any case, if Chris Wright is putting his money where his mouth is, he is entitled to want it well spent.

Another big help would be a settled side. Up until the Sheffield United game, no fewer than 24 players have already been used this season, many of them being youngsters. If I brought a friend along to Loftus Road for the first time, they could be forgiven for thinking team selection works via names being picked out of a hat. When Rangers have a more settled side, maybe we can then enjoy more favourable performances.

But despite everything, QPR are currently lacking that most endearing of beasts — the scapegoat. The former Keyser Soze of Queens Park Rangers, Richard Thompson, has already done the decent thing and taken a one-way trip to Elland Road. The manager who was in charge during last season's demise is no longer with us either. And as much as we'd like to, we can't blame Mark Hateley for the performances displayed this season. At present, the young Rangers side needs time to develop. Already consolidation looks like being the key word this season. It's obvious Stewart Houston has different ideas on how to manage QPR when compared to Ray Wilkins. I hope they are good ideas, because we can't be patient forever.

(Raymond Eaton – issue # 103)

A share for all

The £30million flotation of QPR and Wasps is underway. Chris Wright hopes to raise £12million to improve the ground capacity of Loftus Road as well helping the playing fortunes of both QPR and Wasps. QPR season ticket holders and membership holders at Wasps can buy shares in Loftus Road Plc for 67p each – that's 5p less than the banks and institutions will be charged. Approximately three million shares are on offer, but investors must buy a minimum of 200 shares — £134 with the discount. Maximum is 37,500 shares at £25,125. Any remaining shares will be offered to the general public at 72p. The value of the shares depends on the joint future success of QPR and Wasps. Oh well, at least one of the clubs is heading in the right direction at present…

(Ed – issue # 103)

10 reasons why it should have been great NOT to be in the Premiership this season

1) Learning more about different ways of life, e.g. people in Barnsley still piss up against brick walls and keep their sewerage in open tanks.

2) Not having games at inconvenient times on inconvenient days like 8.00pm on Monday nights.

3) At least now we won't have any of our former players scoring against us for their new team.

4) Finding out that Rangers have got fiercely loyal fans even when playing Port Vale on a Wednesday night — about 11,000 of them.

5) Better media coverage — in fact, Nationwide Football League Extra is on every Tuesday morning at 01.45.

6) We should really look forward to giving teams like Grimsby, Swindon and Port Vale

a really good trashing.

7) Rangers will be able to ruthlessly put teams to the sword in the intimidating Loftus Road arena.

8) Kevin Gallen should score shitloads of goals against inferior First Division teams.

9) We should comfortably clinch promotion back to the Premiership by the first week in April. And finally...

10) Mark Hateley will finally get to show his true class for Queens Park Rangers.

(Paul Maynard-Mason – issue # 103)

A Brucie bonus?

The managerial setup of Stewart Houston and Bruce Rioch appears to be a curious one to say the least. Rumour has it that Houston would only accept the job as manager if Rioch came with him as his number 2, even so it's hard to pinpoint Rioch's motives in stepping down the ladder so much in accepting his position. Already he has been linked with the vacant managerial post at Blackburn, and not many supporters can envisage that Rioch's stay with QPR will be a long one. Whether or not Rioch is simply passing the time until a better offer comes along, or he is genuinely enthusiastic about his current employment, remains to be seen.

(Ed – issue # 103)

Fact or fiction?

As an avid viewer of Eastenders, I have come to the conclusion that the hitman hired to kill Ian Beale was really Mark Hateley in disguise. The gunman almost completely missed his shot – just like Mr Hateley has done so often for QPR – especially at Sheffield United last week!

Also, I can exclusively reveal that despite his vast wealth, Chris Wright likes to save up his 50 pence pieces – he totally refuses to put them in the meter to make the scoreboard work.

(Lee McLoughlin – issue # 103)

So much for our early season optimism...

After the Reading game it was three defeats on the trot with two goals scored and seven conceded, leaving us currently lying in 19th place.

Here was I about to slaughter Stewart Houston for his inactivity in the transfer market, when he goes out and smashes the QPR transfer record by paying £2.7million for John Spencer. It's been all too apparent since Kevin Gallen was ruled out for the season with injury that we needed a replacement, and the acquisition of Spencer looks like being an excellent piece of business. At 26 years-of-age, Spencer has enjoyed a good goalscoring record in the Premiership with Chelsea, but has never really enjoyed a long run in the team. However, Spencer was a big favourite amongst the Chelsea fans, and was their leading scorer last season with 13 goals from approximately twice as many starts. He always plays with 100% commitment and I'm sure he'll prove to be a big success.Also joining us, or should that be rejoining us, is Gavin Peacock. Although on loan for the moment, Peacock will definitely sign for £800,000 as long as contractual agreements can be sorted out. I've always been an admirer of Peacock, who at 29 years-of-age, should be at the peek of his ability. Not only will he add some much-needed class to the midfield, he always chips in with his fair share of goals (20 for Newcastle from midfield in 92/93 when they went up).Judging from the reaction on the terraces at Reading, QPR fans are very excited about the captures, and despite another bad result, our slump in from cannot last much longer.

(Ed – issue # 104)

Gimme gimme gimme

One of the great conversations amongst men at the moment in pubs up and down the country is which one of the Spice Girls do you fancy most (putting a less finer point on the subject). Rather than elucidating on my own personal choice, instead I'll tell you what I want, what I really really want — promotion.

Since Spencer and Peacock arrived from Chelsea, happy times are just around the corner. People are saying we've got a hard job on our hands to gain promotion, well I think not. As I write after the Oldham game, QPR lie in 14th place — 4 points off the play-offs, 11 off 2nd place. When you think there's still 72 points to play for, the difference is minimal.

I've got a bet on with my mate that QPR will end third, reach the play-off final and beat Wolves at Wembley. There's a tenner in it for each of my predictions, whilst my mate reckons Spurs (his team) will end third and win the FA Cup. I've got no doubt who'll end out top.

I accept QPR have been pretty dire this season, but there's such a long way to go no one can be certain as to what will happen. I for one though can't wait for 1997 – it's going to be a great year, I can feel it in my water (quote Brian Moore).

(Dean Bonner – issue # 105)

Thanks Chelsea

After the Reading game, QPR lay 19th in the league. A month later, following the win against Norwich, QPR were in 5th position — albeit for a few hours. The

transformation in form and results has been remarkable, and there are two simple reasons why it has come around — John Spencer and Gavin Peacock. The pair have been outstanding in every game they have played so far, and it was great news that Peacock made his move permanent just before Christmas for the bargain fee of £1million (after a set number of appearances). Spencer brings a whole new dimension to the attack, bringing others into play all the time as well as having a superb eye for goal. Peacock adds some much-needed quality to the midfield — his passing is always precise, he manages to find space in all the time and threatens to score in every game with his runs into the box. We haven't had a midfielder quite like him for many years.
(Ed – issue # 105)

Bad memories

I just picked up FIFA 97 for the Sony Playstation and I was pleasantly surprised to find it loaded with R's video clips... during the opening video there is Trev making a run up the wing then getting tackled, there are other shots of the R's walking on the field before a match, and a shot of them at Man Utd. The teams are all from last year, but QPR are rated the worst team in the Premiership. Ian Holloway is still in the squad, and Hateley is foolishly rated better than Gallen or Dichio, but no Super Ray, which surprised me. I guess it's the only way this Yank will see any QPR footage this year...
(P W Wood – issue # 105)

On the right track

It is now over three months since Stewart Houston took over as manager of QPR — a sufficient period in which to judge the progress made under the management of the man who took over from Ray Wilkins. For his first two league matches in charge, Rangers managed draws against Swindon and Birmingham. In between, Rangers went out of the League Cup, also at the hands of Swindon. This was followed by two defeats against Port Vale and Grimsby Town. Then came a run of eight points from four matches, but after that came a period from which QPR got just one point from five matches around the November period. More recently, we've had that run of good winning form that started with the Sheffield United match. Overall, a pretty mixed bag so far.

Houston didn't take over at the best of times. Relegation was still fresh in the memory, and the new manager would have to do without first team regulars like Bardsley, Gallen, Yates and Quashie. Once again, youngsters were thrown in at the deep end. The results from Houston's first couple of months in charge didn't exactly inspire the supporters — it took him six attempts to win a league match, and from very briefly being top of the league after two matches, Rangers found themselves in 19th place. It was all going horribly wrong. Whilst the situation never got as far as the man being given a vote of confidence, I know that some supporters started to question whether Houston was the right man to manage Rangers. The prospect of losing two managers in one season worried me. This has happened at Man City and as we know, they're in the middle of the biggest crisis imaginable.

The lack of activity in the transfer market was also causing concern, even to this contributor who advocated a cautious approach before making a major singing. However, patience is a virtue and Houston was spot-on when he finally signed John Spencer and Gavin Peacock. The poor transfer dealings of Ray Wilkins always went against our former manager, but Houston can be well pleased with his work in the transfer market so far.

Another improvement since Houston took over concerns the disciplinary record. The caution count for the two previous seasons has reached epidemic proportions. Thankfully, under Houston (and Rioch?) there seems to be a bit more discipline in the ranks. A very good December has seen Rangers climb the table and the supporters can be a little bit more optimistic. Rangers aren't looking like the finished article yet (the 90 minutes at West Brom bares testimony to that fact), but I'd like to think we're on the right track. 1997 will present some interesting challenges to Houston and the team.
(Raymond Eaton – issue # 105)

Mystic Magee predicts the remainder of the season

JANUARY: Kevin Gallen reports back to Loftus Road for training after Christmas having lost two stone in weight after an intensive fitness diet. This is all well and good — but what about the other buttock? QPR face immediate investigation under the terms of the Trades Description Act after signing a lucrative sponsorship deal for 97/98 with 'Winalot'. QPR arrange a glamour friendly with Manchester United, and are on the wrong end of a 6-1 drubbing. Stewart Houston expresses his disappointment, especially as QPR were leading going into injury time. Elsewhere, Kevin Keegan resigns as manager of Newcastle United, and sections of the Geordie crowd accuse him of neglecting his roots. Keegan rigorously denies this, although his grey hairs are there to see.

FEBRUARY: John Hollins is appointed QPR boss and in his first match in charge, Karl Ready almost scores a spectacular overhead kick, indeed he would have done had it not been for an equally spectacular save by Juergen Sommer. Nonetheless, a point against Palace is seen as "an encouraging start" by Hollins, who is promptly sacked. John Spencer grabs his 48th goal of the season in the 0-0 draw at Ipswich. Steve Yates scores the winner from 30 yards at Stoke, who are delighted with the three points. Elsewhere, Dean Holdsworth is given compassionate leave by Dons boss Joe Kinnear after the striker's car park antics with a former porn model. Many believe that Kinnear had been most generous, as Holdsworth must have been absolutely knackered. Steve Yates is voted player of the month for February — by Stoke fans.

MARCH: Don Howe is appointed as the new QPR boss as Rangers make it through to the FA Cup 5th round — away to Birmingham. In the league, John Spencer continues his phenomenal strike rate by scoring both goals in the 1-0 win over Oldham. In the same game Rufus Brevett fractures a cheekbone — it belongs to a linesman. Rangers win through to the FA Cup quarter-finals with a 1-0 win at St Andrews, with Spencer helping himself to a hat-trick. 4000 fans made the trip, 2000 made it back. At a board meeting Don Howe presents his 4-4-2 plan as the best form of attack. In turn, Chris Wright presents his P-4-5 plan as the best form of dismissal — Howe is sacked. Meanwhile, the club announces radical new measures to improve catering for fans at Loftus Road — they are encouraged to bring their own sandwiches. The FA Cup quarter-final match with Millwall at the New Den is delayed half-an-hour by the late arrival of 16,000 Millwall fans who hadn't realised that their team had moved ground. Rangers substitute Daniele Dichio scores the injury-time winner and is subsequently attacked in a New Cross pub afterwards by Millwall fans, who were very apologetic when they eventually realised that Dichio was not in fact Wolf from Gladiators.

APRIL: John Spencer scores the winner in the six-pointer at Bolton, a match he misses through injury. Rangers players hint at industrial action if managerial instability continues. Meanwhile, Rangers fans are in agreement that a strike would be a terrific idea, particularly if it's on target. John Spencer scores an own-goal at home to Grimsby, but surprisingly claims to have been in Spain with the missus at the time. Terry Venables is appointed as Rangers new boss, saying that promotion cannot be gained overnight; he is sacked the next morning. Three tickets are raffled by the club for the FA Cup semi-final with Liverpool at Villa Park. The first ticket went to an Irish based QPR supporter, and the other two were claimed by John Spencer. In the event, Rangers sit back on a 1-0 lead and lose 8-1. Meanwhile in the other semi-final at Old Trafford, Spurs are beaten by Manchester United. Elsewhere, Paul Ince says he doesn't understand the criticism being directed at him by Inter Milan fans — so he orders an Italian phrase book.

MAY: The end of season match at Bradford City sees Mark Hateley make a 30-minute appearance — he is paid overtime for doing so. QPR fail to earn promotion and shares fall to 0.16p each. Richard Thompson buys them all up and regains control of QPR for just four hundred pounds, leaving fans distraught and out of pocket. Juergen Sommer and Karl Ready appear on Capital Gold to promote a campaign declaring war on drugs in sport. The interview is seen as ground breaking as it was the first time the pair had appeared on the same wavelength. Steve Yates sensationally makes history by becoming the only player to have received two caps in one England appearance — his first one, and his bloody last one. During the summer, Chris Wright sees an elderly lady struggling with some baggage and says, "Can you manage love." She replies that she wouldn't even consider his bloody job. Chris Wright's search for a manager is ended however with his surprise appointment of Justin Fashanu, who promises that quality will be brought to the club in the near future. He immediately telephones Alex Ferguson to make enquiries about Butt.

(Aidan Magee – issue # 106)

A sense of perspective

Well, not having put finger to keypad since before Christmas, it is traditionally a time to count one's blessings. Me, I'm simply grateful that it's over and this time of year is cool because it is now as far away from Christmas as it's possible to be. At least I can go into a shop and buy a copy of the Racing Post without having to shout over 'Simply having a wonderful Christmas time' and the 'comedy' version of 'Rocking around the Christmas tree'. And of course those five wins on the bounce is cause for muted celebration, muted in these parts because I only saw two of them — a gutsy but fortunate win over Sheffield United and the slaying of the embarrassingly poor Southend — they were good once, honest.

Up for the cup in the new year though and despite the presence of the admirable Peacock and Spencer we were back to early-season form. Hateley clearly feels that he has kept us in the cup, but I feel that a third goal in 14 months is hardly good cause for getting involved in gesturing to the crowd. In fact the draw was much more down to tactical naivety on Huddersfield's part, having completely nullified us by interposing themselves in midfield they sat back after their goal and allowed us space to play (after a fashion) — a mistake which is even more common at this level. So, at the moment I'm sticking with my pre-season assessment of a play-off spot and then keep your fingers crossed, pray, sacrifice to Satan, whatever's your thing. Still, Peacock and Spencer are excellent signings, Spencer in particular a tremendous difference. Watching Dichio and Slade up front was like watching Beavis and Butt-Head on the pull — you sit there thinking 'these two dumbasses are never gonna score'. We're still being linked with Frank Sinclair and that is a signing I would fully support, so do it!

(Andy Ward – issue # 106)

Port Vale 4-4 QPR

The last time ITV screened a QPR match live, Man Utd were the hosts and you need little reminding of the outcome. The 4-1 win for QPR remains the high-point of the decade. Five years and a bit later, a division lower, with a spartan ground and attendance to match, Vale Park was the venue as QPR came under the scrutiny of live coverage on ITV once again, resulting in QPR's most satisfying draw of the decade.

It was a strange decision that LWT chose not to screen the game though. The nearest regional station to screen the match was Anglia, and it was a great pity so many fans, unable to travel to the match itself, missed out on the most enthralling of games. The scenes when the fourth goal went on in will live long in the memory. Just about every player, with Dichio leading the way, ran straight over to the away end and were engulfed in a massive orgy of celebration. Several QPR fans ran onto the pitch through pure joy, and there stood one lone policeman trying to keep order — a hopeless task.

John Spencer said after the game that he didn't believe QPR could fight back from four goals down, and his performance in the second half certainly reiterated that fact. Then up he popped in injury time, a left foot shot between 'keeper and post so stunning and accurate it defied the pressure he must have been under in the circumstances. It wasn't the hardest of opportunities, but the nonchalant ease with which the chance was taken had to be seen to be believed. Great memories.

You really had to be there to fully appreciate the roller-coaster of a ride it is these days as a QPR supporter, desperate to get out of this crazy division. For 85 minutes we were diabolical, a throw-back to the days early on in the season when the words 'QPR' and 'attack' had no association with each other. On full time, and a miraculous recovery at 4-4 completed, the high in the away end was something else. To say we didn't deserve it would be an understatement. What the thousand-or-so QPR fans had witnessed was nothing short of miraculous.

The opening half-hour of the game was as nondescript as any this season. Apart from a Paul Murray shot that forced an excellent save from Musselwhite, neither side showed much in attack. Then it all went horribly wrong. Glover fired Vale ahead; Mills made it two with a far post header from Guppy's excellent cross on 35 minutes; Guppy made another for Jasson six minutes later and then an own-goal from Brazier direct from a corner completed a totally embarrassing first half for QPR. The defending was as bad as it is ever going to get. Every time Vale got into the box, they scored, taking full advantage of slack marking and a lack of awareness amongst messrs Graham, Ready, McDonald and Brevett.

The second half got under way — seemingly a lost cause for QPR, with Maddix replacing Graham — not the substitution everybody envisaged. With Hateley back to his immobile worst, and Brazier anonymous as ever, Impey and Dichio should have replaced them at half time. Instead, a further 20 minutes of dire action took place until the inevitable substitutions happened. Then, and only then, did QPR start to show any resemblance of an attacking force. Vale should have been 5-0 up by now with Naylor having a goal turned down that appeared to cross the line. Soon after another Vale player, Holwyn, did score through his own net from a Sinclair cross, to give QPR the slightest of lifelines.

The urgency to attack was still not much in evidence though as Vale appeared to be holding on comfortably for victory. Then Impey volley in a spectacular second on 85 minutes from 18 yards, and Murray chipped a delightful third over the advancing 'keeper from Sinclair's through ball three minutes later. Quite amazingly, into injury time Spencer rammed home the equaliser from close range after Dichio's header was palmed out by Musselwhite. Words cannot describe the euphoria that followed. The comeback just never looked a possibility. Every player was off-form — it took the three subs — all excellent — to provide the inspiration, but in the end it was worth waiting for. I just wonder how Port Vale fans must have felt?

(Ed – issue # 106)

The times — they are a changing

Indeed how things change. Pissed as farts at Reading, returning home with nothing but a hangover and looking forward (sic) to another relegation season. Then seven weeks later and a bit pissed up after Barnsley but at least having three points to wake up to and the genuine prospect of promotion.

That match has to be the best we've had at Rangers for a long time — not hard granted — if only for the enthusiastic celebrations as we once again gave the Yorkshire club a right good shafting. Spencer's text book hat-trick — one with each peg and a header, resulted in wonderful scenes of joy and happiness that have sadly not been a regular sight at Loftus Road in recent seasons.

If you want a good laugh, watch Spencer's first goal again. As Murray's cross comes over, watch the guy in the away end wearing a white top, standing up with arms cockily out-stretched to indicate 'WIDE'. Then watch his arms quickly come down as Spencer slots it home. We've seen spot the ball competitions, now how about a spot the prat in the away end? I thought that goal alone was a memorable strike but this guy has unwittingly made its value on the end of season video soar. The Nationwide League Goals Extra also showed Barnsley fans proudly holding a Brazilian flag alongside their own. Apparently they seriously believe that Barnsley are the Brazil of the Nationwide League due to the exciting football they play! Well… like Brazil they field a goalkeeper and ten outfield players and I guess they both start with the letter B and... I would like to believe it's irony on their part but I don't think the average Barnsley fan would know what that meant, let alone how to use it. All I can conclude is that that they put some funny stuff in those Yorkshire puddings nowadays, which incidentally would be a far more apt description of their side.

In the award winning 100th edition of In The Loft — well it didn't really win any awards but it damn well should have done — I was very pessimistic about our chances of promotion. The main reason for my pessimism (and let's face it you'd be concerned if I started being optimistic) is that I could not envisage a side managed, or should that be mis-managed, by Wilkins, making any sort of impression in a league as tough as this one.

I believe Chris Wright shared my sentiments. The was-he-pushed or did-he-jump debate may probably never be settled but I personally believe that Wilkins merely received a slight nudge in the right direction — in his case OUT! Either way who cares? He went and that along with the end of the Thompson reign spelled the best ever news this club has had for a long time. A measure as to how bad things had become is that it took Houston and Rioch, no mugs in the management game, so long to begin to turn things around. Had Ray still been in charge I believe that we would still be languishing at the wrong end of the table. After all he would have never bought Gavin Peacock because he would have provided him with stiff competition for the midfield spot that his over-blown ego still believed that he could play effectively.

With reference to my article in issue 102, I could see nothing but a season of struggle ahead. Thank God it's looking like I was wrong. Apart from the added class that Spencer and Peacock have brought, there's an improved resilience about the team, epitomised by the last minute winner at Huddersfield in the FA Cup and the amazing comeback at Port Vale. There is still a lot to be done, however, with the defence surely the main area to be worked on, but at least now we can look ahead with renewed optimism to the closing stages of the season. It should be exciting at the very least.
(Matthew Holley – issue # 106)

On The Ball with Andy Ward

Maximum respect to Trevor Sinclair for an outstanding goal against Barnsley. If I ever see a goal better than that I'll count myself lucky — absolutely unbelievable technique,

athleticism and skill. It transcended the match itself, the score just didn't matter for a moment, and it will transcend this season in that the strike will be remembered long after what happens in terms of promotion or play-offs — a thing of beauty is a joy forever.

I had to start with that because it would be unworthy to just throw it in the middle somewhere — it even has to take precedence over the remarkable goings on at Vale Park, which I'll come to in a moment. First I'd like to stress that if you get too caught up in our situation, if you feel that promotion is the be-all and end-all, then it's easy to miss out on simply enjoying what's happening as it happens, which would be a real shame. I'm going to set myself up to be knocked down here but I quite like Division One — real fans, competitive matches, some excellent young players who will be big stars in the future and proper fights as well. Yes, I'd prefer the Premiership but looking in from the outside makes you realise what a big playground it is at times. If we're not good enough (which we aren't at the moment) then this is our level — you can like it or lump it, and for me the first option is more fun. I wouldn't want to see the club stagnate and end up here but another season or two of rebuilding won't do any harm if we're prepared to be patient.

For patience is indeed a virtue, not least at Port Vale. I'd really love to know if anyone left at half-time, or have we got more faith? Being a carrot-cruncher I was spared Baywatch and Peter Ustinov but even my sofa support was wavering with 10 minutes left — have a bath or stick to the bitter end? Bearing in mind that having a bath too early on Sunday leads to the Long Dark Tea-Time of the Soul, I resolved to tough it out, and was duly as amazed as everyone else. Because it wasn't as though Rangers were pounding on the door for the whole second half — whatever the programme might say about never-say-die spirit, the second half was an exercise in face-saving and everyone knew it.

Impey's goal sparked off one of those bizarre periods of play which happens from time to time, Vale had completely switched off and were of course unable to lift it again. Worse than that they just fell to bits, you could see the third coming and after that it only takes a second to score; Spencer duly obliging.

It must have been absolutely mental to be there though, I think I would have loved to have been in the crowd but the last place on earth I would want to be was the Port Vale dressing room afterwards — you don't manage for as long as John Rudge without being able to go into one when required. Paint-blistering stuff I'm sure.

In fact, January was a month of blistering action, the FA Cup in particular taking off at least a round earlier than usual with some great games and great goals, Trev's special among others reopening the debate, or should that be playground argument, as to whose goal is the best. As usual the old yardstick "My team good, everything else bad," is used to beat us all over the head rather than measure anything out. In fact it's very difficult to compare different kinds of goals. Goals of individual skill, a la Wegerle, or power a la Ferdinand, lobs, strikes from distance and spectacular displays of technique.

All you can do is apply a sort of 'degree of difficulty,' which I'm afraid (not) relegates Beckham's goal against Wimbledon right down the list. In my experience of playing, I always found it more difficult to score when the keeper was inside his penalty area — that tended to pose something of an obstacle. On top of that there wasn't an opponent anywhere near him and United were 2-0 up and in the last minute, i.e. no pressure.

Waddle's goal against Everton ruled over it because he was running parallel to the goal-line and he only had a split-second to hit it. Etc., but couldn't we just appreciate all spectacular goals without having to list them and say "yar boo sucks to you" or "no way that's not fair" according to the result?

Anyway, has Johnny Spencer started trend for kicking advertising hoardings? Did you see Cantona almost wreck one when a Wimbledon fan (respect) pretended to throw him the ball in their FA Cup clash? That was a fantastic finish to that game, it was great to see two heavyweights pounding each other for the rights to catch up with us in the FA Cup, and what a finish by Schmeichel in the last minute, I almost felt sorry for him. Almost... when that goal went in, Andy Gray said "Trevor Sinclair eat your heart out," — Trev is now the official king of overhead kicks. Actually I take what most commentators say with a hefty pinch of salt but recently when some idiot described Les Ferdinand as "Alan Shearer's sidekick," I nearly put the TV in…

(Andy Ward – issue # 107)

QPR 3-1 Barnsley, FA Cup 4th Round

Breathtaking, superb, spectacular, wonderful, exhilarating, fantastic, tremendous. Mr Trevor Sinclair. His performances this season have been anything but, though when he conjures up one of the greatest goals in the history of football, you have to take your hat off to the man. Sinclair's goal on 75 minutes came at exactly the right time for QPR, who, having come back from a goal down to lead 2-1 with excellent strikes from Peacock and Spencer, were now down to ten men. Andy Impey's career at QPR has had its ups and downs. At the moment, he is on a very big down. A blatant punch on a Barnsley player and the inevitable red card was Impey's 3rd in his last 14 QPR games. He got a standing ovation from most QPR fans for his troubles, but he gets no sympathy from these quarters.

With Barnsley seizing the initiative and throwing men forward, a moment of pure magic won the game for QPR when it seemed Barnsley were about to equalise. Spencer put in a hopeful cross, and we all know what happened next. Just how did Trevor do it? As a mark of how good the goal was, I doubt that for the rest of our lives we will ever see another overhead kick from outside the penalty area, with such precision and speed, ever scored again, from a QPR player or any other.Overall, a fantastic game, but as usual QPR made it hard for themselves, party due to Tony Roberts. To be fair to Tony, for the first goal the ball didn't appear to bounce up as he expected from the free-kick, but to stand with your legs apart in such situations is appalling for a goalkeeper. Dive into the shot Tony. As for Barnsley, they're not a bad side, they've just happened to encounter QPR on probably our three best days of the season.

(Ed – issue # 107)

Love or Hate-ley?

Once again, it's the 'is he good/bad' debate on Mark Hateley. Hateley is getting on a bit, like Waddle, Ray etc. He was signed and came to us after having a good record at previous clubs. He cost a lot, but that's not his fault. He also gets paid a lot (drives a hard bargain — good for him, anyone suggest they wouldn't in his position?). He has no pace — Spencer has no height, a player should play to their strengths. Spencer demonstrates passion (his personality). Hateley doesn't appear passionate — perhaps that's *his* personality. Does anyone REALLY think he doesn't care? His team mates would know, they will also know his personality.

I would suggest everyone in the team tries their best. No one wants to fail. Hateley's speciality is to head the ball — when I watch him he is clearly very clever at what he does (against Crystal Palace he pretty much won all the balls he went up for). He does however require someone clever to head the ball to. Up to now we haven't had anyone like that. We have now.

When he came on against Palace he created a lot of chances — but he is not a Trevor Francis or a Les Ferdinand. He has a particular skill which he uses well. He does not run after balls for the sake of it, he very sensibly goes for the ball when he can do something with it. That may look like he doesn't care but it also shows he saves his energy for real chances. He is not a pivotal player, he is a supplier (although he needs good service).

If we want to win, I say we should back him (almost whatever while we have no real alternative). To boo our own players saps them of confidence. I don't shout at my kids when they get something wrong. When doing badly we should cheer the harder, shouldn't we?

(Jonathan Mercer – issue # 107)

Highs and lows

Whilst there's little doubt that Trevor Sinclair's outrageous goal against Barnsley in the FA Cup will be voted goal of the season in whatever format you choose, there have been at least a dozen QPR performance's this season that could all be worthy of 'worst display of the season'. The latest, at Ipswich Town, would probably do the word 'worst' no justice at all. Just like there are few words that could be used to describe accurately *that* goal, trying likewise to put into words just how bad QPR were at Ipswich would be incredibly hard without the use of expletives. Spectacular goals are one thing, but I don't think I can remember a season that has seen so many performances of a remarkably low standard. I, or any QPR fan, do not want to see any more this season. There is only so much one can tolerate over the course of a season regardless of the division or standard of opposition.

Apparently, Brian Little was at the game to watch Sinclair in action. He must have gone home laughing at seeing 11 players who collectively and individually, were unutterably poor. Before the start of last season, I could honestly say I have only ever been totally embarrassed to witness two QPR displays — at Southampton in the ZDS Cup when we lost 4-0 in 1990/91, and at Sheffield Wednesday in the League Cup in 1992/93, again 4-0. You could add a couple more to that list from last season, but the total is now probably well into double figures after some of the trash on display this season.

Houston called it "The worst since I took over," but he's said that a few times before and undoubtedly will say it again before the season ends on this showing.
(Ed – issue # 107)

Ipswich gloom

Weren't we absolutely pathetic at Ipswich? If anyone harbours the ridiculous notion that we are somehow better with a back five, what do you reckon now, eh? This ridiculous system, combined with Murray's absence has us looking relegation candidates again. Everyone could see we should have gone 4-4-2 about an hour earlier! What a pathetic substitution as well — why not take off Ready who had a shocker? As for Barker — a midfield dynamo, hmmm... Hopefully the formation will change back soon (apparently it is Rioch's doing) and Barker will be watching from the stands.

Having spent four hours getting to the game and paying an extortionate £16 for a ticket, to see Barker passing the ball two yards back to Ready who then hoofed it up to Hateley was frankly pathetic. The five at the back is a dour, negative Arsenal system – we've been brought up on flying wingers, overlapping full-backs and crosses into the box. We clearly do not have the personnel for this system. I really can't see why the management favour it. When that substitution was made (Brazier for Brevett), we had Yates, Brazier and Graham all playing out of position — not fair on the players, let alone the fans! Sort it out Stewart!

I read in The Sun today and I'm more than a trifle alarmed that Houston is quoted as saying "I can't understand what went wrong." Seems obvious to me; team winning lots drops best midfielder for old duffer and changes formation to one that has already proven unsuccessful this season (Reading, all the early games). Is Stu really this stupid? Is he going to ruin our cup chances by persisting with this system?
(Adam Margolis – issue # 107)

Dan's dilemma

This month's 'Four Four Two' magazine, carrying an exclusive interview with Daniele Dichio, sees the QPR striker say that he is proud of his record of never having been caught offside. Rangers manager Stewart Houston attributes this record to Dichio's tendency not to interfere with play.

(Aidan Magee – issue # 107)

Wimbledon 2-1 QPR, FA Cup 5th Round

A performance that, despite the result, you could be proud of, but how times change. Wimbledon away was always the least looked forward to game of the season when we were in the top division, and yet at Selhurst Park QPR had more fans than they have done for any home game this season. Estimates ranged between 12,000 and 14,000 present. Officially, the two sold-out stands hold a combined total of 11,999, add to that loads more QPR in the main stand and the figure probably was nearer to 14,000.

The game itself wasn't a let down. Wimbledon were atrocious in the first half. QPR had more of the ball, took the lead with a fine header through Hateley, and could have had a couple more. The passing was much better than in recent games, and the players actually got stuck in with wholehearted commitment for a change. If we could have held on until half-time I'm certain we would have won the game. But no sooner had Hateley stopped cupping his ears in front of the Homesdale Road Stand (no more now Mark) than Wimbledon were level through Gayle — from a set-piece of course, and certainly the most crucial goal conceded all season. Shortly after the break, Earle got what proved to be the winner with an excellent run and shot from 20 yards that gave Sommer no chance.

It all went a bit quiet amongst the Rangers fans. The game had been won and lost in a matter of minutes, and our attempts to get back in the match were far too sporadic for the occasion. Hateley had a header tipped over the bar, and then had a close-range effort cleared off the line thanks to a remarkable block by Fear, but that was it really. At least the players tried their best, which was more than they did at Ipswich, and I think everyone left with the impression that the Premiership can't be far away if the same sort of attitude is shown week in, week out.

(Ed – issue # 108)

Strange but true

Recently, Rangers gave trials to two Costa Rican internationals in the reserves. Midfielder Maurico Solis, 27, scored one goal in three games while striker Paulo Wanchope, 20, netted six times. Both were rejected by Rangers for not being 'good enough' so imagine my surprise when Derby signed both for an undisclosed fee. Stranger still, a friend of mine went to the recent away match at Charlton. After the game he discovered that his car had been towed away. Fearing that he would have to pay a hefty fine he went to the car pound which turned out to be the car park in the middle of a block of flats! No authorised personnel, no fine! Obviously the police were hoping that the local urchins would right off the car and that would be punishment itself! Stranger still, why is it your car gets broken into when your team has just lost? It never happens when it wins...

(Moreno Ferrari – issue # 108)

Things ain't rosy and it ain't much fun when it's QPR 0 Oldham 1...

Many people find it difficult to see the light at the end of the tunnel. I'm struggling to find the entrance but then again... Trevor Sinclair's goal against Barnsley was indeed one of the most amazing goals seen on our hallowed turf. The athleticism, control and dexterity involved was breathtaking, but the most amazing thing about the goal was that so many people — including many respectable journalists, actually believe that he meant to do it!Sarcastic sod I may be but for a truer representation of Trevor's ability in front of goal and overall standard of play, one has only to watch a video recording of our recent home fixture against that footballing force — Oldham Athletic. Five million pounds? Houston, take it now!

What was particularly worrying about the Oldham game was the manner in which the defeat was 'achieved.' It was like a home fixture from earlier in the season, so devoid of passion, movement, confidence and ideas the team were. It says a lot when Danny Maddix is your most dangerous attacking player!

It was so damn good of you Mr Editor to feature Pamela Anderson on the cover of ITL # 107. I'm pretty sure, nah positive, that if QPR had a cracking pair like that up front we'd be pissing this league. The sudden freak storm which hit W12 before the Reading match was as merciless as it was fierce — no man was spared its terrible wrath, especially this particular man who, selling the aforementioned ITL on the corner of Loftus Road/Ellerslie Road received an almighty soaking, which left me feeling and probably looking like a drowned rat by the time I'd made it to the safety of the directors entrance. Several editions of issue # 107 got a soaking as well. Sob, that's sadly the nearest I'll ever get to getting Ms Anderson wet.

Wonderful to see a large contingent of R's 'fans' turn out for the recent cup game at Selhurst Park. Hardcore and dedicated supporters to a man and woman, their love and passion for the club made one feel a positive glowing feeling in one's heart. A measure to their interest in the club can be found from a conversation I heard at half-time – "Here Steve, is Les Ferdinand injured today or suspended. We ain't half missing him." ... Bloody part timers!

It's been said before but I have to say that I find Mr Hateley's 'hand to ears' gesture after scoring a trifle OTT. Poor old sod, as if being dragged down to London and receiving a massive signing on fee isn't bad enough, he then finds himself earning only six grand a week — my heart bleeds for him. Let's get one thing straight, Mr Hateley was never the victim of a hate mob, merely a small but well informed minority who decided to voice their disapproval at his shambling efforts verbally. I don't condone abusing players but considering what R's fans have had to watch over recent seasons I feel they've been incredibly restrained.

The point is however, that it's not Hateley's fault. He may be performing better now but basically his best years are long gone. If he had been a free transfer, few would have complained but he wasn't and instead cost this club an awfully large sum of money.

Incidentally, the complete fool who decided to shell out over a million quid for him departed a hero, leaving the club he had mismanaged so well in the worst state it's been for years. Which, and I apologise for mentioning again, makes as much sense to me as Ms Anderson falling for and then marrying Tommy Lee Jones when there's guys like me around waiting in the wings.

Quote ITL # 106, "At least now we can look ahead with renewed optimism to the closing stages of the season." Me and my big mouth! After the Oldham game I feel that our defence should get themselves registered with the official charities act. 'Lost confidence in front of goal, desperately need a win? We at QPR are more than happy to help solve your problems.' I'm worried that my cynicism may be terminal...
(Matthew Holley – issue # 108)

Getting back to the point in hand

Well, it looks like First Division football for us next season. Here we are talking about rebuilding and the like... it must say something of our commitment if Impey can't be bothered anymore. What happened to the marauding runs of two seasons ago? He scared players witless, I remember thinking at the time that now finally we would see him reach the potential he had been threatening for years. It must be a measure of his frustration if all he can motivate himself for these days is a punch up. He is and was a good player but if he is unhappy I do not want to see him in a hooped shirt.

We all know that Rangers have the players currently in the squad to gain promotion. We are a match for any in the First Division, we have our stars and we have our moments, but once again we are inconsistency personified. Why?

Is it to do with the management of the team or are there really core first team players that are disillusioned with trips to Barnsley and hanker after the glamour of the Premiership? I feel on the showings so far this season that there are a lot of players currently under performing who do seem to really not give a toss. Names; Impey, Dichio, Barker, Hateley. With injuries to Gallen and the Bard that's an awful lot of potential first team players either not giving it their all or just not available. If we add players in the squad who are simply not good enough full stop, i.e. Charles, Slade and Roberts, it's clear we have a serious problem.

So what do we do? Buy in the talent in the hope of a lift, a la Spencer and Peacock, or do we work on motivating existing players? I feel we need to develop a first team squad that's both familiar with each other and the system they have been asked to play. It's no good playing 3-5-2 one week and 4-4-2 the next. We have a young inexperienced nucleus of players. The future is bright but it needs working on.

Look at the players Rangers currently have under the age of 22 — Murray, Quashie, Plummer, Brazier, McDermot, Graham, Challis and Mahoney-Johnson. Some are good enough to be playing first team football week in week out now, others need developing. Let's develop a system, familiarise the players with it, and stick to it.
(Neil Ingham – issue # 108)

Roll on next season

Since the last issue, QPR's fortunes have gone from bad to worse. Despite a very welcome win against Huddersfield, the season is rather disappointingly petering out into a massive anti-climax. If you thought mid-table in the Premiership was bad (good old days, huh?), then you ain't seen nothing yet. As long as the play-offs remain a mathematical possibility, the team should be going all-out to ensure that at least they make a go of it, even if the likely outcome, on present form is anything to go by, will be abject failure. Roll on next season.

It's all been a bit miserable in the fortunes of QPR in the last six weeks or so. Unrest in the stands and on the pitch has seen a massive loss of faith in Stewart Houston from both players and fans. Unlike Gerry Francis and Ray Wilkins, Houston is not a figure that appears to acquire respect from his players. Certain players are just not performing for him, which may prompt wholesale changes in the squad during the summer. In a meeting between the board and fans last week, Chris Wright revealed there will be a major clearout of players, with five or six players already targeted to bring to the club as replacements. The club are fully aware of exactly how fans are feeling at the moment — they too have been as disappointed as us by events on the pitch this season.
(Ed – issue # 108)

Leadership qualities

Q1) You're losing away to Charlton 2-1. Do you;
A: Get Simon Barker off and bring on Paul Murray sharpish, or
B: Stick your fingers in your mouth and whistle like a lunatic.

Q2) Your team has just conceded a goal in the first minute of a home match against Reading, and don't appear capable of getting back in the match. Do you;

A: Take Simon Barker and Lee Charles off and bring on Paul Murray and Mark Hateley pronto, or

B: Stick your sodding fingers in your mouth and whistle like a sheepdog trainer.

Q3) Your team has gone 2-0 down to Reading, virtually ending your play-off hopes. Do you;

A: Dip into the transfer market and buy a new keeper and a couple of decent defenders, or

B: Stick your fingers in your mouth and whistle like Roger Whittaker.

If you answered A to the above options then you may as well be Alex Ferguson, Roy Evans, Joe Kinnear or any other number of level headed managers working in football. If you answered B to the above then you obviously have a lot to learn about football management and couldn't manage a bunk up in a brothel, let alone a football team.
(Neil Smith – issue # 109)

Can we blame injuries?

Whilst they may not have been the difference between promotion and another season in the First Division, I can't help but think that the loss of four key players has made a huge difference towards Rangers season.

In the past, players like Danny Maddix, Gary Penrice, Les Ferdinand and Ray Wilkins have all been sidelined due to long-term injuries, but they weren't all missing at the same time. This season however, David Bardsley, Kevin Gallen and Nigel Quashie can all justifiably call the entire 96/97 campaign a write off, whilst the man who is perhaps Rangers most consistent player, Steve Yates, has barely managed to get into double figures for appearances this season.

Now you could say that their absence highlights the lack of depth that there is in the QPR playing squad. But if you look at it that way you could also say that if Man Utd lost the services of Eric Cantona, Roy Keane, Gary Pallister and one of the Neville brothers, all for an entire season, then they too would be severely depleted. And what's more, we'd never had heard the end of that either.

We will never know how Rangers would have progressed had these four players been fit this season. Also, you could say by way of a counter argument, that if Gallen wasn't injured, Rangers may never have signed the excellent John Spencer. However, putting any such hypothesis to one side, QPR have not made an outstanding start to a season since the 92/93 campaign when we were briefly top of the Premier League (never thought about them as being the halcyon days at the time). If QPR are going to make another good start next season, a clean bill of health for the entire first team squad would do us no harm whatsoever.

(Raymond Eaton – issue # 109)

A costly mistake

The departure of Mark Hateley to (the other) Rangers came as a bit of a surprise, actually it's completely amazing that anyone would pay the reported £300,000 for a player his age. Knowing how often the press get it wrong, I would be surprised if the actual fee was more than £100,000 and that the rest is made up of wages, signing-on fees and bonuses. Presumably the QPR board jumped at the chance to recover a small portion of the cash wasted by Wilkins and even a small addition to the summer re-building fund is very welcome.

Let's face it, Mark's time at Rangers has been pretty much a disaster and ironically is departing the club when he looked to be showing his best form since arriving. Given time the hand cupped to the ear routine could have gained cult status as a traditional Loftus Road celebration. Mark wasn't fit for most of the time that he was at QPR and when he was fit he didn't score. The huge (outrageous) fee didn't do him any favours, it should have been obvious that a player of his age and diminished pace would be particularly dependent on quality service. This was always going to be a problem and it's difficult to see what Wilkins was thinking of when he signed him.

Perhaps Ray saw himself as the midfield general providing the passes to enable Hateley to terrorise defences. If so, he was living in fantasy land. Wilkins was too slow for top level football when Gerry Francis wisely dispensed with his services. The short duration of his stays at Wycombe, Hibernian, Millwall and now Leyton Orient surely make it clear that he should have gone long before. Clearly there was/is nobody else at the club who was going to provide such service. Wilkins' appointment was a mistake, as evidenced by the wasted transfer money and the lack of a coherent pattern of play culminating in relegation. The Financial Times reports an exceptional charge of £537,000 in the accounts arising from 'changes in football management and marketing rugby'. Presumably, although the split was by 'mutual consent' there was some costs involved.

(Chris Law – issue # 109)

Super Johnny Spencer

Let me acknowledge my undisputed QPR player of the season. Despite only coming to the club around the end of November, John Spencer has without doubt made the biggest contribution towards Rangers cause this season. An outstanding run of goalscoring form since he has arrived at Loftus Road probably indicates that if he was a pre-season signing, Spencer may well have been the top scorer in this division by now. Of course, every striker will miss a few opportunities, but in the case of Spencer, we will best remember the woodwork denying him hat-tricks at West Brom and against Huddersfield. One view that I read of, was that against Barnsley Spencer got the best hat-trick seen at Loftus Road since the much seen one scored by Rodney Marsh back in 1970. If Spencer had a bit more luck against West Brom and Huddersfield, then he would have conjured up equally brilliant efforts to what was managed against Barnsley.

Now, with a bit of luck Kevin Gallen will (hopefully) be approaching something like full fitness come the start of next season. Also by then, Stewart Houston may just have signed another striker. But on the evidence of this season, they or any other contenders will have to compete just to play alongside Spencer come next August.

One striker that can now be crossed off that list is Daniele Dichio. To say his transfer situation has turned into a soap-opera would be an understatement. There is much that could be written about Dichio here (little of it complimentary), but instead I will say just one thing, and that is if Dichio thinks that he will set Italy alight on the strength of this season's performances, then he is in for a very big surprise. The situation with our Sampdoria-bound striker highlights just what a farce the Bosnian ruling really is. It's typical that the first time QPR should have any involvement with it, we should lose out in a big way. And let's face it, there are only winners and losers with this thing.
(Raymond Eaton – issue # 109)

All but over

It does seem strange to be winding up the season before March is out but I can't see any possibility of QPR making the play-offs from here and let's face it most of us would like to see the back of the season ASAP. It's had its moments, giving us hope — for a couple of months either side of Christmas we showed what we are capable of, only to let it slip again.

We're not near the top at the moment because we've lost eight games at home, as many as in the Premiership relegation season, which is terrible. Bolton was excusable but all the rest were winnable, and if we'd only managed three or four out of those seven then we'd still have a shout at automatic promotion, never mind the play-offs. I must admit for a couple of days after the Reading debacle I thought that the dynamic duo should sling their capes but perhaps they should have another season with some more of their own players.
(Andy Ward – issue # 109)

Roll on next season

Following defeat against Bolton, QPR's hopes of making the play-offs can be considered almost impossible. Not for the want of trying though, QPR have giving it their best shot over the past few games but the sad truth is our best simply isn't good enough, even for Division 1. Life in this division won't be getting easier in the future either, but next season will hopefully be a different story. On the whole, this season has been extremely disappointing, but with more than our fair share of off-field problems and injuries, at least we can point a few fingers to where it has perhaps gone wrong.

In our four biggest games of the season — Man City, Wimbledon, Wolves and Bolton, we have taken the lead but conceded goals just before half time to swing each match back in favour of the opposition. These four matches have epitomised the frustration that this season has provided.

It's certainly been a busy last month involving transfers. Gone (or going) are Hateley, McDermott and Dichio. Whilst we're all pleased to see the back of Hateley, the sale of McDermott was surprising to say the least. Let's hope Bardsley is back next season fitter and better than ever before, otherwise Houston may start to regret letting the very promising youngster leave the club when his future with QPR looked so bright.

As for Dichio, after turning down Wimbledon he opted to go to Sampdoria instead on a free transfer under the Bosnian ruling. The move has been on the cards for some time when you consider Dichio was allowed to train with Sampdoria in the summer of 1995 when Ray Wilkins took QPR to their Italian training camp, and if Sampdoria think they have got themselves a bargain, they couldn't be further from the truth.

Then again, if the role was reversed and QPR signed a young Italian striker who scored 13 goals for a relegated club last season, we wouldn't be too disappointed would we? The fact is though, most Sampdoria fans probably haven't got a clue what Dichio plays like, but they're going to be in for a big shock when they find out if he plays anything like he has done for QPR this season. The signing of Steve Morrow reiterates the probability that Houston will use the 3-5-2 system next season. I was hardly ecstatic upon hearing the news of Morrow's arrival, and could possibly now signal the end of Alan McDonald's QPR career.

(Ed – issue # 109)

Super Johnny Spencer, well for half a season at least before life in Division 1 became a drag

Like so many others, Andy Impey found life outside the Premiership a struggle and was sold to West Ham for £1.2million in August 1997 after more than 200 appearances for QPR

1996/97 ~ Division 1

Date	Match	Comp	Scorers	Att	Issue
17/08/96	H Oxford Utd W 2-1	League	Gallen, Dichio	14,703	# 100
23/08/96	A Portsmouth W 1-0	League	Gallen (2)	7,501	
28/08/96	A Wolves D 1-1	League	Dichio	25,767	
01/09/96	A Bolton Wdrs L 1-2	League	McDonald	11,225	
07/09/96	H WBA L 0-2	League		12,886	
11/09/96	A Norwich City D 1-1	League	Impey	14,000	
14/09/96	A Barnsley W 3-1	League	Dichio, Perry, Barker	13,003	
18/09/96	A Swindon W 2-1	Lge Cup	Dichio, Impey	7,843	
21/09/96	H Swindon D 1-1	League	Murray	13,662	# 101
25/09/96	H Swindon L 1-3	Lge Cup	Brazier	7,843	
28/09/96	A Birmingham D 0-0	League		17,430	
02/10/96	H Port Vale L 1-2	League	Barker	8,727	
05/10/96	A Grimsby Town L 0-2	League		5,472	
12/10/96	H Man City D 2-2	League	Sinclair, Murray	16,265	# 102
16/10/96	H Bradford W 1-0	League	Brazier	7,776	
20/10/96	A Tranmere W 3-2	League	Slade, McDonald, Charles	7,025	
26/10/96	A Sheff Utd D 1-1	League	Slade	17,096	
30/10/96	H Ipswich Town L 0-1	League		10,562	# 103
02/11/96	H Stoke City D 1-1	League	Sinclair	12,174	
10/11/96	A Crystal Palace L 0-3	League		15,324	
16/11/96	H Charlton Ath L 1-2	League	Sinclair	12,360	
23/11/96	A Reading L 1-2	League	Spencer	12,847	
30/11/96	H Sheff Utd W 1-0	League	Barker	11,891	# 104
07/12/96	A Oldham Ath W 2-0	League	Spencer, Peacock	5,590	
14/12/96	H Southend Utd W 4-0	League	Barker, OG, Spencer, Peacock	11,117	
21/12/96	A Huddersfield W 2-1	League	Dichio, Brazier	10,718	
26/12/96	H Norwich City W 3-2	League	Peacock, Dichio, McDermott	15,699	
28/12/96	A WBA L 1-4	League	Spencer	19,061	
04/01/97	H Huddersfield D 1-1	FA Cup	Hateley	11,776	# 105
11/01/97	H Barnsley W 3-1	League	Spencer (3)	12,058	
14/01/97	A Huddersfield W 2-1	FA Cup	Peacock, McDonald	11,814	
19/01/97	A Port Vale D 4-4	League	OG, Impey, Murray, Spencer	5,736	
25/01/97	H Barnsley W 3-2	FA Cup	Spencer, Peacock, Sinclair	14,317	# 106
29/01/97	H Birmingham D 1-1	League	Spencer	12,138	
01/02/97	H Crystal Palace L 0-1	League		16,467	
05/02/97	A Swindon D 1-1	League	Hateley	10,830	
08/02/97	A Ipswich Town L 0-2	League		12,983	
15/02/97	A Wimbledon L 1-2	FA Cup	Hateley	22,395	# 107
22/02/97	A Stoke City D 0-0	League		13,121	
01/03/97	H Oldham Ath L 0-1	League		10,180	
04/03/97	A Charlton Ath L 1-2	League	Dichio	10,610	
08/03/97	H Huddersfield W 2-0	League	McDermott, Spencer	9,789	
12/03/97	H Reading L 0-2	League		10,316	# 108
15/03/97	A Southend Utd W 1-0	League	OG	6,747	
22/03/97	H Portsmouth W 2-1	League	Murray, Spencer	15,746	
29/03/97	A Oxford Utd W 3-2	League	Yates, Spencer, Peacock	8,365	
31/03/97	H Wolves D 2-2	League	Spencer, Peacock	17,376	
05/03/97	A Bolton L 1-2	League	Morrow	19,198	
12/03/97	H Grimsby W 3-0	League	Spencer, Murray, Slade	10,765	# 109
19/04/97	A Man City W 3-0	League	Spencer (2), Slade	27,580	
26/04/97	H Tranmere W 2-0	League	Dichio, Spencer	14,859	
04/05/97	A Bradford City L 0-3	League		14,723	

League Record - P46 W18 D12 L16 F64 A60 Pts 66. League position – 9th

In The Loft Player of the Season – Rufus Brevett

Chapter 2

1997/98

Overspent and under-performed

Whilst the 1996/97 campaign sticks in the memory for varying reasons, following ones were to fair less well. Going into 1997/98 expectations were even higher than the year before. Talk of 100 points and 100 goals were common amongst the exploding internet message boards. Kevin Gallen was back, Mike Sheron arrived for £2.35m and super Johnny Spencer was going to blast in at least 30 goals on top of that. No other team in the league could boast such strength up front, and you'd have been hard pressed to find one with better midfielders — the likes of Sinclair, Peacock, Quashie and Murray would have walked into any team. Quite how we managed to nearly get relegated leaves me bewildered even to this day.

After eight games things were looking good. Performances hadn't exactly been up to the standard expected, but to be joint-top after four straight wins pointed to great things. The tide turned following a miserable defeat at Port Vale and we were never to win on our travels again all season. It was becoming obvious that two players in particular who thought they belonged in the Premiership were just not putting in the required effort. Spencer sulked off once the goals weren't as frequent as the season before — Everton eventually took him off our hands in March, whilst Sinclair was anonymous pretty much from the off but perked up considerably when finally offloaded to Premiership West Ham in February. He scored twice on his debut and ended up with 7 goals in 14 games during the remainder of the season — as many goals as he managed for QPR in his 73 appearances in Division 1.

Quite how the man-management of Stewart Houston played its part is hard to say. He never seemed to have any kind of conviction in the role. He had the players, so the buck has to stop with him, although Bruce Rioch seemed to be hated by just about everyone, which done little for team harmony. The signing of Mike Sheron done Houston no favours. "Get me Mike Sheron and I'll get you the Premiership," he reportedly told Chris Wright. Wright fell for it and financially proved to be a major disaster. Sheron simply wasn't worth that kind of money – a decent enough player but a quarter of his transfer fee would have been more appropriate. Any hope that Gallen would supply the goals where Sheron and Spencer spluttered along proved another shattered dream. Gallen was almost like a different player on his return from injury, old before his time yet he was will only 21. Gallen, Spencer and Sheron managed just 19 league goals between them.

Houston lasted until November, replaced by Ray Harford who was poached from high-flying West Brom. He considered it a step up at the time but it would prove to be his worst experience in football. Harford recorded just three league wins until the end of the season. 14 draws and the crazy mind of Jamie Pollock just about saved our soul.

The QPR brand was still proving to be respected. Loan singings Mark Kennedy and Neil Ruddock were major coups, whilst Vinnie Jones offered verbal and physical batterings, if little else. The whole season though had been an absolute disaster and in terms of ability and expectations compared to the eventual outcome, for me the 1997/98 season has to go down as the worst in living memory. ❑

Here we go again then

Another nine months of hard slog, battling against the elements and trying to fight both physical and mental pain. And that's just my job as editor!

At £2.35m, Mike Sheron became QPR's joint record signing when he was signed from Stoke at the start of July after months of chasing by Stewart Houston. QPR have certainly got an embarrassment of riches up front now, and something has got to give eventually. That something will undoubtedly be Trevor Sinclair as the system Houston is expected to start the season with — 3-4-1-2 — simply doesn't have an attacking position available, or even suitable, that our 'star' player can fill. Although currently injured, there has been interest from both Wimbledon and Derby in recent weeks (how sad these clubs are considered bigger than QPR nowadays).

Sinclair is currently one of 13 players on the sidelines. The full list, as at the end of July, reads Roberts, Sommer, Ready, Brevett, Yates, Challis, Plummer, Bardsley, Slade, Quashie, Sheron, Sinclair and Charles. Although most should be fit for the start of the season, it has hardly been an ideal situation to have pre-season. The big bonus of course is seeing Kevin Gallen back in action again, slightly ahead of schedule, although poor old David Bardsley seems to have the injury from hell and looks set to be out until after Christmas.

Sadly, but pretty much as expected, Alan McDonald was released by QPR in the summer and joined Swindon on a free transfer. It is very hard to put into words what a great servant Alan was to the club, and no matter what you perceived his ability to be, there's no doubting he was QPR through and through and incredibly popular with the fans, who recognised his loyalty and commitment to QPR. It's a pity he couldn't have stayed on at the club in some shape or form, and his leadership will be greatly missed. Sometimes you can have the best defenders in the world in your side, but without someone there as leader, it will never work. For that reason alone, QPR will miss Alan immensely, and just the how the defence will fare without him remains to be seen.
(Ed – issue # 110)

Pre-season doubts and questions

I had an overwhelming sense of optimism about the coming season — strange yes, but true. With the new signings, the promising younger players, the return of Kevin Gallen and the prospect of starting the season with Spencer and Peacock the title celebrations for next May were rapidly moving from the planning to the booking stage.

Gillingham away (oh dear)
I wouldn't like to say that the optimism I had disappeared but after this pre-season friendly, I left 'planet QPR' and returned firmly back to earth.

It could be said that it was only a friendly — and after all they mean nothing. It could also be pointed out that big fat Jim Stannard — Gills keeper — produced at least three superb saves. Furthermore it could be said that the team that played and the formation used is not necessarily the one that will start the season, and to do a serious bit of 'straw clutching' QPR were, after all, the away side.

Trouble was that despite the fact we had a new keeper in Harper, a centre back in Rose, a striker in Sheron and Gallen back playing again, little if anything had changed. The team still lacks shape. Take the midfield — we still lack a genuine ball winner, a man who can take the game by the scruff of the neck and go on to 'run it'. Other familiar sight's saw;

- Brevett endearing himself to the crowd by adopting a far from friendly attitude
- Murray showing the temper that appeared a few times too many last season
- The defence being, at times, all over the proverbial shop as Gillingham attacked with pace, power and purpose

Gillingham's players may not have our players' skills but it can't be denied that they looked both physically fitter and bigger than our players. In a physical league such as the Nationwide, I await the new season with increased anxiety and trepidation.

I'll finish this morale boosting cheery article with a few questions on certain subjects. No answers from these quarters either, because I can't do so with any confidence.

1) How is it that although the team produced a great deal of dire performances last season, the play-offs were still within reach until the second to last game of the season?
2) Is there anyone who thinks that they could handle the tension of a play-off final?
3) How come Andy Impey — player of the season two years back — now only warrants a £1.2m price tag?
4) Why did Rangers fans at times last season call for Houston to resign or be sacked when Wilkins never received the same treatment?
6) Just how did John Spencer score his first goal against Barnsley, and the winner against Portsmouth?
7) In FHM's '100 sexiest women 1997', how the hell did Uma Thurman finish as low down the chart as number 54?
(Matthew Holley – issue # 110)

Role reversal

After being linked with just about every vacant managerial position this summer, Bruce Rioch has firmly stated his future lays with QPR. But the question needs to be asked, exactly what is Rioch's role? If ever a high-profile figure has taken such a back-seat role, then Rioch is certainly it. You never see him quoted, interviewed or pictured. Stewart Houston is certainly the dominating figure of our managerial partnership, whereas the role was reversed in their days at Arsenal. Undoubtedly Rioch is an excellent man to have at QPR, although what impact he has made on the team is very hard to pin point as he is very much in the background. There were signs towards the end of last season that the style of football QPR were playing was very Rioch-inspired, but can he take the credit? Or perhaps, will Houston let him? It's about time Rioch stepped out of the shadows and be allowed to express his true worth to QPR.

(Ed – issue # 110)

Golden Brown

The joint-record signing of Mike Sheron for £2.35m certainly raised a few eyebrows in these parts, not least because with Kevin Gallen now fit again, how exactly is Stewart Houston going to juggle his team around to keep everyone happy? To gain a better insight Into the player, we asked the co-editor of 'The Oatcake' (Stoke fanzine), Martin Smith, for his views on the situation.

"He most certainly was a flop at Norwich where he scored, I think, two goals in about thirty games. At Stoke though he was a revelation. He started scoring as soon as he came to the club and for the best part of a season and a half he was finding the back of the net on a very regular basis (42 goals in all during that time).

As much as he was adored by Stoke fans most of us were aware of his fallings; he lacks pace, his passing to fellow team-mates is often atrocious and he cannot head a ball to save his life — he did score a few headers for us but these were of the "my gran could have buried that one" and these efforts dwarf in comparison to all the headers he missed. As well as these faults there are quite a few Stokies who noticed that his form tailed off alarmingly when all the transfer speculation started — he sort of went AWOL for a few matches and picked up a couple of 'mystery injuries.' One of the reasons he gave for doing so well when he came to Stoke was that he had been homesick at Norwich, which is why we found it so surprising that he has chosen to go back south again. Personally I think that £2.35m was a more than fair price, though of course we had to give about £800,000 of that to Norwich — drat! That said, most Stokies would prefer he was still with us.

Despite his shortcomings he was as good a goalscorer as we've had for some time. If Gallen gets fit and Spencer plays to form then I think you'll have a very expensive player in your reserves at which point we'll have him back on loan!"

(Ed – issue # 110)

Gillingham blues

Having just watched us lose at Gillingham, it is worrying me that our team shows a distinct lack of balance. I know it is wrong to deduce conclusions from a tin-pot friendly, but for a team as attacking as the one put out at Priestfield, it was alarming that we managed very few worthwhile efforts on goal.

A team consisting of three strikers, two attack-minded midfielders and two wing-backs is too attacking, and Stewart Houston of all people should know this. I am going to put my neck on the line and say that Houston may have made a blunder by signing Mike Sheron. Although nifty as a youngster, he faded out at Man City, did nothing at Norwich and struggled during the second half of last season with Stoke. £2.35m is a hell of a gamble for a club for us. However, time will tell, and I'll give him the chance — if he does the business, you will see my apology on the front cover of In The Loft.

Regardless of whose names are on the team-sheet this season, I shall be supporting them, not barracking them. There were plenty of twats last year, particularly away from home, that slagged off members of the team and the manager. What makes it even worse is when the person can't even pronounce player's names properly.

I had a feeling we would lose at Gillingham, a progressive club that have made huge strides in the last two years with a bunch of lumbering donkeys. Having moved from Gillingham just just over six months ago and with work colleagues who support the club, perhaps it was inevitable that they would beat us. Another interesting point is that some of my sixth-form school colleagues were serving hot-dogs — with three A Levels. I had to laugh, but then I suppose not everyone can aspire to the heights of an In The Loft match-day seller like me.

I don't know why everyone seems so pissed off about Impey's departure to West Ham. What was it, one really good season and the rest mediocre — particularly the last two. Since relegation his attitude has been far from great. He can consider himself fortunate to be playing Premiership football again (if he ever passes his medical of course).

Finally, what about this for a piece of memorabilia — Terry Fenwick's hooped track-top, as worn by the goalscorer himself in the 1982 cup final, is currently in my wardrobe — sized extra-large. I also saw his match-day shorts—sized extra-tight.
(Aidan Magee – issue # 110)

Come home Les

As I write, it looks pretty certain that Les Ferdinand is going to join Tottenham, and I can't help but feel what "could have been." Had QPR earned promotion last season what would the chances have been of persuading him to come back to QPR? Slim probably, but imagine the thought — Ferdinand, Gallen and Spencer in one attack. We certainly could have afforded him if we are willing to gamble nearly £3m on Sheron. I'm pretty certain Les will return to QPR one day, but wonder if a golden opportunity was wasted by playing like a bunch of plonkers for far too much of last season, determining another season in Division 1.

(Peter Walden – issue # 110)

Are we Arsenal in disguise?

The exciting news is that Arsenal reserves have signed up a new £12 million forward line and are going to try their luck in the Nationwide Division One, borrowing QPR's ground, staff, kit and fans in a revolutionary loan system. In truth I haven't got a major problem with Houston bringing in players he knows, wherever they come from, the main thing is that they're any good. As I said at the start, any genuine optimism has to be founded on what's really going to make a difference since last year, and in fact since last November I reckon we have added more players and made more changes than anybody else in this division (except Birmingham who would even change their name for an envelope full of crumply tenners).

Counting from Spencer and Peacock's debut game at Reading I made it 44 points from 27 games, a ratio that equates to fourth or fifth in the table. That includes the 8 games without a win Feb/March, but it also includes half a dozen wins when the season was all but over. Greeting the acquisition of Sheron with cautious optimism — yes I know I'm supposed to say that either he's the Messiah to lead us out of the wilderness or he's a complete waste of money but why don't we just wait and see — we could push for an automatic spot. The doubt is that, leaderless without McDonald, the defence looks too poofy for my liking — aptly described by Brian Glanville as the thin blue line. The wild card is Trevor Sinclair, a technically gifted player who just does not fit in to Houston's preferred system at all. I might be tempted to play him wide right without a full-back behind him, in the same sort of role as Beckham takes up for England. If that doesn't work it would probably be best for everyone if he moves on.

(Andy Ward – issue # 110)

Honey, honey

Despite QPR ground-sharing with Wasps, I have been pleased to see Loftus Road retain its blue & white appearance — until now that is. As I took to my new season-ticket seat in the Ellerslie Road stand for the Ipswich game, I was horrified to find my bottom now being parked on an ORANGE seat, that I believe forms part of one of two giant wasps made up by seat colours. Next season I reckon I'll have to pay for my season ticket with 200 jars of honey.

(Julian Mahoney – issue # 111)

Not the best of starts

All is not well in the life of QPR. The shocking display at Nottingham Forest has snowballed the calls for Houston to be dismissed, and whilst I believe his position as manager is fairly safe for the time being, any more performances like that witnessed at Forest will surely put his future in doubt. The next four matches are all encoutners QPR should be looking to take maximum points from. Anything less than favourable results and performances could well decide our manager's fate sooner than anyone could have expected. There is still a lot of time for QPR to come good — we all know what the team is capable of. How much time Stewart Houston has though remains to be seen.

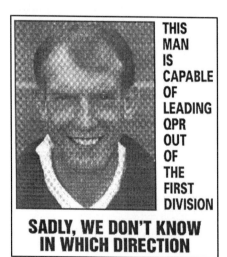

THIS MAN IS CAPABLE OF LEADING QPR OUT OF THE FIRST DIVISION

SADLY, WE DON'T KNOW IN WHICH DIRECTION

One of the most telling aspects towards QPR's less than impressive start to the season has to be the poor form of John Spencer. Last season Spencer became an instant cult figure as his quality and quantity of goals pulled QPR out of the mire time and time again. This season, without a 'big man' to play off, Spencer has found the going tough and an ankle injury picked up in training has hardly helped his cause. Spencer was quoted as saying in the Daily Record pre-season that he doesn't intend to hang around in Division 1 for more than another season, and if QPR failed to do the business this season, he would be looking for a move. If QPR are to make any headway this season, a lot of the burden will surely fall on Spencer's shoulders. QPR will only succeed if Spencer succeeds. Get to it Johnny, make yourself a hero once again.

This is certainly going to be a make or break season for Kevin Gallen. Now back to full fitness, his early form has been terrible and if he doesn't start scoring regularly for QPR soon, the fear is he never will. When Gallen first broke into the first team at the start of the 94/95 season, Gerry Francis commented at the time "he has matured from being a boy to a man." How Gallen must wish there was still some of the "boy" in him. The 1997 Kevin Gallen looks old before his time. He has no pace, his shooting is awful and his physique could do with a lot of working on. He's 21 going on 31, but still with little sign he is going to fulfil his enormous potential showed as a junior. If Gallen doesn't find his shooting boots soon, his career will end up being "what could have been."
(Ed – issue # 111)

QPR 2-1 Stockport Couny

It's been quite a while since I last attended a home match that had such a nasty atmosphere. The period between Stockport equalising and QPR grabbing the winning goal seemed like a lifetime spent amongst fellow supporters who seemingly believed anything less than QPR winning 6-0 was a crime of the highest order.

The performance was poor, especially in the second half as we defended atrociously, but the attitude and behaviour from many fans, at least in the upper Loft where I was sitting, is detrimental to the team, and annoying to others who have far more patience and who simply want to get behind their team instead of listening to such things as "Houston is a wanker," and "Fuck off Barker you c**t.". Arguments start, fellow fans rant to one another why so and so is good/bad for the team. The atmosphere, that should be good natured and encouraging, turns sour. If the players can't find encouragement from one another, at least the crowd should be able to provide something.

Things reached a head when Paul Murray was substituted — he was playing no better or worse than anyone else, but the disapproval from QPR fans was obvious. Murray, like Kevin Gallen, is a big favourite amongst the fans, but when Gallen was substituted, I heard not one word of disapproval. What's the difference? Two minutes after Murray was substituted, Trevor Sinclair struck the winning goal. A great substitution or just coincidental? Full credit to Trevor though, back to his best with both goals today, but can he do it again?

With expectations so high this season, fans are demanding instant results. Last season, despite familiar confidence amongst fans, was like a step into the unknown. This season is different — the squad in stronger, the fans wiser. Stewart Houston is the kind of person who will only satisfy the majority of fans by fielding a team that stays in the top three or four all season, playing stylish football. Anything less and he will get abuse, and possibly the sack.

A time to evaluate how the season has started is around 10-12 games in when the league table starts to take shape. Anything less is premature and unnecessary. That is why there will be no calls for Houston to go in these pages — although a time may arise when that could change.

(Ed – issue # 111)

Mystic Magee – The 2nd

September

QPR announce a brand-new sponsorship deal with a major household name. The deal is worth £1m over three years, and Chris Wright says, "We are delighted to be associated with Domestos." A scandal rocks the club as the 'Irish News' claims that they caught Steve Morrow shagging an invisible person. Stewart Houston calls the report a disgrace, whilst Morrow claims merely to have been doing some press-ups. After the sacking of Alex Ferguson, Manchester United chairman Martin Edwards tells a press conference that he is seeking a replacement who will command the respect of the players and act shrewdly in the transfer market. Edwards added that he had been in touch with Ray Wilkins, but he couldn't think of anyone either.

October

Results begin to go against Rangers in October and Houston and Rioch decide to impose a ban on sex for players, 24 hours before a matchday in a bid to improve performance on the pitch. In the match at Bury, QPR take a 1-0 lead, but end up losing 2-1. When asked to evaluate the effects of his new policy on the team, Houston said "They started well, but in the second half many became frustrated and started humping the ball." Elsewhere, David Beckham appears in his first commercial, as part of his sponsorship deal with Brylcream. Other players follow Beckham's hair-care lead as 'Studio Line' sign up Chris Waddle. Ray Wilkins also signs a similar deal with 'Mr. Sheen.'

November

Cash-strapped Bournemouth embarrassingly reveal that they wrote a cheque for nine pounds which bounced. A club source said that their proposed signing of Karl Ready has subsequently been put on hold. Mike Sheron defies the critics who said he wouldn't make a lasting mark on the club. There is now an imprint of his arse on the subs bench. After the match at Middlesbrough, the Football League begin investigating an incident where John Spencer celebrated his wining goal by parading a flagpole carrying a QPR jersey. At the hearing, Spencer has no trouble convincing the panel that he was hugging Steve Slade.

December

Kevin Gallen begins dating the model from the Wonderbra adverts, and rumours that they plan to marry in the summer are fuelled when she announces that she is dying to get something off her chest. She appears topless in The Sun the next day. Chris Wright makes an astonishing offer to Stewart Houston by offering him a job for life. Houston however declines the offer saying he doesn't have the experience to become a turnstile operator.

January

Houston and Rioch decide that a bit of humour is needed in the dressing room to raise players' spirits. They tell the team they're going up. Fans at Loftus Road become aware of the management's desire to play jokes, as Simon Barker is named at number eight against Bradford. Elsewhere, another foreigner arrives at Middlesbrough, and this time it's Maradona. The Argentine asks manager Bryan Robson where the nearest boozer is, and Robbo points at Paul Merson.

February

QPR make headway in the FA Cup by winning their third, fourth and fifth round ties. After a two-month injury setback, John Spencer declares that the quarter-final will be his round. Midfielder Gavin Peacock says, "It's about time the bastard bought us a drink." The most sensational story of the season comes when former Oxford United chairman Robert Maxwell rises from the dead. His family tell him that since his 'death' in 1991, the Manor Ground has become a labyrinth of shoddy brickwork, cracked terracing, rickety framework, bent railings and smashed windows. Maxwell says he had no idea they'd done it up.

March

Kevin Gallen is criticised over his affair with a buxom blonde porn star. Stewart Houston defends the striker by saying that if anyone can handle the knockers, it's him. However, Chris Wright is more critical of Gallen's love triangle, explaining that "three's a crowd." As if to reinforce the point, he quotes some of QPR's midweek attendances. Meanwhile, Trevor Sinclair says he will be out for the rest of the season, although a friend says that he plans to stay in one night during April. Elsewhere, Crystal Palace's Italian forward Attillio Lombardo drops his biggest hint yet that we will leave Palace on deadline day, by saying that he is determined to leave the Eagles in the Premiership.

April

In the FA Cup semi-final, Karl Ready strips naked on the pitch after committing a dreadful foul. BBC viewers are stunned, and Houston says that Ready took opposition chants of "Off Off Off," completely the wrong way. Houston makes Mike Sheron the scapegoat for the 6-0 defeat by Arsenal by saying that the only time he troubled David Seaman was when he requested an autograph for the missus. Rioch directed criticism at the defensive partnership of Rose and Ready, saying "They are too similar to play together — they're both crap." Trevor Sinclair is banned from driving for a year after being found to be eight times over the legal alcohol limit.

May

Reformed gambling addict Steve Claridge claims to have lost £400,000 in bets before successfully kicking the habit last year. When asked whether he had any tips for other addicts, he said, "Rough Quest, 2.10 at Chepstow." As some feared, Trevor Sinclair emotionally tells the world at a media conference that he has a drink problem — he has trouble getting to the off-license without his car. The Sun's resident baldy git Greavsie suggests that players should consider 'Alcoholics Anonymous' — "At least this way they can drink under a different name." Sinclair took this advice onboard and gave AA a ring. He was slightly surprised to see a big yellow van pull up outside his house an

hour later. On the pitch, Rangers win a close play-off final against Norwich at Wembley, as John Spencer leaps high to head home Brevett's low cross. Despite the twin towers success, Chris Wright assures fans that new faces will arrive at W12 — Stewart Houston has already requested one for himself.
(Aidan Magee – issue # 111)

In defence of Trevor

Actually, I know absolutely nothing about the case of Mr Sinclair's alleged fracas in Manchester. I'll leave that to his solicitor. What I am concerned about is the amount of flak Trevor seems to be receiving from Rangers fans. I find it particularly strange because the people that slag Trevor often argue that if he was white and without dreadlocks, no one would take any notice of him because he's an ordinary player. Trevor's image is very much a media creation — not his own. He was a well recognised figure even before his regrettable modelling exploits with Top Man, and it's hardly his fault that many women find him attractive. It is not Trevor's fault that some stupid clubs seem to be willing to risk £5million on him, so shouting "£5 million Sinclair? Wouldn't pay £500 for you mate," is hardly an insult because he has never, and probably never will, claim to be worth that kind of money.

Clubs today have to think about merchandising, not just the player. Trevor is popular due to his skill and because of his image — he attracts fans to the game, and people will pay money to have his name on the back of their shirts. In the long run, financially, Trevor may well be worth £4million+, simply because of his attraction.

That's dealt with his image then — in today's football world where players are treated as movie stars, many of them have little control over their image — except Alan Shearer, but when you've got a one-dimensional personality it's kind of hard for the media to make up an alternative one. Gazza's a nutter, Graeme Le Saux is intelligent, Iain Dowie is ugly, Paul Merson's a reformed man, and Trevor Sinclair is football's Mr Sex. That's the way it is. Let's move on. Commitment. Where has this incredibly misguided idea that Trevor "simply doesn't care," "doesn't want to know," "just wants an easy life modelling," trash come from exactly? Until the end of the season when a terrible challenge put him out with injury, he'd barely missed a game since he came to QPR. When he loses the ball, he chases and tries to win it back. I can remember a certain famous idol of recent years who'd have half the crowd stunned into silence when he chased back after losing the ball, so rarely did he bother — preferring instead to put his head down and his hands on his hips.

I admit that at the start of last season when there was much transfer speculation, Trevor's form was poor, but the same could be said of all our players except Macca. If you research the goals we scored before his injury I'm pretty sure he was directly involved with well over half of them. And even if he had put over more than just the occasional useful cross, who exactly was going to head them in? Last season Hateley and Dichio proved how poor they both were by probably scoring less headed goals between them than the somewhat shorter John Spencer. In the dark days before before Spencer & Peacock arrived I can remember pinning virtually all my hopes on Sinclair. This may say a lot for the quality of the rest of the team, but even if his shooting is ridiculously poor, his attitude compared with the likes of Impey and Dichio was exemplary — he tries his best for QPR. At times he tried too hard, I certainly got the impression he felt like Juninho at Middlesbrough — no-one else seemed capable of much so he had to do it himself, and too often he held onto the ball for too long. And here is the important point. The team, just like me, looked exclusively to Sinclair. Get the ball, get it to the right wing — especially because of Impey's endless suspensions, where someone will have a go at the opposition. When Spencer and Peacock arrived it improved because the unimaginative back four had more belief in who they were passing to — there were two more quality options, and with Murray developing more and more, things improved. The crunch, as a few have pointed out, was when Sinclair got injured, QPR suddenly started playing better, started passing better, started to win more games.

Sinclair's absence meant that QPR players had to look elsewhere; Murray, Spencer, Impey, Quashie and especially Peacock benefited from this. Peacock's improved play was not due to a sudden turn in form, but was more due to the formation and his new position, with he and Spencer playing just behind a centre-forward, and of course it allowed Quashie to step in to midfield (providing Houston saw sense and played him instead of Barker). The passing improved because the players didn't automatically look to Sinclair, and he wasn't our main attacking option.

Contrary to popular opinion, I believe Trevor can be accommodated into the system. I believe we should play a 3-4-2-1 formation, with Sinclair and Brevett as wing-backs, and only one out of Sheron and Gallen playing centre-forward supported by Spencer and Peacock. However, why we signed Sheron is still a mystery to me. Houston said he had "genuine pace," — next to Ray Wilkins maybe. If he wants to play two strikers, why didn't he sign a tall one who can head the thing, and not someone who plays in exactly the same role as Gallen? With proper coaching I have no doubt Sinclair could be extremely effective in a wing-back role — certainly more so than Mark Graham or any of the other 17 right-backs we experimented with last season, except maybe McDermott, and we all know what happened there.

I don't deny that if someone offered £5million for Sinclair I wouldn't bite their hand off with my sharp fangs, but to be honest that money is nothing more than speculation — I don't believe anyone's offered more than £3million, otherwise Houston would have said goodbye to Trevor months ago. The fact is he is a QPR player, and one that has displayed some loyalty and, I believe, a lot of commitment to the QPR cause. His crossing and shooting are infuriatingly bad at times, but people like to watch Sinclair, and he is capable of skills that the majority of players in the Premiership can only dream about. I don't care if Trevor never produces another goal like the overhead kick, what he needs is to be settled into a system than can become familiar to everyone playing it, where his value does not result in every ball being pumped to the wing. The best can be gained from Trevor when everyone stops seeing him as some kind of failed saviour and more of a talented but hard working player that occasionally produces some unforgettable magic.

(Dan Trelfer – issue # 111)

Progress, at what cost?

Defeat at Port Vale will hopefully prove to be a minor setback as QPR continue to make progress at the top of the league, but things aren't quite smelling of roses yet if recent rumours are anything to go by. Team spirit could be better for a start. An alleged punch up between Kevin Gallen and John Spencer on the training ground suggests there is friction in the air, and Bruce Rioch apparently is hardly a favourite amongst the players. There is obvious tension on display on the pitch at times, with players arguing amongst themselves and lots of screaming and shouting taking place when a move breaks down, or a pass or cross is inaccurate. Progress has been made since the poor show at Nottingham Forest, but the general feeling is that there is a lot of discontent amongst the squad, which unless makes a rapid departure, could have a detrimental effect on the team in the weeks ahead.

Nigel Quashie, a recent star for the England U-21s, followed by a man of the match display in the game against West Brom, will according to John Spencer "be worth more than Alan Shearer if he ever leaves QPR." Spencer went on to say that Quashie is the best passer of a ball he's seen since Glenn Hoddle, and "will be a full England player within a year." We all know Quashie is a great prospect at QPR, but I think Spencer must have been on drugs to say such things about the 19-year-old midfielder. Then again, having spent nearly five years at Chelsea it's rather obvious Spencer knows nothing about football! Quashie repaid the compliment by setting up Spencer for the opening goal at Crewe, but his prospects of being valued at more than £15m are a million miles away.

(Ed – issue # 112)

In defence of the gaffer

With the air of expectancy filling Loftus Road this season, it would appear that any substandard performance is going to lead to calls for the sacking of Stewart Houston. You only had to be at the Coca Cola Cup match at home to Wolves to hear the

'Houston Out.' chants to realise what Rangers fans expect this season. And this abuse in only the first week of the season! I for one am a supporter of Stewart Houston. I think he has the ability to take us back to the Premiership this season despite us having a lot of big clubs to contend with. But, like any other human being, it won't do his confidence any good with people calling for his head so soon into the new season.

To be fair to Stewart, when he came to Rangers last year, he came to a club that was in complete turmoil. We had the reality of relegation, a new board trying to find its feet, a new sponsor, and probably the weakest squad in living memory. The club was in a real mess. Houston had a massive job of finding his way around the club, assessing who could do what, and they buy the players to fill the huge holes in the team. He may not have done things as quickly as we would have liked, but who could doubt that he made two excellent signings in John Spencer and Gavin Peacock? Houston appears to be a man who errs on the side of caution and does not go crashing into the transfer market feet first like his predecessor did. He knows the weaknesses in the team and has tried to address these problems.

It's far too early to say much about his summer signings as they need time to settle in as we all do when we change jobs. Admittedly he has made some odd decisions such as his handling of Paul Murray last season, and the selection of Simon Barker, but recently he has done something about it. Most Rangers fans would agree with at least nine of the team selections he made against West Brom.

So I would appeal to all true Rangers fans to start supporting Stewart Houston and really get behind him as he tries to get us promoted out of this Godforsaken division. We all want him to succeed and I'm sure he will with our support and the players doing their jobs, but if he fails then yes, he should go. Only time will tell if he's good enough. Let's give him it.

(Richard Atkins – issue # 112)

Just Crewe-sing

So there I was, on the train on platform 5 at Euston ready to make my way to Crewe, not with other like-minded R's fans but with the day-trippers and the sadly misinformed tourists. I had managed to get a ticket but couldn't get on the fully booked-up football special — this wasn't so bad as for £3.50 less I could go up an hour earlier and come back three hours later (more pub time). It was a fairly mundane journey up, and Crewe itself was the epitome of a northern town; one long road, at least 12 pubs and the same number of chip shops. It was quite a bland place but was very laid back and I enjoyed it, especially the pubs! There was a police cordon stopping opposing fans getting through to the away end, a bit like the 'ring of steel' employed in the city, and so flashing my ticket like some detective from CI5 I made my way into the ground. Gresty Road is not much to look at, almost like a non-league ground but at least all four sides were covered. I've never ever, as far as I can remember, seen QPR go 3-0 up away from home as Spencer, Maddix and Sinclair put us in a strong position. Both Quashie and Peacock were running the midfield, spraying balls around with unerring accuracy. It was a mystery as to why we were not 7-0 up as both Peacock and Sheron missed golden opportunities.

Although the R's were still carving out chances, the passing started to go astray and the tackles were being missed so it was no surprise that Crewe scored. Adebola shrugged off tired looking tackles from Ready and Morrow to pass for Lunt for a simple tap in. There were more than a few nervous looks from the QPR fans as Crewe got a second through Adebola, although this looked suspiciously offside, a fact backed up on TV.

The QPR fans were now whistling for the final whistle, then relief all round in the away end as Rangers almost snatched defeat away from the jaws of victory. Whilst everyone headed back to the coaches and trains I headed back to the Bank bar for a few pints to toast a hard fought win — only one problem, all the pubs were shut and they wouldn't open for another one and a half hours! I later found out the reason for this was that everyone goes home for their tea! Wandering around Crewe for an hour and a half is not exactly the most entertaining thing in the world to do, although I did manage to have a look round Gresty Road and have a little walk out onto the pitch. I bought the Green 'Un newspaper to read up on the match (they were impressed with Quashie), by which time the Bank bar had opened (Banks Bitter and flavoured vodka shots at £1.20 each).

I didn't get back home till almost midnight but at least we had another three points in the bag and I suppose that was the main thing... that and having a fair old drink up!
(Moreno Ferrari – issue # 112)

No change on the horizon

Houston Out!? After all, out of the last 8 games we lost one 4-0, one 2-0, and we nearly didn't win one or two of the other six. Yeah, what we need to do is sack the management, leave the team in complete turmoil for at least a month and then bring in someone completely different to start from scratch again — that should work. I'm sorry, I know it's the lowest form of wit but I felt like getting my point of view across as well. The difference is, if you want to know what I think you can pick this mag up and read it, or not, at your leisure — I don't inflict my views on everyone in earshot while they're trying to enjoy their free time, OK? OK. Not that I'm dusting off the route maps to Anfield and Old Trafford just yet, but the simple fact that we are top three without having, I feel, played particularly well is some cause for encouragement.

There is still plenty of room for improvement, especially in defence, where Maddix and co are showing their expertise at last-ditch saving tackles but it would be better if a little more concentration was applied to stop these tackles from being needed in the first place. Right back is obviously the major problem — we clearly don't have one so why not do without, tuck Ready or Rose or whoever into a back three, play Sinclair as a ¾-wing ¼-back and switch Peacock off the left wing where he is ineffective and into 'the hole' where he is excellent. A couple of minor tweaks which could make a big difference, particularly at home where opposing defenders would fill their tights at the prospect of having to deal with Spencer, Sheron, Sinclair and Peacock buzzing around the last third.

(Andy Ward – issue # 112)

Tubthumping or Pigbag?

Can someone please let me know why it is that the team runs out to Chumbuwumba's 'Tubthumping' this season? Whatever happened to the fans favourite 'Hoops' sung along to the theme of 'Pigbag'? Is it because the line "I get knocked down but I get up again," is a reference to last season's habit of giving the opposition a goal start?! Or is it because the line "He drinks a whisky drink, he drinks a vodka drink, he drinks a cider drink," etc, a reference to Kevin Gallen's bar order!

On the subject of Kevin Gallen, what a disappointment he is turning out to be. I remember when he was banging in the goals for the youth team and then the reserves, how he was being touted as a future England centre forward, even Alex Ferguson made an impromptu bid to buy him — but his career seems to have taken a nosedive.

It's true that he has suffered his fair share of injuries, but I wish he was built like a brick outhouse so that he wouldn't get knocked off the ball by all these tuppeny halfpenny doggers; I wish he would follow Sir Les's example and work on his upper body; I wish all those heavy drinking whispers would go away and how I wish he was back banging in the goals as I remembered him doing for the first team... because I like Kevin Gallen, he is 'one of us' out there on the pitch and I only want to see him do well at QPR.

(Moreno Ferrari – issue # 112)

Small is not always beautiful

The football produced by QPR this season has ranged from poor to average. Our hopes that QPR would walk away with this division with no shortage of skilled, attacking football have sadly proven way off the mark. The reason is simple — QPR are a good team of individuals, but an ordinary side collectively. We have too many players of a certain ability, and not enough of another. The biggest problem is up front, where a lack of height in attack has meant the team has not been able to earn or keep possession consistently, which in turn has led to a shortage of goals — just 18 in 13 games up to and including the Man City game (it wouldn't be so bad if our defence wasn't so poor).

Spencer and Sheron are trying — and always failing — to win the ball with a defender towering over them from behind. The presence of Dichio has been greatly missed this season, if not necessarily for his goalscoring ability. His number of assists last season speaks volumes. Spencer and Sheron are both good strikers, but are hardly prolific at the moment. If every team in this league was as small as us, they'd score for fun. With that not being the case, there remains a serious problem that needs to be addressed. Again, you have to question the signing of Sheron, we really could have done with a different kind of striker.

I'd go as far as saying that we would be in a much better position in the league with a strike force of Dichio & Spencer, or Dichio & Sheron. For Sheron & Spencer, small is not always beautiful.
(Ed – issue # 113)

The alternative dimension

Why did Houston sign Spencer and Sheron if for at least 70-80% of the game the side are going to resort to pumping aimless high balls up to them? It is boring, lacks imagination and is a fruitless mode of attack with such little height up front to aim at. One would assume that any manager who spends in excess of five million pounds on a strikeforce would be looking to build a side around them that plays to their strengths (i.e. balls played to feet), and therefore bring out the best in them.

Other problems in this side is the lack of a true right back and two players in Maddix and Morrow who are clearly ill at ease playing in a flat back four. Morrow has, this season, become a butt for the fans frustrations but remember last season when he played competently and often very well. His deterioration in form is due to the system which, up to the Sheffield United game, was being played. Other areas for concern are the lack of a genuine ball winner in midfield and an apparent lack of team spirit and commitment — a damning slur on the current management team indeed.

This piece is being penned after the credible draw at Sheffield United and it raises the points discussed earlier. Has Steve Morrow's last gasp equaliser saved both his first team place and his manager's job? Earlier in the season rumours were rife at Reading that had we lost that night Houston was to be sacked. Anyone who attended will testify that the team were awful — at times a complete embarrassment — but they won and that was preceded by three straight wins pushing the R's into second place.

So why then the general level of despondency and lack of genuine excitement simmering around Loftus Road even before a ball had been kicked against Charlton? After all the team were lying in third place and Houston had just been made manager of the month. Basically it's because we're QPR fans and on the whole reasonably intelligent. It's like spraying a dog turd with gold paint — You may fool some but you'll never fool everyone.

Overheard at half-time 2-1 down to Charlton, "We shouldn't be losing this, Charltonaren't a very good side," er...neither are we I'm afraid to say. And 'Not very good' is what we are. Did Charlton play us off the park because man to man through 1-11 they are superior? No, they won because as a team they are superior, are well organised and attack with pace and purpose. It is a major accusation aimed at our current management but I personally believe that defensively we are now significantly worse than we were the season we got relegated. That's why the lack of excitement is around because what happened against

QPR'S DEFENSIVE ABILITIES COME UNDER QUESTION

FANS GIVE THEIR VERDICT

Charlton has been on the cards for a long time. I hate to say it but with only 11 games gone I've seen precious little to convince me that this current management team and this squad of players are capable of making and sustaining a promotion challenge.

Also overheard during the Charlton fiasco, "Come on Slade you were good in the seventies!" Sob, bit like QPR really...

Apparently in another dimension far far away QPR got slaughtered at Reading and Houston got the sack. The new management team had a major task on their hands and defeats against West Brom, Crewe and Portsmouth saw the team bottom of the league. However with new faces settling in and the management's fresh and exciting ideas starting to work, a shaky 1-0 win at Port Vale was followed by the obliteration of Charlton. Now the team are starting to look really good and optimism is abundant amongst the R's fans. Oh yeah and there's this multi-millionaire called Matteus Hollioke who despite living the high life and being married to Pamela Anderson still finds time to visit the R's and also to pen really positive, cheery articles for the award winning club fanzine… or is that a little too far fetched.

(Matthew Holley – issue # 113)

Excuses, excuses

Stewart Houston has spoken about his reasons why he didn't sign Paulo Wanchope last season when he had the chance. Houston said of the player; "The main reason was I didn't see him as a centre-forward, which is what I was looking for. Jim Smith plays him wide on the left of a three-man front line and that's where he is best. He doesn't hold the ball up like Mike Sheron. He is a leggy, spidery sort of a player who likes to go on runs and play out wide. I would say he is more of a raider than a centre-forward. I already have wingers here and I was worried he wouldn't play in 75% of the games and we'd have problems with a work permit. He would also have been heading off across the Atlantic for internationals all the time. But he is doing very well at Derby and I wish the boy all the luck. I have no regrets." About 15,000 QPR supporters do I expect.

(Ed – issue # 113)

Star gazing

There were many guests present at the Manchester City match. Noel Gallagher and his wife Meg, former R's player Alan Brazil, former City player Gary Owen and also recent players Andy Impey and Clive Wilson. Impey was asked what he was doing back at Loftus Road and he replied it was to throw a few rocks at Bruce Rioch. Apparently, the reason why Impey left QPR was that he had a massive bust-up with Rioch. I don't want to worry anyone but recently Kevin Gallen was alleged to have had a punch-up with John Spencer, with reports shortly afterwards saying that Spencer was on his way out of QPR, with Middlesbrough being favourites to sign him — oh dear!

(Moreno Ferrari – issue # 113)

£750,000 Lecce bill

Daniele Dichio surprised us all recently in his underachieving Italian career by moving to Lecce — bottom of Serie A, from Sampdoria in a £750,000 switch. Despite having only made one appearance as sub for Sampdoria in a UEFA Cup match against Athletico Bilbao, Dichio was featured in the November issue of Goal magazine saying how much he was enjoying his time with Sampdoria. Obviously, the club felt differently sending him packing to Serie A's most unglamorous club.

(Ed – issue # 113)

THE PICTURE QUALITY AIN'T GOOD, BUT THEN NEITHER'S THE PLAYER... DANIELE DICHIO'S CLAIM TO FAME FOR SAMPDORIA - REPLACING JURGEN KLINSMANN IN THEIR OPENING SERIA A GAME; HIS FIRST AND ONLY APPEARANCE!

(issue # 114)

Swindon Town 3-1 QPR

Being Guy Fawks nights, fireworks could be seen lighting up the sky all around the County Ground. One such explosive came back to ground on the pitch itself, a four-foot stick pronging out of the turf only yards from where Morrow was standing. It could be said many times this season that Morrow could do with a rocket up his arse, but this was taking it quite literally!
(Ed – issue # 114)

Houston out... done

It was, in my defence, first thing in the morning, but on the day following the Houston and Rioch sackings I naively thought that the, not altogether unexpected, sensation had made front-page news! 'MERCY' the headline on the front of the Daily Mail screamed. Only later was I to realise the headline was of course, referring to the Louise Woodward trial.

Mercy for us fans though nevertheless. The season has been an atrocious one so far with negative tactics and 'up and under' balls providing the bulk of Saturday afternoon 'entertainment' at Loftus Road. As an aside, and a prime example of how bad things have become, the highlight of the bore draw against Birmingham City had to be when the PA announced "and the substitution for Manchester City...". Well when you've seen yet another terrible game against yet another second rate team these human errors are perfectly understandable.

It was all part of Houston's plan to make us more like Arsenal. Although the fans who sang "We're not Arsenal anymore," during the Huddersfield game, should think of the team the Gunners presently field and maybe not be grateful of that fact, but gutted. It's ironic but over the years we may not have had the Gunners support and silverware but we've always had far more attractive teams down the Bush and that is why precious little envy has ever been felt towards them from the average Rangers fan. Nowadays it's a different story. I hate to say it but it's definitely a case of role reversal with us inheriting the 'boring' tag. I can't begin to wonder how the average Arsenal fan is coping with having to watch exciting football and players like Vierra, Wright, Overmars and Dennis Bergkamp week in week out.

In my previous article in issue 113, for the first time I suggested that Houston and Rioch should possibly be allowed to leave. On his appointment last season and the poor run of form that followed up until December I found it hard to be critical. Here, after all, was a man picking up the pieces from the previous disastrous Wilkins & Thompson era. The club was facing one of its biggest crises due to Ray's complete incompetence right through to the board's apparent lack of interest and asset stripping. At QPR it wasn't a manager that was required. At that time a miracle worker was needed!

Of course we didn't get that but instead got an Arsenal assistant manager who slowly turned things around with the — at the time — inspired signings of Spencer and Peacock from Chelsea. In December the team hit form and the second shafting of Barnsley in January suggested not just promotion but the title...yes, we looked that good!

Alas it was not to be as the team slumped, hit form again but ultimately at the end were not good enough. This was the real problem with the management team. Because although a probable disastrous second successive relegation season was avoided (yes, we were that bad before Peacock and Spencer arrived), the team had not moved forward and after a fair few summer singings looked positively worse than the team that was relegated in 1996.

So the sacking in the end came as no real shock. After all, the team were pretty average, bordering on awful even during the four straight wins that left us in a truly false position in second place earlier in the season. It does raise several important, and some may say, worrying questions.

- What a shame that the supporters who waged a campaign against Houston didn't consider Wilkins of worthy, if not worse, treatment. If Wilkins had been sacked in December 1995 would we still be a Premiership club?

- Obviously, who comes in now?

- With the pressure to get promoted mounting as each year passes will the new manager be allowed time or will sackings become the norm at Loftus Road. For example, don't forget that there was intense pressure from Manchester United fans to sack Alex Ferguson at one stage. What state would United be in now had the board succumbed to the mounting outside pressure?

- Does the fact that Rioch only heard about his sacking on teletext give an indication that the current problems at QPR run deeper than just the management?

As I said just questions... but think about it.

Also in my previous article I spoke about Gerry Francis and basically how incompetent he is. On the day after Houston and Rioch's sacking the Evening Standard ran a back page headline — 'Gerry for QPR'. God help us! Talk about out of the frying pan and straight into the raging forest fire. Please Chris don't even think about it!

There was a great deal of anger over the 3-1 defeat at Swindon from both parties. Before the game Swindon had tried to get the game postponed due to the fact that their goalkeeper, Fraser Digby, was only 60% fit. Personally I don't understand why Swindon were so upset at having to play the game. Things could have been considerably worse. Just think, they could have had a fully fit Lee Harper in goal.

The game against Stoke (possibly the best at home this season?) also bought with it a fair amount of talking points which required further discussion. 'Chrissy Wright Wright Wright' the Loftus Road crowd sang, presumably due to the decision to release Houston.

Please don't forget that it was in fact Mr Wright who wrongfully appointed Mr Houston last season and his sacking has cost the extra money in paying him off for the remainder of his contract. Also it is Mr Wright who decided to let Wasps both share our stadium and become an integral part of Loftus Road Plc.

Rugby is a minority sport and therefore has no commercial or marketable value. QPR have for years run at a loss, hence the need to always sell our assets to balance our books. When the club got relegated it may surprise some but the club was one of only a handful that didn't make a financial loss and were therefore solvent. By introducing a financial liability such as Wasps into the equation the company was always going to have extra problems balancing the books. As a consequence Loftus Road Plc share prices have plummeted and the club is now in more serious financial trouble than it's been for years. We are in a potential freefall situation.

I for one am in support of Chris Wright but do events that have transpired since his takeover really warrant such celebration? I'm not necessarily criticising the current board but I can't help but wonder what the general feeling would be if it had been Richard Thomspon who had masterminded the deal with Wasps and was contemplating a move to a new stadium miles from home?

Also against Stoke came a new level of commitment and a greater sense of urgency. This new found enthusiasm could be attributed to the fact that the previous management was so disliked. Then again one cannot help but feel cheated. These after all are professionals and should be giving 100% each game. The fact is that plenty of people have to work with bosses they don't like and a lot of us don't get the money that the current playing staff at QPR are earning each week.

I was thinking back to the Charlton game and how painful it was. At 4-1 down I would happily have left but I had promised to meet my mate, who was in the away end, after the game. Many did leave and I remember one man pointing to the badge on his QPR shirt as he left in anger. It is fair to say that the team have not been playing 'to their badge' and that is what hurts. The applause following the Stoke game was because the team actually looked like they wanted to win and that is the least the average fan can expect. If that level of commitment had been shown all season would we now be in a far better league position? Once again questions and no answers from this side because I don't have them.

The Huddersfield home game provided us with our first win in November. However it illustrated the problems at the club and whoever takes charge now has got an almighty job on their hands — not just in building a promotion winning side but a side that can also hold its own in the Premiership. The gulf between the two divisions is getting bigger all the time. It's a poor reflection on our squad but I believe that from the current crop of players only Nigel Quashie has the potential to be a star in the Premiership and the best the others can aspire to is your general run of the mill journeyman player. That's how highly I rate the current side.

After the Huddersfield win we lay in tenth place. I believe that had we been in the Premiership this season, playing as we have been, we would now be bottom. A sobering thought for any wannabe manager indeed.
(Matthew Holley – issue # 114)

Five reasons why Houston had to go

Yes, alright, stop sniggering those of you who think that five reasons alone, rather than twenty five could possibly sum up why the ex-Gooner assistant manager had to go. The following categories are in no order of importance, neither are they 'Miss World-style' announced in reverse, but instead are all subjects that every Rangers fan will have discussed at some length over the last year or so.

1) Tactics
For me, the Middlesbrough game was just the final straw. How we could go to a place like the Riverside with less firepower than a Swiss Army knife is just unbelievable. It has become plainly obvious that Mike Sheron is seriously struggling just to see the ball recently, and the five-man defence does not work.

After the Man City game, I went home and watched the Sky coverage on tape, and the amount of chances they had was plain scary. Only Karl Ready has looked at all impressive recently, and I will deal with some of the other 'defenders' later.

It was clear that after more than a year in charge at the club, Houston had no real idea of his best 11 — also, with him and Rioch taking different sections of the team for training, the cohesion between attack and defence was non-existent. Just not good enough I'm afraid, and for me I will always remember the Middlesbrough game as the worst tactical performance by a QPR manager for over 5 years.

2) Transfers

Top marks to Chris Wright for making a spot-on assessment of the situation—"It was not Stewart's inclination to buy players from the lower leagues." QPR's speciality in recent years has been plucking players like Sinclair, Brevett and Murray from obscurity and making them into top class players. Splashing out £2.5million on players like Sheron and Spencer, then paying them £8,000 a week makes me bloody sick. Sorry to swear, but it really hacks me off that people can be paid that sort of money to give only 40% in a hooped shirt.

Spencer and Sheron against Bury were a joke — we should have been (no joke) 6-0 up at half-time. Yet I'm willing to bet that Spencer still picked up his goals-scored bonus on payday. Bring back Devon Bloody White!

3) Attitude

Hands up anyone out there who truly liked Stewart Houston, or, for that matter, Bruce Rioch. No-one? Strange that… Houston's programme notes always said something like "…and it was great to see so many of you travelling away from home. What a boost it was to us all…" Yeah right, if he really wrote those, then I believe that 'War And Peace' was written by Joe Pasquale.

Houston really was the most miserable man I have known for a manager — his pathetic whistling at matches really must have inspired the players — not.

His attitude of questions relating to why he let Paulo Wanchope go were embarrassing. He said "I didn't see him as a centre-forward." Well of course not. Wanchope has scored more goals this season that Sheron, Spencer, Gallen and Slade have put together.

Houston could not admit to his own mistakes. After getting the chop, he blamed his sacking on the requirements of shareholders, and that Chris Wright wanted an easy time at the AGM. No Stewart, it was because you were crap.

4) Players

I was very tempted to write just two words – Steve Morrow. Morrow's only saving grace(s) are the two goals he scored (including incidentally a superb goal at Bolton last season) but how Houston considers him to be good enough to be, A) A central defender, and B) Captain, is beyond me. As a leader, Morrow is less inspiring that Tony Blair and with just about as much charisma. However, Blair does win more headers.

Lee Harper, I'm sure, doesn't actually have any hands, as any shot seems to ricochet off his wrists. If he's lucky, he will claim it on his second attempt, or if he's unlucky (eg Birmingham) embarrassment soon follows. Tony, all is forgiven!

The right-back situation is just a disgrace — this should be resolved ASAP — I would love to ask Houston why he didn't sign one. Indeed, after Rufus Brevett's suspension, the left-back cover is almost as much of a mess as Challis is injured.

5) Bruce Rioch

I still have no idea if Rioch was a help or a hindrance to Houston. Eyebrows were raised when it was first announced that he was to be assistant, and the constant speculation linking him with every vacant manager's post can't have helped anyone.

Oh, and by the way Bruce, bad luck in not getting the Sheffield Wednesday managers job. Your self-promotion in trying to land the position reminded me of Alan Partridge in his rubber thong, lap-dancing to the programme controller to try and get a second series. Pathetic. See you guys — you won't be missed.
(Paul Maylard-Mason – issue # 114)

Pack it up, pack it in – let me begin

A new era for QPR? Or a return to the limbo wilderness of the caretaker manager? Why is it always the caretaker who gets to take over? Just for once couldn't someone give the kit man or the receptionist a go instead? It seems to me that by the time a real manager gets here, half the light bulbs won't be working and the first thing he'll say is "Ooh, they haven't flicked a duster around here in weeks." Despite there being no concrete news as I write, it looks like John Hollins will be given back his mop and bucket (have I done that one to death yet) fairly soon, before the press links us with everyone in the world and they have to start all over again at the top.

Teamtalk on the Internet is quite good normally but so far, in strict chronological order, they have linked us with David Pleat, Alan Curbishley, Gerry Francis, Graham Rix, Nigel Spackman, Mervyn Day, Ray Harford, Barry Fry and Colin Lee. Perhaps they're just trying to name everyone so they can go "you read it here first," or am I being cynical. I feel that Harford and Spackman are the most credible candidates although neither would seem to fit Chris Wright's identikit of the man he seeks.

On the pitch we are erratic in the extreme under Hollins, ranging from very good in the second half against Stoke to appalling after the break against Huddersfield. What infuriates me is that no one in the whole club will play Peacock in his best position which is in the 'hole' so beloved of many Premiership imports. The further forward he is the more he will hurt the opposition BUT he's much less effective with his back to goal (especially in the shadow of Andy Morrison's beer gut — I don't think I've ever seen a fatter-looking professional footballer, and that includes Kenny Sansom and Colin Clarke). The line-up which suits our players is the long-forgotten diamond formation, ever so trendy about 3 years ago, but will they listen? I think not. No doubt

the new man will have his own ideas — it is self evident that this is a vital appointment. Wright must be prepared to back his judgement, choose the right (no pun) man and stick with him for as long as it takes. Just for once I'm glad it's not my decision.
(Andy Ward – issue # 114)

Who's next?

If players and fans alike had a problem with Houston's dour outlook, then the likes of Curbishley, Harford and Spackman are hardly going to fare any better, being almost replicas of Houstons in the personality stakes. In any case, it's hard to imagine if either would wish to leave their present jobs at this moment in time (although there may be a case for Spackman as he's without a contract at Sheffield United), so it would seem Chris Wright may have to broaden the horizon for a new man.

In the meantime, John Hollins is ticking along nicely, getting the all important 'feel good factor' reinstated at the club. His record of one win, one draw and one defeat won't get QPR into the play-offs if this type of form continues, but the battling performance at Wolves, despite the defeat, could only earn him more brownie points in his quest to be QPR's next manager. If he does succeed, there will be few complaints from these quarters.

You would have to go back a long way to recall a managerial setup that drew less inspiration. Houston's problem was as much to do with his personality as his capabilities, was Rioch was loathed by many players for his disciplinary stance. QPR have not progressed one bit as a club in their 14 months in charge, despite having a stronger pool of players.

The decision by Chris Wright to let them go could not be put off any longer. In saying that, the whole situation could have been handled better by Wright. The timing (a day before the AGM) was crucial for Wright, and the way in which Rioch found out about his dismissal (on teletext) was shocking in the extreme Nobody deserves to find out such a fate in these circumstances, and it was shoddy business by Wright, reminiscent of the kind of thing his predecessor would do.

Whoever does finally get the manager's job will not have much money available to do any necessary team rebuilding. The squad is large enough to overcome this, but whether the new man can juggle a fine set of individual players into a cohesive playing unit, remains to be seen. This was Houston's biggest problem, chopping and changing the formation week in week out, but appearing on the whole to be clueless with what was best.
(Ed – issue # 114)

Paying the price

Although not having written for the whole of last season I have remained an avid reader of your organ and even more remarkably have continued to possess a season ticket at QPR.

I have been gratified to note that ITL contributors have now ceased to look at Rangers' prospects through rose tinted glasses. Perhaps I missed them but there hasn't been one "this season we will win one of the cups," or suchlike and it's hardly surprising given the current form. After the run of four consecutive victories there has been one win in eight matches and on game 17 with 23 points — we are 7.6 points behind the schedule so helpfully printed in ITL. That means six consecutive victories are need to get back on target. Of course, that ain't gonna be. The reason why is that QPR are mainly a bunch of Arsenal deadbeats, trying to play at being Arsenal. Houston and Rioch have now thankfully departed, but there's still Morrow, Rose and Harper. Good grief! Not that Rangers have had a lead recently, but when they have there has been very little motivation to add to it. The players seem content to try and sit back and defend a lead, à la Arsenal. Add to this the fact that Sheron has now learnt that QPR forwards' method — i.e. shambling about the pitch trying to become an Iain Dowie playalike and this season can be written off.

(Paul Smith – issue # 114)

Houston, the problem is no longer yours

Just what planet was Stewart Houston supposed to be on during his time as QPR boss? The quote attributed to Houston in the press after the Middlesbrough defeat was enough to make even Ray Wilkins blaspheme. Apparently, upon hearing the travelling R's supporters calling for his head to roll, Houston was reported to have said "Unfortunately we just hit Boro on a good day. It's back to the training ground to sort things out." Well, he never got the chance.

Now correct me if I'm wrong, but did QPR just hit Wolves, Tranmere, Nottingham Forest, Port Vale, Charlton Athletic, Swindon Town as well as Middlesbrough on a good day? I think not. And that just chronicles the defeats. The seven wins and four draws amassed up to Boro have been, to say the least, dire. Effort and commitment just don't add up to much if certain players at the disposal of Houston and Rioch are not good enough, and the management team, having assembled and coached the present playing staff at QPR for over a year could not see the flaws.

In my view, Chris Wright made a mistake in appointing Houston as manager in the first instance, and had to take the alternative decision to get rid of him sooner rather than later. Can any of QPR's older supporters imagine ex-Chairman Jim Gregory giving Houston such a long lease of life as manger, considering the awful displays of the team, week in, week out? No, of course not, and that is why Chris Wright had to consider all the options, and having done so, finally made the right decision on the future of Stewart Houston. The decision had to be taken in the best interests of Queens Park Rangers football club, before it was too late.

Any supporter of QPR who had attempted politely to engage Stewart Houston in conversation will confirm that the man has absolutely no charisma at all. In a word, charmless. It has even been confirmed by Chris Wright at the latest Supporters Club meeting that Houston did not attend this meeting because he has a communication problem. Shy or what! Surely this so-called communication problem transmitted itself to the players in training, or not as the case may be! Perhaps Stewart could have attended these meetings and attempted to communicate by whistling and waving his arms about. On second thoughts, it did not work on match days either, so forget it.

QPR were going nowhere the longer Stewart Houston remained as manager, and Chris Wright finally made the correct decision to hopefully escape from the awful malaise.
(Bill Elkins – issue # 114)

Problems, problems

The damage Stewart Houston has done to QPR will be ongoing for a while yet, and we'll have to wait and see if Ray Harford can steady the ship. His appointment has been received with mixed views, but there is no denying the fact he is a man of great experience, with an excellent knowledge of the lower divisions. Having already made one purchase, the relatively unknown midfielder George Kulcsar from Bradford for £250,000, it's obvious Harford means business. He is already beginning to address the problems in the team, and hopefully soon to follow will be a defender or two and a striker at least half a foot taller than Sheron and Spencer. In fact, judging by the way the team played at Oxford, Harford may as well be on the look out for 11 new players.

It was god to see John Hollins being offered – and accepting – the No.2 job to Ray. Although Hollins was guilty of several key tactical mistakes in his last couple of games in charge against Norwich and Sunderland, he instilled a greater belief in the players and certainly got the backing of the crowd. In his brief spell in charge, Hollins spoke constantly in his programme notes about the passion, the spirit, the commitment, "making this club great again," — the kind of stuff we never heard enough of from Houston. Pity about the picture that accompanied Hollins in his programme notes though. He appears to be in a lot of pain — either that or he's having one off the wrist...

So let's hope Chris Wright has got the right man second time around. With the reputation of being a ruthless businessman, Wright will be looking for a quicker improvement in team affairs than he got from Houston. The play-offs are always a possibility, but at this moment in time I'd gladly settle for mid-table mediocrity come May. It's hardly a positive thing to say, and I wouldn't like to utter the words "we're too good to go down," (that doesn't count), although perhaps "too crap to stay up," is tempting fate. We hope.

QPR have recently been linked with a move for Ian Dowie in the press, and as sad as it may seem, he is just the type of striker QPR need at the moment. It's infuriating watching Sheron and Spencer — two undoubtedly talented players, striving from game to game trying to capture a modicum of form. We've had half a season to judge the partnership, and quite simply it hasn't worked. The pair are too similar in style, and lack the height and strength needed in this division. Last season the pair grabbed over 40 goals between them. Stick them together in the same side, and it all goes horribly wrong.

We all know what Spencer can do and can only hope his game starts coming together soon. As for Sheron, well even some of the poorest of strikers have at least one 20-goal season in their career. I just wonder if Sheron has had his.

At the other end of the pitch, QPR currently have the second worst defensive record in the division. It cannot be underestimated just how much we've missed Alan McDonald this season, or at least, a player of similar ilk as a replacement. How can Tony Roberts or Lee Harper hope to impress with so little cover in front of them? The likes of Ready, Maddix, Brevett and Yates have been with the club long enough to know each other inside out but we continually fall to stupid errors, mainly due to a lack of communication and awareness. If nothing else, Alan McDonald provided this necessary link and since his departure, things have just got worse. In this respect, David Bardsley has been missed as well. Stick him out on the pitch in a wheelchair I say. He may not be able to kick a ball, but he could point and shout, instruct and direct—no one else is providing it.

(Ed – issue # 115)

An Evening with Simon Barker & Friends

As part of Simon Barker's testimonial season, a 'Question & Answer' forum took place on Wednesday 26th November at Ealing Town Hall. Present alongside Simon on the panel were Mike Sheron, John Spencer, Gavin Peacock and host John Hollins. About 250 QPR fans paid the £10 entrance fee, and it was a thoroughly entertaining evening.

All that was said was strictly 'off the record' — John Spencer for one should be grateful for this, as most of what came out of his mouth was very expletive, but very funny! All the players and Hollins were very at ease with the proceedings. Given the recent departures of Houston and Rioch, and our league position, there could have been a few tricky moments but everything went smoothly. What I felt more than anything else was that these players really do care about QPR, and badly want promotion.

Simon Barker was asked several questions about his testimonial season. There will be a match at the end of the season, but Simon isn't quite sure who it will be against. Man Utd, Spurs, Chelsea, Rangers and Celtic have turned him down, whilst Blackburn have yet to give a definite answer. Looks like he may have to settle for Barnet... Simon was also asked what went wrong with his proposed move to Swindon in the summer of 1994. Apparently, there was a disagreement between Simon and Gerry Francis, so he spent pre-season training with Swindon with a view to a move. Two days before the start of season, Simon was told that the club couldn't afford to buy him as they needed to use the money to buy a new stand. To much laughter, John Spencer shouted out "And it's fucking falling down!"

Each player was asked what was their favourite goal scored for QPR. Peacock chose his effort against Norwich last season as well as his first for the club as a 19-year-old (forget the game?!). Spencer's choice was the winner against Portsmouth last season, whilst Barker had two — the chip away to Sheffield Wednesday in our relegation season, and the equaliser against Liverpool in the 2-2 FA Cup quarter final in 1990. Bizarrely, Mike Sheron opted for the own-goal against Reading. On the night, both Sheron and Spencer were self-critical about their lack of goals this season, saying they had to do better.

Thoughts on Stewart Houston and Bruce Rioch were mixed. John Hollins had a lot of sympathy for them, knowing what it's like to be given the boot. Barker thought that the pair never made any attempt to endear themselves to the fans, there just wasn't the kind of relationship most managers should try to have. Spencer especially came across as not being sorry to see the back of Rioch. When one question was asked regarding when Paul Bruce is to be given a try out in the first team, Spencer misheard and thought the question was about Bruce Rioch; "No I didn't punch Bruce Rioch, I kicked him in the bollocks".

The panel were asked which was their favourite and least favourite songs. Spencer's choice was "Walking in a Spencer wonderland," to which Gavin Peacock suggested to be changed to "Walking in a Peacock wonderland," as no one ever sings anything about him! John Hollins pointed out that the "We're not Arsenal anymore" song has to stop as the three ex-Arsenal players take it personally — one of which, Lee Harper, was disappointed to be dropped after the Middlesbrough game. Hollins said that Tony Roberts is the most dedicated keeper he's ever worked with (first on the training pitch, last off etc), and deserved another opportunity. "It's my choice, and if I get it wrong I'm out of a job."

Simon Barker was asked which were his favourite games because of the away support. Three sprung to mind — Man Utd in the FA Cup quarter-final, Nottingham Forest on the last day of the 95/96 season, and Wimbledon away in the FA Cup last season. West Ham at home when we were relegated was the most moving experience he'd ever felt, knowing that despite winning the game 3-0, we were down and the feeling was just terrible. Simon pointed out that the fans should never underestimate the impact it has on the players when the crowd are getting behind the team, whilst constant criticism of players can be debilitating.

Do the players read the fanzines? One or two. Barker said that some of the things written about the players does hurt. Karl Ready for one was very upset by some of the things written about him, but Barker suggested that fanzines aren't really meant to be read by the players, it's a fans thing.

The question of who wanted who to be the next QPR manager was asked. Everyone was fully behind John Hollins and hoped he'd get the job. If not, Gerry Francis was a popular choice. Barker picked out that professionally, Francis was the best manager he's ever played under, but his favourite was Don Howe as he'd given him his first real opportunity in the first team and taught him a lot about the technicalities of the game. John Spencer spoke very highly about Glenn Hoddle, as did Gavin Peacock, but his choice as favourite went to Kevin Keegan. Interestingly, Ruud Gullit was hardly mentioned. Peter Reid got Mike Sheron's vote.

One or two of the players have bought shares in the club. Gavin Peacock bought a load in the summer as he thought we would go up (still does). Spencer replied that when he joined the club "some other poor bastards," had purchased all the shares!

In all, it was a very interesting and lively debate. I sensed that the players and Hollins are all fully 100% behind the cause, and that if we don't go up this season, it won't be for the lack of trying. Night's like this help to cement the bond between fans and players, and can only help the spirit as it gives a greater indication as to how each party views each other. I don't think any more nights like this are planned for the future, but I'd like to see them become an annual fixture with QPR. So if and when the next one comes around, you'd be well advised to go along for an excellent night out.
(Alan Smithfield – issue # 115)

The right man for the job?
I'm writing to question the managerial capabilities of our new manager, Ray Harford. Is he really the best QPR could get? It seems to me that Chris Wright went to a lot of trouble to get Harford, after all the turmoil with WBA and the threat of court action, injunctions etc. Just think how pissed off we would be if another club stole our manager.

What has Harford achieved in his managerial career? He did OK at Luton, but apart from that, nothing. At Luton, he was dismissed for showing a lack of good relations with the board and supporters. Sounds like Stewart Houston all over again.

I really wish Ray Harford all the best with QPR, but something tells me it isn't a progressive step up from Houston. After witnessing our shambolic display at Oxford, I don't think it's a new manager we should have gone after — a bloody miracle worker is what we need! This club is rapidly heading for the bottom three. If QPR went down this season, it would be a huge catastrophe. Hmm, then again at least we'd have another trip to Southend to look forward to though...

(Michael Turner – issue # 115)

10 interesting facts about new QPR signing, George Kulcsar

1) His first name is George.
2) His second name is Kulcsar.
3) He cost £250,00 and signed a three year contract.
4) George is described as a 'ball winning defensive midfielder'.
5) An anagram of George Kulcsar is 'Who Are Ya'.
6) Like Nigel Quashie, George has a surname that doesn't rhyme with anything.
7) George once had a part in Neighbours playing Mrs Mangell's long lost son.
8) Whilst at Bradford, George became addicted to curry and spent a lot of time vin de loo.
9) George takes a size 8 shoe – when he was younger it was much smaller.
10) George share's his first name with Eastenders character George Palmer – sleazy bent boyfriend of meatheads Phil and Grant's mum, Peggy.

(Ed – issue # 115)

Not looking good

8,000 gates ... more 0-0 draws ... no entertainment or excitement ... star players set to leave ... welcome to the rest of the season.

If you still side with the theory that QPR are too good to go down, then what a thrilling time we all have got to look forward to until we're finally put out of our misery on May 3rd. And fans used to complain when we constantly ended in the top half of the Premiership!

1997/98 has been a complete waste of a season. With 57 points still to play for, that is still quite something to say. The way we've played all season, the play-offs are never going to be in reach unless a dramatic turn around in form occurs, so Ray Harford should use the remaining games to experiment radically to hopefully get things right in time for next term. The entertainment value at Loftus Road this season has been zero, and if we are to be spared a relegation dog fight, the least we can hope for is a bit of style and a few goals to raise hopes for next season.

The job Ray Harford has on his hands is probably bigger than he could ever have imagined. Initial thoughts that Harford was not the type of manager QPR should have gone for in the wake of Houston and Rioch's departures however seem to have gone away. From what I've read and heard about Harford, the man appears to be a bit of a dude — quick witted, and with an extensive knowledge of all divisions. Houston only had knowledge of Premiership reserve teams. It's too early to say yet that Harford will become a success. It's all very well him coming in, giving the team "eight games to assess our strengths and weaknesses," — Dennis Smith goes to West Brom and says the same thing! All managers have their own opinions, and there's nothing to suggest Harford's opinions are the type all managers should use as a benchmark. If however, they prove good enough for QPR, then that's good enough for me.

24-year-old right-back Antti Heinola became Ray Harford's second signing for QPR when he signed from Emmen for £150,000. With 7 full Finnish caps to date, Harford describes him as the "nearest thing he's seen to Arnold Muhren," — we're still wondering where the 'nearest, actual David Bardsley' is. Anyone got any ideas how he's progressing?

Transfer speculation has linked both Trevor Sinclair and John Spencer with moves to London Premiership clubs. West Ham have reportedly bid £2million plus Iain Dowie and Ian Bishop for Sinclair, whilst Crystal Palace want £2.5million rated Spencer. It would appear QPR would be prepared to let either player go at the right price — a particular shame regarding John Spencer, who looked all set to become a QPR great after last season but has somehow lost his way. As for Sinclair, the longer he stays in a mid-table First Division side, the quicker his valuation will decrease. He'll definitely be gone before the start of next season, that there is no doubting.

Harford has neither said he is or isn't interested in Dowie, but it can only be a matter of time before even he realises the Sheron/Spencer partnership hasn't worked, and brings in a striker that can add a bit of height and aggression to our attack.

Whatever does happen regarding transfers between now and the end of the season, let's hope Harford uses the remaining games constructively, experimenting with new tactics and formations. Nothing has worked so far as QPR trudge from one game to the next looking more clueless by the minute. So come on Ray — give us something to shout about and let's see an end to this constant dross.
(Ed – issue # 116)

Reading the riot act

In 36 years of watching QPR never have I been compelled to write anything condemning about my team, but as of this day especially after the Reading performance I just have to put them on paper to save my poor suffering wife from anymore mental anguish. In days long gone I would watch QPR with my grandfather, going to all the home games in the old Division 3 and watching the R's rise up the divisions, down again and so forth. Even when we took a real tanking you always felt that the team of that day would give 100% and leave the field as dejected as us, the fans. Yes, and so we were beaten but the team sprit showed through and off you went to the following game safe in the knowledge that all would be forgiven in the name of QPR.

QPR STRIKERS FAIL TO ANSWER THE CRITICS THAT SAY THEY'RE "JUST A BUNCH OF GIRLS"

Please someone, tell me what's gone wrong? I feel sorry for Ray Harford taking over this squad but everyone must know that at least eight of the side that faced Reading must go, not to mention certain players languishing in the reserves.

Nobody has a divine right to Premiership football but I believe that we the supporters have a right to watch players performing to their full potential or at least busting a gut for the club. If our talented forward line for this division (how many times have we read that one in the papers) cost £5million+ and are allegedly paid £8,000 a week each, I wish they would bloody well play for it. Sheron's unwillingness to run and challenge for some of the balls in the Reading game was atrocious. Spencer obviously thinks that he is too good for this division and as we didn't go up last season has decided that he is wasting his time. Who the bloody hell do they think pay their wages? We do every time we attend a game. On my journey home I turned this thought over in my mind, the day at a game costs me £65.00 in travel, tickets, programme etc. Luckily I can afford this, but what of the people who have to struggle and give up other luxuries watching Sheron and Spencer ponce around up front watching Sinclair run down blind alleys and providing no movement for him even if he kept the ball. "Oh well, we lost that one but I still pick up me dosh thanks."

We have some talented youngsters and we have a fair share of dross journeymen and our supposed superstars. If we have some superstars, why pray? Tell me we are no better than a mid-table division 1 side.

This question I am sure our new manager will have resolved by next season and I think we can see a different Rangers next season. I'll still go to the games but sadly not my wife who will not part with her hard earned cash to, as she says, "watch players who do not look as if they care what the outcome is." So this is a small part of the clubs' income, but we need people like my wife to watch us at every game possible otherwise the crowds will slowly diminish and so our hopes of rising amongst the elite again will be long gone, and I will be sitting in a shrinking attendance because I feel for my club.
(Gary Weller – issue # 116)

Can someone slip me the answer?

"At the moment, QPR are playing like relegation candidates. There, I've said it," (ITL # 115). Isn't it amazing that as human beings, we are constantly seeking the eternal truth! Answers to questions like "Why are we here?," "is there a God," and, perhaps most important of all, "Who's better, Aqua or Whigfield?." And yet, when the truth reveals itself, it's often at the most unexpected time and place.

Portsmouth, December 1997. As the words "playing like relegation candidates," sank in, I was almost blinded by a light brighter than I'd ever seen before. Yes, the true power of floodlights is only really revealed when you try to hang yourselves from them. Fortunately (though some would disagree), like everything else associated with the hoops that day, all my efforts ended in dismal failure and I was left to trudge away with all the other mugs who stayed to the end, much to the amusement of the Fratton Park faithful (and who can forget their charming accents? "You moight as well not have curm, moight, hurr hurr.")

I guess what I'm trying to say is that I thought the tone of the last ITL was on the mark. We are playing like relegation candidates, and it's about time someone said so. For all the talk from management and players alike as being one or two results away from the play-offs (well, I suppose they've got as much right to tell jokes as the next man), we have as I write conceded as many away goals as anyone in the division and scored 1.2 goals per game. The play-offs? No, but we're only one or two results away from the magnificent defensive records of such giants of the game as Reading, Tranmere 'None shall pass' Rovers and the mighty Port 'Iron Curtain' Vale. Who would have foreseen a season of such greatness?!

Okay, so sarcasm isn't the answer, but nor are performances like the one at Portsmouth (or against Reading). Over the years, the phrase "never seen them play so poorly," has been used a lot by QPR fans. The Portsmouth game, my (anorak alert) 113th of watching the lads, fitted the description pretty well and from the fact that no-one applauded the players at the final whistle, I wasn't the only one who felt that way.

The fact that our present prospects seem so bad despite the departure of the despised Mr Thompson, the arrival of an infinitely more committed and forward-thinking chairman, and, in my opinion, better players than in our relegation season (Holloway, Hateley and a past-it Wilkins for Muzza, Spencer and Gavin anybody? Thought not), is an irony not lost on many of us.
(Neil Perry - issue # 116)

Positivity is a difficult thing

Time to check the old profit/loss accounts I think. One season, written off. Value: None. It would be nice if, just for once, someone would tell it like it is in football. "Well, the league and cup are bonuses really, now we can concentrate on flicking our plums till August." The cup replay exit was probably as much for the best as it was predictable. After all, I don't think "We're not Arsenal any more," would have cut much ice by the time Bergkamp knocked in number five.

Apparently we would have got Arsenal in the next round anyway, I didn't know due to being in hospital because when the draw was made Kevin Keegan saying "anyone got a house yet," was so funny that my sides actually split, with the tearing of the skin and the intestines on the floor etc. And they say sarcasm is the lowest form of wit. Well it's pretty close but professional football men being paid to arse around on TV takes the biscuit I feel. The thing is, TV used to make me angry but now I just don't watch it. It's very sad, but I can feel football going the same way. Well, much of this can be put down to Rangers being so pants at the moment, and with no money it's not going to turn around overnight.

In particular, if the Tranmere game is life without our two most saleable assets, we should be busting a gut to hang on to them. Perhaps I should wait until we turn the corner, because it will happen however long the road may seem, before considering the question "Is football crap nowadays or am I just getting old. Discuss." I would like to make one point from the Tranmere game, which was indeed an awful, awful game. I've not just seen better games at Southend, I've seen better nil-nils which is saying something. So it's not wrong for people to voice their disapproval at the end. But it was totally out of order to give Steve Morrow the bird. The defence wasn't the problem, they did everything that was asked of them — that might not have been much apart from those bazooka-like long throws, but they can't do any more can they? Morrow had had a decent game and had done nothing wrong. OK, he's had some mares this season but he's not the only one. Houston and Rioch have gone. Yes, they wasted a lot of money. But making Morrow the scapegoat and taking it out on him is thoughtless, extremely unconstructive and if it really makes you feel better then you're sad.

If only we were in the Premiership then we'd be happy. That's what everyone seems to think, but is this really true? Whose fans are happy in the top flight? Well, Manchester United obviously, but then again Jack Nicholson was happy in One Flew Over the Cuckoo's Nest after they lobotomised him. Chelsea ditto, until some ****ing $£*%& %"&*@$ scores against them. Derby fans are probably pleased, I should hope so anyway, maybe West Ham (those who don't travel) and, err, hmm, Leeds? Not sure if they're still playing crap football. Blackburn? Most of their crew only signed up to watch Shearer and win trophies. Southampton and Coventry at a pinch but I hardly think they're jumping up to click their heels together in mid-air (try to picture it). The rest just whinge to high heaven. Lighten up dudes, take it from us — things could be a hell of a lot worse.

In the meantime, chins up guys! Remember when we lost nine on the spin under Don Howe — you only beat us 2-1 etc? Two months later we bagged 20 points from 8 games including a 3-1 win at Anfield. It can happen — just when you least expect it.
(Andy Ward – issue # 116)

Not fit to wear the hoops # 1

We're a month into Ray Hartford's tenure and he must be wondering what he's let himself in for. At least I guess he has an easier journey to work to face each day.

It's been a poor season. Following the mind numbingly boring game against Tranmere we now stand a mere seven points above the relegation zone. Worrying thing is, it's hard, nay on impossible, to see things getting much better. Here we saw a Rangers side devoid of ideas and enthusiasm, not only fail to beat a Tranmere side languishing in the bottom three, but also fail to threaten or create any decent opportunities. It's hard to see where the next win is going to come from, what with the confidence crisis currently infecting the club and with the team creating so little in the way of attack.

To quote Ray Harford in the Sunday Mirror stating how he understands the fans frustration; "But I have to admit I'm not as unhappy as they are, because I saw things out there that encouraged me." Read it and try not to weep. Please Mr Harford, if you're reading this please can you reply to the usual address and explain what it was exactly about the Tranmere game that encouraged you because to be frank, I'm perplexed.

All I saw on Saturday was a bunch of overpaid so-called professionals leaving the field and no doubt off to count the ridiculously large sums of money that they no doubt earn. Not fit to wear the hoops? They're not fit to grace the hallowed turf. They're con artists and frauds, masquerading as a football team whilst wearing the colours and badge that many of us have followed for years. They're a total disgrace and are an insult to this proud club and every devoted fan that paid good money to watch them and will probably continue to watch them and support this club for years to come. Why? because we're QPR fans and even though the current ambassadors are not worthy of praise or affection we will still continue to turn up. Sad isn't it?

On the subs bench for the Tranmere match was Antti Heinola, our new signing. What must he be like if he can't instantly command a place in this current side? A glance at the youth and combination league tables inspires little confidence and suggests that the situation at this club is indeed terminal.

Things are not good. A stream of dreadful managers has crippled this once decent little club and left us now the laughing stock of London football. The appointment of Ray Harford has made no tangible difference and although it's still early to make judgements the team now look as clueless and demoralised as they ever did under Houston's reign.

If you have a copy, refer to the programme for the Reading home fixture. In the interview with Tony Roberts the blurb informs us that apparently "The new managers' tactical changes have been interesting for the players and fans alike." What, you may ask, are these revolutionary new ideas? Take it away Tony; "My role is to play the ball down field to Mike Sheron's head and then we go from there." Sounds familiar doesn't it but then the club programme wouldn't be the same unless it churned out material which is both patronising and insulting to an IQ which is only marginally higher than that of a goat.

Tragic when you think that it was only five years ago that we were the pride of the capital. It's bad for us fans, it's clear that the current playing staff doesn't care enough but what can we do? The team currently deserves all the abuse in the world, and considering what we've witnessed this season our fans have been reasonably restrained so far, but unfortunately this approach is destructive rather than constructive. One suggestion forwarded on Saturday was a mass boycott to make it crystal clear what we think of them, but then do you think they would care and this would only serve to destroy morale even more. We could of course strive to get behind the team but that is becoming increasingly difficult.

Whatever course of action the fans decide to take, and I could understand any of the above being taken, it is clear that once again we will be the ones left to pick up the pieces. After Saturday relegation is a real possibility, make no mistake about it. Confidence is at an all time low and disillusionment amongst fans is rife. We are in a

free-fall situation, only being a few defeats away from a crisis. Not fit to wear the hoops? If those players had an ounce of decency and any self-respect they will want to prove those fans wrong. Somehow I fear they'll be too busy counting their money and dreaming of pastures greener.
(Matthew Holley – issue # 116)

Torquay here we come?

It was only a couple of years ago that QPR were entertaining the likes of Manchester United and Arsenal. In six months time, there is now the real possibility that it will be the likes of Macclesfield and Torquay coming to Loftus Road. The result and performance against Port Vale was not even up to non-league standard, let alone good enough for the Second Division. With just four league wins from the last twenty-five games, Second Division football is becoming more of a reality with each passing game. Just five points separate QPR from the bottom three — a figure that is slowly reducing week by week. Who would have thought at the start of the season that the match against Bury on May 3rd could well be a relegation decider, instead of a match full of joy and celebration, heralding our return to the Premiership?

I'm sure I've witnessed enough dross at Loftus Road in these current Division 1 days equal to ten years worth before that. And now the thought that this once fine club could be playing the likes of Wrexham and Carlisle next season is starting to become a reality.

It's certainly a new-look Rangers at the moment despite the same old results. As expected, Trevor Sinclair ended months of transfer speculation by signing for West Ham for £2m plus Keith Rowland and Iain Dowie — who have made good starts to their QPR careers. Yet judging by Trevor Sinclair's form so far for West Ham, you have to feel QPR have got the poor end of the deal, especially considering Sinclair's valuation once stood at £6million. However, I don't think there's too many QPR fans who are sad to see him go when considering his form over the past couple of years (but then there's a few players you could say that about).

In return, the signing of Mark Kennedy on loan from Liverpool with a view to a permanent move has gone down well in most quarters. Still only 21 and with less than a hundred professional appearances under his belt, Kennedy is still very much a raw talent but if his move were to become a permanent one, he is one player that we will have genuine cause to get excited about in years to come.

As for Rufus, his transfer to Fulham was a surprising one as he was never one of Ray Wilkins' favourite players in his time as manager at QPR, and he will certainly be missed by many fans who appreciated his wholehearted commitment rather than his sublime skills. I can't really say the same for Juergen Sommer, one of the worst goalkeepers I've seen in my time supporting QPR. His greatest weakness was his positional sense — his inability to stay on his line cost QPR so many goals in our relegation season (especially in the fated game against Man Utd), it was almost comical. *(Ed – issue # 117)*

Longing for the good old days

It's probably about time I stopped evading the main issue and faced it head-on. This has been an awful season, by far the worst in my 10 years, and a lot of it goes well beyond results and performances.

But what concerns me most is this. Everyone seems to be forgetting what I've always thought that QPR really stands for. Simply, I liked it when we were the underdogs. What attracted me to Loftus Road in the first place, and what made the top-level years so enjoyable, was that this was a club who couldn't match most of the division in terms of finance, support and influence. But they made up the difference with skill, good management and bloody hard work.

There was nothing better than caning one of the big boys, whether it was the real top dogs or, in many ways just as good, the wannabes like Tottenham, Everton and Chelsea. How great it was, home or away, to see their fans, arrogant and disrespectful at 3 o'clock, turn on their team or sneak out in silence at half past four. And best of all, more often than not Rangers didn't do it by spoiling tactics or luck, but by playing the suckers off the park. It was a privilege to watch and support players as good as Ferdinand and Wilkins (who both cost a pittance); players who worked hard to improve their game beyond recognition such as Wilson and Bardsley; top-class honest professionals like McDonald and Falco; even the likes of Holloway and White who knew that this was their one and only chance at the top level and busted a gut just to keep up.

I may be guilty of using rose-tinted glasses to view the past, but OK, let's look at the present. There's only one player at this club right now who deserves to be mentioned in the same breath as the above, and that's Gavin Peacock. The spirit is willing in Barker, Maddix and Bardsley but I fear the flesh has gone. Obviously give the new players a chance, but the rest have all got their price, every last one of them, and that includes Quashie. Still, players come and go, and both chairman and manager are making encouraging noises about complete rebuilding.

What is of much more concern to me is the fact that the character of this club is rapidly changing for the worse. Within this division we see ourselves as a big club. As the guy from Huddersfield pointed out a few issues ago, there is very little to back this up. Only the money we've spent. But we're acting like a big club all the same. Overpaid players are poncing around and pointing at each other instead of rolling their sleeves up (top cliché) and fighting for each other. A minority of supporters, but it's growing all the time, are showing the same arrogance and disrespect that we used to get from the Tottenhams of this world. Next time you join in with "oo are ya!!" when someone from Huddersfield, Reading or Crewe takes a corner, just imagine being one-on-one with the bloke. He would be well in order to make three points. 1) I'm someone that you've always wished you could be, a professional footballer. 2) We're making your lot look pretty stupid, and 3) Just who the fuck are you exactly? It's no wonder opponents and fans are up for it against QPR and it's no wonder they love it when they beat us, especially when they play us off the park. Does that sound familiar? Am I out on my own here or are we turning into, at this level, the kind of club I used to think was, and still think is, pathetic?

Now, I've tried in the past to spark some discussion without much success. This time I would really like to know, do you think that's bollocks or do you agree? It's not that I feel I need others to agree to be more sure of my opinion — quite the reverse in fact, if a lot of people feel that we don't really stand for anything and that league position is all that matters, then I'll be even more convinced that I'm right. All the same it would be encouraging to know that other people feel the same way, and if they do, then the club should be made aware of it.

But if I'm on my own here and if I believe that the QPR I used to love is dead, not just asleep, I would have no hesitation in applying the ultimate sanction with a clear conscience.
(Andy Ward – issue # 117)

Let the exodus begin

In my review of the Ipswich game in the last issue I questioned Trevor Sinclair's desire to play for QPR. I'm sure everyone will have realised the implicit irony when he scored two goals on his debut for West Ham, but why did he run himself into the ground as soon as he gets back into the Premiership? Was QPR's current predicament in the first division something beneath him?

All these questions are by-the-by now, which only runs amok in the feverish mind of a discontented fanzine writer. But still I can't get my head around the fact that Harry Redknapp bought Sinclair on the strength of his current form. He's hardly been tearing first division teams apart this season has he? But after a moment's thought to consider why we are getting into a froth about this, we all know in reality as well as Mr Redknapp, was that a couple of years ago Sinclair was one of the most exciting players in England — fully deserving his place in the England squad. I personally thought that when we went down to the first division his class would show — and perhaps it has been the absence of his own high standards of football for us in the last two years which has disappointed me the most about this sorry story.

At QPR we have got used to the fact that we have been a stepping-stone for up and coming players. Fair enough. Sinclair has turned 24 and is hoping for a late push into the England squad for France '98, but if he wanted to put himself in the shop window for a club, why didn't he work his socks off while he was still at Rangers? Instead all we got was occasional flashes of his brilliance interspersed with a lacklustre attitude to winning the ball back (known in layman's terms as defending).

In fact, what the Sinclair transfer has highlighted is the two-tier player system that we currently have at Rangers. Take a moment to consider whether any of our 'better players' would stay at Rangers if an offer from a Premiership club came in. I'd bet they'd be off before you could say "I'll see you on Sunday at four on Sky Sports 1."

Lest we forget the other tier — the no-hopers. Players that are consigned to the dearth of forever playing in the 'Nationwides'. We seem to be overloaded with a lot of these kind of players at the moment. Still, I'm sad that we don't have the opportunity to see Rufus play at Loftus Road again when Fulham get promoted and Rangers do down.

And what about the influx of new 'talent' in the last couple of years? Is it just me or are we getting players who are Premiership rejects — Spencer, Peacock, Morrow, Harper, Rose — added to the new chaps — Kennedy, Dowie (hooray!) and Rowland — compared to just a few years ago when we were buying the international bright young things on their way up — Sinclair, Ferdinand, Sinton and Seaman. The only new arrival that has really excited me is Mark Kennedy, who has shown when representing Ireland how good he is — but he's only here on a six-week loan.

Are the bright lights of the Premiership just too alluring? Yes, most probably, but if any of the In The Loft readers played for Rangers we'd burst our lungs trying to get back to cover a Morrow slip-up, even if we've all got crocked knees. I don't expect the same sort of devotion from players as a lifetime fan, but when someone like Sinclair is being paid in the thousands to play a game of football one or twice a week, shouldn't we expect a little more than the dire performances we have seen this year?

As a fully fledged Division 1 minnow, is playing for QPR now a step-down the ladder of a players' career? Is there no honour and pride in wearing the hoops? Are players' mercenary attitudes to clubs really symptomatic of a take-your-money and run attitude prevalent in the game today? Will I stop posing annoying, pithy, little conundrums? The answers inevitably to all these questions is yes.

(John Crowley – issue # 117)

Ready or not?

Did anyone see the 'week in the life of Karl Ready' article in the Express a couple of weeks ago? He has the lifestyle of a superstar (what I'd expect someone like Beckham to have). According to this article he does two and a half hours training sessions five days a week, and a bit less the day before a game in case he gets injured!

He earns 200k a year, has 3 cars including a BMW Z3, goes to swanky restaurants most days and goes out the piss and clubbing with his mates in Bicester most nights. All this for an average 1st division centre back. Still he's just a normal bloke really!
(Chris Tozer – issue # 117)

Robbie James R.I.P.

I couldn't believe it when I opened the papers this morning and read that Robbie James had died during a game last night. I knew Robbie when he was at Rangers and he was one of the nicest guys you could ever meet in the world. I used to work in the lottery office and Robbie would always come in after training and blag a cuppa and some biscuits and just generally have a chat about how things were going. He knew he wasn't the most gifted player in the world but just accepted it and worked to his strengths by working extra hard on the training ground and during a match.

After the cup final of '86 we were all supposed to go to the Lancaster hotel for the celebration meal after the game but I just couldn't face it and just drowned my sorrows in the pub. When I went to work on Monday as expected the atmosphere was terrible. Robbie came in and just sat there still not believing what had happened and he shed some tears in the office while we drunk our usual cuppa. His wife Karen came in as well that day and she was just fantastic trying to lift everyone. In the end she did manage to get a few smiles from us but she knew we were all hurting badly inside. That Christmas Rangers had a junior christmas party for the fans at Guinness and Robbie and Karen brought their children along. I think they were the only ones to do it and just generally had a good time with the fans, answering questions and just talking to people. That's why I'm so sorry about what happened to him. He will be badly missed, not only as a footballer but as a really fantastic bloke.
(Williams Wall – issue # 117)

QPR 5-0 Middlesbrough

Middlesbrough had beaten us with ease in the cup a few weeks before and I'm sure that I came along with everyone else to Loftus Road expecting us to be comprehensively slaughtered. We'd been playing so crap as well, but as each subsequent goal went in people were jumping in the air to celebrate and then looking at each other as if to say "What the...?"

Everyone has their own perspective on the game but I thought that our performance was actually better in the second half than the first! Early on Merson had sent Branca though — if he had scored the game could have been very different. But for once this season Rangers dug in and struck a rich vein of luck — in the last twenty minutes of the first half something very strange happened.

Without a doubt, everyone played their hearts out after we scored. Morrow revelled in his new left-back role (with less responsibility), whilst Yates and Ready looked just, well, at ease. Bardsley was masterful (great to see him back), Quashie a revelation, Kulcsar for once got stuck in.

Kennedy really came to the fore in this game and for the first time during his brief loan spell it seemed a few other players were on his wavelength. The first goal from Kennedy's deflected shot was a reward for the professional way we had come out. Bruce's first goal for QPR was pure luck – that's the only way to describe it; his miss-hit cross was completely misjudged by Dibble.

The third goal was completely different entirely — Harford must have been pleased to see a classic counter-attacking move finished off by Gallen who rounded the 'keeper and somehow managed to hit the ball past two defenders on the goal line. And then Sheron's first goal came just before half time — a classy curling twenty yard shot into the top corner.

The second half was the best that Rangers have played all season. The ball was brought out controlled from the back and when Townsend was sent off, Sheron and Kennedy had the space in the middle to spray the ball around.

Everyone wanted to score but in the end we managed just one more. A classic move from Kennedy found him on the byline, but somehow he managed to curl in a pinpoint cross that was met on the full by Sheron. If you wanted to complain you could have said that we should have scored more. It was pleasing as well that when 'Boro refused to lay down and die, Harper made some great saves. He is fast becoming the first cult keeper at Loftus Road since Seaman and he actually seems to care about the cause as well.

Andy Dibble at the other end was mercilessly taunted by the Loft. It seemed to me rather harsh but looking around it soon became apparent that a lot of people were releasing a lot of pent-up tension. People were singing (and standing up) and generally having a good time. The tannoy announcer at the end conveyed the general sense of dizziness by saying that he had just looked at the teletext and it said that Rangers had won 5-0!

A game sure to go down in people's memories not only because we'd been waiting so long for something like this to happen but perhaps for a fleeting moment we caught a glance at a player in Mark Kennedy that could have become a true legend.
(John Crowley – issue # 118)

We're not staying up?

With eight of the current bottom nine clubs due to play each other on the last day of the season, QPR's future in this league might not be decided until the very last kick. If we stay up, it won't exactly be a time for celebration — more like a time to evaluate quite how QPR could come so close to the drop, and how we must not be faced with a repeat performance next season. If we go down, it will quite possibly be the worst day in the history of QPR. And unlike when we lost our Premiership status, I don't think there will be too many fans thinking we will bounce straight back up next time around.

The players, who have let us down for 95% of the season, must now fight with every last ounce of energy they have — if not for the pride of QPR, then that of their own. 50 points should be enough to stay up, but it could be higher. Unlike 1995/96 when QPR were relegated, there was some pride amongst the players wearing the blue and white hoops. Whether or not the current squad can display the same attributes, remains to be seen.

One things for sure, if we go down there won't be no 'Nottingham Forest' style finish to the season amongst the fans, none of the "hard luck boys, we'll support you ever more," type feelings. There will be bitterness and anger, frustration as to how and why it's been allowed to happen.
(Ed – issue # 118)

QPR 1-2 Swindon Town

There's been quite a few contenders, but undoubtedly this has to go down as one of QPR's most embarrassing performances of all time, let alone this season. It would be pointless trying to describe the complete and utter ineptitude displayed by the players once again — I've done it so many times this season, words fail me. It would be far too agonising anyway as this once fine little west London outfit continue to put us through hell. To lose against ten men without a proper goalkeeper for the majority of the match is simply unbelievable.

The day certainly belonged to Alan McDonald — a true QPR man who must have squealed with embarrassment, seeing the shambles of a football team he's left behind. Deep inside, he was probably laughing to himself. 70 minutes in goal and all he had to do was make a couple of routine saves and catches.

The character of the man in undeniable. Volunteering to go in goal following the unfortunate dismissal of Digby, McDonald's first return to Loftus Road should have ended in disaster, as we sat back and anticipated a goal feast against the leagues most out-of-form side. Not only did this not materialise, Swindon went on to win the game against all expectations, whilst QPR fans were left to fight amongst themselves in Q-Block after someone shouted for Harford to be sacked. The fighting spilled out into Loftus Road, where, for some peculiar reason, a man in his 20s with a Chelsea tracksuit top on, was walking in the opposite direction. It wasn't his lucky day, or that for QPR.
(Ed – issue # 118)

Not fit to wear the hoops # 2

So went the chant against Swindon. But QPR don't wear the hoops. Despite my protests hoops are still missing from the sleeves. Someone in charge must know that there will be no success until hoops do reappear on the sleeves.

Really there seems little point. For years I have expressed my misgivings about QPR. Usually it has been against the flow of optimism and hopeful prediction. This season I have felt the urge only once (sorry matron). Most of ITL's correspondents have foretold gloom, doom and Division 2 — and quite rightly so. I couldn't imagine any circumstance in which I would be compelled to write again this season. I actually did think that QPR would drift to fairly comfortable safety at lower mid-table. Indeed, the Middlesborough result and performance reinforced this feeling. The defeat at Birmingham was, of course, expected. What other result could befall the team with the worst away record in the division?

But Swindon was something else. I missed the Port Vale match (phew) but my fellow season ticket holders in the Lower Loft vouched that there was little to choose between the two games in terms of hitherto unknown levels of incompetence in the face of useless opposition.

It is often stated by football cognoscenti that it is easier to win with ten men than with eleven because of the motivating power of being one man down. So, as soon as Swindon had lost their goalkeeper, Harford should have immediately removed two QPR players, thus returning the advantage to us and ensuring a win. However, such is the cunning and subtlety of McMahon that he would have removed two Swindon players so that their eight could beat our nine.

Now, and I'm sure you're with me here, QPR would get the best of the strategy by removing a further two players to leave our seven to beat their eight — and Swindon couldn't do anything about it because if they removed two more they would have forfeited the match 2-0 under the laws of the game. Perhaps Harford could field seven players from the outset for the remaining matches of the season thus ensuring the overwhelming advantage that having fewer players on the pitch provides. The underdog scenario is our only hope.

Just for one ludicrous moment let's imagine that it's actually an advantage to have more players on the pitch than your opponents and that if it is the goalkeeper who is missing that it's even more of an advantage (silly I know, but stretch your incredulity to humour me). If this did happen what should the team with the more players do? How about test the new goalkeeper (Macca) with shots on target? Well, a mere 22 minutes after Digby was sent off QPR managed it. How about send over a few tantalisingly difficult to catch high crosses? Well, 23 minutes after Digby was sent off QPR managed it. And what happened at the first corner — yes, it was taken short.

I must say, Macca deserved his triumph — especially after Quashie tried to stir things up by pathetically waving goodbye to Digby. It's shameful to see that happening. Dennis Wise, maybe, but please not QPR players.

In the second half there were great hopes that Dowie would double his two-year goal tally but he was too busy with his headless chicken impersonation. The loss of Kennedy is hurting badly. Without him there are no decent corners or crosses and the galvanising effect he has on the other players is lost.

Time for a statistical appraisal of Ray Harford and John Hollins (who I think should have been appointed ahead of a bloke who just wanted a job nearer home). This season under Houston in 16 league matches there were 6 victories — a 37.5% success rate. Under Hollins then Harford in the first 22 league matches there have been 4 victories — an 18.2% success rate. This is an intolerably low level of wins and shows that Houston was twice as successful as Harford/Hollins. Yet so many fans still express the opinion that Harford should be given more time when it is obvious that he must be sacked now or else he will be leading QPR back to where they were when I began sinking my granddad's hard earned into the club in 1960. But at least they had hoops on their sleeves then.

(Paul Smith – issue # 118)

Lend us a fiver Si

A near full-house witnessed Simon Barker's testimonial against Jamaica, netting the semi-popular midfielder a nice payout in the region of £200,000. It was quite a coup by Barker getting Jamaica to turn out for him as their fans populated more than 80% of the ground, resulting in a sea of green and white and an air of a particular smoke, resulting in an atmosphere rarely experienced at Loftus Road. Fielding a team made up of regular first-teamers, reserve team players and Dennis Bailey and Steve Hodge (?!),

Jamaica won an entertaining game 2-1 but I doubt that would have bothered Simon Barker after netting all that money — but he deserved it for displaying the one thing missing from too many of today's players — loyalty.

(Ed – issue # 118)

Andy Ward has left the building

Hmm — how to put this? I've had enough and I'm off — there I've said it. Actually I said a lot of it last time around and what has happened in between has made up my mind. Port Vale I left early, for the first time in 300-odd games even by a few seconds. I left because we didn't deserve to score and I just didn't care whether we did or not. Middlesborough I skipped, and in fact I suspect everyone else did too, and when the powers that be, that anti-Middlesborough conspiracy we heard so much about last year, realised no-one was going to show they slipped a few quid in the appropriate media pockets and Bob's your auntie's live-in lover. No way did the team I've been watching this season notch five against the joint leaders, even if they are crap. Finally Swindon, the most out-of-form side in the division coming straight off a 6-0 caning, gave us a goal start, lost their keeper to the most ridiculous decision I've seen in 10 years bar none, and won comfortably. Not to belittle their efforts, their commitment and football were top notch, but my point is that I just laughed.

There was a time when I would be depressed on Monday and beyond if we lost to one of the top sides in the country. No more. It's like ending a relationship with someone you used to love because you've both changed, and it's just gone. I think it's very much like that except in one important way. Most of us have experienced both sides of the coin, I certainly have, but when the dumper decides enough is enough, the dumpee may not concur and can be, well, heartbroken. This is easier because I doubt if the current club gives a toss about one more or less — it might have been different when the likes of Neil Roberts worked for the club, but now? Now, after all that, I had finished this article (flashback!), and a little spark remained. I wasn't quite sure if the old club was really dead, not quite. Then Vinny Jones signed. As player-coach and manager-in-waiting. Ashes to ashes, funk to funky…

Anyway, football as a whole has changed irrevocably over the last 3-4 years. I believe that the period in between Arsenal taking the championship off a stunned Liverpool at Anfield, and up until Blackburn buying the title and then Manchester United dominating it, will, or anyway should, come to be viewed as a golden age. I've gone into it before and anyone with half a brain and both eyes open can see it for themselves anyway. The game is obsessed with money. The flood of cash into the game is washing away the many cultural differences between clubs until only two types remain. The haves and the have-nots. The haves will do anything to maintain their status, the have-nots would skin their Granny to join them. And despite this vast quantity of money coming in, how many professional clubs turn a profit? Less than a dozen. So what will happen when the money stops coming in? Not my problem mate, I'll be out by then, look a sponsorship deal, quick! Oh well.

So, at Loftus Road, a team totally bereft of the two qualities I value most in footballers, pace and intelligence, goes through the motions. Above, several clubs who are having their best season in years don't seem to even enjoy it — no time, keep chanting the mantra, 42 points 42 points 42 points — we've survived! Thank God for that, now next year we can concentrate on, er surviving again. Their supporters entertain themselves by, when an opponent evades a challenge and whistles a long-ranger two feet wide, standing up and going "WIIIIIIIIDE, ha ha you're shit." This coming from people who consider it a feat of co-ordination to walk and eat chips at the same time. Below, clubs who still value their community and their background struggle to survive, the word having a completely different meaning. Too many of their fans spend their free time and hard-earned cash being consumed by bitterness and envy, more so among the has-beens than the never-weres.

So what about you, you might say. QPR will always be my team, but from a distance. I just haven't got the desire to spend my free time in such a miserable atmosphere, I don't want to become bitter and envious, and the bottom line is I derive very little enjoyment from coming to Loftus Road any more. I've had more fun watching the likes of Watford and even Southend this year than Rangers where it just gets to me. In fact, I think someone else has been to Watford too, as the pre-match and half-time "entertainment" for Swindon was basically thieved from Vicarage Road with a couple of cones stuck on the top.

I shall be back every now and then, less to support than to observe, as the wonderful Robert Rankin would say, whilst remaining unobserved. As my inspiration, you can blame him for some of my more drug-induced submissions over the years. I don't want this to sound bitter, or self-justifying, and I hope it doesn't. I had seven great years watching Rangers, including three brilliant seasons following them all over, plus three mostly depressing ones at the end. QPR will now either sink into total obscurity or, in a few years, regain a seat at the top table: the reward — oodles of cash; the cost — everything we ever stood for. Oh whatever, like so many articles before, it's off my chest now and I feel better for that. If bits of it made one person laugh, or made one person think "Oh yeah, I suppose so," so much the better. Be seeing you!
(Andy Ward – issue # 118)

Praying for time

It seems like a lifetime, but two and a half months have passed since the Tranmere home match, which incidentally is the last time that I put pen to paper. Funny how often time really doesn't fly, no doubt the substandard 'entertainment' being served up by the R's at present contributing to Old Father Times current lack of pace.

Since the diabolical game against Tranmere things haven't got much better either. The magnificent victory over Middlesbrough apart the team have shown their failings on a regular basis.

(Issue # 118)

The win over Crewe will be remembered for Mark Kennedy's two superb goals but the fact that a two-goal lead was nearly lost highlighted the problems in the current side. This was further seen at Charlton where a reasonable first half display was followed by total collapse in the second half. The defending was frantic and the team struggled at times to put two passes together. Just looking at this match you could see which side had played in this league for years and which side just thought they had a divine right to return to the Premiership.

After being outplayed by Port Vale at home an improved performance against Sheffield United and a point at Norwich — a side whose path from respected Premiership side to obscurity we seem to be uncomfortably following — followed.

The Swindon match saw the 'Return of the Mac' and when they had their goalkeeper dismissed I said to my sister that if we lose this one we will get relegated... gulp!

I'm writing this on the morning of 4th April. I don't need to spell out the serious trouble that the team now find themselves in. When you look at the commitment shown against Middlesbrough and also in that period when Houston was first sacked, you can't help wondering whether we are in a false position. I don't believe that the team are as bad as the current table suggests but we find ourselves in trouble due to a lack of commitment and effort — UNFORGIVEABLE.

One such individual with an overblown ego and an inflated opinion of his abilities is of course Trevor Sinclair. A player once rated at £10million by Ray Wilkins (says it all really) and a player now blossoming at Upton Park after leaving for just over a fifth of that estimation. It had been, prior to his 'dream move', "a miserable past eighteen months." Well Trevor, for the average QPR fan that period hasn't been the happiest of times either, especially having to watch your substandard performances in addition. The fact that Trevor seems to have finally learnt where the goal is and at present by all accounts, playing superbly, merely rubs salt into the wounds and confirms that he was cheating us and stealing from the club.

Not that anybody cares that he's left. He'd had enough of us and we certainly had had enough of him, but with players like him wearing our colours this season is it any surprise that we're in the shit at present? Still maybe one day Mr Sinclair will fulfil his number one ambition and get to play for a big club.

After a short spell with the club it looks like John Spencer has had enough as well. Currently on loan at Everton and at the same time failing to make an impact he's yet another reason, and there are many, why we are in the very unfortunate position we find ourselves. When Spencer first joined he was dynamite. His work rate and effort seemingly rubbing off on the rest of the side and lifting them out of the slumbers. Last season he helped, ahem, awake a sleeping giant.

Sadly, loss of form and it has to be said, loss of interest, has seen Spencer — like West Ham's new wonder boy — have a nightmare season. Maybe as supporters we are often unfair. It must be difficult for world class players such as Spencer and Sinclair to lift themselves playing for a little club such as QPR and at the same time only earn about 8k a week. How can we expect them to show commitment to us when their wonderful God given talents deserve a larger stage?

One player I was very sorry to see leave is Mark Kennedy. It's a sign of the times that players see a move to Wimbledon and West Ham as being better than playing for QPR nowadays, and is yet another pointer, if indeed they are needed, as to how low we have sunk.

Kennedy was the first class winger we've had since, and I can only rely on older fans opinions, Dave Thomas. His exceptional crossing of the ball and his ability at free kicks and set pieces really does put into perspective Mr Sinclair and the drivel that we've had to endure from him over the past few seasons. With Kennedy in the team we really did have cause to get excited when awarded corner kicks. Take the Middlesbrough match. What we witnessed that evening was an exhibition by Mr Kennedy on the art of taking corners and set pieces. With a man like Ferdinand in the team that evening the team could have easily doubled their win. Sadly he decided his future lay elsewhere but in an otherwise miserable season he was like a glowing ray of sunshine and will be sadly missed.

The spectre of relegation has been hanging over us for a while but a trip to Stoke and yet another poor performance gave Chris Kamara his first win as manager. Not that any of us were really surprised that a dreadful side like Stoke would end up with three points, so low in confidence this side have become.

A solitary cry of "Wright Out" at Stoke was not added to but interestingly was not contested. The future of the club is very unsure and since Houston's departure things have not improved. It is fair to say that the team looks as clueless and as demoralised as they ever did under Houston and the figures speak for themselves. The R's have failed to win away from home since September. The only thing keeping us afloat at present is the inability of any teams below us to string together a row of wins. Since October the team have won a game a month, January being the exception where they failed to win even that much.

The players brought in have hardly inspired any confidence, is there anybody out there who believes Keith Rowland is a better left-back than Rufus Brevett, and is also worth more money? Iain Dowie looks worse than I even thought he was. I thought he might do well for us, giving us much needed height up front but after a reasonable start he just looks like another waste of money. I feel sorry for Steve Slade and think that he's been unfortunate to not be involved more this season.

I thought that when we got relegated we would have a hard time in this division but not even I thought that after just two seasons in this league I would be discussing the 'R' word again. Things are not looking good as we go into our final run. The thought of having to win at Maine Road to stay up has been playing on my mind since last year and it's looking like my worst fears could be realised. All the 'die hard romantics' who saw our drop into Division 1 as a brief loan period whilst we make our glorious return renewed and invigorated, must be feeling sick.

Don't think either that another drop will be good for the club. I can just hear it now, "We'll piss this league," "We'll beat all that inferior opposition with ease." Sounds familiar doesn't it? Another drop and we're in serious trouble both on the field and financially. I've lost faith in the current side to perform any miracles — for the next few weeks I'm just going to be praying for one.

(Matthew Holley – issue # 118)

Manchester City 2-2 QPR

Superb game, superb atmosphere – it was just like being in the Premiership once again. The players turned it on at the latest available opportunity to avoid the drop by the skin of their teeth, and how we laughed at City.

It wasn't looking great when Georgi Kinkladze hit a stunning 30-yard free kick past Lee Harper in the opening minute. The roar was deafening, but soon the Maine Road faithful had very little to cheer about. Sheron equalised minutes later after quick thinking by Gallen, then the moment came that will haunt Jamie Pollock for the rest of his life. His own goal would have been something special had it been scored by a striker, just what was he thinking?

The rest of the half was end-to end stuff. Sheron fluffed a one-on-one (though he was crocked when scoring), Pollock and Goater both hit the wood work and QPR should have been awarded a penalty when Kit Symons brought down Gallen, somehow the ref deemed it legal and City equalised just after half time through Bradbury. It was pretty much one-way traffic after this as City piled forward, knowing nothing less than a win would do.

Maybe without the likes of Ruddock and Jones we would have buckled, and captain Bardsley looked as good as ever, but proved to be his penultimate game for the R's. Quashie got his marching orders late on, but this was to be our day. A completely miserable season had somehow not ended in utter disaster with relegation. Of course, there are bigger teams than QPR to suffer this fate, and it's a bit tastier when we're the ones to send them own…

(Ed – issue # 119)

Joy at Maine Road as Neil Ruddock and Vinnie Jones (boo) celebrate staying up

Matthew Rose, aka 'The Glassman', endured a torrid first season at QPR but went on to make over 250 appearances for the club in just under ten seasons

1997/98 ~ Division 1

Date	Match	Comp	Scorers	Att	Issue
09/08/97	H Ipswich Town D 0-0	League		17,614	# 110
12/08/97	H Wolves L 0-2	Lgc Cup		8,355	
15/08/97	A Tranmere Rvs L 1-2	League	Peacock	7,467	
23/08/97	H Stockport Cty W 2-1	League	Sinclair (2)	11,108	
27/08/97	A Wolves W 2-1	Lge Cup	Peacock, Murray	18,398	
30/08/97	A Notts Forest L 0-4	League		18,804	
02/09/97	A Reading W 2-1	League	Spencer, OG	10,203	# 111
13/09/97	H West Brom W 2-0	League	Sheron, Peacock	14,399	
20/09/97	A Crewe W 3-2	League	Spencer, Maddix, Sinclair	5,348	
24/09/97	H Portsmouth W 1-0	League	Spencer	12,620	
27/09/97	A Port Vale L 0-2	League		7,197	
04/10/97	H Charlton Ath L 2-4	League	Sheron (2)	14,825	# 112
18/10/97	A Sheffield Utd D 2-2	League	Murray, Morrow	18,006	
21/10/97	A Bury D 1-1	League	Spencer	4,602	
26/10/97	H Man City W 2-0	League	Ready, Peacock (p)	14,451	
01/11/97	H Birmingham City D 1-1	League	Barker	12,715	# 113
05/11/97	A Swindon Town L 1-3	League	Peacock	10,132	
12/11/97	H Stoke City D 1-1	League	Barker (p)	11,923	
22/11/97	H Huddersfield W 2-1	League	Quashie (2)	16,066	
29/11/97	A Wolves L 2-3	League	Sheron, Peacock	23,645	
03/12/97	H Norwich City D 1-1	League	Peacock	10,141	# 114
06/12/97	H Sunderland L 0-1	League		15,266	
12/12/97	A Oxford Utd L 1-3	League	Peacock	6,664	
21/12/97	H Bradford City W 1-0	League	Peacock (p)	8,853	# 115
26/12/97	A Portsmouth L 1-3	League	Sheron	12,314	
28/12/97	H Reading D 1-1	League	Spencer	13,015	
03/01/98	H Middlesbrough D 2-2	League	Spencer, Gallen	13,379	
10/01/98	A Ipswich Town D 0-0	League		12,672	
13/01/98	A Middlesbrough L 0-2	FA Cup		21,817	
17/01/98	H Tranmere Rvs D 0-0	League		12,033	
24/01/98	H Notts Forest L 0-1	League		13,220	# 116
31/01/98	A Stockport Cty L 0-2	League		7,958	
07/02/98	H Crewe W 3-2	League	Kennedy (2), Ready	13,429	
14/02/98	A West Brom D 1-1	League	Dowie	19,143	
17/02/98	A Charlton Ath D 1-1	League	Peacock (p)	15,555	
21/02/98	H Port Vale L 0-1	League		14,198	
25/02/98	H Sheffield Utd D 2-2	League	Sheron, Ready	9,560	# 117
28/02/98	A Norwich City D 0-0	League		12,730	
04/03/98	H Middlesbrough W 5-0	League	OG, Bruce, Gallen, Sheron (2)	11,580	
07/03/98	A Birmingham City L 0-1	League		18,928	
14/03/98	H Swindon Town L 1-2	League	Quashie	13,486	
21/03/98	A Stoke City L 1-2	League	Barker (p)	11,051	
28/03/98	A Huddersfield D 1-1	League	Jones	13,681	
01/04/98	H Wolves D 0-0	League		12,337	
10/04/98	A Sunderland D 2-2	League	Sheron (2)	40,014	
14/04/98	H Oxford Utd D 1-1	League	Gallen	12,859	# 118
19/04/98	A Bradford City D 1-1	League	Gallen	14,871	
25/04/98	A Man City D 2-2	League	Sheron, OG	32,040	
03/05/98	H Bury L 0-1	League		15,210	

League Record - P46 W10 D19 L17 F51 A63 Pts 49. League position – 21st

In The Loft Player of the Season – Karl Ready

Chapter 3

1998/99

Francis returns and keeps us up... just

Having just about done enough to secure at least another season in Division 1, there was very little pre-season cheer around all things QPR going into the 1998/99 campaign. The year previously bookmakers made QPR second favourites for the title. Such was the catastrophe both on and off the field, the club were now considered relegation fodder and not many fans disagreed.

Matters weren't helped when the only cash left available to spend during the summer went on Richard Ord. Six hundred and fifty grand on a player who pulled up after his first pre-season friendly and never kicked a ball again. Truth was, an on-going back problem was his real problem after an injury ravaged last 18 months at his previous club, Sunderland. Full marks to the medical team there then.

Such comical pieces of business had been common place since Ray Wilkins washed away Les Ferdinand's transfer fee. Perhaps Chris Wright should have been more on the ball, but he was to prove anything but. Ray Harford lasted just nine more league games as QPR manager, with the club adrift at the bottom of the table. Vinnie Jones went AWOL after Iain Dowie was preferred to take on the role until someone else came in, resulting in another sorry episode in this once respected Premiership outfit.

The debts were now mounting as Division 2 loomed large. An SOS went out to Gerry Francis – not everyone's first choice – but after telling all that listened that he didn't need to get back into management, his heart ruled his head and he agreed to take on one of the toughest jobs in football.

Somehow Francis breathed life into a side that looked as clueless as any in our modern history. Starting in November, six wins and two draws from the next ten games had the optimistic few looking at a surge into the play-offs as relegation started to look ever more unlikely – an unthinkable situation prior to his arrival. The turn of the year saw a change in fortunes though as the old habits crept back in and just three more league wins were attained until the final day of the season.

Sunday May 9th 1999 is a day that will live long in the memory of all QPR fans. Any kind of win against Crystal Palace at Loftus Road was all that was required. It was a scorching hot day, the ground was full, and the rest is history. 6-0. Six bloody nil from a side that had barely averaged a goal a game during the entire season was as surprising as it was spectacular.

To survive in such a way whilst truly memorable, but only papered over the cracks of a club in turmoil on and off the pitch. Financially stricken, with a squad stripped of just about its last quality players, keeping QPR up was nothing short of a miracle by Gerry Francis. The key word was now simply survival, applicable at all levels. ❑

Bury the memories

It hardly seems like two minutes since the referee blew the final whistle at the end of the Bury match to put us all out of our misery after the most dreadful of seasons. We escaped relegation by the narrowest of margins imaginable — just one more defeat would have been enough to send us into Division 2, and no one would have been saying we were 'unlucky' this time around. Even QPR's performances in 95/96 didn't come close to the awful standards witnessed last season. We all know Ray Harford inherited a squad made up of many overpaid Premiership wannabes who either had to get out or buck up. In many respects Harford has achieved this, but the football on display and results achieved just got worse and worse until Vinnie Jones and Neil Ruddock arrived, bringing with them the extra ounce of commitment required — though not a winning formula — to just about secure another season in this division.

The same cannot be allowed to happen this season, and Ray Harford along with several players with a point to prove have to deliver the goods from day one. The talent in certain areas of the squad is unquestionable — Nigel Quashie and Paul Murray are are capable of forging an excellent central midfield whilst Mike Sheron and Kevin Gallen should get their share of goals, but only if the service is right. This proved to be a major struggle last season, and the team still lacks quality down the wings. Tony Scully is our only genuine wide player, and the jury is still out on his capabilities. In defence, the signing of Richard Ord doesn't exactly inspire so don't expect to see any great improvement there.

I don't think anybody really expects us to cause any great commotion at the right end of the league this season, but maybe with our expectations so low the players may just surprise us and deliver the right results. If not, there won't be the same anguish around Loftus Road as last season, just a few more puzzled looks as to how this once respected Premiership club has fallen from grace so rapidly, and with probably another change in manager.

With Vinnie Jones manager-in-waiting, the pressure on Ray Harford to strike the right formula is greater than ever. We can all accept defeat, but we will not accept another season where the players, individually and collectively, do not give 100% to QPR every minute, every game, every week.

(Ed – issue # 119)

Gone, but not quite forgotten...

Whilst the summer didn't quite see the mass clearout of players many forecast, amongst those who were shown the door — David Bardsley, Simon Barker and Tony Roberts — QPR were saying goodbye to a trio of players with a combined service of 30 years and over 800 appearances between them.

No doubt the biggest mistake Ray Harford has made yet in his short time as QPR boss was letting David Bardsley leave on a free transfer. Bardsley was, in my opinion at least, the best defender I have seen play for QPR. At 33, he still had a lot to offer the club and he certainly looked fit enough after 18 months out with injury. At the same age, Clive Wilson was joining Spurs — poor old Bardsley now finds himself back at his first club Blackpool, one year short of completing 10 years with QPR and of course missing out on a deserved testimonial. But being a high wage earner, Bardsley's days at the club were always numbered as QPR slowly but surely lose all traces of being a Premiership club.

More importantly though, Bardsley was one player who you could rely on to give 100%. Deemed good enough to be captain for the crunch game at Manchester City last season ahead of the likes of Jones and Ruddock — but now surplus to requirements. Upon leaving for Blackpool, Bardsley was reported to have said, "I still love the club (QPR) and I hope they do well. I was there a long time and I didn't want to leave, so there is no way I will be wanting them to have a bad season."

My favourite memory of Bardsley has to be when he scored against Leeds in the 1992/93 season — one full-back crossed (Wilson) for the other to head home in front of the Loft. Great days for Bardsley and QPR, but ones that now seem a long time ago.

The case for Barker is a little different. With a surplus of midfielders at the club, Barker was never going to be offered a new contract, especially following his testimonial. Ten years is a long time for a player to stay at any club, and having played under eight different managers, those years were certainly up and down.

Barker's best season with the club was in Gerry Francis's first term in 91/92. His goals and overall performances, more so in the first half of the season, nearly earned him an England call up — instead Graham Taylor opted for Andy Gray, so no major shame for Barker there. I think QPR fans were split on their overall judgement of Barker as a player, mainly because he could look so ordinary one game, then pretty damn good the next. His legendary shaking of the head when he misjudged a pass or shot was a regular feature most games, but he gave everything for the cause of QPR. As I write, Barker has yet to find himself a club for the coming season, and I hope he doesn't find himself travelling along the same road as Kenny Sansom and Paul Parker to oblivion. At 33, Barker can still do a job at this level, but wherever he may end up I think most QPR fans would give him a warm welcome back to Loftus Road if and when he ever returns as an opposing player.

The same cannot really be said for Tony Roberts, on the contrary he wouldn't get abuse either — fans would probably just laugh. Every club has a joker in the pack, and Roberts was ours. Unfortunately, too many of them occurred on the pitch as one

minute he'd be pulling off a blinding save, the next letting in the softest of goals — as his new club Norwich could testify. It's actually a good move for Tony, although I would be surprised if he joined to be their new first choice 'keeper. He was approached by Millwall — a division more apt to his chaotic standards, but when he informed new manager Keith Stevens of his wage demands, Roberts was told to "Disconnect your phoneline as you won't be getting any offers." Funny and true. They say goalkeepers aren't born until they're 30. Well, there's not long to go now before Roberts 'comes of age,' although something tells me he may be an exception to the rule.
(Ed – issue # 119)

McCoist no-go

QPR's hopes of signing Ally McCoist from the other Rangers were thwarted by the players' apparent lack of commitment to the club. With the BBC studios just around the corner, McCoist's blossoming career as a TV personality was seen to be a too big a distraction. Vinnie Jones must be thinking he can walk on water — player, coach, movie star and currently seeing out several weeks worth of community service — whilst all McCoist wanted to do was film a few rounds of 'A Question Of Sport'. QPR may live to regret the decision...
(Ed – issue # 119)

Pre-season chatter with Matthew Holley

Joke: How do you turn a duck into a soul singer? Put it in the microwave until it's Bill Withers. Er... and that's about as funny as it gets today. Not for a long while has a new season been so uneagerly anticipated. Even the 'We're too good for this division' crowd are now silent and must now realise that like Wilkins — the great man (sic) who took us down — that they, just like him, haven't got a clue. It's hard to believe that 1998 has seen the R's manage only two wins. It's also worth pointing out that 49 points would normally have seen us dead and buried, Millwall making the drop a few years back on 52. Continue in the same way we finished last term and it's curtains. These are just a few facts I share with you to let you know that I'm always here to spread cheer and to put a smile on everyone's faces.

Pre-season activity with two new players — a goalkeeper and a defender joining us, who's names at this moment I cannot recall, will hardly have temperatures rising in W12. Maybe the soppy optimists that predicted a quick exit from this division did have a point after all. A largely forgettable season climaxed with a typically lack lustre defeat at home to Bury. A stream of similar results and performances where at times the teams' commitment could be questioned was enough to make even the most die hard fan question their sanity whilst turning up each week. After all why should we bother when at times it seems that the majority of the team doesn't care?

One game however answered that question and reminded this particular fan why he supports QPR and continues, despite the shit we've seen in recent years, to turn up on a regular basis. A magnificent day in Manchester saw the R's gain the point needed to secure their Division One status. An electric soul pumping white-hot atmosphere awaited the R's fans that went to Maine Road that day. Not for a long time has a game seen the old butterflies go so totally crazy in the stomach. This could of course be attributed to myself, editor Prosser and his brother, attempting, and almost succeeding, in drinking Manchester dry on the Friday night.

However it was only on arrival at Maine Road that the enormity of the situation suddenly sunk in. This was a game the R's couldn't lose. If they did relegation could beckon. It was a heart stopping affair with the majority of the away end living each tackle and probably feeling afterwards like they had played 90 minutes themselves. Like Quentin Tarrantino said when he made Reservoir Dogs — "We'll sell you your seat but you're only going to use the edge of it." As exciting as it was though, a mediocre mid-table finish with no relegation clouds hanging over us will do quite nicely this time around instead... management, team please note.

(Matthew Holley – issue # 119)

Early season woe

We've got problems, and major ones at that. QPR have not progressed one iota since last season, and the early signs suggest we'll be faced with another relegation battle on our hands this season.

Whilst the first team squad has great depth, it lacks real quality. The three problem areas — central defence, wide midfield and attack, desperately need reinforcing. Richard Ord, if and when he gets fit, will walk straight into the first team following the defensive shambles at Norwich. Ray Harford has no money to spend despite the sale of Nigel Quashie to Nottingham Forest, so if we're only in the market for free transfers, so be it.

There's no denying out of the four matches played so far, we could have easily won all of them. Unfortunately, Kevin Gallen and Mike Sheron have missed enough sitters between them to last a whole season. At least there appears to be more commitment in the team so far, but that can only take us so far. The present team is the least skilful and enterprising I've seen in my time supporting Rangers. We've always had a potential match winner who could produce a goal from nothing, but we haven't even got that to cling on to. Our reputation as being a 'footballing' side has all but gone. Half our players can't even run properly—stick a ball at their feet and they look about as graceful as Giant Haystacks practising ballet.

It really is a case of making the most of what we've got and hoping for the best. The five-man defence Harford is employing hasn't worked at all. Generally, if you play with wing-backs you shouldn't play with an orthodox winger as well. As a result, nearly all our attacks stem from the right with Heinola and Scully. The balance isn't right. The team would have more shape to it if Peacock played just behind the front two (easily his best position), and Scully was sacrificed for an extra midfielder.

Ray Harford is running out of games to start turning things around. He has done little in his time here to get the fans on his side, and he comes across as being far less charismatic that Houston and Rioch ever were, which is really saying something.

Judging by his post-match comment at Norwich — "We keep taking one step forward, two steps back. It's going to be that sort of season I think" — suggests he has lost the plot already. They're not the words of a man with apparent drive and ambition, but words from a man who has already lost belief in his players. I only hope I'm wrong.

Considering the rough ride Houston and Rioch got from the fans, Harford has been fortunate enough to escape any significant amount of abuse despite having a far worse record. That will soon change unless we see a marked improvement in team affairs — I fear we will be waiting for a long time yet.
(Ed – issue # 120)

Mystic Magee – The 3rd

After last season's shameful run of predictions where virtually everything I predicted would happen, didn't, I have spent all summer working my arse off to scrape enough money together to fund the purchase of a brand new crystal ball — so here's hoping I'm a little closer to the mark this time around.

August

QPR announce yet another new sponsorship deal, this time with Butlins, for whom a spokesman has said; "It's so uncanny — our season ends in October as well." As Vinnie Jones' period of community service begins, some of his critics say that Asian style 'strikes' would have been more appropriate... Brian Clough says "There's nothing like giving a damn good hiding to show him that violence gets you nowhere."

September

Iain Dowie stuns the R's faithful with an unforgettable free-kick at home to Barnsley — he becomes the first player in forty years to hit the floodlights. Ray Harford announces that Nottingham Forest goalkeeper Dave Beasant will be his first big signing of the season — he is 6'4". Elsewhere, sports wear giants Nike are to print a warning on the packaging of Ronaldo's new boots. It will read, 'In case of bad fit, pull out tongue.'

October

The month starts with a sensational 'smash and grab' as the trophy room at Loftus Road is robbed. Shepherds Bush police are appealing to witnesses who may have seen two men running down South Africa Road with a blue and white carpet. Ray Harford as last reveals why Neil Ruddock was not signed on a permanent basis; "When I signed Vinnie Jones, you could tell he was hungry for success, whereas Rudduck was hungry, and that's it." Meanwhile, Iain Dowie is kicked off 'A Question of Sport' for failing to identify a football on the picture board.

November

Ray Harford expresses his disgust at the team's lack of commitment after yet another away defeat. He says, "Some of our players out there thought it was some kind of game." Harford is sacked, although he walks into another job straight away, where he will be expected to deliver the goods — he is to become a postman. Elsewhere, Tottenham's financial crisis deepens, as directors are now having to pay for their drinks at the forthcoming AGM. One director said, "I don't mind paying for my tea or coffee, but forks in the sugar bowl is taking it too far."

December

After a solid display away to Crystal Palace, midfielder George Kulcsar is asked whether he will be going to Euro 2000. He says, "It depends if I get a ticket." A tabloid newspaper report claiming that '55-year-old Chris Wright will be grateful to sell Iain Dowie for a pile of dung' prompts Wright to say that the papers have got it wrong. He says, "I'm 56, not 55." Vinnie Jones ends a glittering career at Loftus Road after disemboweling Swindon's Steve McMahon.

January

Brit-pop band Space perform a hit single live before England's friendly with Romania at Wembley. The song is called 'The Female Species Is More Deadly Than The Mail' — try telling that to Graham Kelly, who is killed by a letter-bomb. On the pitch at Loftus Road, Vinnie Jones causes a rumpus by 'bum-butting' Michael Owen in the third round of the FA Cup, causing severe concussion to the youngster. In the referee's match report he sums up by saying that Jones really doesn't know his arse from his elbow.

February

Speculation that defender Karl Ready is moving to Chelsea is confirmed by the man himself, who says, "Yes I really like the place, and it would suit my family right now, but it would be a bit further to commute to QPR's training ground." Trevor Brooking appears live on 'Match of the Day' with a broken shoulder, after stupidly volunteering to help carry Graham Kelly's coffin to the funeral.

March

Iain Dowie is kicked off 'They Think It's All Over' for failing in an attempt to recite the lyrics to the famous football song 'Ere we go.' Chris Wright fails to appear at a press conference amidst rumours that he is suffering from a penis infection. Fans are hoping he doesn't go the same way as Matthew Harding, who died as a result of his own faulty chopper.

April

Transfer deadline day passes with Kevin Gallen leaving to join Fulham for a cut-price £1m. Rangers were holding out for £1.5m, although the Cottagers said they were not prepared to pick up his bar-slate. Chris Wright says that there is to be a clearout in the summer, as he threatens to sell Rangers prize assets, "I've already had an offer for the Scoreboard," claims Wright, who also confirms that a convicted thief is to join the board of directors. The mystery man is mobbed as he tries to take his seat in the directors box — unfortunately for him it is screwed firmly to the floor.

May

Fans are aghast to read the news that Big Ron is to become the new QPR boss after months of searching for Ray Harford's successor. At the press conference, Big Ron says that managing Rangers is a massive step up from running a market stall in Albert Square, but Chris Wright believes that he is the man to attract star names such as Fowler.

(Aidan Magee – issue # 120)

The super-Ray syndrome

"Super Rays Blue & White Army," the Rangers fans chant. Who the hell is this Super Ray? Following the Norwich match it is now 14 — 14 competitive games that is without a win. Incredible to think that the last win was the 5-0 thrashing of 'Boro. In addition it's also almost a year now without an away win. Things are, to say the least, not looking good.

Overheard at Walsall; "We should beat these, they're a second division side." Well I'm afraid that's exactly what we currently have at QPR — a second division side that is, through good fortune, playing in the first. Make no mistake about it, in a normal season 49 points would have seen us dead and buried, we were lucky. Midway through last season the fans wanted Houston and Rioch out, and they got their way. So in comes Ray Harford who turns us from a mid-table side going nowhere, into prime relegation candidates! With nothing changing over the summer, and the team carrying on this season as they finished the last, we are, at present, still that. No wonder the Rangers fans chant "Super Ray's Blue and White Army"!

It's almost like history repeating itself. Last time we got relegated the bloke who took us down was also refered to as "Super Ray." No wonder the club treats us like morons. Houston may be a bad manager but compared to the two super-Rays he walks on water in my eyes. Not that many agree with me. Wilkins could do no wrong and 'Super Ray mark 2' seems to be escaping any real criticism, although I feel that may soon change. Who comes in though? Don't ask me, I haven't a clue and I fear the board is equally devoid of ideas.

It looks like Rioch is doing a good job at Norwich. Maybe that's because now he's working with proper professional footballers that are prepared to work hard and don't fear a little discipline. Rioch's rein at QPR was obviously too much for our overpaid, overrated prima donnas. I heard shocking rumours from his spell. Apparently he had the team going on long runs and other heinous crimes! And of course the players reacted in exactly the way you'd expect — complaining about their "QPR nightmare," and not playing to their badge whilst picking up a large pay cheque. The Norwich game highlighted the severe shit we now find ourselves in. It's hard to imagine where the next win is coming from let alone the 50-odd points, which should guarantee survival.

Last season Harford bought Kulscar to add steel to our midfield. He didn't really make an impression so Jones was bought in. He now stands in the dugout barking orders, not even warranting a place on the subs bench. With five at the back we're left woefully lacking in midfield and because of this the defence is overexposed and against sides like Norwich that attack with pace we will struggle. Of course in Scully we have a bit of pace up front, but I fear that although willing he's not very able. We also have a predictable strikeforce lacking pace or presence. In a nutshell we've got a long hard season ahead. In Quashie we sold the one player we currently have who has the potential to be a good player in the Premier League. There are two ways of looking at it. On one hand getting that amount of money for an unproven youngster is good business. On the other though, it sums up the ambition at the club.
(Matthew Holley – issue # 120)

No ordinary injury

Having read many of the, unflattering, comments on the arrival of Richard Ord from Sunderland I thought I'd set the record straight.

I watched most of Sunderland's promotion season in 1995/96 when at university in Sunderland and Ord was the rock they built one of the meanest defences in the country. He could tackle, head the ball and generally put himself about a bit. More importantly, he shouted endlessly. There were hardly ever moments of confusion as all the defenders knew what to do and where to do it at any particular time.

He may have struggled in the Premiership, but at this level, if he played, he would be nothing but an asset to QPR. I can assure you that had he been fit, he would have featured last season for Sunderland and we wouldn't have witnessed the joke defending which gifted goals to us and Birmingham amongst others.

So am I happy with his signing? Well, not really. The key is in 'had he been fit.' He has been out now for around 18 months, not with any particular nasty injury, just never quite fit. He also needs a back operation but is refusing because it could end his career.

I think there is every indication that we have bought ourselves a lemon, to use a motoring expression. I only hope I'm wrong. It's a lot of money to pay for a physio's couch warmer.

(Matthew Mannion – issue # 120)

Clinton confesses all

"This afternoon in this room, from this chair, I testified before the Office of Independent Counsel and the Grand Jury. I answered their questions truthfully, including questions no citizen would ever want to answer. Still, I must take complete responsibility for all my actions, both public and private. My inappropriate behaviour constituted a critical lapse in judgement and a personal failure on my part for which I am solely and completely responsible. The shame and embarrassment it has brought my wife and family has been intolerable, but I ask for forgiveness as it was I, and only I, who decided to call my daughter Chelsea."

(Ed – issue # 120)

Another no so super-Ray

As football supporters up and down the country could sympathise with, following QPR these days is not much fun at all. The football is poor, we haven't won a league game since March, our manager keeps telling us he's "doing a good job," when he blatantly isn't, and our chairman looks like he's finally had enough. All these ingredients arrive at a point where you can safely say QPR are a club in crisis. One look at the current share price tells its own sorry story.

No matter who you wish to point the finger at, everyone is equally to blame, from pitch to boardroom level. A change of manager or ownership may appease fans short-term, but the club is rotten to the core at all levels and there appears no immediate answer to our problems.

I had my doubts about Harford's credentials in the first place, but neither I or anyone could have imagined the depths he has taken this club to. In his favour, Harford has not had the money to spend like Houston, but surely there must be something left over from the sales of Sinclair, Spencer and Quashie? I hate to use the term 'asset stripping' but unless Wright can prove otherwise what this money is being used on, the doubts amongst fans that Wright is trying to get back as much money as he can before selling up will grow stronger. Some vital questions need to be answered.

Such as... Is Ray Harford actually still in charge of the club? Vinnie Jones and Iain Dowie were supposedly given the reigns prior to the Tranmere match, with Harford 'moved upstairs.' Harford has strenuously denied this, saying he will be spending more time in the office following the departure of Clive Berlin, but otherwise his role remains unchanged. Even so, Sky Sports text went as far to quote Harford as saying, "I'm happy with my new role. I'll pop down to the training pitch once a week to see how things are going." Jones and Dowie were certainly more active on the touchline during the Tranmere match than at any other this season. QPR fans are no fools — we need to know the truth.

(Ed – issue # 121)

During the war...

OK, you tell me why the present Rangers outfit resemble the Teletubbies? There could of course be many and varied answers to this question. I would favour the answer that they could play all day and not one of them would know where they are!

'A bunch of girls' was the appropriate caption on the cover of ITL # 116 to those that wear the hoops — my comments are that we would be better off playing the ladies with a band of gold, they at least must know that a goalpost is a vertical structure if the ball goes between them, a goal is scored!

Can I say as I fight against appearing an old fogey, now only 4 years from being 70, and as one who has sleepless nights and driving my poor wife crazy to get the Rangers score all over the world through thick and thin, I can truly say I have never known a trough like we are in as I pen these words. We all thought things could never get any worse at the nail biting end to last season but after leaving the ground against Bury with yet another goalless draw my feelings must have been the same as many of you — as one of rage, frustration, dashed hopes and a gloom bigger than the whole of W12.

After following the R's for 60 years — good God is it really 64 years since my father propelled me from the school end to get away from the bad language being used around me — I've stoically borne bad results since Dave Mangnall was manager (look that one up chaps), but it will come as no surprise that I have never, never known such impotent play as being currently served up for us. There have been lows of course as for many years it seemed it was our destiny to be in the lowest division but at least the games were entertaining in the main.

Yes we lost some, drew some and even won some. Leaving the Walsall game, the thin crowd brought back memories when all my classmates of St Clement Danes School in Ducane Road went along and were the main vocal group in the 1940s. At least then we were a poor but honest club. Now with fairly long standing director, Clive Berlin, leaving the club for what we are told is a cost cutting measure, nothing for our manager to spend after Quashie's departure, Sinclair gone, Impey spirited away and Dichio now banging them in for Sunderland, it is difficult to see where salvation is coming from. It's not our fault we were given the genes of a QPR supporter when we came on this earth. Certainly we know how to suffer whilst our neighbours across west London gorge themselves on the caviar. We might be in the minority in London but we're very special. What a pity the team isn't!

(Geoff Donald – issue # 121)

Hitting rock bottom

Pre-season there was a feature in the Captain Cash section in the News of the World where Vinnie Jones and other players pledged a donation to charity when the R's manage to record their first league win of the season. Captain Cash is, for the sensible amongst us who never read, let alone even look at that rag, here to 'Help the needy and bash the greedy.' People basically write him begging letters and the good old cap'n comes to the rescue with a cash donation. So, seven games into the season and the Captains still waiting and so are the rest of us. Any players reading this please remember that not only are you ruining our weekends at present but you are also depriving these important charities of much needed help. Give them the money you pledged now. They don't deserve to have to wait — they're innocent. Or is this appalling run of form a devious public relations ploy where QPR will be seen to be giving charities a large boost at Christmas time?

At the beginning of the season I felt sure that the most common score in QPR matches would be 0-0 or odd goal defeats or wins. The opening game at Sunderland reinforced this belief with Harford adopting a defensive approach playing for the scoreless draw. It may amuse some to know that the only time I've actually laid down money on the game being scoreless this season was at Carrow Road.

So now it's a year. A whole year, 365 days, 12 months, 52 weeks since a Rangers side has won away from Loftus Road. The way things are progressing at present, in March 1999 it's frighteningly possible that we may be saying something like, "It's now a year since a win at Loftus Road," (gulp). Pessimistic in the total extreme maybe but what else am I meant to think at present? The game at Watford was typical of the season so far and highlighted all the problems which are currently infecting this club. The defence can appear OK at times but only when the opposition is not attacking with any real purpose. Richard Ord has not been seen all season and Chris Plummer, who earned rave reviews pre-season, is not even challenging for a place.

We need a hard man in midfield to give the team variety and balance — someone that can do that vital holding role. Harford knows this and attempted to address it by signing Kulcsar and then Jones. However what we need is a Rottweiler not a Yorkshire terrier to boss the midfield minefield.

Although the team has not been performing well so far, they have missed enough chances to have won at least half of the games — Tranmere at home was a dreadful game but Gallen missed two clear opportunities. Think back to last season and the four straight wins, which put us in a false position — second from top, last September. Those games were classic examples of grinding out wins. Those four wins also provided us with the cushion, which ultimately stopped us from dropping out of the First Division trap door after the dreadful run which was to follow.

This season we don't have that cushion and we look like a side destined for the drop. It may be early days but it's hard to imagine where one win is going to come from let alone the run of results needed to push us to mid-table safety.

(Matthew Holley – issue # 121)

As if further proof is needed...

Below are the league records of QPR's last ten managers, with a win percentage calculated for each. Ray Harford's record so far isn't just poor, it's bone-shattering catastrophic. He'd have to win 19 of the next 23 games to equal Stewart Houston's record, which itself was deemed not good enough. How much longer will Ray Harford be given? As the prophetic John Lennon once sung, "I'm living on borrowed time"; must surely be the words reverberating around Harford's head.

MANAGER	P	W	D	L	F	A	WIN %	AV PTS*	AV GLS F*	AV GLS A*
TERRY VENABLES	157	81	30	46	250	152	51.59	1.74	1.59	0.97
STEWART HOUSTON	56	22	14	20	77	78	39.29	1.43	1.38	1.39
JIM SMITH	139	52	32	56	166	181	37.41	1.35	1.19	1.30
DON HOWE	61	22	15	24	75	78	36.07	1.33	1.23	1.28
RAY WILKINS	70	25	12	33	85	98	35.71	1.24	1.21	1.40
GERRY FRANCIS	140	48	46	46	193	188	34.29	1.36	1.38	1.34
TREVOR FRANCIS	37	12	13	12	40	40	32.43	1.32	1.08	1.08
FRANK SIBLEY	25	8	5	12	30	43	32.00	1.16	1.20	1.72
ALAN MULLERY	17	5	6	6	23	29	29.41	1.24	1.35	1.71
RAY HARFORD	33	3	15	15	28	42	9.09	0.73	0.85	1.27

*AV PTS - AVERAGE POINTS PER GAME. AV GLS F - AVERAGE GOALS FOR PER GAME. AV GLS A - AVERAGE GOALS AGAINST PER GAME.

(Issue # 121)

Oxford United 4-1 QPR

We have witnessed enough humiliation on the pitch over the past eighteen months to last a lifetime. We all have our own 'worst yet' opinions, but this performance would surely top the lot.

Oxford, beaten 7-0 the previous week, were simply too strong, too quick, too good for us. It's obvious the players are going through a confidence crisis, but if Oxford are able to pick themselves up from a 7-0 thrashing to demolish us with ease, then lessons can still be learned from defeats.

As we stood on the open terrace, soaking from the rain, it was embarrassing being a QPR supporter today, certainly enough for Ray Harford to finally call it a day. He claimed he'd run out of ideas — I don't think he had any in the first place.

Returning home in his posh Merc, nearside window smashed for the third time this season, he thought he had it bad. Poor soul. In nine months at the club, Harford hadn't achieved a thing. A smashed window or two is little hardship for the crap we've had to put up with in his time as manager.

It would be wrong to say all our current problems are Harford's fault, as they aren't, but we all expected him to do so much better. I had my doubts about him in the first place, and it's yet another sorry chapter in the history of QPR. His win percentage must be, without checking the record books, the worst in QPR's history, and the sheer lack of entertainment under him has made the last nine months for me, and most others in all probability, the worst ever experienced.

(Ed – issue # 122)

Welcome back

So, the Rangers fans that were singing Gerry Francis' name at Watford have finally got their wish. With Ray Harford finally calling it a day after the shambles at Oxford, the hunt was on to find someone willing and able to take on one of football's hardest jobs.

Amongst the names bounded about, Gerry's was the one that stood out with the most credibility. A lot of fans have their doubts, but many more have welcomed his return, myself amongst them. Will it be third time lucky for Chris Wright? We can only hope, for if Francis can't rescue QPR from the mire, I don't think anybody can.

So what will constitute success for Gerry Francis? The league tables don't lie — we're bottom of the league on points as well as merit. It will be no mean feat if Francis can equal last season's position of 21st come May. He has inherited a side with limited potential and zero confidence. There is no money to spend — he has to rely purely on his ability as a man-manager. We cannot start planning for the long term when the short term is so important. It's vital QPR preserves its standing as a First Division club as, if reports are correct, the debts the club have, combined with relegation will see us in a position of no return, or even worse. Of course, what Francis does have that neither Houston or Harford possessed, is a genuine love for the club. In these money-orientated days, love is something you can't buy.

Under his first stint as manager, we enjoyed one of our best ever periods in the history of the club. The entertainment level was usually high, goals came in abundance and there were some memorable victories — the exact opposite to our present standing. It would be foolish to expect the same again under Francis, at least in the short term.

We can only start planning for a return to such days once we can prove we are anything other than relegation candidates, and that is one hell of a task in itself. Let's give Gerry our full support to prove we need him as much as he needs us.
(Ed – issue # 122)

Vinnie Jones

Love him or loathe him, you have to feel some sympathy for Vinnie Jones. He's become something of a black sheep at QPR for very obscure reasons. It's only taken a couple of TV appearances promoting his film (which took six weeks to film before he was even a QPR player), combined with rumours of a less than friendly style of coaching the team, to turn him into something of a hated figure. After being snubbed for the manager's job, Vinnie obviously feels there is no future for him at QPR and he hasn't been seen since the Oxford match. His heart is in the right place, but sadly with the wrong team. There is only one place Vinnie will ever feel at home, and that is at Wimbledon. A costly mistake he may be, but he's not alone.
(Ed – issue # 122)

The state of the Rangers

So it's bye bye Ray Harford... hello Gerry Francis. QPR and stability certainly don't mix, and even though I considered myself to be a staunch supporter of holding on to Ray Harford, I rapidly changed my mind after the most embarrassing defeat I have ever witnessed as a Rangers fan at Oxford United.

Chris Wright must be wondering where it all went wrong. After selecting Ray Harford purely on the basis of his being the "Wright man for the job," (arf!) we have seen Harford prove himself to be the worst manager Rangers have ever had. However, there is no doubt the gradual erosion of QPR as a football force began long before "Super Ray'," (arf!!) appeared from the half-decent team he had assembled at West Brom.

So whose fault is it that Rangers sit proudly near the bottom of Division One? We can discount Gerry Francis, whose departure was certainly a catalyst for the slide into obscurity, but here, for what it's worth, is my analysis of where the blame lies for the state we are in (with handy percentage scores for those who can't be arsed to read the words).

1) Richard Thompson

Seen by many as the devil incarnate before jumping ship as soon as Rangers were relegated, however, all he was guilty of was just keeping Rangers competitive. A truly ambitious chairman would not have sold Darren Peacock at such an important time, and would have invested serious money after our fifth-placed season in 1992/93.

Thompson's game was to balance the books and make money where possible — don't forget, all the money from the sale of Sir Les was made available. If only Thompson could have been more of a gambler, who knows... and by the way, talk to a Leeds fan and see the similar story up there now — spend only what you earn. Richard Thompson, you take 10% of the blame for Rangers predicament.

2) Ray Wilkins

Good, nice, bald, great-bloke, genuine, super Ray. No. £6million spent on Zelic the frightened Aussie, Hateley the crocked 'striker', Osborne — too much of a threat to Ray's playing career, Sommer — another typical (i.e. no good) Rangers keeper. Truly, Wilkins had, and still has, no idea of how to manager a football team.

And yet, I still remember the sort of people who pretend to know about football (whose knowledge generally stretches no further than Manchester United's first team) telling me how great Ray was at the time... "He'll get you out of trouble, don't worry," ...Bye Ray, keep commentating on live football so I can turn the volume down, eh? Ray Wilkins, you take 33% of the blame for Rangers predicament.

3) Stewart Houston & Bruce Rioch

What a great pair of guys... likeable, full of character and if I remember correctly at the time, Houston was tipped by Alan Hansen to be a genuine find for any team who employed him. Alan, with your knowledge of football, how can us genuine fans who watch football every week possibly know more than you? You are omnipotent, and I bow down to your superior knowledge. Except I don't.

Houston & Rioch, the guys to whom the words 'out of position' mean nothing. Something like nine right backs played under them when we never had one. Steve Morrow — central defender? Matthew Rose — right back? Gavin Peacock — centre forward? One up front away to Middlesbrough — Trevor Sinclair. Kings of motivation, Sinclair and Spencer, both loved the time spent under the clowns — not! I could go on... oh, you want me to stop. OK. Stewart and Bruce, you take 15% of the blame for Rangers predicament.

4) Ray Harford

Yet another clown prince of motivation; "If we finish one place above relegation, I will be happy." ... "That's the kind of season it'll be, one step forward two steps back."... "I don't know what else I can do, I've run out of ideas." ... "Can someone wipe my arse for me." ... no, he didn't say that last one, but would it have surprised anyone if he had?

Ray, some ideas for you in retrospect — use different players? — don't play five at the back when our problem is scoring goals? — watch the reserves occasionally? — don't obviously crap yourself at anything Vinnie Jones says? Ray saved his own hide last season by bringing in Ruddock (top player) and Jones — his main mistake being not getting Vinnie purely on loan as we would appear to be stuck with an unfit, past-it workhorse now. See ya Ray, you really won't be missed.

Oh, and by the way, if you "sensed a coldness from the fans," perhaps you may now realise in hindsight that it would have been a good idea to actually win some games? Ray Harford, you take 20% of the blame for Rangers predicament.

5) Chris Wright

Hmm, what can I think of next? Unique in that he is the only person left who can actually do something to reverse the mess he has made of things. Chris Wright is the total opposite of Richard Thompson in that he gambled nearly everything on getting Rangers back into the Premiership at the first attempt. This didn't work because of the personnel who were entrusted with carrying out this task.

Chris, you still have the chance to make yourself a real Rangers hero... don't mess up this time, please? For Rangers current predicament, Chris Wright you take 10% of the blame.

The other 12% of the blame must lay squarely at the hands of the players, many of whom plainly couldn't be arsed to play at anything like their full potential — Sinclair, Spencer, Sheron, Morrow... and of course, many plainly haven't been good enough — Kulscar, Baraclough, Jones and Dowie can all stand up. However, as with Chris Wright, some of these players can do something about it.

For the sake of Queens Park Rangers, Chris Wright and Gerry Francis, please lads — play like you mean it.
(Paul Maylard-Mason – issue # 122)

JUST HOW DID WE LET THAT ONE IN?

ONE-NIL DOWN AT OXFORD, THE QPR DEFENCE DO THEIR LEVEL BEST TO MAKE SURE IT WOULD BE RAY HARFORD'S LAST GAME IN CHARGE...

HARPER, YATES AND MADDIX FAIL TO CLEAR THE BALL ADEQUATLEY, UNDER PRESSURE FROM THE OXFORD ATTACK...

READY HOOFS THE BALL 20 YARDS TO MURPHY, WHO PINGS IT BACK TOWARDS GOAL...

IT LOOKS LIKE AN EASY SAVE FOR HARPER...   ...OH NO, JUST HOW DID HE LET IT IN?

(Issue # 122)

A question of faith?

The more astute amongst you will have realised by now that we are unlikely to join the yellow brick road back to the Premiership in the near future, if ever again. This fact alone raises many questions that I would like a few answers to, some of which I have listed below. They are not all major factors in our demise, some are even light hearted, but I do believe in their own way that they are all very relevant.

Was Ray Harford's league record of 4 wins from 35 matches the worst record of any QPR manager in history? Where is Derek Buxton when you need him?

Why did Ray Harford spend the last of our available cash on an injured centre half, when most people would identify our biggest problem as a lack of goal scoring power?

Why do we keep buying injured players and who is it that examines them before we buy them? It wouldn't be Doctor Nick from the Simpsons by any chance would it? He's cheap and totally incompetent.

Why did Ray Harford only sign one player from a lower league club when Chris Wright said that was what he was brought here to do? Think about it, Baraclough is the only one who was playing for a lower division club when he signed for us.

If there were no decent forwards available for free, or at least for very small fees in the summer, how come so many other teams found them?

What will happen when QPR come up against some decent opposition this season?

Can anyone remember three so poorly supported away sides as Walsall, Bury and Tranmere Rovers? Take note — this could easily be us in a couple of years.

Has anyone else noticed the similarity between Tony Scully and Odie in the Garfield cartoons? They both run around all day with boundless energy and enthusiasm and achieve absolutely nothing.

Why does Steve Slade still look like a Biafrian immigrant and does he eat at the same restaurants as Chris Kiwomya?

Do any members of the existing scouting staff have passports? If so, when was the last time they used them to look at foreign players? I can only imagine they found Antti Heinola from an advert in a contact mag (come to think of it, I think it was John Hollins that found Heinola before Harford even arrived at the club).

Does anyone in the squad know how to take a throw in?

Why is Karl Ready playing at the back for us when he is probably the worst defender in the division?

On the same subject, who were the journalists that voted Karl Ready as the best defender outside the Premiership last season and what mental institution do they live in?

How many defenders will we have to pay in the same team before we stop giving away absolutely pathetic goals as soon as we leave Shepherds Bush?

Why do the most unskilful members of the team take most of the free kicks?

Has anyone ever seen the squad train? Do they actually practice ball skills and free kick routines, or do they, as I suspect, run around in circles desperately trying to become "The fittest team in the league," as our beloved coaching staff love to say?
(Paul Davidson – issue # 122)

Gerry the miracle worker?

So, has the tide finally turned, or will QPR's fine run of form turn out to be a false dawn? I wouldn't like to commit myself either way on this one, but three wins out of three can't stop us from hoping that better times are just round the corner.

So just what difference has Gerry Francis made so far? The players certainly look fitter than they did under Harford, and the new-found confidence the players possess has to be credited a great deal to Francis.

Harford was a great coach technically, but in his all jobs as manager he's been accused of being too soft on the players. Gerry Francis certainly can't be labelled in the same bracket. Remembering from his first time as manager, if ever QPR put in a bad performance, the players, media and fans would be made fully aware of that fact, whilst Harford would utter a few misgivings, and say something along the lines of how it would be an achievement if QPR stayed up this season. Francis won't settle for second best. He may not be able to produce a winning side for every game he's in charge, but it won't be for a lack of trying.

With Francis apparently having to make up £5million worth of debt, he's been quoted as saying that if an offer comes in for any of his players, he'd be hard pressed not to turn them down. There are a lot of players surplus to requirement at QPR, and these should be the ones first to go. The squad is simply far too big for QPR's current financial standing and has to be trimmed.
(Ed – issue # 123)

WHO'S THE BEST?

VOTE NOW FOR YOUR QPR MANAGER OF 1998

RAY HARFORD: 3 WINS IN 9 MONTHS

GERRY FRANCIS: 3 WINS IN 10 DAYS

PHONE 0891 309 310 TO REGISTER YOUR VOTE NOW!

A new beginning?

This article was to run close as one of the most depressing I've ever written in a QPR fanzine. I was, to put things mildly, pissed off. It's not just the fact that we were bottom of the league but it was the dreadful lack lustre performances that got us there. I had visions of us being relegated by Christmas, down as they say without even a fight. I personally didn't want Gerry back and merely saw his appointment as another public relations move by Wright to get the man the fans demanded and therefore keep them on his side.

Of course this article has had to be changed and for that I'm very happy. A lot of what I've begun to address in this brief forward will be touched on again in this re-edited article. I could of course have totally disregarded the previous article but it's amazing how things change in life and by including this little preamble I'm providing an example of life's little ups and downs.

At this moment I would like to say that for the first time in ages during the two wins over Barnsley and Bolton I felt that I was watching QPR again and I thoroughly enjoyed myself. If Gerry continues in this vein I'll take back everything I've ever said about him. In fact if the R's avoid relegation this season I think he should be made Lord Mayor of Shepherds Bush.

To take my first serving of humble pie here's a quote that was to be included in my original article — 'Gerry's appointment although welcomed by many, is surely the final nail in the coffin as Chris Wright's disastrous tenure brings us ever closer to oblivion. Second Division football and bankruptcy are now all we have to look forward to.' This article was to be called 'The end of QPR.' This one has a new title. Before you read it I would like to finish this opening with some food for thought — Fear can hold you prisoner. Hope can set you free.

I personally was starting to find it hard to envisage this Rangers side winning another three games all season. Before the Barnsley game I felt that if we didn't win at least one of the next three fixtures we would be down. Early days maybe to make such a dramatic statement but we were at that time six points adrift at the bottom. That gap had to at least be closed. You all know the rest. Of course I'm not getting carried away and stating that now everything's OK. It's not. We're still in trouble but the two home wins in a week were not only welcome but were achieved with no lack of style. For the first time this season we saw football played and the level of commitment was admirable. The way that Gerry has turned not only the worst but also the most disillusioned and demotivated side I've ever seen at QPR around deserves praise of the highest order. Long may it continue.

What a difference a week makes. The beating at Swindon, which followed one of the most ineffective displays seen at home for a long time against Birmingham, had me thinking that it wasn't a matter of if but when our relegation to Division Two was confirmed. I recalled a remark I overheard after the Portsmouth debacle earlier this season — "We're nearer to the Vauxhall Conference now than we are to the Premier League."

As an aside, and just to remind ourselves that the club is still in the shit, when welcoming Gerry back you have to ask yourself this question — Why didn't Chris Wright appoint him last year? The reason is of course because he never really wanted him here, hasn't got a clue and only bought Gerry home to appease the fans at this difficult time. It's exactly the reason he sacked Houston because the fans wanted it and it coincided quite nicely with the annual AGM. If the Gerry Francis revolution continues I depressingly expect to hear *"Chrissy Wright Wright Wright"* to be chanted by the moronic few once again.

Gerry has indeed introduced not only new pride and passion into the side but has actually made them look like a team. I could talk about the entire team but it's worth highlighting the individuals who perhaps haven't had the best of times but now are ensuring their first team places with their superb performances at present. A lot of it's about confidence and also about playing players in positions that they are comfortable. Take Steve Morrow. A butt of the fans frustrations last season but to anyone with half a brain it's always been clear that he is not comfortable playing in a flat back four. Against Barnsley, had it not been for Langleys superb home debut, he was man of the match for me and against Bolton he was superb. Why? Because he's playing the sweeper role — a role he is both comfortable in and in this division can excel. Also he has turned in some reasonable displays playing the holding role in midfield. This is a role he should have been allowed to make his own last season when the midfield was crying out for someone of his ilk. Instead the management went out and signed Kulscar and Jones.

Also Richard Langley has been superb. It may still be only early days but one has to ask where the hell he's been all season? Is it my imagination but did he get more tackles in against Barnsley than Vinnie has in his whole QPR 'career?' Add to that the fact that he possesses a good football brain, is composed on the ball and has good pace and it's easy to see why Ray Harford never selected him.

Although I've doubted in the past that the Sheron/Gallen strike force can ever be effective it is at present yielding goals — Kev's goal against Bolton epitomised that all important ingredient in life — confidence. You know something Gerry old mate I'm starting to feel a bit of that ingredient about you nowadays.
(Matthew Holley – issue # 123)

The kids are alright

If you were led to believe that our youth team wasn't up to producing much decent talent recently, then the emergence of Richard Langley would have surprised many. His introduction to first team football has been a highlight in recent games, scoring on his full debut against Barnsley and then laying on the first for Peacock at Crewe. Similarities between him and Nigel Quashie have already been drawn, but one thing's for sure, in his few appearances to date, Langley has shown more skill, awareness and intelligence than Tony Scully has in the entire season. Langley looks a genuine prospect, and if his attitude is only 50% better than Quashie's, he could go a lot further than our ex-player.
(Ed – issue # 123)

Can Gerry reproduce the goods?

During a ten-day break in Toulouse recently I had managed to avoid discovering how Rangers had been doing in my absence until a day or so before I was due to return home. Then somebody asked me if I wanted some bad news. As I knew she knew I was a QPR supporter, I had a pretty good idea what the news was. Of course, I had to know the full details, however unpleasant, and she confirmed my worst fears when she told me that Rangers had lost to both Birmingham and Swindon.

I was surprised and upset by the news, especially as I had literally dreamt of a Rangers victory a few nights before. However, despite the initial depressing effect of this unwelcome knowledge on my spirits, I didn't allow it to ruin the rest of my holiday and I returned to London refreshed and ready to face the rigours of a British winter.

However, I was not so sure that I could face the rigours of regular visits to Loftus Road over the ensuing months. I arrived home on Monday 2nd November but it was not until the Wednesday that I finally decided I would go to the Barnsley game that night. The weather was reasonably clement and in a straight contest between a night spent watching QPR or the television, QPR just shaded it.

As it turned out I made the right choice and Rangers beat the Yorkshireman, although they came close to throwing it away. Had Barnsley scored just before the interval, as they so nearly did, then I think the result may well have been different. But Rangers held on and deserved the victory. There have been other victories this season — not many, but some — and they have proved to be false dawns. The real test would be if Rangers could string two wins together — then we might have some real justification for optimism. Well, if the Barnsley game was a refreshing change then the Bolton game was like the world turned upside down. The atmosphere was buoyant, Kevin Gallen scored a wonder goal right in front of the East Paddock where I was sitting, and the team played the best game I'd seen all season.

Suddenly being a QPR supporter did not seem such a trial of loyalty versus common sense. To complete the change from night into day Rangers won a third game, and this one away from home. Alright, so it was against Crewe, the side who had kindly taken over the arduous job of holding up the rest of the division, but a win is a win.

Of course, Rangers are not out of the woods yet, but they are climbing the table, and if they carry on as they have done in recent weeks, then fears of relegation will rapidly subside.

There is no doubt that the reason for this turnaround has been the appointment of Gerry Francis as Director of Football (or manager, to the traditionalists amongst you). I have to confess that he was not my first choice for the job. I would have liked to see Nigel Spackman in the post — a man just starting out on his managerial career who has performed well at Sheffield United, who is keen to make his mark, but who also, like Francis, has a past with the club.

However, it was clear that Chris Wright had his heart set on our old manager and so far things are looking good. One can see why Wright wanted him. He is one of the great QPR heroes, a man who has brought success to the club both as a player and a manager. It has been easy for the fans to get behind Francis and he has brought a new confidence and organisation to the side. The question of the wisdom of returning to a club where you have had success in the past will only be answered in time.

Others have discussed the ups and downs of his previous stint as manager. For me, overall it was a positive time, although I do have reservations. On the plus side, he instilled a belief and discipline in the side that saw it compete with, and beat, the best teams in the league. There were those marvelous victories over Leeds United at Loftus Road and Manchester United at Old Trafford (surely this will always rank as Rangers greatest league win). On such occasions the team provided high quality entertainment. Under Francis the team also showed a resilience that saw it bounce back from adversity time and time again. And finishing fifth in the league was a substantial achievement.

For me, however, the highlight of those years was the emergence of Leslie Ferdinand as one of the country's most formidable strikers, and Ferdinand himself has testified to the importance Francis played in his rise to the top. We all remember how for so long before his arrival Ferdinand was unable to realise his undoubted potential.

On the down side, I was not too pleased at the way Don Howe was unceremoniously kicked out to make way for Francis. That, of course was none of Francis' doing. More pertinently, although the team did at times provide great entertainment, they too often lacked the sparkle of previous Rangers teams. He brought much needed stability to Spurs after the audacious excesses of the Ardilles era. But in the end he did not manage to take the club a stage further. He could not produce a team to live up to the Spurs fans' ideal of success with style.

So, in welcoming Francis back home and while thanking him for all he has achieved already, I would implore him to remember that Rangers fans desire some flamboyance in their teams and that the game is not all about hard graft and "consistency." As he should know, we like to see a certain impish brilliance, especially from the player in the number 10 shirt (no offence to Kevin Gallen).

Francis has revitalised the club and given us all a boost. I hope he brings some much needed stability and that he can maintain his enthusiasm for the difficult job he has taken on. But I also hope he can provide us with the level of entertainment that he produced, together with the likes of Stanley Bowles and Dave Thomas, in his playing days. A tall order perhaps, but something worth aiming for.
(Peter Tajasque – issue # 123)

A happy new year?

Reports of QPR being £6million in debt — a million over the agreed overdraft figure — is not the sort of news we want to hear, especially coming at a time when the players are finally getting their act together on the pitch.

Selling players to raise capital and thus breaking up the team at the present moment could undo everything Gerry Francis has achieved since his return to the club. Whereas once we wouldn't give two hoots if the likes of Sheron, Gallen and Morrow were sold, these players, amongst several others, have finally found their form and have to stay if Chris Wright has an ambitious future planned for QPR.

Wright gambled all his eggs in one basket when he gave Stewart Houston a virtual endless supply of money to get QPR back in the Premiership at the first attempt. It didn't work, and now we are suffering for it, despite the fact the club is level on transfer fees in and out since Wright's arrival. If Wright cannot see that Francis has at last found the right formula in getting the club heading in the right direction at the very least, then his credentials as an astute businessman go right out the window. With a personal wealth exceeding £50million, would it really be too much to ask of him to bail us out?

QPR fans were critical of Richard Thompson for not dipping into his own pocket, but under him we were never in the red. Thompson run QPR on a tight budget, but a realistic one at that. Wright has displayed extreme naivety in his running of the club since becoming chairman, and the current financial situation is of far greater importance than at any time under Thompson. The whole future of QPR could be at stake if the financial crisis isn't sorted out soon. If the debt is reduced at the detriment of the team, the end result could be far worse than it is presently.

With Gerry Francis also occupying the position of Director of Football, he will be well aware of exactly what is required to pull QPR out of this mess. He should have a far greater say in which, if any, players are to be sold, so there should be no repeat of recent events involving Everton and West Ham where players have been sold without the knowledge of their respective managers. So at least if a player or players do depart, it would be done so with the permission of Francis, who should have immediate plans and ideas to compensate for the loss, i.e. is Steiner being groomed to replace either Sheron or Gallen? If it is the case, it is a smart move by Francis, thinking one step ahead of the game.

In a nutshell, our advice to Chris Wright would be; don't be too hasty in selling our assets, and try to raise funds from another source. If present form and results continue through to the end of the season, the play-offs and promotion could be a realistic consequence. QPR's debts would be wiped out through season ticket sales alone...
(Ed – issue # 124)

Moreno Bares All

So how smug was I after the home win against Barnsley? After extolling the footballing skill and virtues of Richard Langley to just about anyone who was within earshot of the Loftus Road members stand for about the last year, I felt pleased as punch when he scored on his full home debut inside 10 minutes. I had in fact asked Nick Blackburn, the vice-chairman, as to why Ray Harford would repeatedly overlook the extremely promising youngster. Even Blackburn was completely perplexed and agreed with me totally that Langley was good enough to be in the team no matter what his age. It was very shortly after that conversation that Ray Harford left and Gerry Francis came back home — I'd like to think I was instrumental in hurrying Harford's departure!

~ ~ ~

What do you think has been the deciding factor in the R's resurgence of late? Gerry Francis coming back in charge of the team? Kevin Gallen and Mike Sheron finally on the same wavelength and clicking together? New fitness regime? Danny Maddix playing out of his skin, probably at his best ever? Peacock, Langley, Rose and Morrow finding their form? All good points but I think it's the loan signing of Ludek Miklosko. It's a tremendously long time since I actually felt comfortable with any of our keepers — we probably in all truth haven't had a half-decent 'keeper since David Seaman. A couple of friends who are Ipswich Town fans think we have an outside chance of making it to the play-offs and believe that a major part in us achieving that will be down to Miklosko. Ludo has the experience of getting promotion to the Premiership, after all he did just that for West Ham in 1992-93. My message to Gerry... sign him up — permanently.

~ ~ ~

Surely there must be a club out there somewhere where Vinnie Jones can bugger off and go to? The press has linked him with several clubs, Burnley and Wimbledon among them, but as time goes on the chances of him joining another club for cash seem remote. What galls me though is that we are still paying him a wage even though he hasn't played or coached at QPR since Gerry came back. Vinnie's been keeping himself busy in the meantime, not with football but promotional book tours, doing PR work for the Wrestling Foundation, and even help launching ITV2. Please Santa, please come in and take him off our hands.

~ ~ ~

I'm getting quite used to the PA announcer at Loftus Road, although he was an annoying sod when we were losing but now phrases like, "Let's hear if for Queeeens Parrrrk Rannnngggerrrrs," don't sound so hollow and pathetic. Even after the Ipswich game he commented, "We wuz robbed." One of the funniest things I've heard was at the Port Vale match. After battling back to lead 2-1 the R's faithful came out with "Can you hear the Port Vale sing." I couldn't tell if they were singing or not as the Vale contingent numbered just over 300!

~ ~ ~

Four Four Two magazine are running a series where footballers choose a fantasy team made up of players they have played with during their career. Les Ferdinand was first up and his choices were interesting. Five QPR players made it in his team, which were Ray Wilkins, David Seaman, Clive Wilson, Danny Maddix and Les himself. No Spurs players were included, unless you count Wilson and I don't as he's been a Spurs reserve player for the majority of his White Hart Lane career.

(Moreno Ferrari – issue # 124)

147

QPR 3-2 Port Vale

Over the past ten years of selling In The Loft on the South Africa Road, I have been offered many things in exchange for a copy of the latest issue, apart from the cover price itself. Mainly from away fans, I have been offered a can of lager, a packet of fags, even the matchday programme itself. Nothing though compares to the offer of a ticket for the Sponsor Lounge executive box for a copy of the last issue, by a Vale fan slightly worse for wear. Result! Being just about acceptable to pass the strict dress code in appliance, I escaped from the cold and made my way to the half-empty executive box over looking the centre of the pitch, just as the game kicked off.

I expected my entrance to be akin to gate crashing a party, but I escaped a potentially tricky situation as I hardly got a second look from the suited and booted employees of West London Construction Network. Perhaps the occupiers were too engrossed in the game to notice me, but whatever the case I didn't bother them and they didn't bother me. Thinking "I've got away with this one," I quickly acquired a pint of lager and took my seat in the front row.

Somehow we went in at the break one-nil down thanks to Martin Foyle's precise header on 31 minutes. I was consoled with another pint and a plate of food from the buffet, which was surprisingly foul. A slice of chocolate gateau soon took the taste away as I glanced through the programme — looking and reading much better compared to the start of the season, even if the statistics page is completely erratic. The line-ups and appearance chart at the back simply don't correlate to each other — will Kevin Gallen ever get credited with two goals against Stockport, and does anyone else remember Chris Plummer making a couple of appearances as substitute?

We changed from 3-5-2 to 4-3-3 — a move which reaped benefits in the second half as we run out 3-2 winners. First man of the match Maddix, then a bizarre own goal from Talbot quickly put QPR ahead. A couple of efforts from Gallen and an overhead kick by Steiner threatened a rout as we looked capable of scoring through every attack, but we always looked vulnerable on the counter attack by Vale who duly equalised in the 78th minute through, of all players, Simon Barker. It was a vital goal for Vale, and a particularly poignant moment for Barker, but he kept his dignity and didn't milk the celebrations, unlike Bradley Allen a couple of years ago when he scored the winner for Charlton Athletic.

Having been dealt a second cruel blow in four days, it appeared we'd have to settle for a solitary point once again. Credit to the players though, they didn't give up the cause but it took a moment of magic from Mike Sheron to finally secure all the points. Cutting inside his man just inside the box, he struck home an excellent left-footed shot from eighteen yards with just two minutes left on the clock.

As for the executive box, well it was a nice experience and certainly stopped my nads from freezing up, but you can't really beat being up in the stands amongst like-minded supporters. That's not to say if the same offer came up in a future game, I wouldn't think twice about accepting...
(Ed – issue # 124)

QPR in crisis?

So now it is now five wins out of seven. Incredible! With a bit more luck against Sheffield United and no injury time against Ipswich it could well have been seven. However I think it's safe to assume that most R's fans would have settled for 16 points out of 21 on the eve of the Barnsley match. Gerry is indeed performing miracles. How would the club be faring now if he had been brought in last year when Houston was sacked? It certainly makes you wonder. Would we now be pushing for promotion? Would we have got better prices for Sinclair, Spencer and Quashie? Would we have been involved in a relegation battle at the end of last season?

All questions and the truth is that a lot of things could have happened but to dwell on them here amounts too little but hypothetical speculation. Just why Chris Wright, however, thought that appointing Harford and at the same time pay West Brom considerable compensation for his services was a better option than appointing Gerry, only he can answer.

What we have now is a revival that several months ago would have been unimaginable to even the most optimistic supporter. The victory over Port Vale was a hard fought game, but in fairness it should have been all over at half time, so superior were the R's.

Considering a victory was achieved with Peacock and Langley absent — far and away two of our most influential players recently — speaks volumes for Gerry's managerial ability. Add to that Morrow's early departure and just like against Ipswich we found ourselves with a weakened side that nevertheless battled hard and gave 100% for the cause. What a difference to the gutless capitulations at places like Portsmouth and Oxford to name but two.

Going back to the Port Vale game — was there anyone in the stadium who didn't expect Simon Barker to score? Also I

(Issue # 124)

149

thought that he received an excellent reception from the R's fans on the day but according to the Sunday People he was jeered throughout. Wouldn't it be nice if those idiot reporters who work for the gutter press would consider attending a game once in a while instead of merely inventing reports?

The victory over Port Vale, which dragged us away from the relegation zone, was soured on the Sunday with confirmation that Gerry will have to sell two players before the new year to keep the club afloat. Gallen, Sheron and Murray were three players mentioned. To lose Gallen or Sheron now will be a blow as we ease ourselves out of the relegation mire. Regular readers will know that I've doubted that this can be a fully effective strike force but now both are playing superb and look like men reborn. It's unlikely that we'll get our money back on Sheron though. He has his critics and will probably never justify the price that was paid for him but currently he's playing well and will be a loss. If the club have got to sell him I say wait until the end of the season because I've got a feeling that we may be able to get a better price for him then. Murray however would be no loss but the clubs' debt amounts to millions and the 'two bob' we are likely to receive for him will not alleviate the serious financial state the club finds itself in.

The current revival although fully welcome is currently covering up the serious issues and the worrying predicament the club finds itself in. The debts and discontent in certain quarters don't bode well for the future and when the team hit another bad patch, especially if this is triggered by the impending sale of key players, then the aforementioned discontent could be rife.

Vinnie Jones got plenty of publicity in the tabloids on Sunday. "Shut yer Gobs," was his message to Rangers fans in the Sunday People. I believe that he is planning a new book soon — 'How to win friends and influence people' to follow on from his latest effort. My opinion of Jones as a footballer and a member of the human race are not particularly high.

However, the reputation that Jones has 'earned' throughout his turbulent career as being a dirty bastard, equally applies to the likes of Robson, Gascoigne and Steve McMahon to name but a few. What concerns me in this particularly regrettable episode is that the Rangers fans are currently turning on him and they are of course justified in this. On the other hand though he is distracting the fans wrath from the individual who should be the main source of their frustrations... yes, the chairman. The club accepted Jones' high salary, bonuses and he was promised an assistant managers role and a chance to become manager if Harford left. Whatever you think of Jones, and I for one hated the thought of him ever managing the club, the promises made to him have been broken. Of course the issue goes much deeper than that. He's currently collecting four grand a week without breaking sweat and has cost this club a huge sum of money. He then attacks the fans, a lot of who struggle to collect his month's wages in a year. But you have to look higher to find the real problem at this club.

A similar situation involving yet another old carthorse was Mark Hateley. Another target of the fans abuse, but if you was a 35-year-old footballer well past your best and some idiot offered you a new start and a large pay packet to boot would you turn it down... I don't think most would. The fans of course took it out on him and not the manager who signed him.

The Jones situation epitomises the inept way that this club has been run by Wright. If Thompson had sold the players Wright has he would have been accused of asset stripping. Also when Thompson left the club, although he could be seen as a rat deserting a sinking ship, the club were solvent — something that they were for most of his reign.

I shared fans' frustrations during the Thompson era. With a little bit more investment we maybe could have aspired too much greater things. But then again maybe not. Once again I'm back to the hypothetical stage. We never will know. Saying this I never joined in the chants for Thompson's resignation or partook in any of the demonstrations. My argument was that if Thompson leaves, who comes in? None of the various campaigns against our ex-chairman ever, in my eyes, had any thought, direction or substance to them. The fans got Thompson out and now look at the shit we're in.
(Matthew Holley – issue # 124)

Early exit not like it used to be

Going out of the FA Cup at an early stage many years back (i.e. before 1995) would usually, at least for those with a bleak outlook on life, leave us with 'nothing to play for.' This however is certainly not the case this season, likewise the last campaign. Apart from the obvious goal in avoiding relegation, of which giant strides have already been made, it's time QPR finally found a period of stability. Since relegation in 1996, QPR have hardly had the opportunity to lay down roots in this division and really suss it out, such has been the quick turnover in managerial and playing staff. Hopefully, that time has now come. Each match in this division for QPR is still very much a learning experience.

The huge debts reported at QPR prior to Christmas brought with them chilling headlines regarding the sale of our biggest assets to help reduce the cashflow. The recent AGM proved to be inconclusive as to where we really do stand.

Reports earlier in the season suggested Aston Villa were about to make a £4million move for Murray—have they ever seen him play? Murray was superb in his first full season with the club, but since then his form has dropped dramatically to such an extent, he's probably been our most ineffective player this season. In turn, the form of Matthew Rose in midfield has been most encouraging. Very comfortable on the ball and with a certain air of superiority about him, Rose also possesses the most effective yet simple skill known in the history of professional football — the ability to pass the ball on the ground. Be it five yards or thirty, the ball always skims nicely along the surface, making it easier for the receiving player to control and go forward. Murray and Peacock — please take note.

It's great news to see Ludek Miklosko finally signing on permanently with QPR, even if the tight-fisted Hammers forced QPR (and Ludo himself) to pay a fee. The future of Rob Steiner though appears unclear. His three-month loan period is up at the end of this month, and it's hard to see where the funds will come from to finance his £300,000 fee. Judging by the performance of Iain Dowie in the second half against Huddersfield, perhaps we don't necessarily need to splash out on a 'big man' up front. OK, so it was an easy game for Dowie to play — stand on the edge of the penalty box for 45 minutes and win a few knock downs, forget all this running about lark. With Slade and Kiwomya also in the ranks, can QPR really afford to have six strikers on their books? *(Ed – issue # 125)*

From the horse's mouth

I found myself in a small gathering around Chris Wright after the AGM in December. During the discussion he mentioned that Alan Curbishley had agreed to join QPR after Houston's departure, but Charlton decided not to let him go. He said that Ray Harford was the worst manager ever at QPR. I confirmed this by telling him that 'In The Loft' had produced a table of recent QPR managers

(Issue # 125)

showing that Ray Harford was the least successful by some distance, and I also pointed out that Stewart Houston was the second most successful behind Terry Venables. This brought a look of surprise to his face.

(Richard Aitkins – issue # 125)

Words of wisdom from the pen of Matthew Holley

My previous article 'QPR in Crisis' coincided with the home defeat at the hands of that 'footballing force' Crewe Alexandra, which, in turn, gave us a sharp, and some may say bleak, reminder of the dark days before Gerry (bloody prophet of doom I hear you cry). Still a cracking performance at Palace deserved more and a comfortable if not entertaining win over Norwich pulled us ever clearer from the dreaded drop zone. However following defeat at Barnsley the club now sit in a kind of dodgy state of limbo.

With games coming up against fellow strugglers Bury, Portsmouth and Bristol City, not to mention the small task of Sunderland preceding them, we are a couple of wins from comfortable mid-table mediocrity or a couple of defeats from drifting into danger once again. Hopefully the players will respond and successfully steer and navigate (can't believe I'm about to say this) the good ship QPR safely through the dangerous treacherous waters that lie ahead.

This Christmas has certainly given a few R's fans a certain sense of Deja vu. Going back two years — Norwich at home on Boxing Day — home win, and once again Huddersfield at home in the third round of the FA Cup. Also just like last time the events coincided with a dramatic uplift in form and fortune. In both games against Norwich Peacock did indeed score superb goals but there the similarity ends. Steiner and Gallen combined superbly to set up Gavin to cut inside his marker and blast the ball cleanly past the Norwich keeper. As someone said after the game — what a shame that such a crap game had to be ruined by such a superb goal.

The previous cup-tie against Huddersfield is the last home match that I've missed. Sadly on this occasion I was in attendance. The previous tie saw Mark Hateley score a last minute equaliser. How surreal it would have been had our current 'big man up front' — Iain Dowie — connected properly with that cross in the dying minutes. What with that ominous, almost alien sky, which was accompanied by the apocalyptic storm which held the match up at half time, such a surreal event would have been most apt.

Indeed at times one was left wondering whether we weren't at Loftus Road but instead had, by some weird extraterrestrial occurrence, been momentarily shipped to a scene from Flash Gordon. After all, the PA did rather helpfully state before the action got underway that, "This is Loftus Road." Maybe he isn't such a gormless twonk after all.

Sadly there was probably a greater chance of an alien invasion than the R's getting that elusive equaliser in the second half.

To be fair the R's should have scored and created enough chances to do so but it was all so frantic with a lot of emphasis on pumping the ball high onto Dowie's head. The problem is that the midfield minus Richard Langley loses its balance as we miss his creativity and guile. It comes to something when a 18-year-old straight in from the youth team does things with the ball that seasoned professionals find difficult a lot of the time — naming no names of course.

Things will have to improve if the season is not to end in tears. I think a lot of us foolishly began looking at the top 6 during the recent improvement. Indeed had the season started in November I think we would have been top. At the time of writing we sit 12 points behind Huddersfield in sixth spot. More importantly we are 5 points clear from the bottom three — remarkable considering where we were at the start of November. But relegation still is the more likely of the two options and I'm sure and hope that Gerry knows this.

(Matthew Holley – issue # 125)

He's done a Jensen on us!

Anyone that's been a regular visitor to Loftus Road over the years will probably have seen or heard of at one time or another, a certain Mr John Salt (pictured) — more affectionately known as 'Catweasel'. Never short of a word or two, John, who was voted Mr Rangers 1993, used to be a familiar face at Loftus Road for many years until he suddenly disappeared a

 couple of years ago, seemingly vanishing from the face of the earth. His undeniable support for QPR was never in question, always turning up wearing a QPR shirt and scarf, to match his equally two-coloured trousers. His disappearance was certainly something of a mystery. And then, whilst selling the last issue at Crystal Palace, who should walk by clad head to toe in Palace gear? You've guessed it, Catweasel himself. He's done a Jensen on us!

(Issue # 125)

154

Reality check

Defeat at Tranmere now makes it nearly two months without a win, and once again fans are getting restless. Scoring goals is proving to be a problem — expect Rob Steiner to come back on loan very soon, but at least Gerry Francis has made us hard to beat, with the defence tightening up considerably — we haven't lost by more than a solitary goal for nearly four months.

We're still perilously close to the relegation zone, but I hope there will not be the same frenetic finish to the season like last. Games since Christmas have been a mirror image of many before Gerry came back, and we saw enough of them to last for many a season.

The free-signing of Tim Breaker should hopefully prove to be a useful acquisition by Gerry Francis. With the jury still out on Antti Heinola's abilities, coupled with his current injury, Breaker has the opportunity to make the right-back position his own — he certainly impressed during his loan period back in October, albeit appearing in just two matches, but he looked a great deal less affective on his second debut at Tranmere. Breaker's signing though really shouldn't have been necessary in the first place — personally, I've never forgiven Ray Harford for letting David Bardsley go, when he still had so much to offer.

On the subject of Ray Harford, upon his recent appointment as First Team coach at Derby (it's a bit further to travel than West Brom, eh Ray?), Derby midfielder Lee Carsley was quoted as saying, "He's got the respect of everyone in football." Quite a few thousand QPR fans would, I'm sure, disagree with you there Lee.

In the meantime, stay out of the black and keep in the red — you get nothing in this game from Kevin Gallen's head.

(Ed – issue # 126)

Words of wisdom from the pen of Matthew Holley

For starters here's a quick couple of questions for all the trainspotters out there.

1) QPR as we all sadly know have not hit the target at the Loft end very much this season. Exactly how many times have they achieved this feat (including cup games) so far this season and who is currently the top scorer at the Loft end up to and including Portsmouth at home?

2) The R's as we sadly know are yet to win a match in 1999. Who though up to and including Tranmere away currently is the top goal scorer in 1999? (Answers at the end).

Only a short one this issue but due to recent lack of inspiration on the pitch and a nightmarish weekend up north following the Tranmere match the brain ain't exactly working at its normal up-tempo rate. But I digress, following a comfortable win against Norwich on Boxing Day mid-table mediocrity beckoned. Following a bad defeat at Tranmere we're suddenly once again checking the fortunes of the bottom three clubs and looking forward (sic) to when we have to travel to Port Vale on May 1.

The Tranmere match had "we're in trouble here," written all over it with the R's leading twice and throwing it down the drain against a team whose home form has hardly been inspiring of late. It's a good job really that we've still got easy away games to come against the likes of Birmingham, Bolton and Ipswich or else we really would be up shits creak... altogether now, "If you're all going to Bournemouth clap yer hands."

Far too many points have been thrown away of late. Take the Sunderland game. How many would have quite happily settled for a point before the game but felt choked afterwards (ditto Ipswich)? Forget the fact that Sunderland were the better side and still were when down to ten men. It was STILL a game that should have been won and may well have been if Francis had made at least one substitution. The midfield were being run ragged, our strikers were out on their feet and we were crying out for changes if only to break up the pattern of play. You all know the rest and wasn't it just bloody obvious who was going to get the equaliser. Add to that yet another lead blown against Pompey and not even a glimmer of ambition to even get one at Bristol and you can see why May 1st could be a very important date for your diaries (gulp).

One glimmer of sunshine (I won't say Ray and I think you know why). Although there is no money to spend on new players despite selling due to economic necessity the team that lost at Tranmere was missing one or two faces — notably Langley and Rose. Notice how I didn't say asset stripping because for some strange reason that phrase doesn't seem to apply to the current board.

A measure of Langley's impact on the side is that in his five full appearances in the team in November, he helped inspire four victories and he has been badly missed in the centre of the park. Rose has surely got to be the surprise package of the season and I feel that when fit he could be the ideal foil for Langley in the centre midfield. Hopefully we won't have to wait long because I fear the current side has got to be broken up if a repeat of last season's relegation battle is to be avoided. Note when I say repeat that's fine if like last season we do avoid the drop but this time we won't have 'The most Important man of the Millennium' around to help us out.

Answer to earlier questions. 1) 6 times. Top scorer at Loft end — Maddix, 3 goals. 2) Top scorer in 1999 for QPR — Maddix, 2 goals

(Matthew Holley – issue # 126)

£170,000 a goal – a costly mistake?

He cost a club record £2,750,000. He earned £8,000 a week. His name was Mike Sheron. Having been at QPR for a little over 18 months — roughly 80 weeks — his 20 goals for the club cost QPR £170,000 a piece. It's little wonder why we're in the financial state we currently find ourselves in. But was Mike Sheron a costly mistake or a player that contributed well to the side? The debate continues.

Personally, I grew to like Sheron as a player, but I had my doubts when we signed him that he wasn't the type of striker we required, and this proved to be his greatest downfall. Of course, this wasn't Sheron's fault, but the man who bought him — Stewart Houston. Houston had been chasing Sheron for months, and I continually had to ask myself why.

With John Spencer, Kevin Gallen and Steve Slade giving little aerial threat, Sheron's arrival didn't exactly give QPR any greater options. Having lost Daniele Dichio and Mark Hateley, there was no one to turn to, to provide height in attack — a problem that had to be rectified by Ray Harford with the signing of the ageing Iain Dowie.

However, pre-season 97/98 and the thought of seeing Sheron, Spencer and Gallen in a three-pronged attack certainly seemed a mouth-watering experience, with Peacock and Sinclair providing ample service. When reality saw through though, we were to be greatly disappointed.

With Gallen struggling for form and fitness, Spencer looking half the player he was from the season before, and Sheron starting the season off injured, Houston's dream three-pronged attack just never got off the ground. Indeed, all three players were to never start together in the same side.

By the time Sheron made his debut at Reading, it was obvious to all that Houston had bought the wrong type of striker. Somehow we managed a 2-1 win at Reading, with Spencer getting off the mark for the season and a Sheron-assisted own goal giving QPR victory. Three games later we were joint top, but not any more convincing. The partnership of Sheron and Spencer just didn't spark, and it never looked like doing so.

By now most QPR fans had formed their own opinions of Sheron. He was skilful but not overly so, possessed average pace, but he just didn't look a natural goalscorer. Worst of all, too often he was virtually anonymous. In short, he simply wasn't worth the money Houston had paid for him. Dropped for the first time against Stoke following 5 goals in 25 rather inauspicious appearances, not only was Sheron struggling but the team was as well. Many pointed the finger at Sheron, but he was one of many contributing factors.

Records show that Sheron never really was the prolific striker we hoped he would be. As a promising youngster at Man City, his best goal return in a season was 11 goals from 33 starts in 1991/92. Overall he hit 24 goals from 84 starts in the top flight for Man City, before Norwich splashed out £1million to take him to Carrow Road in July 1994. Sheron had a miserable time at Norwich, managing just a solitary goal in his first season — ironically, the goal was to come against his future employers, QPR, in a 4-2 win.

Things weren't to get any better at Norwich, and Stoke took him back to the north west in November 1995 for a cut-price £200,000, where his 34 goals in 64 appearances made him a hero. Quite why Sheron was such a success at Stoke remains a mystery. Perhaps they played to his strengths, although it's hard to define exactly what they are.

Back at QPR, and Sheron continued to be in and out of the team until he finally hit some degree of form, and finished last season with 6 goals in his last 12 games, including two precious goals at Sunderland and another at Man City. Without them, QPR would currently be plying their trade in Division 2. His partnership with the fit-again Kevin Gallen was showing signs of promise, but it wouldn't exactly be fair to say Sheron's goals kept us up as he contributed to our plight as much as anyone else in the first place, but the goals certainty earned him some breathing space, with hopes for a better second season with QPR.

Back alongside Kevin Gallen, Sheron failed to build on where he left off last season, and the pair between them missed enough sitters to drive fans to despair at the start of the season. Sheron proved to be the scapegoat and again found himself dropped, coming in the final days of Ray Harford's managerial reign. Under Iain Dowie, Sheron returned to the side against Wolves with two opportunist strikes in the opening minutes to provide a first away win for over a year, but it wasn't until Gerry Francis took over that Sheron started to look comfortable in a QPR shirt.

November turned out to be a fantastic month for the team and Sheron, who's partnership with Gallen yielded 6 goals, helping QPR to four wins out of five and the Manager of the Month award for Gerry Francis. For the first time in eighteen months, QPR resembled a football side, and were finally getting good value from Sheron.

A fine match-winning goal against Port Vale continued Sheron's rise up the goalscoring charts as he looked set to notch up twenty odd goals, but it proved to be his last telling contribution in a QPR shirt. An injury after barely ten seconds of the game against Norwich on Boxing Day was the last we were to see of Sheron.

With the financial problems effectively meaning every player had his price, Barnsley's offer of a reported £1.5million proved too good to turn down by Chris Wright, but still meant a £1.25million loss on the player. I believe Sheron would still be a QPR player had he not picked up that injury against Norwich, and I feel his best days for QPR were yet to come. Sheron has said himself he didn't want to leave, but ultimately he proved too expensive to keep — especially when sitting on the treatment table.

There are a lot of QPR fans who were sad to see him go, but probably just as many pleased to get the money received for him. Me? I'm somewhere in between.
(Ed – issue # 126)

Too good to go down?

From a position of relative safety at the start of the year, just one win since Boxing Day means the run in to the end of the season is going to be just as frantic as last season, if not more so.

Despite going to the wire, we didn't actually spend any time in the bottom three last season. Having spent two months there earlier this season, it's a position we can hold quite comfortably — all of a sudden the words 'QPR' and 'relegation' do seem to go with each other.

Just a couple of points separate us from the bottom three. Too good to go down? Not us. Was the month of November really a false dawn? Apparently so.

Yet still we're no pushovers. We're only a clinical striker away from being much higher up the league, and we've yet to be thrashed under Gerry Francis. The players are far fitter and better organised now than they were under Harford, but the results just aren't coming. The longer this goes on, the longer it will be before the confidence comes back, and our drop into Division 2 will come that much quicker. 10 games left lads — don't let us down.

As suggested in issue 124, Chris Wright has finally dipped his hand in his pocket, ploughing in up to £4million as part of the much mooted new share issue. After failing to win planning permission to build housing on the newly acquired Wasps training ground, Wright has been forced to bail the club out during these critical times.

With shares on offer at 20% of their original offer price, shareholders willing to add a few more to their existing number won't exactly need to break the bank, but it really would be an act of faith. If relegation becomes a reality, the value of a share will plummet to just pennies.

The new share offer coupled with the sale of Mike Sheron ensures QPR stay in business for the short term at least, but long term it's a bleak picture. It could be years before the current financial situation is rectified, and god only knows which division we'll be in by then. Strangely, Chris Wright still goes on about moving QPR to a brand new all-seater stadium, when his long term plans should be much closer to home.

(Ed – issue # 126)

Goodbye and good riddance

Vinnie Jones has finally parted company with QPR and football, but not without further cost to the club. QPR have agreed to pay Vinne his wages up until the end of the season — a figure in the region of £100,000, when his contract will then be terminated. It will bring to an end an ugly chapter in the clubs' history, and a huge financial outlay to go with it. A year ago Vinnie was seen as our saviour, just the kind of player required to get us out of relegation trouble. To an extent, his contribution proved significant — but who have we got to turn to now, as we find ourselves in a similar situation?

(Ed – issue # 127)

Any now, my day has come...

'Food For Thought'

To name a couple who instantly spring to mind; David Platt, David Beckham. These players at certain times in their careers have been referred to as 'free scoring midfielders.' Does that make then our very own Georgie Kulcsar a 'No scoring midfielder?'

Defeat against Bolton now means it's just the one win this year. Still, with the easy fixtures left remaining, our superb pacey strike force, free scoring midfield, watertight defence and our managers' superb tactical genius we're far too good to go down surely.

Disturbing things to report in the upper Loft as well. It first came to my attention during the Portsmouth game that where I sit, nutters surround me. It's fair to say that people who know me well, often doubt my sanity, but I'm talking the nutter at football who stands out in the crowd head and shoulders above the rest. In fact closer inspection showed that not only am I surrounded but also they appear to form a weird mystical 'Magic Circle' with me at the core. A true life X-File if ever there was one — Scully get your ass out the reserves you're needed in the upper Loft. I'm kind of worried that one Saturday the men in white coats are going to come down the Rangers and they won't have enough vans to take us all away.

Anyway, 'and now the end is near,' ... My dad first brought me to Rangers when I was but a toddler. I've grown a bit since then physically but not much mentally. In those days we had Bowles, Francis (and he was a damn sight more inventive player than he'll ever be a manager) and Givens etc. I made sporadic, often regular appearances down the Bush and didn't come once in the season of Mullery's reign. I've now been a season ticket holder for over 12 years. I've seen some good and bad times, good players and bad. Football though just isn't the same anymore. Sky TV, Premier league, overpaid players, all-seater stadium — the death of the game as we once knew it before it became all trendy.

The seasons standing on the Loft — never better times at football have I ever had.

'Don't push me 'cos I'm close to the edge'
I also remember when we came close to losing our club when I was only about 15. The fans protested and ultimately won the day.

'It's like a jungle sometimes, it makes me wonder how I keep from going under'
And now our club is once again faced with a very unsure future. I consider the current owner and board the biggest threat that this club has ever had to face. However the protests against them are almost to the point of non-existence. One of the reasons that I started writing for this rag was because I believed in the importance of an independent voice for the fans. This followed the aforementioned merger back in 1987 and the fanzines and the independent supporters clubs were a sign of unity.

'I've said it before time after time... woooahh'
I never joined in the considerable protests against the Thompsons. I shared fans frustrations at the lack of investment and ambition but the club was run as a business. Even when we had a decent side we weren't packing the stadium each week and Thompson was aware of the consequences of an inflated wage structure. Defenders of Chris Wright state that he's run this club with the best of intentions but then the same could be said of Richard Thompson who tried to run the club so that it could finance itself and this he achieved. Don't talk to me about asset stripping either. Since the outset of Chris Wright's disastrous tenure more money has been gained through sales than has been invested. Also don't forget who fronts the bill for the majority of Wright's appalling financial decisions — the shareholders.

'And as everything fell apart nobody paid much attention'
The farce with Vinnie Jones is typical of the Mickey Mouse way this club is being run. I believe we, as fans, deserve an explanation from Mr Wright as to how such an unskilled moron like Jones was allowed to cost this club so much. The Thompsons were criticised as being able to read a balance sheet upside down but know nothing about football. Ditto this current owner although unfortunately his financial decisions have matched his football ones. One has only to look at his terrible three choices of managers. Not only that but his worst choice, Ray Harford, was appointed at once again great expense to this club with the compensation that had to be paid to WBA. I

include Gerry as well who was only appointed by Wright because of fan pressure. I don't believe Mr Wright really wanted Gerry back here and his re-appointment is typical of the style of manipulative public relations that he has exercised since taking over.

'Hear the drummer get wicked'

I still warm up to Public Enemy on a Saturday match day morning. I like wicked clothes as well, just like my man Lennox — FCUK FEAR — love it. Must get the T-shirt. How about one for QPR fans — FCUK THE BOARD — nah, didn't think you'd like that one, he's a Rangers fan after all so give the man a break.

Used to like wicked football as well but we don't get that down the Rangers anymore — "We'll slide down the surface of things" and on and on...

My sister told me to watch 'Lock Stock and Two Smoking Barrels,' says it's a great film. Told her to FCUK off, ain't watching nothing that's earned that asshole money. Hope Jones beats his neighbour up again and this time gets bird. Hopefully a few of the boys will sort him out if you know what I mean.

'Living life too close to the edge hoping that I know the ledge'

Does anyone know the name of Chris Wright's Public Relations geezer? Got myself a bit of a bad reputation recently and I need a top professional to make my name gold dust again as opposed to dog shit.

(Matthew Holley – issue # 127)

Just one more win...

Defeat at Birmingham made it three defeats on the trot — if the last three matches of the season end in a similar way, we'll be as good as relegated. Our only saving grace at this moment is the four-point cushion between us and 22nd place. Just one more win should be enough

It was good to see Arnie, the QPR mascot, bring his family along to the recent game against Wolves.

(Issue # 127)

to make us safe for another season at least, and hopefully that win will come against Bradford — but who actually fancies our chances?

We can only hope Chris Wright has contingency plans already planned for if the dreaded 'R' word becomes something more than a dreadful dream, so from May 10th we can start operating efficiently as a Second Division outfit rather than considering ourselves to be a First Division side 'on loan' for a season — the lessons learned when relegated from the Premiership should hopefully be of great benefit.

Looking on the positive side, if Gerry Francis can keep us up, I believe we will be in a better position going into next season than we were for this. Financially, we'll know where we stand at least. The mere fact that Chris Wright allowed his club to amount huge debts without even realising it, whilst shocking, in many ways opened his eyes to the fact that without Premiership TV money, QPR need to be run as a self-sufficient entity.
(Ed – issue # 128)

The honeymoon's over – now when's the divorce?

They say that the only things guaranteed in life are death and taxes. However, if you are a football manager there is one more. At some stage you will get sacked. Now, like it or not, this applies to Gerry Francis as much as anyone else, especially as he has now apparently had a vote of confidence from Chris Wright. If John Rudge can get the sack then so can anyone, Arsene Wenger and Alex Ferguson included. I am not wishing any ill will on Gerry Francis. I thought at the time and still do, that he is the best possible man for the job given the current circumstances and hope he stays for a year or two at least.

There are though worrying signs that the honeymoon period is over and for the first time, to my knowledge anyway, as early as the Watford game I heard people, if not exactly calling for his head, then at least severely questioning his methods. I must say that to a certain degree I have to agree with them. He is definitely baffling me with both his tactics and team selections.

It is said that apparently we could not get any forwards to sign for us on loan and yet we turned down taking young Arsenal player Omer Rixa. Francis allegedly said, when rejecting the offer, that Rixa was a midfield player and he only wanted to sign forwards. What a shame neither Francis nor any of his scouts (with the obvious exception of bullet brain Dowie, who spent the game elbowing teenagers at the other end of the pitch) had bothered watching our reserves just before Christmas when they were comprehensively beaten by a young Arsenal side whose star of the day was, of course, Omer Riza. Not only did he score the first goal and make the second, but he ran rings around our defence all day.

Talking of my friend Iain Dowie, my feelings on the man are pretty well known by now. Quite simply, he is the worst player to ever pull on a hooped shirt and a disgrace to the club. I cannot believe that I wrote an article at the start of the season praising him for his running of the reserve team. His latest programme notes for the reserves game at

Watford are amazing. I quote, "They equalised but we went 2-1 up which was nice. Academy player Adam Rustem came on and nicked a little goal for us." It would indeed have been nice, except that Adam Rustem equalised for us three minutes from the end after Watford had scored twice, making it 2-2. Even then we managed to throw the game away in the very last minute to the sort of goal that the first team let in week in, week out. Nice to know that the manager cannot even remember the score isn't it?

And now we come to transfer deadline day and a quick look at the signings. Ross Weare, OK, no complaints. Big, strong, quite quick and looks good in the air. Seems totally unfit and will take maybe a season to get used to our level of football, but still a teenager so a good signing for very little I think. He already has his knockers amongst those that follow the reserves, but he looks better than Lee Ferdinand did when we took him from Hayes, so we will have to wait and see.

Jermaine Darlington? Strange signing. Despite still being quite young (25?) he has knocked around a few clubs already. Not a regular in the Aylesbury team which I find a bit worrying and I have to say that on the couple of occasions I have seen him play against Harrow Borough, I haven't noticed him at all. Saw him for the reserves at Northampton though and he does look both two footed and quick, so probably worth the gamble.

CHRIS WRIGHT RECENTLY STATED THAT THERE ARE TOO MANY PLAYERS AT THE CLUB EARNING OVER £100,000 A YEAR, BUT ARE NOWHERE NEAR A PLACE IN THE FIRST TEAM. JUDGING BY KEITH ROWLAND'S MODEST SEMI, HE CAN'T BE ONE OF THEM!

The youngster Luke Cornwall from Fulham, who knows? Apparently he is very highly rated by the Fulham fans that have followed his progress from the youth team into the reserves and he played quite well at Northampton.

Finally we come to Andy Linighan. As ever he is still almost totally dominant in the air (great headed goal for the reserves) and as quick as a constipated camel on the ground. Apparently Francis says he's a leader, which I have to admit we sorely need at the moment though how much we are having to pay him is anyone's guess. With Ready's legendary lack of concentration and Linighan's total lack of pace, it could get a bit scary in our box for the rest of the season. The shear fact is, that none of these players, with the dubious exception of Linighan, will be of any use to us this season at all.

Word is that our beloved senior talent scout Keith Burtenshaw is telling everyone that he contacted every club in the top two divisions in the weeks leading up to deadline day but was unable to get any players whatsoever on loan. Is it possible that word about the shameful way we conned Bradford over the Steiner issue has got round to other clubs, or is it just that Burtenshaw spends more time watching QPR than scouting other teams? Surely someone out of Marshall, Newell, Bradbury and all the rest that moved in the few days leading up to deadline day would have played for us. Several people, Tuttle for example, seemed to prefer to play for someone else's reserves than our first team. There must be something wrong somewhere surely.

Also has anyone noticed the almost total silence that met our last signing before deadline day? In case you haven't heard, QPR signed Iain Dowie's brother, Bob, to be our non-league scout. This is a bit like hiring the Pope's brother to audition page three girls. Just ask the fans that have suffered from his juvenile antics at the teams that he has managed. He has been slung out of more clubs than George Best. His favourite trick is to severely abuse his own fans at the top of his voice and threaten to beat them up if they have the audacity to disagree with him. If we suddenly sign a journeyman midfield player called Ian Rutherford then it's time to pack up and emigrate.

Hopefully by the time you read this he will have buggered off to St. Albans. I do hope he has taken his brother with him, but don't hold your breath. I do not know what this obsession with the Dowie family is, but for those couple of weeks when we actually employed the Dowie brothers and Vinnie Jones at the same time, we were just one nutter away from the worst quartet since the four Horsemen of the Apocalypse!

On the playing front, what is Francis's obsession with centre halves? He appears to have caught George Grahamitis. We are not going to score many goals (the miracle of Swindon excepted) until we play a few attack minded players.

I am almost ashamed to say that I just couldn't be bothered to go to Ipswich. I was so upset after transfer deadline day and the Huddersfield game. The bank holiday traffic, no guarantee I would get in, not one decent forward in the club, no it just wasn't for me. After 35 years and over 400 away games, I just could not be arsed.

The point I am making is that, instead of going to Ipswich, I spent the afternoon sitting in the garden listening to 'Talk Radio' and drinking lager. The 'summariser' for want of a better word for Talk Radio's football coverage is none other than our old manager Alan Mullery, the same manger that had the players practice 'hugging after scoring' prior to our UEFA cup match in Reykjavik a few years ago (I kid you not). It's nice to see that he still knows nothing about the game, spending all afternoon getting confused about different players and who they have and have not played for. His finest moment though came when he twice said that Dynamo Kiev were Russian and came from

Moscow. Probably just as well we got knocked out by Partisan Belgrade, 'cos Mullery could have taken us anywhere in the next round.

No, the honeymoon is definitely over for Gerry, I just hope that divorce proceedings don't have to start in the near future!
(Paul Davidson – issue # 128)

Player of the season – Danny Maddix

Considering this season has mirrored much of the last one, it's strange that there's quite a few candidates up for winning this prestigious honour. In comparison to last season when no one really deserved it, Karl Ready won it on the basis that he was a permanent fixture and steady performer in a side that constantly chopped and changed, yet he wouldn't have come close most other seasons. This season however is a much better contest. Going through the team and weeding out the muck, the following players stand out — Miklosko, Rose, Maddix, Peacock and Gallen.

All five players have enjoyed their own spells when performing better than any other player during some stage of the season. Until his injury against Huddersfield, Matthew Rose was the last player to take centre stage in this respect, and he certainly earns the most improved player of the season vote. Ludo Miklosko is, in my view, the best goalkeeper we've had since David Seaman. Sure, he's made a couple of blunders but has won us far more points that he's lost since coming from West Ham, and is a big favourite. Gavin Peacock, as usual, has run his heart out for QPR this season and is always capable of getting on the scoresheet. He remains our only Premiership-quality player. Then there's poor old Kevin Gallen. Up until the confidence-sapping lack of goals caught up with him in recent weeks, Kevin was playing his best football in a QPR shirt, but his failure to put the ball in the back of the net is both surprising as well as annoying, and he probably now can't wait to see the back of the season.

And finally, to Danny Maddix. It was a close call between him and Peacock, but Danny takes top spot on virtue of being a consistent performer in both penalty boxes this season. His goals have proved to be a handy bonus on top of his high standard of defending, where he remains one of the best man-markers in the game.
(Ed – issue # 128)

Crunch time

I'm sure every player will give absolutely everything today, but doubts remain whether we have the required class to go with it. One thing is for sure — it's going to be one hell of a tense afternoon.

Needing a win against Palace would have been hypothetical had QPR got it at Port Vale instead. With QPR laying on at least a dozen free coaches, and in front of a huge away following, the performance unfortunately was like many others witnessed this season. Just as concerning was the actions of a minority few who tried to cause trouble both during and after the game. I've also heard that one of the trains back to London was severely trashed after the buffet bar was closed ten minutes into the journey home. Sad days.

(Ed – issue # 129)

Did you go to?

A round up of QPR's 25 away games this season

Great support, shame about the result

Port Vale — A win would have guaranteed safety, but as always QPR fail in front of a huge away following.

Watford — Nearly five thousand odd made the first trip to Vicarage Road in ten years, but witnessed another poor defeat.

Ipswich Town — The away section was packed and sung all afternoon, pity the players weren't equally on song.

I didn't think we'd win that one

Wolves — QPR's first away win in over a year, and long overdue it was too, the only surprise being how we didn't win by more.

Bradford — City were on top form, but this was QPR's best away performance for over two years.

Just about worth the effort

Sunderland — Superb ground, and we definitely deserved a share of the spoils.

Walsall — A pleasant night out, and how I laughed at that Gallen miss.

Tranmere — Funny old match but I still didn't think defeat would actually mean anything come May.

Bolton — Strange ground, OK performance.

Birmingham — Atrocious conditions, but a nice ground and a battling display.

That was a rare event

Norwich — 4 goals in the first 8 minutes. Great entertainment despite the defeat.

Bury — Dowie! Dowie! It's always a privilege to see Iain Dowie's annual goal.

It was a false dawn after all

Crewe — Easy enough win, but how we failed to beat Sheffield United a week later I'll never know.

Crystal Palace — Haven't come close to playing as well away from home since.

Grimsby — Thought we'd easily stay up after a decent enough display, but how wrong I was.

What exactly are we doing here?

Portsmouth — A sunny August Bank Holiday, but the players just couldn't be arsed.

Charlton — 2-0 down from the first leg, we were already as good as out of the League Cup.

West Brom — Officially, Gerry's first game back in charge, not that we could tell the difference.

It's raining in our hearts

Oxford Utd — Both team and fans were thoroughly pissed on, but at least Ray Harford had the sense to call it a day afterwards.

Swindon — Nothing worse that open seats in driving rain, especially if you've lost.

Stockport — The rain was the only thing I remember about this one.

Zzzzzzzz

Huddersfield — What was the score again?

Barnsley — Three days after Christmas, but there was nothing festive about this dour 1-0 defeat.

Bristol City — I felt sorry for those watching at home, but it was far worse actually being there.

Sheffield United — A dull, lifeless performance — and that was just me in the pub afterwards!

(Alan Smithfield – issue # 129)

No knob joke

Following Antti Heinola's injury at Birmingham, Gerry Francis was quoted as saying; "I don't want to go into too much detail about it, but there was blood coming out of his penis." Well, you can't get much more detailed than that, but it couldn't have been more eloquently put!

(Ed – issue # 129)

Where has it all gone wrong?

I've got to admit that with the season progressing the way it has, I've been distinctly unimpressed, completely and utterly miserable and totally fed up making my way down to Loftus Road every other Saturday. There was a time when I actually looked forward to making my way down to W12 but now every step along the road is filled with dread and fear.

The streets which once looked clean and bright and now graffitied and filled with rubbish. The stadium which once had dignitaries from all over the world coming to voice their approval at the all-seater splendour before them now looks like a poky old hole with seating leg room only for those of 5ft and under. The ticket touts which were once a nuisance corning out of White City tube station have now disappeared because, let's face it, who in their right mind would want to make the trip up to west London to watch Port Vale, Crewe, Bristol City etc. How I miss these touts, even the smell of the burger and hot dog sellers to me now make the place unattractive and unappealing to be in. The team which boasted such skilful gifted players that played such attractive open attacking football which was a joy to watch, have been taken over, with notable exceptions, by brainless inadequacies who can't pass, tackle, shoot or do anything generally decent with a football.

We were told that there wouldn't be another season like last when we ended a point and a position above the relegation zone, and like fools we believed them. The writing surely was on the wall. No notable transfers had taken place before the start of the season and so therefore a poor team from last season wasn't necessarily going to be any better this time around, however we still kidded ourselves that we would still challenge for a place in the play-offs at the very least. How I miss those middle of the table finishes in the Premiership, we kidded ourselves that we were unadventurous and unambitious yet now half of the teams in the top flight aspire to just that sort of 'lofty' position.

The flotation of the club together with Wasps was to generate capital for the Plc — for the improvement of the playing staff and to make up for the shortfall to pay for higher wage bills because of the removal of the parachute payment system from the Premiership — seems to have backfired badly. Even the reissue of shares this year has failed to generate extra cash from already disillusioned investors. Had the money been there perhaps the transfer of Rob Steiner from Bradford City would have been permanent. Admittedly, the cavalier attitude with money that the previous incumbents of the managerial chair have certainly not helped the fiscal side of the club.

Reports in The Times and Guardian suggest that at least 20 professional players will have to be sold off or released in time for next season (although denied by QPR). I personally would welcome such a blitzkreig on the playing staff and I'm sure there are other Rangers fans who would gladly see the back of some players who quite frankly are 'swinging the lead.'

Although the above might sound like the ranting of someone completely disillusioned with QPR, it's far from the truth. This is a club that I'll support the rest of my living days and as such I would like to see them succeed and not just fall by the wayside, otherwise the next 40 years for me are going to be extremely dull. I would like to see

the club going forward, picking up all those supporters that we seem to have lost from the 1970s. I would like to see kids in the W12 area and other parts of London and the home counties walking around in QPR replica shirts, and not just those of the so called 'big clubs.' Me? I'm "Rangers till I die."
(Moreno Ferrari – issue # 129)

Going back to our roots?

I'm writing this the day after the 1-0 defeat at Birmingham — I thought that I wouldn't write at all this season for reasons eloquently expressed by Matthew Holley in his valedictory article in issue 127. And I wouldn't have written except for an article in the Evening Standard on Monday 19th April. It said that Gerry Francis would be giving his players extra shooting practice in preparation for the Birmingham match. Francis is quoted thus; "To get something out of a game we've got to score goals." This dramatic insight explains why Francis was so sought after — it's a pity that he didn't think of the idea before the new year and perhaps then we'd have had more than two away victories since he arrived.

While he's at it perhaps Francis can also get players to forget the training methods which result in corners and crosses landing on the head or at the feet of the nearest defender.

I haven't been to any away games this season so I may not be qualified to pronounce on this topic, but it seems to me that QPR have set out to achieve goalless draws in the last three. Even in the West Brom home game the players seemed to be playing for 0-0 until that weird 45th minute. With no hope of keeping a clean sheet in away games there seems little point in not going on all out attack — you never know! And anyway, a 4-2 defeat is no worse than a 1-0 defeat, in fact it boosts the goals scored column.

But I still don't think QPR will be relegated. Crystal Palace will come to the rescue by playing their part in the 'old pals act' (with or without a suitcase full of folding at half time) allowing Rangers to win the last match to stay up at the last push.

The last four seasons have witnessed three relegation struggles which is where I came in. I first watched QPR in the 1957/58 season. Rangers were in the 3rd Division South. At the end of the season the top halves of the 3rd North and South would make up the new 3rd Division and the bottom halves would make up the new 4th Division.

Rangers were knocked out of the FA Cup 6-1 by non-league Hereford and by the beginning of March were well adrift in the bottom half of the table. What followed was a run of 12 games with only one defeat, including an Easter double over Crystal Palace. Rangers survived by 6 points. Gerry Francis's demand for one win in the last six games seems pathetic in comparison. Whatever does happen this season, at least ITL only went over the top once with optimism. There was talk of a play-off position in the first flush of success after Francis's arrival but I don't think that it was ever repeated.

So what of next season? I'll renew my season ticket come what May as far as the division is concerned — but I'll probably give it up when Rangers move to the new stadium somewhere in the M4/M40 corridor. The silver lining on a relegation cloud would at least postpone that evil day.

(Paul Smith – issue # 129)

Message to Gerry: keep your hair on

IT IS an inevitable by-product of journalism, alas, that try as you might to avoid it, people sometimes take offence at what you write.

"Collateral damage," we call it in the trade. Even so, it inevitably makes it none the less distressing and I am particularly distraught to have offended Gerry Francis (below).

Mr Francis is a minor eccentric. Despite being wealthy enough not to need to work, and despite having little recent success in his chosen career, he persists in football management.

For this dedication, he is to be congratulated. What he is less to be

applauded for, is his reaction to what we used to know, before Ron Atkinson rewrote the lexicon of rhyming slang, as his Barnet (Fair).

It is this that has caused the unpleasantness.

"Gerry Francis must be tearing his hair out," (well, it won't make it look any worse)," it said in *Standard Sport's* Friday Analysis.

A few days later, the poor lamb refused to answer a question from a reporter working for this newspaper, threatening to withhold all co-operation until his displeasure had been relayed to us.

It now has been, and I personally am more sorry than words alone (and I've looked them all up in the dictionary) can even begin to suggest.

By way of apology, and in lieu of damages, I wish to conclude with a word of lavish praise.

After losing 3-1 to Bradford, QPR are in a desperate state and have a fair chance of being relegated to Division Two.

Despite this worrying position, London W12's best-loved Wurzel finds the time, and the heart, to become agitated by a mild remark about his hair.

This sublime gift for keeping sight of his priorities while under intense pressure does him great credit, and holds out more than a gleam of hope for his team. Hats off to you, then, Gerry. Or, perhaps in the circs, hats on.

The Evening Standard, 26/4/99

QPR 6-0 Crystal Palace

So they finally came up with a performance to justify their existence in the blue and white hoops and wasn't it fun?

It was, by sheer coincidence my one hundredth game of the season (45 of those, QPR games) and by God was it worth struggling through the other 99 or what? There have been times during the season when my deep and long-standing love of our club had started to wane, but I stuck with it and had confidence that it would all turn out well in the end. Well sort of.

My other half had gone abroad with her mother for the week, presumably so as to be away in case I demolished vast chunks of our house in my grief if we lost. I had drunk vast quantities of cheap red wine the night before so as to make me sleep and not spend the entire night worrying myself to death about the result the next day.

I had tried to convince myself that it did not matter, but it did. It seemed to matter more than life itself. And it seemed to matter more and more the nearer the big day came.

On the morning of the fateful day, I was in a bit of a mess and not all of it was to do with the red wine. My heart was telling me not to worry, it would all come out OK in the end. My head was arguing with that logic, asking who if anyone was going to score the two goals we would probably need to win the game. Somewhere in the middle, I had a lump in my throat the size of an orange.

The journey to the game was a nightmare. The Western Avenue was so stuck up with traffic, I cut down the back roads to get around it. So had everyone else. It took an age to get to Shepherds Bush, but when I got there at about 12 o'clock, I had never seen so many people there so early in my life. Not just Rangers fans with vacant looks on their faces, but also thousands of Palace fans milling about with equally pained expressions, thinking they might be seeing their team for the last time ever. The LSA was packed almost to capacity and the queue for a couple of pints of lager took over 20 minutes. Still, it passed a little time before kick-off and it helped a little, nervously chatting with others with the same hopes and fears of what was to come.

And then, there we were in the ground. Too late for the team announcements we wondered who was playing. Then they came out onto the pitch, eventually. Somebody yelled that Maddix was there, great relief all round. Then someone noticed Scully, what the hell was he doing out there? It was generally agreed that Francis had to try something different and the fact that he was going to play a flat back four and push a few men forward seemed to be a relief to most people.

We dire for the first few minutes, but to be fair Palace did not look up to any great shakes either. And then the first sign that God really does come from Shepherds Bush and is a Rangers fan after all, he sent us down a miracle. George Kulcsar — who although has some admirable qualities as a footballer, could not be relied upon to score from the penalty spot into an unguarded net — stunningly blasts the ball into the goal from outside the box like he had been doing it that way every Saturday afternoon for a year.

Kevin Miller, normally as good a goalie as there is in the division, just stood there and watched. He was as stunned as we were. For a split second nobody seemed to move, then suddenly the whole place erupted. We had scored. We had got the early goal we needed, we were surely on our way.

The half ticked on with everyone saying we needed another goal. Then just before half time miracle number two appears. Chris Kiwomya, with the aid of a defence so static you would have thought it was ours, ran through and hit the post. Now we know all about hitting the post, we have been doing it all season. Every time we do, the ball either rebounds for a corner or lobs gently into the outstretched arms of the 'keeper. Not this time. God, who obviously likes a good laugh the way he has treated us this season, flips the ball gently back on to Kiwomya's head for such an easy chance that Iain Dowie would have knocked it in (now that really would have been a miracle). Half-time 2-0, now we knew we really had a chance.

The second half will go down in legend. Kiwomya's comedic dance routine around in circles before chipping the ball gently into the, again, unguarded net; Scully's unbelievable volley (surely miracle number three); Miller's good save from Kiwomya's penalty, with Slade taking Kiwomya down from behind on the rebound, only for Breacker, with possibly his first truly worthwhile contribution to the club since he signed, on hand to tap the ball home. And there was still time for Kiwomya's practically farcical head-tennis exhibition, from Scully's stunning cross it has to said, before almost apologetically knocking the third attempt in off the post.

And still there could have been more. Slade missing a sitter, Gallen driving a shot just wide, it could have been eight. By this time nobody seemed to care. As the song said, we were staying up and didn't we let everyone know it? The noise was outstanding. People were laughing, hugging, crying, singing, jumping, waving, you would have thought we had actually won something. And still the Palace fans stood and watched. Fair play to them I thought. There can't be that many fans that would almost all still be in the ground at the end of a 6-0 hammering but there they were. They were quiet sure, wouldn't you be, but they were all still there, seemingly waiting for the death knell to be sounded.

And then it was over. Despite all the announcements, about half the crowd were on the pitch, as if anyone really expected anything else. Me, I was outside in Loftus Road. My heart was pumping away telling me how it knew all along/ Kulcsar, Scully, Breacker, yeah no problem, knew it all along.

The lump in my throat had gone to be replaced by a small tear in my eye. And my head? It was wondering how much of that cheap red wine was left and how long it would take to get home to find out.

And God? He was, no doubt, sitting back in his great big armchair in the sky and pissing himself-laughing, now he really did know all along what was going to happen!
(Paul Davidson – issue # 130)

Ray Harford chats with fans prior to the pre-season friendly at Millwall. Two months later his disasterous spell as manager came to an end having recorded just 4 league wins from 35 games. Harford died of cancer on 9th August, 2003, aged 58

174

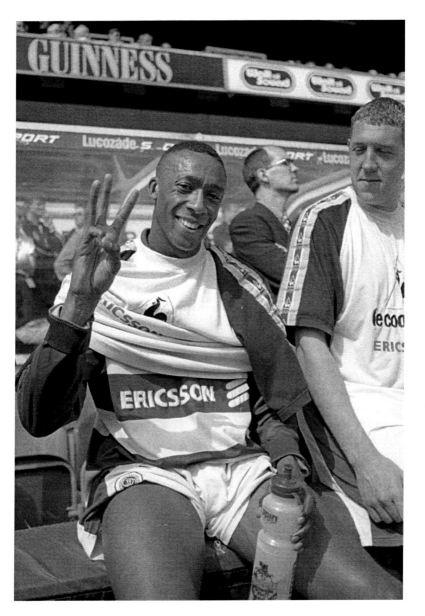

Chris Ki-wom-ya takes a breather after leaving the field following his hat-trick against Crystal Palace on the memorable final day of the season

1998/99 ~ Division 1

Date	Match	Comp	Scorers	Att	Issue
08/08/98	A Sunderland L 0-1	League		41,008	# 119
11/08/98	A Walsall D 0-0	Lgc Cup		3,691	
15/08/98	H Bristol City D 1-1	League	Ready	13,337	
22/08/98	A Norwich City L 2-4	League	Peacock (p), Sheron	16,317	
26/08/98	H Walsall W 3-1 (aet)	Lgc Cup	Sheron, Slade, Maddix	5,052	
29/08/98	H Bury D 0-0	League		8,652	# 120
31/08/98	A Portsmouth L 0-3	League		12,106	
08/09/98	H Tranmere D 0-0	League		8,070	
12/09/98	A Watford L 1-2	League	Slade	14,251	
16/09/98	H Charlton Ath L 0-2	Lge Cup		6,497	
19/09/98	H Stockport W 2-0	League	Gallen (2)	8,205	# 121
22/09/98	A Charlton Ath L 0-1	Lge Cup		11,726	
26/09/98	A Oxford Utd L 1-4	League	Scully	7,489	
29/09/98	A Wolves W 2-1	League	Sheron (2)	20,201	
03/10/98	H Grimsby Town L 1-2	League	Maddix	10,240	
17/10/98	A Huddersfield L 0-2	League		14,290	
21/10/98	A West Brom L 0-2	League		11,842	
25/10/98	H Birmingham L 0-1	League		10,272	# 122
31/10/98	A Swindon Town L 1-3	League	Sheron	8,500	
04/11/98	H Barnsley W 2-1	League	Langley, Gallen	8,218	
07/11/98	H Bolton Wndrs W 2-0	League	Gallen, Sheron	11,814	
14/11/98	A Crewe W 2-0	League	Peacock, Sheron	5,001	
21/11/98	H Sheffield Utd L 1-2	League	Peacock (p)	12,558	# 123
28/11/98	A Bradford City W 3-0	League	Peacock, Gallen, Sheron	15,037	
02/12/98	H Ipswich Town D 1-1	League	Gallen	12,449	
05/12/98	H Port Vale W 3-2	League	Maddix, OG, Sheron	10,498	
12/12/98	H Crewe L 0-1	League		11,926	# 124
19/12/98	A Crystal Palace D 1-1	League	Steiner	17,684	
26/12/98	H Norwich City W 2-0	League	Murray, Peacock	15,251	
28/12/98	A Barnsley L 0-1	League		14,287	
02/01/99	H Huddersfield L 0-1	FA Cup		11,685	
09/01/99	H Sunderland D 2-2	League	Maddix, Gallen	17,444	# 125
16/01/99	A Bury D 1-1	League	Dowie	4,609	
30/01/99	H Portsmouth D 1-1	League	Peacock	12,852	
05/02/99	A Bristol City D 0-0	League		13,841	
13/02/99	A Tranmere L 2-3	League	Maddix, Rowland	5,896	
20/02/99	H Watford L 1-2	League	Peacock	14,918	# 126
27/02/99	A Stockport D 0-0	League		7,649	
03/03/99	H Oxford Utd W 1-0	League	Steiner	9,040	
06/03/99	H Wolves L 0-1	League		13,150	
13/03/99	A Bolton Wndrs L 1-2	League	Rowland (p)	17,919	
20/03/99	H Swindon W 4-0	League	Steiner, Kiwomya (2), Rowland	11,184	# 127
03/04/98	H Huddersfield D 1-1	League	Baraclough	11,113	
05/04/99	A Ipswich Town L 1-3	League	Kiwomya	22,162	
10/04/99	H West Brom W 2-1	League	Ready, Peacock	11,158	
13/04/99	A Grimsby Town L 0-1	League		4,789	
17/04/99	A Sheffield Utd L 0-2	League		14,341	
20/04/99	A Birmingham L 0-1	League		20,888	# 128
24/04/99	H Bradford City L 1-3	League	Gallen	11,641	
01/05/99	A Port Vale L 0-2	League		9,851	# 129
09/05/99	H Crystal Palace W 6-0	League	Kulcsar, Kiwomya (3), Scully, Breaker	18,498	

League Record - P46 W12 D11 L23 F52 A61 Pts 47. League position – 20th

In The Loft Player of the Season – Danny Maddix

Chapter 4

1999/00

Consistency is the key for Francis

Of the many seasons spent at this level over the last 15 years, for me the 1999/00 season has been the best of the bunch. Coming slap-bang in the middle of two near-relegations and a most definite relegation, looking back it makes it all the more surprising. Consistent from start to finish without pulling up any trees, the ship had somehow been steadied, and it was a refreshing change to all that had gone on previously. Relegation was never an issue, and we were only a clinical striker away from pushing for promotion — sadly never a realistic proposition with the club running on a shoestring budget.

It's hard to pinpoint exactly why this hiatus occurred during the club's startling decline in status from 1997 to 2001. Gerry Francis and Iain Dowie more than played their part of course, and several established players enjoyed their best seasons for the club, notably Lee Harper, Matthew Rose and Gavin Peacock. Even players with few admirers added something at various stages of the season, the likes of Morrow, Breacker, Kulcsar and Ready playing their part. The pressure was off to an extent — after the previous two seasons things couldn't exactly get any worse, and all the Premiership-wannabes had long gone. Add all these ingredients to the pot, throw in some fresh blood from the non-leagues that proved great value for pennies (Wardley and Darlington), and hey presto.

Financially, things had levelled out somewhat with the sale of Wasps' training ground for £8.5million (the only good thing to come from the partnership), though most of that was swallowed up in the repayment of loans to banks and Chris Wright, and the black hole that was the club's wage bill. It wasn't just first team players bleeding the club dry, many still on Premiership contracts (though to be fair, most earned their corn this season); a dozen youth team players were enjoying wages of £40,000 to £90,000 a year, similarly ten directors were on the same sort of money — amazingly unbeknown to Wright, who's biggest regret he has cited as being, "not hands on enough."

Francis though remained a cautious man throughout the season, usually referring to the need to attain 45/50 points in just about all of his after-match press conferences. Once these figures were surpassed by early March, he didn't exactly get overly excited, and often remarked how his team had over achieved. I guess he knows his players better than anyone, but the feeling amongst many fans was had Francis been a little bit more adventurous, the play-offs could have been within our reach. Either way, it was still a fine season after the shambles of those previous, and had we not endured some appalling referee's and a crippling injury list mid-season, even Gerry's cautious approach could have reaped greater reward.

If you look at how things went the following season, maybe Francis was right after all. If we really did over achieve in 99/00, then we certainly under-achieved in 00/01. ❑

Inane summer ramblings

So it's official then. The management of QPR was quoted in the middle of June as saying that, as most of us suspected, all of the current playing staff are on the transfer list. No reasonable offer would be refused for any of them apparently and every club in the league had been circulated to that effect. The real sad part about it is that this has been the situation since last October and the only offer we have had was for Sheron from Barnsley and off he duly went. So, as most of us already thought, nobody, but nobody wants any of our players. Another struggle to come this season? Bet your mortgage on it! There's even some sarcastic sod in our office who wants to bet me that we don't score a goal before Christmas. Problem is, looking at the fixtures, he could be right.

I wonder at times exactly just how close to extinction QPR really are. I have seen three different stories during the summer, in three separate papers all relating to the fact that Barclays insist we pay them back the apparent £8.5 million we owe them. The biggest of these reports stated that Barclays were fed up that we have shown no signs of paying back any of the debt whatsoever. This makes me wonder exactly what happened to the money for Sheron for a start. The reports all say that Chris Wright intended using the money from the sale of the old Wasps ground to pay off the debt, but that as we all know won't happen until planning permission is granted and by all accounts the land there is only worth around £5 million even then.

What really worries me is that we apparently owe £8.5 million. This debt was, as far as I knew, about £5 million tops not long ago, so where the hell has all the rest come from? The only slightly amusing thing about all this is that these reports said that if we did not repay Barclays then they would sell off all our assets. That would be good, as apart from the ground I was unaware that we had any. We have, as already said, been desperately trying to sell off any of our players that are worth any money for months and nobody wants any of them. I wonder if Barclays could do a better job of unloading them than our current management?

I dare say that the new player situation will have changed by the time you read this, or at least I hope it has. As of the time of writing, the day of the Bournemouth pre-season friendly, the rebuilding of the team has stalled with us signing no new players whatsoever. We have been linked with just about every available player in Christendom and beyond and signed nobody. Gerry says we must sell before we can buy. Great except we can't sell anybody because nobody wants any of them. We might be lucky and pick up a couple of players just before the season starts that have been unable to get a contract anywhere else and are prepared to play for peanuts, but I can't believe that Chris Wright will authorise any real increase in the overall wage bill. Until we can convince players like Paul Bruce, Ademole Bankole et al to bugger off and play for someone else rather than sit in our reserves picking up a couple of grand a week for doing nothing, then I'm not sure I can see us signing anyone — hopefully, I'll be wrong.

To sum up our pathetic scouting attempts, I read in late May that we sent two scouts to Sweden to watch a Jamaican forward called Onandi Lowe play for his country against Sweden. This man was apparently so desperate to come and play for us that he wrote every day to the club from his Jamaican home asking for a trial. I wonder how much the little jaunt to Sweden cost us? Might have been worthwhile if he had put up a good performance, but as you might have already guessed by now, he didn't play.

I have really enjoyed the last two years pre-season tours to the West Country and Belfast. It was with great anticipation that I waited for news of this year's trip. Gerry had apparently said we were going back to Sweden. That will do me I thought, I've got some air miles saved up. Where do we end up then, bloody Bournemouth and Basingstoke. Christ, are we so broke that we couldn't afford to stay anywhere or what? Or is it just that no one wants to play us anymore?

(Paul Davidson – issue # 130)

Things can only get better

There seems to be an air of discontent around at the moment because of a lack of transfer activity at QPR, when we really should be just thankful we're still in this division. Considering the club is millions in debt, it's hardly surprising — just look at how long it took Danny Maddix and Chris Kiwomya to agree new contracts. Umpteen players have been linked with the club, but only Stuart Wardley and Rob Steiner have made the move. The hoped-for clearout of deadwood hasn't happened because the majority of players are still under contract, so QPR will start the season with more or less the same squad as last time.

The size is there, but sadly not the quality. The annual wage bill must still be way above our means, so we have to face the fact that financially, this season will see another struggle. The days of QPR splashing out millions for average players seems many years ago, but the implications of which are now hitting us hard. It's a fact we have to accept.

Despite this, I feel a lot more confident about our chances this season. Confident in that I can't see another season battling against relegation, but our aspirations will certainly be no better than mid-table — it may sound dull, but it would be a significant step. The key word may well prove to be 'fitness' — the likes of Langley, Rose, Maddix and Peacock form a good base to build a team around, but they need to stay fit. Gerry Francis needs to decide what formation he intends to use, be it 4-4-2 or 3-5-2, stick with it and keep changes to a minimal whenever possible. A period of consolidation is what we really need, but a team that continually chops and changes will not bring that.

Looking at the far from successful friendly matches played, there were very few clues as to what team Francis will start the season with, but with injuries to key defenders looking likely to preventing him from fielding his first choice XI from the start, let's hope this won't be the shape of things to come as the season progresses.

(Ed – issue # 130)

Bright spots

I'm guessing that the vast majority of stuff in these pages is going to be all about anger. Anger over Chris Wright not having any funds to help Gerry buy players. Anger that our wasters who we don't want any more are simply not leaving, either because they're so crap that no one has come in for them (understandable); or someone has come in for them, but the players are reluctant to take a pay cut, or drop into non-league football where a couple of them undoubtedly belong. I'm not naming any names, but here are three anagrams — Reayd, Scuyll, Bankloe. Anger that some fans really do believe that Scully is a great player after his one-off performance against Palace. Anger that Fulham are now a much bigger club than us. And anger that players who were out of contract but wanted to keep, took so long to put pen to paper.

So instead of wasting a paragraph about all that depressive stuff (what? oh, I see your point), how about looking at the good things that happened last season? Shouldn't take long.

Danny Maddix

Without doubt this man was the single most important factor in keeping us in the First Division last season. After that disastrous series of sending-offs the season before last, I thought we should give him to Brentford or Millwall. Then, due to injuries and inept performances he came back into the side and played well for a couple of games. Then a couple more. Suddenly he was our most valuable player, someone who I was proud to have as captain of QPR. The relief that I felt when he was fully fit enough to play in that last game against Palace was unbelievable. A player hasn't deserved the player of the year trophy more than him since the immaculate displays of Clive Wilson in the early 1990s.

Ludek Miklosko

Following closely behind Danny in the 'thank God he's playing' stakes is Ludo. I can't say I was ever a great fan of Harper, and I don't think the QPR defence were either judging by the return of their confidence once they had Ludo behind them. He's still a bit of a Dracula, and he did make that one awful mistake in front of the Loft (was it against Portsmouth?), but he saved us on more occasions than I can remember or be bothered to write down. The man responsible for stabilising the defence.

Matthew Rose

Hands up who thought this man would be a contender for player of the season this time last year? I put him behind Maddix only. He steadily improved over the season and was nothing short of a revelation as sweeper. I think we would have stayed up with a lot more ease had he not missed those last six games or so. I've never been a fan of the sweeper system, but a back five of Heinola, Plummer, Rose, Maddix and Baraclough would change my mind. Expect to see a lot more from Rosey this season.

FORGET NOSTRADAMUS -
THE FUTURE IS HOOP SHAPED

YOU COULD GET TWO OF ME IN HERE

ERICSSON

RICHARD LANGLEY TRIES ON
KEVIN GALLEN'S SHIRT FOR SIZE

The youngsters

QPR always seem to have one or two youngsters on the verge of the first team. Just when one nips off to achieve obscurity somewhere else, a new talent takes his place that looks even better. It was Richard Langley who hauled us out of our rut with his home debut goal against Barnsley, and masterful displays that followed that game. He looked calm, talented, quick, strong and mature. And he has one of the best midfielders of the last 30 years coaching him. Leon Jeanne will sparkle for us when we start winning, but clearly it was too early to start pitching him into a team that kept losing. However, some of the skills he showed I don't think I've ever seen before, particularly one trick he did in front of the Loft on the byline which was beyond description. Chris Plummer also impressed me after a shaky start, and I can't see any argument for keeping him out of the team and continuing with Karl Ready, who, as we know, had an absolutely shocking season — even by his standards. And finally, I think we're all looking out for the emergence of Richard Graham, who we've heard so much about but rarely see, unless you're more dedicated than me at attending reserve matches.

The glimmers of hope

The 3-0 trouncing of Bradford — eventual winners of promotion, sticks out as a real high point. It showed what QPR can achieve when they actually get their act together. That and the 4-0 thrashing of Swindon Town highlighted that we have maybe eight good players that can occasionally carry the rest of the team if they all play well at the same time. However, our main problem for most of last season was not scoring enough goals — we only looked threatening up front in about five or six games. And arguably, the best partnership we had — Kiwomya and Steiner, only played together on, I think, one occasion.

QPR 6-0 Crystal Palace

Yeah, it was a great day. Yeah, it was sunny even though the forecast said rain. And yeah, we deserved to win. But everybody needs to get a grip. The complete overreaction by the club and the fans is mystifying given the circumstances. QPR we're embarrassing in the first ten minutes. Then the unlikely hero George Kulcsar scored a goal that looked impossible for the keeper not to save. We were gifted another goal just before half time when Palace had been well on top and should have equalised. It was only in the second half that Palace finally proved to be the collection of two-bit reserve players that they were. Two sending-offs — both fully deserved (despite biased press reporting by journalists sulking that their story had been ruined), some defensive work that even Ready would have been embarrassed of, and a goalkeeper that couldn't save a shot from Arnie of the R's (Arnie, what are you? A football-head? What is that?). Kiwomya's second two goals were scrambled in, as was Breaker's, and only Scully's effort really stood out as being a truly fantastic goal achieved through skill.

Don't get me wrong, I'm not complaining — it's the best I've felt at a QPR match for a long time, but to judge by the idiotic ramblings on the internet from club and fans alike, you'd think we'd just beaten Manchester United 6-0 to win the Premiership. Everyone seems to think that now we'll be okay. Well, wake up, because Palace were the worst side I've seen at Loftus Road (apart from QPR) since Southend United.

That girl that stripped in the South Africa Road stand

Now that is how to celebrate — paint your boobs with blue and white hoops and waggle them around while dancing on top of the fat-cat executive boxes. Best moment was when she waved her mammaries in front of an old couple who thought they had come to watch bowls. I wish I could have seen their faces, but my eyes were busy elsewhere. Anyway, if that girl wants to send her phone number into ITL, the editor knows how to find me.

(Dan Trelfer – issue # 130)

Where were you all?

Welcome back for another season in Division 1. I hope this one is different from the last two, but this is not what I want to talk about, nor is the 6-0 thrashing of Palace, although I will say I was very disappointed that we only scored six — it should have been nine or ten. But I do want to question the poor turnout in the pubs afterwards. I imagined it would be better and louder than at the end of the previous season, but I was wrong. 'The Fringe & Firkin' was closed until five and Shepherds Bush looked like we had just played Bury on a Tuesday night.

We went and got a McDonalds and then went back to the Firkin, expecting to see fellow R's, but no. Where were you all? We decided to find out and so we went round the corner to the 'Bush Ranger' and outside there were about seventy R's fans all singing. Then someone produced a football, and after a while the ball comes to me and let I let fly with a beautiful shot — and then people start accusing me of being Tony Scully! The bloody cops then turned up and told us to calm down, and the pub actually locked us out, bastards!

Soon after everyone started leaving and before we knew it there was only about six of us left, so we stumbled back to the 'Fringe & Firkin' where we were confronted by a load of Suede fans, most of which were women and pretty fit — short skirts and knee high boots 'fit' that is. Unfortunately (or perhaps fortunately given our condition) we didn't have fifty quid each to give to the touts to join them for the gig.

By this time it was about 9pm and we were now just numbering four, so I decided to make my way back home to Southend. Shepherds Bush was, by now, a ghost town, and I'm upset so few fans could be bothered to celebrate us staying up and absolutely slaughtering Palace.
(Paul Lewis – issue # 130)

Moreno Bares All

Welcome back to another season that on paper could be just as miserable as last season. Rangers have been virtually non-existent in the transfer market, something that perhaps every die-hard QPR fan in their heart of hearts would have expected considering the club's financial plight. What perhaps surprises the more pessimistic amongst us is that we haven't got rid of any players, admittedly who would want anyone except for perhaps Gavin Peacock or even Richard Langley. The expected clear-out of the 'deadwood' hasn't materialised and players haven't even been given away on a 'free' to lessen the clubs wage bill which seems very strange if the club is losing so much money. Gerry Francis said that the start of the season is exactly the same for all clubs, rich or poor they all begin with nought points, let's just hope we have a little more than that when the season is over.

~ ~ ~

I'm sure most fans would agree that the final game of last season against Crystal Palace was a day that will live long in the memory. The scoreline of 6-0 was extremely

185

flattering against a Palace side that seemingly couldn't even care, nevertheless it was against London opposition and it was 6-0! The post match celebrations were just the best that I've experienced for a long time and for once it actually felt good to be a QPR supporter. Running onto the pitch was fun and only the third time I've managed it in my supporting career. Even the stewards relented and helped those who weren't quite able to get onto the grass. The after match drinking also went down incredibly well, outside the 'Bush Ranger' the fans were in full voice and had even welcomed Palace fans into the general festivities — fans even attempted to board buses that were trying to drive past into Shepherds Bush bus garage. it was pretty hilarious. I remember at the start of the day a father and his son were dropped off in front of the ground. His wife enquired at to what time he could be expected to be back home, to which he replied, "If we lose I'll be back in an hour, if we win I'll be back sometime next week." He just might still be out there somewhere!

~ ~ ~

The pre-season matches are well under way as I pen this article and so far the progress has been slow and steady, if perhaps a little uninspiring. A 1-0 win against Bournemouth has been followed with a 1-1 draw against Weymouth with Gerry fielding two different sides in each half. I never used to take much notice of these pre-season jaunts in the past but they seem to be an indicator of what we can expect in the coming months. Last season's match against Brentford was a classic example, we were terrible while the Bees were quite exceptional — what happened later that season... Rangers struggled while the Bees concluded a very successful season with being crowned Third Division champions. So pay close attention to those results.

~ ~ ~

What does everyone think of the new home and away shirts for the new season? Personally I quite like the home shirt even though it'll only be used for one season. The away shirt really is a big steaming pile of pooh. Predominantly white with very thin red and black hoops it seems to me to be a complete waste of time and money. You need a completely different colour scheme so that the difference between the two shirts would be striking enough as to be able to be worn against any team — this is not possible when both shirts have a large amount of white in them. Certainly the yellow third kit will be making more than one appearance this season...

~ ~ ~

Although there hasn't been any activity in the transfer market one of our most favourite characters has departed from the Loftus Road scene. Arnie, the favoured (sic) QPR mascot has been put into retirement and has been replaced by a black cat called Jude. Quite what someone with a football for a head had as an association with QPR is beyond me — it's true that we can't have a mascot that compliments our nickname, it's damn difficult to make something out of Hoops or R's, but Arnie was something else — almost in the same class as Ricky Rockett, as some older supporters will remember; He seemed to come from the penmanship of a really bad graphic designer's inane doodle. Goodbye Arnie, gone but sadly not forgotten.

(Moreno Ferrari – issue # 130)

Swings and roundabouts

Following a hard-earned draw against Wolves, it would be fair to say we can be reasonably satisfied with QPR's start to the season. When considering we could easily have four wins out of four by now (football is never that simple or gratifying), all the same there's not too much to complain about. Of course we all still moan and groan at certain things, but having only just avoided relegation in each of the last two seasons, there are more positives than negatives so far as we aim to restore some credibility in the face of mounting adversity.

No matter what league you are win or which position, supporters hope to see their team win every match. This of course is impossible, so despite how disappointed we felt when we couldn't get a point at Bolton or claim a winner against Wolves, a look at the overall picture paints a far better picture. For a team that has played like relegation candidates for what seems like an eternity, the early signs seem to be pointing towards a top half finish at the very least for QPR.

Putting my manager's hat on, I like all other supporters like to think Gerry Francis could be doing this or that better, but we all have to accept in the end the choices Francis makes. Would Scully make a better wing-back than Breaker? In some respects he would, in others, no. Morrow or Murray in midfield? Most would prefer Murray, but over the last 12 months Morrow has proved himself to be the more consistent performer. Should Ready have been an automatic choice after suspension? Has Steiner done enough to prove himself ahead of Gallen?

There's always arguments for and against, but as a team, QPR have put in four reasonable performance thus far, and look a far more organised outfit than last season. We have made as good a start to the season that we possibly could have, and with a positive feeling around Loftus Road, let's only hope we can build on it.

(Ed – issue # 131)

Full-backs

Everyone seems to be going a little over the top about Jermaine Darlington I tend to think. I must admit he is looking exceptional going forward and considering that this time last season he was not even a regular choice for Aylesbury, he has made great strides forward. I would just like to see him learn a little more of the art of tackling before we go too overboard about him. Mind you, if he is going to score a few more like that one on the opening day, who cares if he can't tackle?

What a shame it is about Antti Heinola. He was just beginning to look the part down the right hand side in pre-season and now he is out for the season at least. He must be just about the unluckiest man to ever pull on a hooped shirt and by God there have been some unlucky ones. I for one have not been overly impressed by Tim Breacker since he signed for us. It's not his fault I don't think, he is a perfectly adequate right back for our division but not a wing-back, he just hasn't got the pace to gallop up and down all afternoon. With Heinola out for the season we would seem to need another right back with some haste.
(Paul Davidson – issue # 131)

A man of his word?

In the final issue of last season, I came to the defence of Chris Wright on the grounds that although he had made mistakes in the past, I felt he had learned from them and that at least he was a fan of the club and not some faceless businessman.

I believed that most Rangers fans still supported him and wanted to see him turn things around. Essentially, I still hold to that view, but over the summer there have been some worrying developments which have caused me some concern.

First to set the alarm bells ringing were the comments of our chairman as reported on the official website immediately after the last day escape from the drop. Instead of adopting a cautious, pragmatic approach, Wright was telling QPR fans to forget about the past and look to the future and that Rangers would be challenging at the other end of the table next season. He envisaged players leaving and new ones arriving as Francis rebuilt his team. I found the tone of his remarks very worrying. For two successive seasons the club had escaped relegation at the last gasp, but despite that, Wright still seemed to have his head in the clouds.

Alright, so Rangers did eventually secure the services of Steiner on a permanent basis, and captured a promising young defender from a non-league outfit, but this hardly constituted the major surgery to the squad that one might have expected of a club determined to challenge at the right end of the table.

And the point is that anyone with any knowledge of the club's plight would have not been surprised at the lack of activity on the transfer front (nobody wants to pay the wages of any players we might wish to sell, and we are certainly not in the market for lashing out vast sums on top quality replacements). Perhaps Wright was just talking the situation up in an effort to boost the share price, but these were not the words of a man with his finger on the pulse or an eye of steely realism on the immediate future.

Another thing that has concerned me has been all the talk of a move from Loftus Road. Apparently, the club declined the opportunity to purchase the site at the west end of the ground which would have improved the possibilities of enlarging the present ground. This suggests that the club has already made up its mind to move away from Loftus Road. That in itself would not necessarily be a bad thing. What is surely frustrating for all supporters, however, is the sense that all of this is being decided behind closed doors without proper consultation with the fans. Charlton, who Wright has identified as some sort of template for clubs like QPR, are also considering moving, but they have publicly stated that their fans will be fully consulted before any decision is taken.

And Wright's favoured option seems to be some sort of super stadium to the west of London. Once again this smacks of someone with his head in the clouds. Surely such a move would be one hell of a gamble. The last time Rangers moved to a larger stadium, the old White City, the whole affair ended in tears and the club rapidly moved operations back to Loftus Road. Some might say that this time it would be different, as by moving to the proposed site Rangers would be able to attract more fans, but I see it as a serious gamble with the club's future and worse, a move that could easily rip the heart out of the club.

Then there was the Fiorentina story which appeared in the media a few weeks ago. The proposed link-up with the Italian giants was reported in convincing detail, although the fact that a Fiorentina spokesman was said to have referred to Rangers as "legendary" cast some doubt in my mind. But where did this interesting tale come from? The club remained tight-lipped, only confirming that an approach had been made by an unnamed party and that this was being considered by the board. There was no mention of the affair in the programme for the Huddersfield Town game, or on the web. And yet, it did have an air of plausibility, and one is led to the conclusion that there is some substance to it, and that it was probably leaked by someone at the club. But all this cloak and dagger stuff leaves the fans in the dark. It could be argued that the club has to negotiate in confidence with potential purchasers but once again it appears that Rangers' future is being decided without an input from the fans.

And this is the really disquieting thing. I support Wright essentially because he is a fan and as such should have the interests of the club close to his heart. I have been disappointed at the way things have gone over the last few years but we all make mistakes and I have been willing to give our chairman another chance. But I am worried. He appears to be behaving in a cavalier and unrealistic fashion, relying on the fans' good will but not seeking to involve them in any meaningful way with plans for the future.

Of course there is the example of Jim Gregory to point to as a strong willed, independent chairman who did things his way, whatever the fans thought. But most of Gregory's decisions were the right ones. Having a wealthy autocratic chairman need not be bad news for a club, as Gregory proved. But it is like a monarchy — just because one is lucky enough to have a successful King at one time does not mean that his successor will be as good.

Whilst it is not fair to expect Chris Wright to be another Jim Gregory I feel it is reasonable to expect him to stand by his own words. He claims to be a fan, and yet he does not seek or act on the views of other fans. He points to Charlton as the template Rangers should be following, and yet neither in his actions nor his words does he back this up. Charlton discovered the valuable contribution that supporters could make to the well-being of a club and recognised this by the inclusion of a fans' representative on their board. It is time for Wright to follow this example.
(Peter Tajasque – issue # 131)

Time for recognition

Gavin Peacock threatens to show our strikers how to do it once again by scoring in each game so far (albeit including a rather dodgy effort at Cardiff). Even by his own standards, Peacock's ability to find the back of the net has proved a real bonus, but I still don't think he gets the credit he deserves. His brilliant ability to get a cross in from the tightest of spaces and his general all round effort goes largely unnoticed by fans and media alike. Of all signings in recent years, Peacock's has turned out to prove best value for money by quite some distance.
(Ed – issue # 131)

That's the way it is

Well, we all hoped for a great day out at Fulham — our first visit to Craven Cottage for 17 years, but quite predictably the 6,000+ QPR fans present went home with faces down, with a minority few adding further cause for disappointment by being hell bent on causing trouble. The performance was so poor, even Houston and Harford would turn in their grave — not a sniff on goal or even a period of pressure to raise expectations.

Fortunately, we've got a few excuses to point at, and the defeat could have been far greater, but the fact still remains that QPR just didn't perform. A game to simply forget — as always seems the case when QPR are followed away by a huge travelling support.

Things didn't get much better at Birmingham, but two highly disputed penalties robbed the game of a fair outcome. Time and time again the man in black ruins the game for everyone (well, at least for us on this occasion), and something has got to happen to ensure this game of ours is ruled to the book. The case for video evidence has never been stronger, but will it ever happen?

Some of Gerry Francis' post-match comments of late portray a confused man. When we play and win well (Port Vale), he moans about concentration. When we play poorly (Fulham) he lauds many positive things when I couldn't see any, whilst at Birmingham, he moans about the players' commitment when it was much better than that on display at Fulham, where I don't recall a bad word said about the team. His newest moan has been about how the opposition have million pound players sitting on the bench, when we have none. So what? If they were that good, they wouldn't be on the bench in the first place. Come on Gerry, be more positive — you knew the score when you accepted the job last year.

We all know what a difficult task it is as manager of QPR in this day and age, but just for once could Gerry at least raise his hands and say, 'my tactics were wrong on the day? He got it right at Forest, and told the world about his master plan when reduced to ten men. The same plan didn't work at Fulham though when Steiner got his marching orders, and never looked like doing so. Be frank, be hard, but at least tell it the way it should Gerry.

The meningitis scare that was announced by QPR on the afternoon of Thursday 9th September could so easily have turned out to be the biggest disaster to have ever hit the club. The worst case scenario — and one not too unlikely — could have seen several players dropping dead from the illness. Once taken a grip, meningitis is highly contagious amongst groups of people in close contact, spreading like wildflower before proper medication can be administered to save the life of the victim. We can be incredibly thankful that the form of meningitis to hit George Kulcsar was not the deadly bacterial strain, and that all other players under suspicion at the time were in the clear.

(Ed – issue # 132)

Rambling on

It looks like this season is going to be no different from the last couple, with our main trouble being scoring goals. Mind you when we play with what are virtually six defenders, as we have been (a back five plus Morrow/Wardley just in front of them) then it's no surprise that we are struggling to score. The bad news is that even with all these defenders playing, we still give away dumb goals. Still, the good news is that whereas last season we would have no doubt given away a late goal at Cardiff to draw, we hung on to win and we also got a draw out of the Wolves game where last season you just know we would have lost 1 -0. And then we went and blew this theory out of the water in the home game against Cardiff. Ah well, hopefully it's the exception that proves the rule.

~ ~ ~

Now I still like Chris Kiwomya, he tries hard, he runs like the clappers and he scores the odd goal. I know he misses chances, but let's face it, if he didn't, we would not have picked him up for nothing. When he plays up front with Steiner, we look a different team, but when will Gerry learn that Kiwomya and Gallen are a disaster as a partnership? In the Wolves game, they had at the heart of their defence two of the oldest and slowest defenders in the league. Did we run at them with pace? No, we just stuck Gallen out wide on one wing, Kiwomya on the other and pumped high balls up the middle to no one. It was only when Slade and Scully came on and the others started to run through the middle that we started causing them problems. The entire Loft seemed to see this early on, but it remained totally oblivious to the bench until two thirds of the game had gone.

~ ~ ~

What would we do without Gavin Peacock's goals? It is nice to see him up near the top of the goalscoring charts and breaking Mark Lazarus's record is fine. Mind you, apart from the penalties against Bolton and Cardiff, has he really scored at all? Against Huddersfield, I thought from my angle that he pushed the defender over and fell on top of him causing the defender to head the ball into his own net. The replays on Sky seemed to confirm this, even Ray Ray Super Ray said it looked dubious. The one at Cardiff was going out for a throw in, if it was a shot at all (despite what the programme said) and not a cross and the one against Wolves I don't think would have hit another goal placed alongside the one already there. Still C'est La Vie as the French would say. Last year none of them would have gone in. As long as they do go in, I'm not much bothered how they get there. Classic goals like the first two against Huddersfield are wonderful to see, but if it's an own goal that gets us a point, then who really cares?

~ ~ ~

The big question is, has Gerry started to lose his marbles, or is he a grand master of reverse psychology? One minute I read that he has told the press that with a lot of effort the current squad could aim for a play-off place, the next he is telling them that if we try really hard and things go our way then we might not get relegated. So which is it? I think that the poor soul is getting old like me and can't remember what he said the day before. Of course, that's just my opinion. He could just be getting old like me and can't remember what he said the day before.

Talking of Gerry, when will he start to accept part of the blame when we have a real stinker? He has insisted on playing a back five when any fan of the club can see that we do not have a proper wing-back in the entire squad, with the possible exception of Darlington. Why on earth did we need six defenders again to start the Cardiff game? And why is it that Gerry is always going on about the great young players we have, and yet he doesn't even put them on the bench. If Richard Graham or Leon Jeanne cannot get a place on the bench for a League Cup match against a lower division team when we have already won the away leg, then they might as well pack up and move on.

And while on the subject of the Cardiff game, is it any wonder that so few people come to games like that when the Rangers charge such ridiculous prices? My season ticket in the Loft costs just under ten quid a game for a league match, but to sit in the same seat for the Cardiff game cost me twelve quid. I suppose that the only good thing about the result is that we can't be ripped off like that again this season, assuming we are drawn away in the third round of the FA cup of course.
(Paul Davidson – issue # 132)

Hero or Villain?

Apparently we are more likely to change our spouse/partner than our bank account. Well, I've had a bank account since 1973 and a wife since 1979, but QPR, well, that goes back to 1967. Apart from proving that I am an old bastard, I suppose it shows some degree of loyalty.

This thought came to mind after the first 44 minutes on a sunny afternoon in Nottingham — Darlington sent off, Wright sure to score from the resulting penalty, not a murmur from fellow Rangers fans. Last year, of the five away games I went to, I saw only one goal scored and one player sent off. Next stat, one goal to two off. Suddenly spending every Saturday morning in Barclays with the family seems eminently more sensible. Ian Wank misses, perhaps Barclays can wait.

The next 45 minutes go a long way to show the changes at Rangers since Francis has returned. Under Harford the team would have surrendered. We came back, battled well. Scully, Peacock and Maddix were excellent, but Langley seemed out of sorts and

Wardley will be one for the future. Ready scores, and Peacock could have won it near the end. Great performance.

The future? If only Scully could cross the ball and a forward could head it towards goal, we could possibly make the play-offs.

The share price has doubled, planning permission has been granted for the Wasps ground, the football management side is spot on, so what is Chris Wright doing? Perhaps some more informed reader could enlighten me. We are very fortunate to have a manager so committed to this club, and who can find good players for next to nothing, but not even Francis can build a really successful team based on non-league signings and it would be unfair to expect him to do so.

Wright needs to release sufficient funds to enable Francis to compete effectively in the transfer market. Chris Wright — hero or villain? It's time he let us know. Our future depends on it.

(Paul Vince – issue # 132)

Not so friendly

If this is what Mohammed Al Fayed meant by a friendly welcome for the visit of QPR, then he was obviously spouting out of his arse (as usual). The ludicrous ticket arrangements for the game meant too many QPR fans were forced to snap up tickets in Fulham sections, before Fulham announced they were freeing up more tickets for away fans. Too little, too late. There was always going to be trouble on the  day, but a great deal of it could have been prevented if Fulham had got their act together well in advance of the match.

(Ed – issue # 132)

Moreno Bares All

I was extremely disappointed, as I'm sure you all were, with the recent result against Fulham. What is it about QPR that every time we take a substantial amount of support away from home the performance just doesn't live up to the expectation of the massed ranks of Rangers fans?

Huge amounts of fans went to the FA Cup ties against Manchester United and Wimbledon in recent times yet the performances were pretty mediocre. Is it because the players are not used to the large vociferous numbers cheering for them and just freeze on the day or are they just not up for it? The only entertaining high spot at Fulham wasn't the crowd trouble that flared up early in the game but the chap who threw a traffic cone 20 feet towards their fans after the match... if we ever needed someone to replace Geoff Capes in the Olympics then this was your man.

~ ~ ~

On the subject of crap performances there can't have been many to rival the Worthington Cup game against Cardiff City at home. I'm sure that the players know that the financial plight of the club depends on how far they can go in one or either of the two cup competitions, so why the below-par showing? This just leaves the FA Cup which means that we'll probably be knocked out by some non-league minnow away from home. I had a feeling that John Hallworth, the City 'keeper, was going to do well in the penalty shoot-out and he proved it wasn't a fluke by saving a penalty against John Hartson of Wimbledon in the following round.

~ ~ ~

It seems that I've become a little bit of a celebrity now that I've appeared in the 'Mars' television commercial. For those that haven't seen it the story is about a young boy who dreams of the Loft choir chanting his name, then low and behold it happens with me and his mum leading the chanting for Jeffrey. A lot of people have been coming up to me complimenting my acting ability... at least that's what I think they've been doing... It was fun to do and at least I got paid for the three hours shooting time it took, and I get recognised in the street — just the other day I heard a wino shouting "hey it's that one off the commercial," — feeling quite smug it suddenly dawned on me that in his alcohol stained memory he might just be getting me confused with the yellow techno puppet on the 'Levis' ad ... oh well.

~ ~ ~

I can't believe how absolutely galling the One-2-One commercial starring Vinnie Jones is. With a touch of a button his wife, son, agent, ex-manager, his bloody ex-football manager, his midget jockey friend and even his fishing partner can always get hold of him on his mobile phone, which begs the question, why is it that everyone could speak to him yet Gerry Francis couldn't track him down!

~ ~ ~

Have the referees declared an open season on QPR? I only ask because some of the penalty decisions awarded against us recently — the two penalties which Birmingham City had and the one for Bolton Wanderers — looked decidedly dodgy. I only point this out as Rob Steiner was sent off for 'diving'... pray tell what was Holdsworth doing then? He looked as if he was shot by the gunman from the grassy knoll. I'm not surprised that the players' heads went down after the second penalty at St Andrews — if two highly debatable decisions had gone against me mine would've too. I was standing next to the editor at the Fulham game when the Steiner incident occurred and couldn't tell if he had taken a dive or not — this isn't because I'm sitting on the fence on this decision but that we could not see one third of the pitch tucked away as we were in the left hand corner!

(Moreno Ferrari – issue # 132)

Uber October

What a great month it's been so far. Unbeaten in four games, including winning the last three, whilst improving our awful away record no end in the process. After losing at Birmingham, prospects didn't look great but we've bounced back superbly, and any doubts we were in for another relegation struggle can now be firmly put to rest. At the same time though, we have to keep our feet on the ground. Three straight wins do not make a season, and it's important the home games against Portsmouth and Birmingham do not see a return to losing ways. All the same, it feels good to be a QPR supporter once again, as a healthy position in the league table stares at me after a great night at West Brom.

(Ed – issue # 133)

The numbers just don't add up

Driving home from work the other week I was pretty stunned to hear our director Nick Blackburn being interviewed by Tom Watt on 'Talk Radio'. I think his remarks adequately sum up the ambition in the club at the moment. He said that the team he admired the most and wants us to be like is... Charlton Athletic. I personally find this a bit of a blow. For the entire 35 years I have supported the Rangers, Charlton have been above us in league terms about three times. Now we are trying to emulate them.

The only saving grace I can see about hoping to be like Charlton is at least they do not appear to be in such severe financial shit as us. I just cannot believe that the company debts have gone up from £5.5million to £9.5million in just 12 months, as was announced recently. All we have read this season is how well the club has done to reduce the debt and that there is light at the end of the tunnel after all and then we are hit with a number like this.

Gerry Francis is quoted as saying that the figures are not as bad as they seem, it is just that the accountants are looking at the figures "in a different way." I reckon they are.

One thing for sure is that the AGM this year is a not-to-be-missed event. It certainly won't be such a pleasant little gathering as last years was, not with a debt like this to be explained away. Mind you, let's not kid ourselves, explain it away they will. I'm willing to bet that some bright spark accountant at the AGM will have everyone believing that we are making a profit, not a loss, and that none of the debts are anything to do with Wasps whatsoever. After all they did last year. One day we will find out the exact state of our finances. Yeah right and one day Chris Wright will explain why on earth he let Ray Harford sign Adebloodymole Bankbloodykole on a £100,000 a year contract. No wonder we are in so much trouble when 'players' like him are making that much money!

(Paul Davidson – issue # 133)

He's at it again!

"Last season, we'd have crumbled after conceding an early goal, but we are showing much greater resolve nowadays," so said Gerry Francis after the Ipswich game. So what went wrong at Fulham and Birmingham?! This continual comparison to last season has been overused to beyond the limit now, even when it barely makes any sense. So let's hear no more of it, from Gerry and our supporters, please?

Poor old Gerry was criticised by Danny Kelly on his talk show recently as being, "One of the worst managers ever," on the basis of his time as boss at Spurs. Harsh words indeed, especially coming from the man who voted In The Loft fanzine of the year in 1997 for a reason that escapes me even now.

Gerry's time at Spurs was hardly a success, but certainly not a failure. In his time as boss at QPR, there isn't much evidence to back up Kelly's claims either. One thing is for sure, if Ray Harford was still in charge of QPR, we'd currently be plying our trade in Division 2.

(Ed – issue # 133)

Another George in the news

The failure to sign George Ndah for a reported £1million from Swindon Town I'm sure will turn out best for all parties concerned. Two goals without a game (Fulham and Birmingham), and panic sets in. The trouncing of Ipswich should put on hold Gerry's search for a striker, and I don't believe we could acquire that sort of money to pay for Ndah or anyone else in the same price bracket.

Whilst it would make sense to try and sell off some of our surplus stock before entering the transfer market, the problem is of course no one appears to be making any offers for our players. I'm sure Wright and Francis would accept any half-decent offers for the likes of Slade, Rowland, Plummer, Bankole, Scully, Morrow, Kulcsar, Breaker, Murray and probably even Gallen, but there are no bidders. The wages of these 10 players — all currently fringe players to the first team — would probably be in the region of £80,000 a month, or more or less £1million a year. You don't need to tell Chris Wright that's a hell of a lot of money for so little in return, and it's also a figure that doesn't need adding to.

(Ed – issue # 133)

One year on...

On the 17th October 1998 we made the long trip to Huddersfield, mainly to welcome Gerry back to Rangers. We were 24th in the First Division. The weather was cold, wet and windy and the football was even worse. Sunday morning 12 months later a 4-1 win at Ipswich, sun shining and 10th in the First Division. But for injury, probably 8 of the team who played at Huddersfield would have been on duty at Portman Road. What a difference a year makes.

We all expected Gerry to wheel and deal, but Sheron has been the only major exit. I suspect many more have not left because of their high wages as reported many times in ITL. On the positive side, perhaps they stayed because they saw a better future for Rangers (no, I don't believe that either). Whatever the reason, it's credit to Gerry.

Whilst I liked Sheron, he had to go — and Steiner may prove a better player. He is the first number 9 to score in two consecutive games (home and away) since Sheron (Bolton at home, Crewe away last November) and the first number 9 to score two away goals in one match (other than Sheron) since Spencer against Man City in April '97. Gallen is QPR and Kiwomya is OK, but I'm more likely to score with Posh Spice than either of those two hitting the back of the net at the moment.

Peacock leads by example, and it's good to see Wardley on the goal trail. The last time Rangers scored 4 away in the League and won was in the 93/4 season — both at West Ham Norwich in March. We went on to finish 9th in the Premiership — when will we be back?

(Paul Vince – issue # 133)

Big support equals better chances of winning?

Following the terrific support at Fulham, it got me thinking — when was the last time QPR won away from home in front of more than 3,000 visiting supporters? I certainly can't remember it happening in this decade. QPR's top ten games in the 1990s for visiting supporters have produced the following results. All figures are approximate, and apologies if I've missed any matches out.

1) Wimbledon, FA Cup 5th round, 96/97. Score: 1-2, away fans - 13,000.
2) Manchester United, FA Cup 6th round, 94/95. Score: 0-2, away fans - 7,000.
3) Fulham, Division 1, 99/00. Score 0-1, away fans - 6,000.
3) Chelsea, Premiership, 92/93. Score: 0-1, away fans - 6,000.
5) Watford, Division 1, 98/99. Score: 1 -2, away fans - 5,000.
6) Port Vale, Division 1, 98/99. Score: 0-2, away fans - 4,000.
7) Coventry City, Premiership, 95/96. Score: 0-1, away fans - 4,000.
8) Southampton, FA Cup 3rd round, 91/92. Score: 0-1, away fans - 4,000.
9) Liverpool, FA Cup 6th round replay, 89/90. Score: 0-1, away fans - 3,500.
10) Chelsea, Division 1, 91/92. Score: 1-2, away fans - 3,500.

...who remembers us having 13 supporters at Sheffield Wednesday for a Simod Cup tie in 1989 — and winning!
(Ed – issue # 133)

No one likes us, we don't care... or do we?

Are we becoming the new Millwall and if so, why? No one likes Millwall, or at least that's what they would have us believe. Nowadays no one seems to like us either. We are ignored completely by Sky TV for their televised matches, we cannot buy a decision from a referee it seems this season (although unlike Fulham we probably haven't tried), and now the rest of the media world appears to hate us as well. What the hell have we done that's so wrong?

I must admit I am confused as to why not one of our games is on TV. I know we can be pretty crap, but just look at some of the matches they have chosen ahead of us — Port Vale v Grimsby and Crewe v Tranmere. Come on, be serious. I heard that Gerry Francis had upset some of the Sky bosses when he was Spurs manager, but that can't be the reason surely, can it? If it is then we may have to wait forever to see us on the box.

The referee thing would be becoming a bit of a joke if it weren't so serious. Everybody that falls over anywhere near our penalty area is given at least a free kick, away from home it's normally a penalty, no matter how hard they elbow one of our defenders. After the Blackburn game, wow it's 'shall we or shan't we' send off the other teams' goalkeeper. The answer — 'nah lets not bother'. A truly amazing decision that one. If Filan didn't bring Kiwomya down, or the referee didn't see the ball hit his arm, then why did he give us a free kick? When he made contact with Kiwomya he had to be the last man, because Kiwomya had gone past the two defenders involved. Why didn't he send him off? Simple, he bottled it. The fact that Filan then went on to save Rovers on several occasions only made it all the more galling for us. Then, to cap it all, the report on the game carried by the Daily Telegraph on the Monday morning appears to blame us, the fans, for the problem. How the writer of the report, a Nicholas Marling, had the bottle to put his name to it, I shall never know. At least I suppose he had more bottle than the referee, John Kirkby.

The report starts as follows, and I quote: 'It's official. The average fan is blinkered, so full of prejudice and hate that he would want to see a football match ruined by a debatable decision to send off an opponent, even if it meant his own team having an unfair advantage. The vitriol that poured forth from Loftus Road when referee John Kirkby made the courageous decision to keep John Filan on the pitch was an education of a sort for the party of schoolboys in the stand.' Yeah right, I can't imagine schoolboys spouting obscenities at a football match, can you?

He goes on to say that the incident was far from 'cut and dried' and that Rovers manager Brian Kidd was "surprised that people thought he should have been sent off." Now that's a surprise. No it is, really. Nowadays I thought it compulsory for managers to say that they had not seen the incident in question. I often wonder if the managers still actually go to the games at all, the amount of 'incidents' they claim not to see.

But back to the report. How can a professional sports writer imagine that we all go to football every week to watch a good game? We go to see our team win first, last and always.

And as for us having an 'unfair advantage', what does this sad hack seriously expect? Are we supposed to clap politely when two extremely dodgy penalties are given against us, or laugh cheerfully when a referee is so biased against us as to make a football match a total farce? I didn't notice the Birmingham or Fulham fans objecting to getting an unfair advantage. I don't suppose Mr Harling did either, but then again he was probably not at football those weekends, he was probably writing drivel about a sport he understands more, maybe rowing or deck quoits, something completely devoid of passion. It is the passion about football that makes it the greatest game in the world, although Mr Harling might disagree.

I remember many years ago a story about a reporter from one of the tabloids, the Mirror I think it was, getting banned from Loftus Road for writing some load of cobblers about us. We didn't get a decent report in the paper for donkeys years afterwards. I sincerely hope that the club takes the same action against Mr Harling. We surely won't miss the odd one-week in fifty that they deign to write about us.
(Paul Davidson – issue # 133)

End of the century? It's nothing special...

So sang Blur a few years ago, and Squeeze as well, actually — a nice acoustic number, and to be honest, I have to agree with them. I was going to select my QPR team of the century, but realised I couldn't do anyone before the late 60s any justice whatsoever. So I was going to go for a team of the 90s, but realised that arguing over which two out of Darren Peacock, Paul Parker, Alan McDonald and Danny Maddix should play in the centre of defence was just too dull.

So, looking for something to write about and having nothing better to do I trawled the QPR internet pages and read all the chat from fans who also had nothing better to do. And it emerged that the two burning topics of the moment seem to be the fate of Paul Murray and the state of our various strikers. No one was debating about whether Alan McDonald should be ahead of Paul Parker in the team of the 90s because of his outstanding commitment to QPR. So, bowing to the masses, I thought I'd offer my view.

The Ruby Murray debate has been cropping up every once in a while for about three years now. In my opinion he has been unfairly treated by all of the four managers he has had experience with since arriving at QPR at the start of the current turbulent period. First he had Wilkins who almost didn't buy him for fear of being edged out of his own precious midfield spot. Rioch and Houston insisted on either playing him as a substitute or bringing him off after an hour when he was our best player. Harford simply played him out of position, and then he had that awful injury.

The rumour is that he and Gerry are not best mates so he's not getting in the team. I've also heard that he's sulking in the reserves and not doing anything to help himself get picked. But this is just idle gossip. I, like many others, love Muzza. But after his injury he failed to regain the form that he previously displayed. He gave the ball away too often and in dangerous areas, his trademark long passes started missing their targets more frequently and he stopped making those dangerous forward runs. On top of that, Stuart Wardley, despite a couple of quiet games (only to be expected for one so inexperienced), has done enough to keep Murray out with his surging runs, determined play and, not least, his valuable height and strength. Another argument is to rest Langley, particularly as he has not impressed greatly recently, but I think that as far as possible we need to persevere with Wardley and Langley, and not damage their confidence by dropping them as soon as they have a dodgy game. Murray could still get in the side, but I fear his heart — despite his obvious love of QPR and us, the fans, may not be in it.

As regards our forward line, I share the frustration of the many fans that believe our approach work deserves more than it is currently producing. A great striker can turn a mediocre team into a great one, even a poor one into a comfortable mid-table side. He can inspire confidence, gain valuable points when they aren't deserved, and (obviously) provide a superior goal difference.

QPR have been scratching around for the 'new Les' since, well, almost as soon as he left us, and without much success. There can be little doubt that if Gallen had been properly nurtured at that time, he wouldn't be the shadow of the player that first broke into the first team that he is now. And so Gallen got injured and Dichio's head grew to enormous proportions. And John Spencer came and scored a load of goals (again, briefly making us look like a half-decent team) and Sheron was occasionally successful. But none of them came close to replacing Les.

Which brings us to the current debate surrounding our favoured three strikers (Steiner, Kiwomya, Gallen), and our three fringe strikers (Slade, Jeanne, Graham).

While I admit to laughing uncontrollably at the suggestion by some of our players that super Robbie Steiner might force his way into the Sweden squad for Euro 2000, I can't understand the criticisms of this man that come from some sections of the crowd. Rarely have I seen a forward so committed to the cause, so willing to fight for his team, and so keen to encourage younger players like Jeanne. Criticisms about his pace are mainly unfounded — he's a lot quicker than he looks, he is an excellent, if seemingly incredibly lucky dribbler, he holds the ball up well and he wins his fair share of balls in the air. My only doubt is over his fitness, as he seems rather injury prone. His skill, determination and strength can be amply demonstrated by the superb goal he had disallowed at the end of the Tranmere game when the linesman forgot you can't be offside from a throw in. When he plays we look dangerous, when he doesn't we don't. It's that simple, and while I don't pretend to believe that he's the kind of striker who'll get thirty in a season and propel us into the Premier League (that player is one that we're unlikely to ever see), at £215,000 Steiner makes superb value and I'd take him over Akinbiyi for £3million any time.

Other people seem more interested in getting Jeanne, Graham, even Mahoney-Johnson into the side, but the main arguments revolve around Kevin Gallen, as they have done for the last few years. I remember someone once writing (it may even have been the editor of this publication) years ago that when Gallen finally made his first team debut, we would see the birth of the greatest British striker since Gary Lineker. Brave words. And for a while it looked as if they might even come true thanks to his raw confidence and the tremendous support of Les Ferdinand (will his ghost ever leave?). But Kev never recovered after Les left and was damned again by that injury. Initially everyone backed him — he's a local lad and deserved it. But when he turned in one goal-less performance after another the fans in turn began to turn, if that's not too many turns. He still has his supporters, but I think there are many more people who have simply lost patience. There were complaints that he was booed against Tranmere — although I didn't hear any — and while that is unfair on him, I can see the point the fans were making. Kevin hasn't had a decent game for QPR for about a year now, and there is a strong feeling that with Jeanne and Graham knocking on the door, his chance has come and gone.

Maybe the answer is to loan Gallen out. His passing ability and vision is at times superb, yet his eye for goal has all but disappeared and his confidence is extremely low. Perhaps a spell for a lower league side might result in a few goals and we might get the Gallen back that we all want. But I don't think that will work. I used to think that it would, and I used to think that if we sold him then he would score loads of goals for his new club and we'd be gutted. But now I don't.

Now I think the time has come to sell Kevin Gallen to the highest bidder — if, indeed, there are any. And the same might be said of Paul Murray. He was superb for us at times, but his continual failure over three years to cement a place in the team suggests to me that something is wrong. I did believe that it was his feud with Quashie, but he's gone and still Muzza hasn't made his mark, so maybe there is an attitude problem. It's a shame because these two were and are two of my favourite players and I hate to see them struggling, but QPR are not, as certain players and fans might think, a charity.

Overall, though, we are doing all right, especially compared with this time last year, when we were rock solid bottom. We can't expect some massive improvement in such a short time and we shouldn't expect too much too soon. The midfield looks good, although it tends to fade, the forward line is dangerous when Steiner is there and Kiwomya is on song, and the defence looks solid... sometimes. Which brings us back to the start: I'd definitely have Macca in there, and maybe Maddix, but perhaps Parker, or did he leave before 1990? I don't know anymore.
(Dan Trelfer – issue # 133)

Blasts from the past

I nearly crashed the car on the way to the Blackburn game when not one but three West Ham fans phoned 'Talk Radio' to congratulate the Trevor Sinclair on his inclusion in the England squad. What got me was that they all said that it was entirely due to his consistency. Two words I never saw in the same sentence when he was here were 'Sinclair' and 'consistency', unless of course the words 'lack of' were included. He had some great games for us and the goal against Barnsley I shall always remember, but consistency, never. Yet more testimony to the managerial qualities, or lack of them, of Ray Ray Super Ray, I suppose.

Why did a section of our fans boo Darren Peacock during that Blackburn game? He was one of the best defenders we have had in recent years and he never wanted to leave. He was sold by Thompson, probably to finance the building of a new toilet in the Director's Bar or something similar. I can still remember driving back down the M6 from working in Preston when I heard the news he had been sold. I pulled into the first services, pulled both my little QPR kit dangler and car sticker out of the back window, ripped them in half, threw them in a waste bin and drove off. I swore I would not go back to Loftus Road until Thompson went and I was as good as my word. Or nearly. I lasted the best part of four whole days before I cracked and gave in!

Similarly poor old Rufus was the butt of some serious booing during the game at Fulham. Like Peacock he did not want to leave the Rangers and said so publicly at the time. You could never accuse old Rufus of not putting 100% in when he played for us, sometimes a lot more, so why the hell boo the man? Sometimes I am almost ashamed of some of our fans. I can only imagine that these 'fans' never saw the players in question play for us. Boo Seaman yes, he was a skunk, as was Spencer. Boo Sinclair if you like, maybe even Sinton (although there is some serious doubt about the circumstances under which he left), but don't boo Brevett or Peacock, they never had anything but good words to say about our club when they left.
(Paul Davidson – issue # 133)

Be positive Gerry!

A major gripe amongst fans this season has been Gerry's use of substitutes and tactical awareness. The fact remains, we've done well so far with what we've got and employing the 3-5-2 formation. As for the use of substitutes, sometimes they work (Stockport), usually they don't (Palace) and sometimes we never get to find out (on numerous occasions).

Even if we were 15 points clear at the top, fans would still find certain things to complain about, and why is it we always have to have a boo-boy in the side? What has Keith Rowland done exactly to annoy so many people?

My point here is, QPR are doing far better than most fans could wish for this season — let's not follow Gerry's lead and continue to feed on the negatives rather than the positives. If watching QPR was always the most perfect of experiences, it would be bloody boring. We'd all like to think we have the answers to everything, but nobody does.
(Ed – issue # 134)

Take me to the place I love

Shall we take the kids away for half-term asked she who must be obeyed. No, I said. Rangers home to Portsmouth and Birmingham. Four points to be sure.

I thought we were unlucky against Portsmouth — we could easily have won by at least two goals. The first goal against Birmingham restored the balance of good fortune, and then CK scored an excellent goal — that will keep him in the team for at least the next eight matches (I'm still not sure he is the answer). Without Peacock I though the midfield lacked penetration and a fair deal of creativity compounded by Langley's inability to rediscover last year's form. Birmingham score twice and to make matters worse they were scored by a forward making his debut for his new club within 24 hours of signing. The second time this has happened this season — a certain Ian Wright scoring for Forest.

For the Birmingham game, instead of our usual seats we find ourselves directly behind the Directors Box (£25 a seat and still no leg room). Eyes began to wander. On the R's side Gary Parker (Leicester) — who leaves 5 minutes before the end. On the Birmingham side John Wark, Kenny Jackett, Tony Parkes, Gavin Peacock and father. Jackett, according to The Mail, looking at Rob Steiner. I can also report Chris Wright is alive — getting quite animated when one or two things went wrong.

Watching the Stockport match on teletext, three down and yet still a feeling we could come back. We did and all the better because Gallon scored two — a rejuvenated Gallen would save the club a fortune and perhaps allow Gerry to play Gallen and Steiner up front with CK playing just behind the front two. Whilst our recent away record is excellent, three home draws is not good enough — a more attacking formation should help our home form improve.
(Paul Vince – issue # 134)

Rambling on

I wrote at some length in the last issue of this esteemed magazine that the Rangers do not seem to be getting the rub of the green from the media this season. This is now in danger of reaching epic proportions and I am becoming more than a little paranoid about it.

Following our superb win at West Brom, I thought I would stay up and watch the highlights on Carlton TV's midweek football show. Having sat through over 25 minutes 'highlights' of Fulham getting stuffed by Wolves and about the same length of action from the Ipswich v Charlton game, I thought that maybe they wouldn't show too much of our game as time was running out. I was absolutely staggered though to see our game highlights encapsulated in three seconds as they were going through the results right at the end of the programme. That's right, three seconds (I was recording the programme and timed it). You could just about make out Breaker crossing the ball, you could plainly see Wardley nodding it in and then half way through his goal celebrations the pictures ended. Now I know that we are not the most glamorous team in London, but three seconds of highlights I think is disgraceful. Especially given the fact that of the three London first division teams in action that night we were the only ones to get any sort of positive result.

I only hope that the next time Carlton asks to show one of our matches, we tell them to piss off. We won't though 'cos I believe that they pay us money to show them and we aren't gonna turn down cash now are we?

To cap it all off, the Daily Telegraph (who really do seem to have a vendetta against us this season) treated the game as if it hardly happened. There were four First Division reports the next morning in their southern edition, Fulham and Charlton naturally being two of them and the other two were of northern teams. The ultimate insult though was that they hadn't even credited us with the three points we had won in their published league table and we were about six places below what we should have been!

~ ~ ~

I noticed in the Birmingham programme that Ross Weare got his first mention of the season, he was mentioned in an article about what good young non-league players we have uncovered. It's just a shame that they omitted to tell us where the hell he is and who if anyone he is playing for.

~ ~ ~

Well, who would have thought it? Kevin Gallen. Blimey! After everyone at the club had written him off, the boy has started to come good. I did not go to either game at Blackburn or Stockport as I was away with the London Towers in Croatia (pose, pose). To be absolutely honest, I am not sure I would have gone anyway, but what a couple of performances. I am not sure how many times I have seen us win north of Birmingham, but I know it's not as many as it should have been. And then to come back away from home, oop north from 3 goals down, magnificent. It is just amazing what a little confidence can do for you. The team is more or less exactly the same as the one early in the season that couldn't score goals to save its life, now it's banging them in like there's no tomorrow. Great stuff and long may it continue.

Talking of Kevin Gallen, what a lovely ovation he got as he ran onto the pitch against Man City. I suppose it's difficult not to like Kevin, he is and always has been a QPR fan through and through and I suppose everybody deep down really wants him to succeed at the club. I must admit though it has been a painful last two years, but let's all just hope that is all behind him now. The way he sprinted up the right wing and smashed that lovely cross into the box late in the game, it just might be after all. Bring on the Magic Hat!

WALKING WITH DINOSAURS

This week's programme features the Dowieasaurus, one of the last of the great dinosaurs - a remarkable species from the late 20" century.

For a relatively lumbersome creature, the Dowieasaurus could be found wondering the great planes of the Premiership fields. It rubbed shoulders with the greatest dinosaurs of its time, although evidence suggests the Dowieasaurus was often an easy target for fiercesome predators.

Towards the end of its lifespan, the Dowieasaurus was reduced to ploughing the rotten trenches of the Nationwide Greens, often failing to have the ability or agility to procreate, thus leading to its extinction. This almost lifelike computer generated picture show how the Dowieasaurus may have looked (right) - this painting by man on the walls of a cave in southern England was recently uncovered, aiding us greatly with our research.

PRESS RELEASE

(Issue # 134)

It also has to be said what a great part in our revival Karl Ready has played this season. So long the butt of so many jokes (mostly mine I have to admit) and so much abuse, but he has risen above it all (literally) and is not only playing the best football of his career, but in my humble opinion looks to be worthy of a recall to the Welsh squad.

~ ~ ~

What a masterstroke putting Stan the Man in the programme every game with some betting tips. Surely no one on the face of the planet can know more about betting than our Stan. His predictions in the first one were so uncanny (not only getting the score and first scorer right, but naming the other scorer as well) that my missus wants to know if he will fill in her pools coupon every week!
(Paul Davidson – issue # 134)

Our George

I saw George Kulcsar before the Crystal Palace game, looking fit and healthy (or at least as fit and healthy for someone that has always looked like a refugee can be). Of course, it would be nice of the club to keep us up to date with his progress once in a while...
(Ed – issue # 134)

The R's are going up (oh bugger!)

Once again I've been trawling in a bored kind of way through the numerous QPR news and chat sites searching for bits of interest, and apart from the obsessive and frankly stupid tirades against Rob Steiner (and in one case Jermaine Darlington), the supposed resurrection of Kevin Gallen, and Gerry's reluctance to use substitutes before it's too late, most people are discussing the p-word.

Now call me a misguided fool if you like, but the last thing I want us to do is get promotion, at least, not this season. I'm not that worried, actually, as I can't really see it happening — as soon as we get a couple of injuries we'll soon consolidate a comfortable position around the 10th or 12th mark. But a lot of people seem to be getting carried away with our recent run of form and are already tub-thumping on about our Premiership credentials. At the forefront of these people is every mascot's favourite player, Danny Maddix, who recently stated that he wasn't interested in the play-offs, because the talk of the Rangers dressing room was of automatic promotion.

Quite mad talk of course, but you've got to applaud this kind of blind optimism especially when it comes from someone apart from Gavin Peacock (who has been tipping us to go up every year since we went down). And as glad as I am that the players are dreaming happily of the Premiership rather than sweating every night about relegation (no, I'm sure most of them really do care), I really hope we don't pull off the promotion 'dream'.

Now a few years ago, I went to Ipswich to see a then even more lowly than usual Walsall play a then mediocre (so what's changed?) Ipswich team in the FA Cup. But as me and my Brummie mate knocked back our cold Becks a guard walked in, took one look at us, smiled with menace, and with a lot of satisfaction told us that the game had been called off because of a frozen pitch.

We went to the ground anyway, and found a few sympathetic Ipswich thugs who were annoyed that the game had been called off and were drunkenly demanding to see someone called 'Sheepshags' (I later realised that his real name was Sheepshanks), and trying to claim some money back for travel. When it was finally clear that Sheepshanks wasn't going to make an appearance, our new Ipswich friends said they'd buy us a drink because they thought we'd come all the way from Walsall. Anyway, the point of the story is that we asked them whether they thought they might get promotion that year, and they all said that they didn't want to because they were much happier in the First Division.

At the time I thought they were mad. Why would anyone not want to be in the Premiership? QPR were fighting for their lives that season, and I couldn't think of anything worse than relegation to the bloody Endsleigh. Then we got relegated, and after a season of singing 'You're not very good,' in that superior way we all did to teams visiting us, then watching them beat us because of our players' appalling attitude wasn't much different from our own, and only gradually realising that we weren't actually very good either, I started to understand exactly what they were talking about.

I started to lose interest in the Premiership. Slowly I began to take more interest in the division we were actually in. Sure, the fact that we were sliding quickly towards the bottom end of it helped focus my mind, but everything was starting to seem far more real than the dreamland of the Premiership.

Teams at this level could actually beat any other team in the league — home or away. Teams like Bradford, Watford and Barnsley stood great chances of gaining promotion (and did) because of the financial constraints most teams had to operate under, making this league a more even playing field. And now I love it, this league. Of course I went nuts at the Crystal Palace debacle — they were three of the worst decisions I have ever seen as a sequence (if nothing else, how could Lynch justify booking Kiwomya on the second occasion when he was clearly being held back by a Palace player and was in possession of the ball? Yet the free kick went to Palace and Kiwomya was sent off). And with one minute remaining and in front of a vociferous crowd, with the game safe, he stupidly decides to send Ready off for what was at worst an innocuous challenge which may not have even been in the box, and Harper looked like getting to the ball first so it wasn't a goalscoring opportunity anyway.

Now, this ref was kicked out of the Premiership but given to us — yet another reason to hate Premiership football — if he's not good enough, surely he's not good enough for our league either. But secretly, deep down, I was quite pleased about losing. It stopped our run, and hopefully stopped all this rubbish about us being promotion contenders. The fact is that we are a marginally better side than last year, but because this league is so tight we have dramatically improved our position through the hard work of the team. But I think we all know that if by some Watford-like fluke we found ourselves back in the top league next season, we'd have a miserable time.

I'm more than happy to finish about tenth this year, get rid of the dead wood currently floating around our club that's desperate to hitch an easy ride on the Rangers tidal wave (yes, I am rushing this last bit), and bring in a bit more quality. A goalkeeper, a centre back and a striker are needed to enable us to launch an assault on the title.

Let's not expect miracles, and let's enjoy the fact that we can go into every match this season with a reasonable chance of winning. But let's not ruin it by trying too hard to join the primadonnas, money-mad tub-thumpers, and Ken Bates in the top league. In my view, this is the real English league right here where we are, where coaching, tactics, and decent scouting can still overcome the dull one-dimensional approach of throwing money at every problem.
(Dan Trelfer – issue # 134)

Defensive crisis

As we go to print, rumours are rife that Phil Babb is about to join us on loan to help solve our defensive crisis. The stumbling block appears to be his wages (no surprises there), but if Gerry needs some advice on the player, he could always get Matthew Rose to ask Roy Evans for advice — after all, they did use to be neighbours in Albert Square before Rose got banged up.

Seriously though, the problems in defence could well jeopardise the good work that's been done so far this season. Maddix and Ready are out "for a long while yet," according to Gerry. Ready has a trapped nerve in his back, whilst the problem with Maddix is less clear, but annoyingly both injuries were picked up in the same week of training rather than during a game.

Added to this. Morrow will be out of action for at least two months after dislocating his shoulder against Barnsley, and both Chris Plummer and Rose have been playing with injuries when they really should be on the treatment table. With Ian Baraclough soon to start a suspension, we really are down to the bare bones. Even so, Wardley was bought as a central defender and should provide adequate cover, whilst Breacker should be able to fill in as a centre back if required. To sign another defender probably isn't wise considering the numbers we have in defence (when fit) and our financial situation, so if we do manage to secure Babb or any other defender on loan, this would be the best action short-term.

There's no such problems up front though where the signing of Sammy Koejoe makes it nine professional strikers on our books — Steiner, Kiwomya, Gallen, Slade, Dowie, Mahoney-Johnson, Weare, Currie and now Koejoe. Was his signing necessary? Can we really afford to keep so many strikers? Considering since when Gerry took over as manager he has had only two offers for any of our players (Sheron from Barnsley — accepted, and a £300,000 bid for Scully turned down from an unnamed club), it must be frustrating for him to not be able to shift out a few players before he can start buying. It's hardly a case of squad rebuilding, more squad saturation.

With three away defeats on the trot, Rangers aren't quite 'back' yet, but we're still in a good position in the league, still unbeaten at home and nobody is getting an easy game from us. Few can complain how this season has gone so far, but it has been full of 'if only's'. With Manchester City suffering defeats in their last three games, it proves anyone can beat anyone in this division, which always makes it a far more interesting league than the Premiership.
(Ed – issue # 135)

Rambling on

London derbies. I remember when we used to be good in London derbies, very good in fact. Back in the eighties the London Evening Standard (or was it the old News?) used to publish league tables as to how all the teams in London had done that particular season in London derbies and we always seemed to be in the top two or three. Nowadays if they published such a table we would surely be bottom. Apart from the glorious last game of last season against Palace, I have a feeling that the last time we won a London derby was the game against West Ham on the day we were relegated from the Premiership. Now I fully realise that we do not play as many as we used to in the top division, but surely we should be doing better than we currently are.

If you include Watford as a London club, that makes it to my calculation just one win in fifteen attempts. I only really mention this, as we desperately need to reverse this trend for February 26th when we play Fulham. There are fans of many teams to whom the results of the matches with their local rivals mean more than the rest of the season put together, Spurs-Arsenal for instance, but I don't think that this has ever been the case at the Bush, whatever the seemed rivalry with Chelsea. This season however, with a safe place in the division seemingly almost assured, but with little chance of making the play-offs, the game with Fulham is going to reach epic proportions. After the way things went at their place, we just cannot afford to lose this game. We only have the home game against Charlton just before Christmas to try to reverse this trend in time, so let's hope for a bit more luck than we have had lately. It's starting to get important!

~ ~ ~

So the latest theory is that the linesman that missed the blatant offside at Crystal Palace probably confused a fan wearing a replica shirt with one of our players. OK, I can live with that, I would just like to know exactly which of our players he thought looked like a sixteen stone drunk with a beer belly, standing ten feet up in the air!

~ ~ ~

So Ross Weare is not only alive and well, but is actually being given a chance in the first team. Apparently he has had a back injury that even required an operation and has been out since the summer. I only know this because of the internet, not a word was there in the programme until he had already played two first team games. Personally I think that this is disgraceful. What's the point of having a matchday programme if it doesn't give you the news on injuries etc? I wondered if Weare was even still at the club for a couple of months so little was the news.

~ ~ ~

Now I like Rob Steiner. I know that some fans don't and given his propensity for missing quality goalscoring chances, I can understand that. I do however think that he holds the ball up very well and his distribution for a big man is excellent. Let's face it, if he could stick the ball in the net more regularly, he would be playing in the Premiership. Having said that, I wish the big fella would stay on his feet a bit more. He tends to fall down like a sack of potatoes if anyone gets near him in the box. It may be all right for the likes of Bergkamp, Ginola and Shearer to drop like they have been shot, playing in the Premiership, but we don't want that and certainly don't need that in the First Division. So please Gerry, tell him to stop it, it's embarrassing.

~ ~ ~

I, along with many others wondered why Simon Crane had left a huge company like Coca Cola to come and work for QPR as Group Chief Executive. Having gone through my copy of the Loftus Road accounts it becomes pretty obvious. With a basic salary for the year of £106,000, a 'performance related bonus' of £20,000, and 'benefits' of £35,000, no wonder he left Coca Cola. Most disturbing of all I find, is that he was also paid no less than £90,000 for 'other payments', making a total of £251,000. Not a bad year for Mr Crane then. No doubt Chris Wright and the other 'suits' will give a little arrogant laugh that anyone should question the worth of such a man to the club. If they only understood that fans that pay their hard earned money week in and week out find it offensive that a director should be paid over a quarter of a million pounds a year, then they might begin to run the club properly. No bloody wonder the club has been in so much financial shit the last few years, would you seriously let any of our director's play with your bank account?

(Paul Davidson – issue # 135)

"Look who it is, it's, er, thingamajig"
— name-dropping Ed on his brush with the rich and semi-famous

Ever since discovering the potency of Red Bull and vodka (thanks Mat), not to mention the damage it does to my wallet, my nights out have become stranger and stranger recently.

So there we were, enjoying a few beers at 'Bad Bobs' in Covent Garden (£1 a time on Tuesdays — top value), when Rufus Brevett walked in. I was 95% sure it was him, confirmed when Geoff Horsfield and Paul Peschisolido quickly followed afterwards. Before we knew it, just about the entire Fulham team were surrounding us at the bar — Lee Clark, Kit Symons, Chris Coleman, Karl Heinz-Riedle, Barry Hayles — they were all there. Not only that, half of them were already worse for wear for drink, and it was the middle of the week!

(Issue # 135)

Now, what are you supposed to do when the entire first team of your newest local rivals are suddenly swarming round you? Surreal indeed, but you had to be there to fully understand how strange the situation was. These were the same players who made sure our trip to Craven Cottage back in September proved fruitless, and for all the money that they're worth, at this precise moment in time they were just like any other ordinary blokes you get in these establishments, and actually proved to be a right good laugh rather than the aloof figures many players no doubt are. Just seeing Peschisolido walking round in a drunken haze, all five and a half foot of him, painted quite a different picture from the triumphant one when scoring the winning goal against us — in this state, he wouldn't have been able to tell a golf ball from a football.

Of all the players, only Maik Taylor and Rufus were the only ones not really drinking, but still had a better time than Lee Clark who sat on his own all night in a chair staring into space. Taylor said QPR were one of the better teams Fulham have faced this season, but I failed to agree with him. "For the first 25 minutes they were all over us," — anyone remember that?

Despite most probably all being happily married, there was no shortage of interest in the opposite sex — but there wasn't any of the 'do you know who I am' lines, and most were only having a laugh. At one stage Chris Coleman actually put his arm around me and, and in his broad Welsh accent said, "Let's go and pull some birds big fella." I was too busy pissing myself laughing to actually take him up on the offer, and by this stage we were both probably in no fit state to try anyway.

A top night indeed, and I now probably don't hate Fulham as much as I used to...

A few weeks earlier, I met ITL columnist Moreno Ferrari after work for a drink, and discovered when passing through Leicester Square that Paul McCartney was in town, launching his new album 'Run Devil Run' at the Equinox. Being a fan, this immediately drew my attention and despite the huge crowds gathered outside, we managed to blag a couple of free tickets for entry. Sorted. No free beer or food unfortunately as we weren't VIP's, but we weren't complaining. Paul McCartney came and went, done his stuff, talked about his album etc, but another highlight was meeting the ultimate footballing geezer-bird and Torquay fan — Helen Chamberlain.

Quite why she was downstairs with us plebs when she had tickets for the VIP lounge was beyond us, but firstly we had to think of a way to get talking to her without sounding like the typically sad football fan she no doubt meets all the time. Being editor of a fanzine was an obvious talking point for me, and by pure coincidence the new issue (132) out a couple of days later had a picture of Paul McCartney on the front — it would perhaps have been sad of me to mention that McCartney once had a hit record called 'Helen Wheels', so luckily I saw sense. Anyway, we eventually got round to talking to her, and very nice she was too (hello if you're reading). Apparently, Soccer AM are desperate to get some QPR fans on the show (maybe even for the Torquay game), and the reason she was downstairs was because it was too stuffy amongst all those VIP's, and Dean Gaffney.

She couldn't stick around for too long as she had to be up early to present her slot on XFM, so it was back to the bar and time to nick every souvenir that wasn't nailed down before everyone else got in on the act. After discretely hauling down a 15ft long PVC promotional banner, it dawned on me exactly of what use it would be to me. Then some old nonce approached me and offered to swap it for a press pack (he had about 6), including the CD and everything... another great result on the night thank you very much.

Then there was the time, when on holiday in America in the summer, we were in this bar in Atlantic City and there being served was a man with a QPR shirt on. Not only was he a fan, but also a professional referee — the name? Graham Poll.

Stranger still, I recently found out one of my best friend's cousin is Michael Currie, the QPR reserve striker who has just returned from a lengthy loan spell in Singapore. Apparently, Michael was something of a star out there, and became a regular face on TV. Not everyone took a liking to him though, and it would probably be best to not write too much on the time when he and his mates got beaten up in a night-club (in case the gaffer is reading)...
(Ed – issue # 135)

Gerry and the Play-off-makers

Cast your mind back to November 1994, the Liverpool game, now let's change the course of history: Rodney never turned up that night, Gerry stayed and at the end of the season Thompson sold QPR to Chris Wright. Chris gave Gerry £7 million to spend and two seasons later with a squad of England under 21's and two full internationals mixed with QPR youth and classy non-league acquisitions we finished fifth in the Premiership and qualified for Europe.

Fantasy land!? I think not. I believe that if Gerry had stayed we would have been doing as well as West Ham are now. We were certainly always as good as them, if not better during that period (early 90s). Harry Redknapp has had the time and a few quid to build his team, we certainly could have matched that.

Look at Leicester, even they have got into Europe. We could have been contenders, honest! So you may ask (wandering along in this fantasy) what is my point: I am alarmed at Gerry talking about packing it in next year, he must stay and continue what good work he has been doing and re-build this dub.

This season has been like a breath of fresh air compared to previous ones. Yes we all know he's a moaner, can't say anything positive, clichéd press conferences, etc, but does any of that matter when he is turning things around on the pitch like he has done? Maybe this is the moan to beat all moans and he is having us on but I doubt it.

He was the only man who could have taken on the challenge last year and someone who cares about the club, 'QPR through and through', who can work with what little or no money we have to get us up.

Take one minute to think about who else has the ability and the desire to get this dub out of this hole? Look at our situation; we can no longer attract medium name players because of our financial situation let along decent managers. He has stated that he will make his decision about leaving next season and it will be non-football related. I believe that we can sway this decision. If we are doing well and he gets an unbelievable amount of support from the fans he will stay, his heart is here.

We must try to keep him or in five years time we could be sitting in Division 2 looking down on all that might have been.
(David McLean – issue # 135)

We're just not good enough

Pleased as I was with the result against Sheffield United, and the good performance for the first 60 minutes or so, I still believe that we're still a way off the position that we need to be in to challenge for promotion. It's a difficult situation, as I couldn't really be more happy with the players we have, especially as they are mostly the same ones that had to endure three or four pretty traumatic seasons.

And I look at the team, and think, "well, we definitely need a new goalkeeper as Ludo is too old and Harper's kicking puts us in trouble several times in every match." And I think, "well Breaker is okay, but we could do better and I'm still not convinced about Antti Heinola (if he ever stops getting those ridiculously painful injuries) so we could do with a decent right back. And we probably need another centre back, and possibly even two strikers." All this and at the time of writing we're seventh in the league. And so I think, "well, we're just not good enough." The problem, for once, isn't that we've got too many crap players or players performing below their capacity, but the fact that we've got a group of competent players playing pretty much to the best of their abilities (with one or two young midfielders excepted).

The unmistakable fact is that Gerry has once again coached some of our poorer players into better ones, and our better ones into very good ones. But I can't see us really improving on our position without three or four reinforcements. But then there is the problem of the club's new and sensible policy of having a reasonable wage cap on new players and refusing to pay signing on fees. Now, I'm not sure which ones, but there are certain overpaid players that are at the end of their contracts this summer and they will be on their way out. So not only will we have to buy better players in the key positions (centre back, right back, goalkeeper, striker), but perhaps a couple of versatile squad players as well. Recently Gerry has been complaining about how difficult it is to get players to come without a signing on fee, which begs the question of how are we going to get better players than the ones we have when bound by these terms? Surely the only way is to sign fairly unknown players who have potential (Darlington, Wardley etc). I was hoping that next season we might actually mount a title challenge based on the fact that we should have improved even more within a year. But now I wonder if the plan is more long term, with promotion perhaps not being likely for another two or three seasons. This is especially so when you consider the noises being made by Chris Wright about the fact that we are still losing millions every year. This suggests that we are going to have to sell to stay alive. Are we not just what we have been for the last decade or so — a selling club that as soon as success starts to filter through is forced to sell our best players?

I hope not, but it does seem something of a vicious circle — we need money to get players to get us into the Premiership, but the only way we can get the money is to be in that league, which we can't do without better players which we can't get until we get there. If that makes sense.

Steiner & Wardley

I'm getting really fed up with people criticising these two players. Over the last three or four years one of the biggest complaints in this fanzine and by fans generally was that we had too many fancy Dan's (literally, in one case), who cared for little other than collecting their huge pay cheque at the end of every week. There were monthly tirades about the primadonna nature of our team, and how we were being out fought every week by teams who didn't necessarily have as much natural talent as our players, but certainly wanted the points more.

Finally we have come into a bunch of players who are working hard for themselves, the team, the club, and us — the fans. And in this team, which has got nothing short of phenomenal team spirit in comparison to recent years, there are a few who stand out. Not perhaps because they are a brilliant talent, but because they are leading this team, pulling it together and dragging us along with them. In particular the skill, speed and determination of Jermaine Darlington, the excellent defensive and distributive qualities of Baraclough and Rose, the defensive prowess of the fantastic Danny Maddix, and the jewel in our crown, Gavin Peacock.

I don't think many people would argue with those assumptions, but when it comes to Steiner and Wardley the arguments begin to start. Let's take Steiner first. He's got six goals so far this season — not a massive total perhaps, but not too bad and he is averaging about a goal every three games, which, if he were to keep it up, means about fifteen or sixteen goals by the end of this season — hardly a poor return for £215,000.

I think much of the criticism levelled at him is because he doesn't actually look like a very effective player. He bundles around as if he's a very clumsy player, yet his style is hugely successful at unsettling defences, and, just as important and something enough people don't give him credit for, he makes space for other players by dragging defenders out of position. It's no coincidence that since he's been playing for us, Peacock, Kiwomya and Wardley have scored regularly. They've clearly benefited hugely from his presence. And not enough people remember the sorry state our forward line was when he left for Walsall at the end of last season — virtually unable to muster a goal until the Palace match.

I find the criticism of Stuart Wardley even more amazing. Here is a player who, from midfield, is averaging about a goal every other game in his first season in the football league! Here is a player who gives everything for QPR. Here is a player who runs all day for QPR. When an opposing player suddenly finds himself in acres of space because a Rangers player is out of position, Wardley is invariably the player sprinting to cover it. And when we attack he is ALWAYS in the box, trying to score.

For years we have been crying out for a midfielder that can get up and down the pitch and get in that box and stick some chances away. How many times last season did we get crosses into the box only for no one to be there? His shooting is excellent and there is still more to come from this man. Against Sheffield United he had six attempts on goal — more than anyone else in our team — he scored with one (another fantastically hit shot with his right foot), hit a great shot just wide after making a good tackle and going on a short dribble (that was with his left foot — yes! he's two footed as well), had three headers saved by Tracey and had another go just wide.

While Rowland, Langley and Murray have all put in patchy and inconsistent performances all season, Wardley has been one of the constants that has kept us largely in the top 10. I can't for the life of me work out why people are saying he should be dropped in favour of Langley, who is struggling at the moment and can't seem to get to grips with the pace of the division and has barely had a shot on target all season.

Steiner and Wardley may have their shortcomings. Their first touch may let them down sometimes, they might struggle slightly against the better teams (Wardley did look out of sorts against Barnsley, but then so did everyone and he soon put that to rights with his performance against the pitiful Blades), but it is their drive and attitude that has got us where we are. And while I don't think Steiner will ever be a first class striker I do think that Wardley has a great future ahead of him, and with experience could become a very accomplished player. While Langley definitely has more natural talent, I still think Wardley is the real prospect of the two. I think he has more hunger, more determination and a greater mental strength — give me that over Langley's fancy touches any day.

What gets you out of this division is power and strength — these two players help provide that for us, so lay off them and start appreciating their abilities instead of shooting them down for the dubious crime of not having enough class for QPR.

(Dan Trelfer – issue # 135)

All I want for Christmas is...

Chris Wright - "A few more fans."

Gerry Francis - "45 points."

Iain Dowie - "Just one more goal for Northern Ireland."

Ludo Miklosko - "My first team place back."

Stuart Wardley - "A new set of dentures."

Karl Ready - "A few more cans of Bleach Blonde."

Jermaine Darlington - "Nuff respect."

Rob Steiner - "Another number one hit."

Keith Rowland - "A right foot."

Matthew Rose - "A re-trial — I'm innocent."

Richard Langley - "Time."

Steve Slade - "Some ability would be nice."

George Kulcsar - "An English passport."

Paul Murray - "A move, anywhere but Norwich."

Tony Scully - "FIFA 99, it's the only way I'd get a game."

Tim Breaker - "A rest, I'm knackered playing wing-back."

Lee Harper - "A ball that doesn't swerve when I kick it."

Gavin Peacock - "Promotion, that's why I'm here."

Danny Maddix - "The new album from Steps."

Ian Baraclough - "A place for England down the left-hand side."

Chris Kiwomya - "Common sense."

Kevin Gallen - "A six pack — both varieties."

Steve Morrow - "Hair."

Ademole Bankole - "Advice."

Sammy Koejoe - "I don't understand the question."

(Ed – issue # 135)

Still plenty to play for

You can blame the referee as much as you like (it's getting tiresome to continually do so), but the fact remains Charlton were better than us and deservedly took their place in the 5th round of the FA Cup after their 1-0 win against us. With Gallen doing his hamstring yet again after just 15 minutes, with Dowie and a totally out-of-sorts Rob Steiner up front, it was always going to be hard for us to create any decent openings, which sadly proved to be the case.

The only time Steiner and Dowie touched the ball came via Harper's goal-kicks, with possession almost always given back to the opposition straight away. A simple change of formation could have made a big difference, but instead we're left with another frustrating defeat. Time to concentrate on the league as they say...

In winning our last two league games, a healthy position in the league has been maintained just as it looked as if we were heading for mid-table respectability. We can't quite manage to break into the top six, but if we can do so come May it would be quite an achievement.

Forget the fact it would be an almighty struggle to survive in the Premiership, and Gerry Francis's obsession with getting those 45 points to secure safety, the play-offs represent a very realistic escape route out of this division for QPR.

Even if promotion to the Premiership would see an immediate return to Division 1, the financial benefits would still be enormous and would provide invaluable experience for our players. If you take 75 points as a bookmark to reach 6th place, which is probably the best we could hope for, then we'd need to find 36 points from the remaining 20 games. 10 wins, 6 draws and 4 defeats should do it. I don't see why that shouldn't be within our reach. Our record over the last 20 games is won 8, drawn 7, lost 5, points = 31, so a slight improvement in our results is required, but probably just as important would be some an improvement in refereeing standards — it's been like playing against 12 men in many games this season.

Looking at the league table as it presently stands, expect the top four clubs (Charlton, Man City, Ipswich and Barnsley) to occupy these places for the rest of the season. You can forget looking out for their results from now on, hoping to see them lose, as they certainly won't be caught by QPR. From the remainder, everyone down to Bolton can consider themselves to be in within a chance of the play-offs. Its going to be very tight come May, and there's every chance only 70 points will be enough to clinch 6th place. Blackburn have finally sorted their act out and should continue to rise the table, but I don't think there's too many other teams to be unduly worried about. Whether or not we prove good enough to mount a serious challenge for the play-offs remains to be seen, but there's certainly no harm in trying, and there would be very few complaints if we missed out.

(Ed – issue # 136)

Cyberdine saviour

'Rob Steiner — Does he look like Ricky Martin or what?' — A question asked on the cover of issue 134 of In The Loft and perhaps a question I, more than most R's fans, should have the answer to. For, having spent many years in near footy exile I now find myself frequenting Loftus Road about one and bit times a month, with number one son in tow. He's only 7 and every time we've visited the hallowed turf's he's coerced yours truly into creeping ever nearer the pitch, culminating in 2 row A tickets in the Ellerslie Road stand for the Barnsley match.

As I found to my cost this is a popular haunt for juniors... I was surrounded by the little blighters. They have an almost magnetic ability in luring players over by waiving pens and autograph books at them. Before I knew it there were Ian Baraclough and Rob Steiner standing about six feet away from me. Now, I'm no great psychological expert and so I have no real explanation for what happened next... perhaps it was all those years viewing proceedings from the distance of the upper Loft or South Africa Road stands.

Perhaps it was the lack of any autograph books as a youngster, but there I was standing next to two first teamers and I just couldn't help saying the words... "Can you sign the programme Ian,"... and he did, just like that. Blimey, this is easy I thought so I tried again. "Rob, can you sign my programme," again he signed it. Then, just as my lad swiped the offending article out of my grasp one of the other youngsters next to me asked, "Rob, Where's Peak?" Steiner paused as if weighing up a number of pre-selected answers: "He's injured," replied the big Swede in a cold monosyllabic manor. I'd heard that voice somewhere before... It was more Bavarian than Swedish. Could it have been Boris Becker?... Nope. The Great Franz Beckenbauer maybe? No, not him. And then it dawned on me... Rob 'The Terminator' Steiner is in fact a 'Model T-800 Cyberdine Replicant'. The close cropped hair, the chiseled looks, that strange awkward running motion, it all made sense. Could it be that Rob (short for Robot) was sent back in time from the year 2020 in an attempt to save Rangers from relegation in the pivotal 1998/99 season?

Forget the Palace match, without Rob's 3 goals last season (effectively gaining 7 points) Rangers would now be on the slippery slope to oblivion. Who knows what reaches of local non-league football the R's could have been playing in by the year 2020 if we hadn't beaten the drop! I know this theory seems a little far-fetched but give the man a leather jacket, shades and a Harley and there you have it. So next time Rob miss-hits a shot or sends a stray pass straight to the opposition, don't be too vociferous with your criticism. He might have his own way of exacting revenge.

(Robert Thomas – issue # 136)

Rambling on

So Chris Kiwomya says that it is not his fault that he keeps getting sent off, it's the fault of the referees. I am afraid that I just cannot agree with him. He seems to be a right 'pain in the arse' on the pitch and always seems to be rucking with one defender or other. As he says that he has never been sent off before this season began, I assume he now plays with a different attitude than he did previously in his career. Either that or he was the luckiest player in the world. All I know is that if he doesn't cut this arrogant attitude of his out and replace it with a bit more hard work, this could be his last season at the Bush!

~ ~ ~

I have to say how impressed I was with the result at Torquay. A nasty flu bug ruled out my intended journey down to the West Country and when it came up on the text that we were one down, I felt even worse. I have no idea how many times I have seen the Rangers lose cup-ties at smaller clubs over the years (Doncaster, Huddersfield, Bury and Watford spring immediately to mind) but it is an embarrassingly large amount.

The relief that came over me when the goals started to go in at the right end cheered me up considerably. I know that we still managed to make the ending exciting, with Ludo giving away a bizarre goal (what has happened to Ludo, he looks more like the idiot Bankole every time I see him?), but we hung on for an important win and that was most commendable.

I would also like to say how pleased I am with the two loan players we have got hold of to cover for our defensive injuries. Ward looks a good and solid, if unspectacular centre half and ideal for this division. Whether or not he will prove to be any good in the Premiership later this season for Watford I have no idea, but I will bet he looks a good player back in this league next season. McGovern I think looks superb. He looks to enjoy coming forward and until Wardley's goal against Crewe, he looked the most likely Rangers player to score. I cannot believe that Arsenal would sell him to us on the cheap, but as with all young players at Highbury, he will be looking to get away when his current contract is up, due to the clubs' current 'foreigners or nothing' policy. I would like to think that we would be in pole position to snap him up as and when it happens.

Talking of injuries, I am led to understand that excesses in training caused at least two of the current long-term central defender's injuries. I have written before that I am not sure about Gerry's fitness policy and that instead of having a team of super-fit players charging around for ninety minutes, half of them look totally knackered mid-way through the second half. If it is true that the training is now injuring the players as well as wearing them out, then maybe it is time for a rethink in training policy. I seem to remember that Gerry's time at Spurs was blighted by the amount of injuries he had to whine about. Coincidence? Maybe, maybe not.

~ ~ ~

So yet another version of 'The Ranger' newspaper has hit the streets (or should it be street?). How many editions do we all think that this one will last, three, four? Every few years this publication is reborn only to die a death a few months later. Why this is so exactly I have no idea, but it must be down to a combination of two things, content and distribution. On the content side, what is the point of half filling it with month-old match reports? Even any Rangers fans stranded on the moon will have seen a match report within a month of the game if they want to.

On the plus side of this, I thought it was a very good interview with Sammy Koejoe in the first issue, it's just a shame that factually it was different to the version in the official programme. The Danny Maddix interview was quite interesting too, if you like that sort of thing. As for distribution, I have no idea where exactly the club intends to distribute it. Going on past results, if it is in the local area then it will be lucky to survive issue two. A much better idea would be to maybe hit the areas outside Shepherds Bush that all the recent surveys showed to contain the greatest Rangers support, but as I have said, those people that are bothered would surely already know what is going on at the club. Maybe it is just an attempt by the people involved to write inane articles just to see their name in print, after all, it works for me!

~ ~ ~

So Leon Jeanne has apparently walked out of the club, at one stage, following his failure to get a regular place in the first team squad. My initial reaction was sod him, if he wants to be like that, then there is no place for him at the Rangers. After a while though, having given some thought to it, I could perhaps see his point. Gerry is well documented in all forms of the media with his continual moaning about the amount of injuries and suspensions we have had lately (like we are the only team in history to get them) and yet at no time during this 'crisis' has he turned to the younger players at the club to help him out.

I know Chris Plummer and Paul Bruce have been getting games, but I wouldn't really describe either of them as being youngsters any more. I firmly believe that the only reason Richard Langley has had such a run in the side was because of the injury to Peacock as his playing performances this season hardly merit a place on the bench.

Every month or so a report surfaces that Richard Graham will definitely 'at least be on the bench on Saturday' but it never happens, so exactly what chance do Leon Jeanne and the like have at the Rangers nowadays. With Gerry's insistence on playing five at the back no matter who has to play out of position to achieve this and the only clear offensive tactic seemingly to bash the ball up the middle as hard as possible for Steiner to hold up, then skilled players like Graham and Jeanne appear to have no future here. Is it right therefore to condemn Jeanne for wanting to get away? Maybe his chosen method of achieving this is wrong, but I find the sentiment behind it difficult to disagree with.

~ ~ ~

I just don't know what to say about referee Robert Styles. I was going to write a blistering tirade about him hating our club and how could he possibly send off Plummer and give Charlton a penalty? I was going to write what a disgrace it was and how it cost us the game etc, etc. Then I saw the replay on TV. I have to now admit that it was definitely the right decision (god that hurt). Plummer clearly dragged the player back by the shirt and the referee was standing right behind him. A penalty yes, a booking yes, but what really annoys me is that I have absolutely no idea what the hell he booked Plummer for the first time.

I still think that the game was very badly refereed against us, but I cannot now disagree with the games' major talking point. This brings me back to my main point. Is referee Styles a) dead biased against us? b) The 'homer' to end all 'homers'? Or c) a cheat that took the Arab's money in the game at Craven Cottage? I wonder if we will ever find out, as I just cannot see the Rangers letting him referee another of our games this millennium!
(Paul Davidson – issue # 136)

Praise where it's due

In front of me at the Charlton game was some idiot who spent the entire game slagging Iain Dowie off. He was right of course. Dowie is slow. He's clumsy. He's old. He's not much good. But what he didn't mention in his disgusting vitriol was that Dowie has played a large part in turning Rangers from no-hopers into something resembling a team, one that might well seriously challenge for promotion next season. It also escaped his attention that, under normal circumstances, neither Francis nor Dowie would want Dowie in the first team. But with Kiwomya and Koejoe suspended, Gallen, Slade, Graham, Peacock and Weare injured and Jeanne off on one of his petulant little tantrums, there was no one else, barring inexperienced youngsters.

What's the point in slagging off a player who just wants to do his best for QPR in such a dire situation? There was nothing else we could do, so why not give the guy some support, and stop all this tired, lazy, and, frankly, hypocritical joking about his looks. If every QPR player over the last few years had had the determination of Dowie we might still be in the Premiership now.
(Dan Trelfer – issue # 136)

Spoke too soon

It had to happen. I soon as I start waffling on about QPR being in with a chance of the play-offs, we haven't won a game since. It's not a case of 'I told you so' — when you consider the position we were in before the Bolton game, it's only natural to start speculating. There's nothing wrong with optimism, especially when Gerry Francis is doing his level best to play-down our chances with his 'happy to get 50 points' scenario. Even if Gerry doesn't consider us serious contenders to make the play-offs, his ambitions for this season should by now extend further than merely surviving another season in this division.

QPR have finally got round to offering Gavin Peacock a new contract, but the early signs suggest Peacock is not too happy with what he's been offered. I can't believe the club cannot afford to offer him an improved deal to what he's on now, or at least the same again — it's an insult on behalf of the club if reports are true that he's been offered vastly reduced terms. If we could afford to pay £1million for George Ndah, it proves there is money available.

Of course, all the power is with the players these days. Peacock could make a small fortune if he chose to move on elsewhere compared to what's on offer at QPR, so it's down to the club to make him feel wanted. Besides, if we were to lose Peacock on a 'free', how much would it cost to replace him? There will be plenty of players available for nothing at the end of the season, but we wouldn't exactly be in a good position to go for them due to the wage situation. I heard Wardley is on just £400 a week, so you get an idea the kind of market we find ourselves in.

Peacock is one of a number of players whose contracts are up in the summer. It's quite extraordinary that we have only managed to sell one player since Francis returned, so understandably the annual wage bill has hardly altered during this period. This will all change in the summer as contracts come to their end and Francis decides who he wants to keep. QPR must make sure our better players and most valuable assets are secured on long-term contracts, and that would include Langley, Rose, Harper, Ready, Baraclough, Murray and of course Peacock. But at the same time, the club needs to avoid any further repeats of the Vinnie Jones situation, where players no longer wanted can hold the club to ransom. Losing any of these on a 'Bosman' would be terrible for the club, but at the same time trying to keep them happily employed certainly won't be easy.

In the meantime, it would be hard for the club to refuse any decent offer for any of our players. Murray is continually being linked with Newcastle — it's obvious Murray is not a big favourite of Francis'. In regard to Langley, although the rumours linking him with Tottenham have quietened considerably, Spurs have had him watched in every home game so far, and an offer for his services may not be far away.

With the news that Rob Steiner looks set to be out injured for a while yet, Francis has expressed his wish to bring in a striker on loan with the same capabilities. It's early days yet, but all the signs suggest the purchase of Sammy Koejoe appears to be money wasted (maybe we can recoup some if he sells that invisible caravan he appears to be pulling when he runs), and Francis doesn't seem to have much faith in his other strikers. This obsession with having a big man up front has always been a characteristic of Francis' managerial style, even though when you play the 3-5-2 system it leans more towards keeping the ball on the deck — which we have players capable of doing, but it would be nice to see it more.

(Ed – issue # 137)

Moreno Bares All

I'm sure that there are a great many Rangers fans out there who have been somewhat saddened at the slide down the league table as we currently stand 10th from an exultant high of play-off contenders having taken only 5 points from a possible 15 from the start of the year. I pin all this blame in our reversal of fortune on one man, if you can call him that. David Mellor wrote in the 'Evening Standard' just before Christmas that he would put some money down on QPR obtaining a play-off spot — since then it's been downhill all the way. I know it's a damn sight better than last season and we really shouldn't be complaining but how many Rangers fans would be content with a mid-table finish? Maybe our expectations of what this season was to be was perhaps slightly more expectant after the success of Bradford City — the Bantams were relegation contenders two seasons ago yet 12 months later they were a Premiership team — surely we could do the same? I'm sure that we could point to our injury crisis but let's face it every team has one of those and the better teams are the ones that cope with it the best. We also know that the money is not there so we can't spend our way out of this league so it boils down to hard work and team spirit.

Gerry has said on many occasions that he would just like to see the team finish mid-table, is this just a case of reverse psychology or is this really our most realistic position? If mid-table is all we can hope for then maybe the long awaited clearance of 'deadwood' can start immediately, after all there's no point hanging onto players if you just intend staying in the First Division as all that occurs is a wage bill that that far exceeds income. We all want our team to do well and not just settle for second best therefore this negative attitude that Gerry has does not sit well with me. Bloody David Mellor... he's got a lot to answer for!

~ ~ ~

On today's official website it states that Gerry is to look into the transfer market (for about the fifth time) to bring in a new player as it seems that Rob Steiner's knee injury will keep him out for longer than was first expected. Gerry says that he needs a forward player that can hold up the ball and is good in the air as we are somewhat lacking in that department at the moment. When you have players such as Gallen, Slade, Kiwomya and even Mahoney-Johnson who all like to operate in the same way — playing with a tall target man — why did Gerry go out and splash the club's dwindling cash on a player such as Sammy Koejoe, who's style is exactly like the players above?

This transfer outcome is even more difficult to swallow when it seemed the club were very eager to sign tall target man George Ndah from Swindon Town but instead had to make do with a poor facsimile copy, surely Gerry should have bided his time and waited for the player with the right criteria to come along, after all Koejoe hasn't exactly made himself a permanent feature of the team.

I just hope that if Gerry is handed some money then he might find it more useful to put into Gavin Peacock's new contract before he walks away in the summer on a 'Bosman' as God knows we need to keep hold of our decent playmakers.

~ ~ ~

Congratulations go to Stuart Wardley on winning the 'Evening Standard' player of the month for December, unfortunately it seems that the award has exactly the same effect as the Nationwide manager of the month, as the prolific goalscorer failed to find the net throughout January and in doing so missed a hatful of chances. Thankfully that was put right in the away match at Port Vale.

~ ~ ~

It was interesting to see the reaction of the QPR faithful to Nigel Quashie's return to Loftus Road. There was an enormous amount of barracking, as there should be when any former player returns, which unfortunately instead of just playing along with and having a joke back, Quashie decided somewhat unwisely to retaliate. The Loft boys were having none of it and decided to wait for him after the match. The doorman explained to Quashie that it would be foolish of him to go out just yet as there were some 20-30 Rangers fans waiting for him.

Unfortunately Quashie, being a little bereft of the grey matter, decided not to take any notice of the good advice and walked out closely followed by the Rangers fans hurling even more abuse at him. The abuse you get from visiting fans is all part and parcel of a footballers life and the better ones adjust to it and some even thrive in it — Robbie Savage, Dennis Wise and more recently Alan Shearer have all shown how you can cope with it. As for Quashie he probably left Loftus Road a little wise... well here's hoping.
(Moreno Ferrari – issue # 137)

Rambling on

I'm so glad that Iain Dowie thought he had quite a good game at Charlton, at least that's one person that did. Surely I am not the only one that gave up all hope of us scoring the minute he charged onto the Valley pitch like Genghis Khan with the hump. I just cannot understand why Dowie (who incidentally gets my vote as the all time worst QPR striker, even over Dean Coney and Allan Thompson) can ever get on the bench at all. I know that Leon Jeanne supposedly walked out temporarily on the club but the fact that Dowie gets put on the bench before him, Richard Paquette and Alvin Bubb (no younger than players playing with other teams) then it's probably no wonder he did walk out.

I have nothing against Iain Dowie personally (just his brother) and I can see the day coming when he takes over from Gerry, which I don't think will be such a bad thing. I just cannot understand why the hell we bother having junior teams at all if we are not going to give any of them a chance. Let's face it, Iain Dowie was renowned as being a crap centre forward when he was in his prime (if he ever had one). For him to still get wheeled out when we are a bit short is an insult to the admission paying fans. Please Iain, just stick to the coaching and leave the playing to people that can play the game without resorting to criminal assault every time the ball is played near them!

It's not just Iain Dowie at Charlton though, every week now I am getting more and more fed up with Gerry Francis' team selections. The line up for the Forest game said it all I think. To my mind he had two main choices, given the injuries to Steiner and Darlington. Firstly he had to pick between Tony Scully — a player that surely now must

rate as one of the worst ever to play in the hoops; and young up and coming starlet Richard Graham — a player continually praised by Francis himself. Selection: Scully. Secondly, he had to pick between Steve Slade — a player that has failed miserably more times than Saint Jude himself; and Leon Jeanne — who appears to be banging goals in for fun for the reserves and juniors. Selection: Slade. Neither of the two youngsters even made the bench, no bloody wonder that they feel like walking out. The overall result was that our first shot on target was in the 76th minute. Thank Christ it went in or we would have had the ignominy of losing to the worst Forest side to leave Nottingham since the days of Robin Hood. Come to that Francis was quoted in the papers as saying what a terrific side Forest were and that their midfield would not look out of place in the Premiership. I have no idea what the view of the pitch is like from our dugout, but it must be bloody awful if Francis thought their midfield played that well.

To be fair to David Platt though at least he gave the kids a chance. In the same circumstances what would the chances be of Gerry picking Ricky Lopez, Richard Graham and Terry McFlynn to play together in the midfield, which would be the equivalent of what Platt did? Absolutely none. Francis obviously has absolutely no confidence in his young players whatsoever.

~ ~ ~

Talking of Gerry Francis, just what is it with him? The more points we get the more bloody miserable he seems to get. It used to be "our priority is getting 45 points," now it's either "our priority now is to get 50 points," or the amazing "I don't know how we have got so many points."

With the ultra defensive tactics we have used so far this season I'm damn sure that I don't know how we have got so many points either. Why doesn't the man lighten up a bit and maybe go for three forwards once in a while? You never know, we might even start to score a few more goals and some of the home games might even be worth watching again. His press briefings on a Friday must be a right laugh. I'll bet that the pressmen all draw straws as to who gets to go, with the winners going into the Springbok instead. Mind you, they would probably get more relevant team info for the coming game in the Springbok than in the press room. I cannot see what the big secret is as to who may or may not play the following afternoon, it's easier to get Britains military secrets out of MI5 than it is to find out who is or isn't injured down the Bush.

One theory that was being talked of in the LSA before the Forest game was that Francis doesn't have a clue what his best line up is, so he probably picks the first eleven players to turn up Saturday morning. God help us if Bankole ever gets a new alarm clock. If any more players come back from injury soon, Gerry will have to have a tombola machine installed in his office to help him with his selections.
(Paul Davidson – issue # 137)

An Audience with Iain Dowie
A report on the 'Meet the Players' evening

I love kids. Love 'em. You know, not in the Graham Rix kind of way you understand, more in a Jim Henson kind of way. The kids, though, have got their 'Open Day' haven't they? — in the bright sunshine before the optimism has been dashed by a thousand Chris Kiwomya misses and a million visions of Tony Scully not controlling the ball. They've got their day when they can meet the players and people like Sladey and Keithy and Scully can all believe for one day that they've got some real fans in the crowd. It's a lovely day where the kids can run around, eat hot dogs and popcorn, and have their shirts signed by footballers wearing shades.

That's the kids day. The 'Meet the Players' session, though, that now seems to be pretty much a once a year fixture — as traditional as the 'World Club Championship' — should be a time for adults, meeting with and chatting to the players whose wages we pay. Parts of the evening were very interesting, but some of the questions were unbelievable. Once a year you get to ask some of the questions that you sit around every week wondering about you can finally get to ask, and, brilliantly, it's a time where the players are refreshingly candid.

So why do people go to these things and ask questions like: "Can anyone in the team do somersaults?", "What do you do to relax?", "Can you believe you're a footballer?", "Do you have to pinch yourself when you think that you're a footballer?" (I know it's the same question, but it was still asked twice), and most pointless of all, "Are you upset when you lose?" (what did they expect them to say? "Nah, it's just a laugh innit?").

Yeah, forget questions like, "Any chance we might sign Darren Ward?" or "Is Gavin Peacock going to sign a new contract?" (these were questions that were asked, thankfully) — I'm just desperate to find out whether Ian Baraclough likes to play a bit of golf on a Sunday and whether George Kulcsar's favourite TV programme is 'A Question of Sport'.

Anyway, while there's still space left I'd like to just tell you all about the more interesting things that were discussed over the course of the evening. I managed to have a chat with Iain Dowie before the 'formal' Q&A, so some of his opinions from that chat will be included here, and weren't necessarily repeated during the later session. Dowie, by the way, was absolutely superb throughout. He came across as a man with massive determination and enormous enthusiasm for the game and for QPR. He is very intelligent, and like his persona on the field, is clearly a very hard worker. Dowie was never a great player, but he worked extraordinarily hard at his game and made himself into the best player he could be with his limitations in speed and skill. He has no such limitations in the world of coaching, and I fully expect the man to be an excellent manager (and yes, I was sure that 'Super' Ray Wilkins would make a great manager, too). I hope Gerry stays on for as long as possible, but when he does go we already have his heir.

The actual panel consisted of Dowie, Gavin Peacock, George Kulcsar (an odd choice, maybe specifically so we could ask about his illness?), Ian Baraclough and Stewart Wardley. In the bar mixing with the fans were Langley, Darlington, Kiwomya, Harper, Slade and maybe one or two others. Gerry was away on business, and none out of Maddix, Gallen and Ready attended which seemed strange seeing as those three are probably our longest serving players.

Gavin Peacock & his contract

Host Tony Incenzo made much of the fact that the information we received from Gavin on this subject was an "exclusive," but in reality it was nothing I or any other QPR fan could have told you. Gavin said he was keen to stay at Rangers and had tabled his wishes and the club had gone away to think about them. Pretty standard stuff. Later, however, when Dowie was fielding a question about new players he moved back to the subject of Gavin. He said that Gerry's and his own policy was to keep the best players at QPR, and that included Gavin. He said that everyone had to do what was best for their family, but that we must all hope that Gavin sells one of his houses, takes a pay-cut and stays at QPR. Gavin, I thought, although smiling, didn't like the inference that he was a rich man demanding shed loads of more money even though he didn't need it. He certainly gave Dowie a strange look.

A few people have said that it looked likely that he would be staying, but I have to say I'm guessing that the opposite is true. I spoke to Lee Harper and he said just about everyone's contracts are up at the end of this season or next, and when I mentioned the likelihood of Peacock staying at QPR, he said that the club was really struggling financially... and that was it. It's a bit much to expect Gavin to take a pay-cut after he's been one of our most loyal performers over the last three seasons, and could justifiably claim to be our best and most important player. Dowie's speech even sounded a bit like emotional blackmail — how could Gavin refuse in front of 150 season ticket holders who had just clapped vociferously at Dowie's suggestion that he had to stay? In fact he was very noncommittal and I don't blame him.

New signings

Iain Dowie fielded all questions dealing with the possibility of new signings at QPR. First of all he spoke about Darren Ward and said how he would love to sign him. The stumbling block is whether Graham Taylor will let him go, and of course whether we can afford him. In relation to that second problem, Dowie stressed that if we were to go in for him, 'people' (i.e. the board) must realise that he is a central defender and would represent an investment in our future — a rock for ten years or so. There had been a rumour that Ward was out of contract in the summer, but when I asked Dowie he said that in fact he had only recently signed a four-year deal. However, Watford are certainly not in a lot better position financially than we are, they will almost certainly be relegated and their wages are not at the usual Premiership heights. He also praised Brian McGovern but it was clear that Ward was the one QPR are really interested in, and I can't see any reason why Dowie would go to such lengths to say we liked the player if he didn't think we stood a chance of signing him. Personally, I think Ward could well be one of the best defenders we've had in twenty years. It is, of course, early to say, but his performances have been solid, he doesn't give away silly fouls, he's a good tackler, a big presence in the air and distributes the ball well. In every aspect a perfect central defender, and I can't believe bigger clubs aren't sniffing round him.

New ground

Dowie again on this one. Basically, he believes we cannot survive in the Premiership without a new ground with a 30,000 capacity, which he does believe we can fill — citing recent large away support at Wimbledon a couple of years ago, Port Vale, and Fulham. Incidentally, all expressed their gratitude for the Fulham turnout, and Baraclough slyly remarked that "I understand we infiltrated some of their areas as well!" I respected the use of "we" there — spoken like a true fan.

Stuart Wardley

Stuart was put on the panel as the hero of the season so far, and he presented a decent image of himself. He's not the best public speaker in the world, and was clearly a little nervous — which wasn't helped by some of the comments coming from certain players at the back of the room. But the overriding image is of someone who loves the game, loves QPR and wants to stay at Loftus Road for a long time — he even suggested he would like to coach youngsters at QPR when he retires! Has Gerry been on at him to sign a 12-year contract or something?

Rob Styles

Iain Dowie and in fact all the players were very vocal on this subject. Dowie started off with a literary joke which a couple of the panel sniggered at, by saying that he thought the ref might be Bill Sykes from Oliver, as he obviously hadn't caught up on rule changes from the 19th Century, which was fine except Dowie really did think this guy's name was Sykes, and not Styles, which confused matters slightly. Dowie said he should know better than to argue with refs, but couldn't help himself, it's the way he is. He went on to say that an official complaint had been made, and that he would be surprised if Styles ever refereed one of our matches again, which is a relief. He confirmed that the ref did make a comment about Dowie being the one who mouthed off about him after the Fulham game just before booking him. Dowie was obviously still upset about our treatment by this referee, and said that after the Fulham game he just posed the question to Sky of "How was it possible to get our first 'decision' after 37 minutes of the game? How was that fair?" — and he was right.

Formations

As may have been expected, there was the question of whether we should switch to 4-4-2 from 5-3-2/3-5-2. Dowie replied that we were playing the system that best fits our players — something I have discussed in this mag before and don't propose to do so again, suffice to say, they're probably right — we don't have the players for 4-4-2.

Gerry Francis

I have to say that the overwhelming feeling I came away from the meeting with was that Gerry may be going sooner rather than later. His absence from the meeting 'on business' may have been quite truthful, but I couldn't help thinking that it was a good chance for Dowie to help us get used to thinking of him as Francis' successor. Before the meeting, Dowie suggested that Francis always wants to take the club forward, but there wasn't any money. He said he was like a fan, and would want a push for promotion next season after this season of decent consolidation. What he seemed to infer was that Francis didn't necessarily think he could take these players any further. In which case, why carry on? And I can see his point. Gerry has nothing to prove, and as we all know, he 'doesn't need football.'

Dowie on the other hand, does need and loves football. He told a very moving story about how he and his Dad would discuss football and tactics for hours. How his dad was a huge Ulsterman, yet when Dowie captained Northern Ireland in a match his dad was crying during the National Anthem. Dowie wants to manage Northern Ireland, and while he is in no rush to get there, he is very ambitious and wouldn't hesitate to take the QPR job. He spoke of how he rarely gets home before midnight due to scouting missions, and how working hard is the best way to learn the managerial game. You got the impression he didn't think he was quite ready, but he's certainly not far off. You also got the impression that people like David Platt were jumping in too early and not learning the game properly.

Overall, Dowie was the big story of the night for me. Articulate, fascinating, intelligent and fiercely determined — I could have spoken to him all night. You really felt like you were in the presence of someone who knew their subject well and loved it. It was a useful evening as well, as we managed to get a few things straight that cause so much debate.
(Dan Trelfer – issue # 137)

Where now for the Hoops?

With any luck, this season should see QPR consolidate a position somewhere in mid-table. Such has been the progress recently that many will be disappointed not to see the team in contention for a play-off place, these people I suspect, have very short memories.

Compared to what we have come accustomed to over twenty years or so, the past two seasons saw QPR plummet in relative terms, to rock bottom. It was at this time in October 1998 that Gerry Francis resumed control of the reigns. I am well aware that football moves on very quickly these days, but our survival last season was nothing short of a miracle.

With no money to spend, even to the desperate point of Ludek Miklosko financing his own transfer from West Ham, and having been forced to sell his best player in Mike Sheron, Gerry managed to motivate a very limited group of players, scraping enough points together to escape the relegation trap-door.

Gerry has even managed to build on those foundations this season, and despite spending very little, the fact that his injury-ravaged team has remained in the higher reaches of Division One makes it simply mind boggling that he should attract criticism for not being positive enough.

Gerry moans a bit because he is a perfectionist, and his realisation that he is never likely to reach perfection makes him very realistic. There is no bullshit with Gerry, you won't find him linking the club to Roberto Baggio and Frank Rijkaard, or signing the likes of Mark Hateley, Ned Zelic, Mike Sheron or Vinnie Jones. He knows QPR's limit to the point that he has never spent more than £750,000 on a player in his time at Loftus Road.

Indeed, his best signings since his return have been Stuart Wardley and Jermaine Darlington. This was an example of Gerry at his best, that is, trawling through lower leagues to unearth some uncut diamonds for modest fees, and then throwing them into the action to let them sink or swim. Fortunately, they have learned to swim very well. Criticism of Wardley is similarly stupid, especially when £15,000 wouldn't pay for the average weekly wage of a Premiership player. Even if he did have nothing to offer the side besides twelve goals in half a season,

As for the future, there still exists a fair amount of dead wood at the club, and this needs clearing at some stage. The problem is that nobody appears to want players like George Kulcsar, Steve Slade, Ademole Bankole and Tony Scully. These players are a legacy of a bygone era and their very presence brings back awful memories. Even Kevin Gallen is living on his past reputation, and it's only the reluctance of sections of the crowd to let him leave that enables him to avoid the wrath of the fanzines.

Criticism of Gerry has been forthcoming even on the occasions when he has been positive. Despite what I have read this season, he is correct in saying that some of the results achieved this season would not have been possible last season. Take Swindon away in driving rain, on a ground where we regularly return empty handed. With a very patched up team, even allowing for the poor opposition, Richard Langley's late strike was remarkable, and Gerry would be right in saying that this would not have happened last season. If things had been the same as last season, then we would be in the bottom three instead of the top ten.

Despite some poor results in recent weeks, I can say with a degree of certainty that QPR have turned the corner at last. Those who continue to attack Gerry should remember who we are indebted to. Our manager will not allow the club to be messed around by idiots like Zelic, Jones, or even John Spencer, who didn't seem to realise that QPR were doing him the favour when they signed him, and that his improved form was more attributable to a drop down into a lower division than his own abilities. A point proven by his failure at Everton, and the fact that he is now plying his trade with Motherwell before he has even reached 30 years of age.

As for Danny Kelly, who claimed that Gerry Francis was the worst manager ever, does anyone listen to this fat moron? He clearly doesn't remember Ossie Ardiles and Christian Gross. This was a man so frightened of success that he didn't want George Graham to reign at White Hart Lane. This was a man whose bulk was such that 'Under The Moon', that hilarious late night sporting chat show, had to limit their number of high profile guests from the world of roller skating and hop-scotch to just one, as there simply was not enough room on their MFI sofa.

(Aiden Magee – issue # 137)

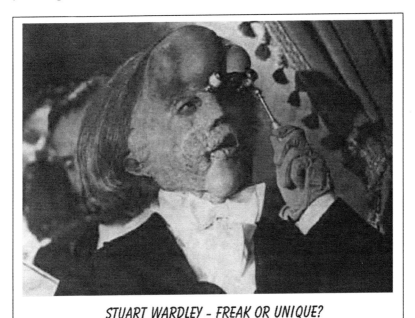

STUART WARDLEY - FREAK OR UNIQUE?

(Issue # 138)

Play-offs (again)

It's safe to say that now we can forget about any hopes of making the play-offs, QPR should aim to finish as high up in the league as possible. Anything less than a top-ten finish would be disappointing, but hardly a disaster, but come the summer Chris Wright & co would need to crucially evaluate exactly where we go from here, and the fact that if our ambitions really do aim towards promotion to the Premiership, a great deal of chopping and changing will be necessary amongst the playing staff, and no small amount of money given to the manager to add to the quality rather than the quantity of the squad.

One player that would certainly add to the quality is Darren Ward, and we must be in with a decent shout of capturing him permanently. For the first time in ages our defence looks reasonably assured — down in no small part to the performances of Ward. We never get thrashed, rarely concede more than a goal a game these days, and if we were a bit more clinical up front we'd definitely be sitting amongst the play-offs contenders.

(Ed – issue # 138)

Rambling on

I fully realise that it must be me, I have after all admitted often enough that I know nothing about this great game of ours, but I just cannot understand what is going on tactically at the Bush. There are some amongst us that think Gerry Francis is the Second Coming of Christ. There are also some of us that think he is practically the reincarnation of the Devil himself. Me, I used to be somewhere in the middle, but I must admit I am currently dropping down the slippery slope towards Hades.

I have read all the efforts to explain our current tactics, in this publication and others, whether it's 5-3-2, 4-4-2, 3-5-2 or even 5-0-5, to me it makes no odds. The team is playing extremely poorly at the moment, certainly compared to before Christmas and most of that must be put down to team selection and tactics. For instance, what tactical genius thinks that Peacock, Wardley and Langley will make a good midfield? Without a ball winner and like him or not George Kulcsar is about our only one we've got, we just cannot compete in the middle of the park. Also Francis moaned and moaned almost non-stop for the three weeks prior to the Stockport match that without a good strong centre forward we had no bite up front. So what did he do? He signed one on the Thursday before the game and promptly left him on the bench, mysteriously thinking that Slade would overnight become a dominant strong running striker. I assume that he left Beck out because he didn't think that he would cope with the system so soon. Tricky thing our 'system'. Get ball, kick ball hard up field to our 'striker' and hope he can desperately hold onto it until the massed ranks of midfield players can get into the box. How long for Christ's sake does it take to learn that?

Because of this obvious faux pas, we were, against Stockport, within ten minutes of recording our third consecutive home game without a shot on target in the first half! Now that's the sort of record to tell your grandchildren about, I don't think. Again, against Fulham, we had only one first half shot on target even though we made two great chances. In the second half I can only remember the keeper having to make two saves as well. With the formation and players that Gerry insists on playing, especially at home, we are purely and simply not getting in enough shots on goal to win matches.

I cannot believe that Gerry has suddenly gone completely mad. Similarly I cannot think that he is taking bribes from the other teams to deliberately put out the wrong players and use such negative tactics. So why week after week is he picking a poor side? The only reason that I can think of, as strange as it seems, is that he just purely and simply doesn't particularly want to win. Maybe he is so frightened of getting into the play-offs, with the possibility of promotion with a squad of no-hopers, that he thinks he must avoid winning games. I know it makes no sense, but if anyone can come up with a better theory, I can't wait to hear it!

While I am 'Gerry bashing', can he be the only manager in football that signs players on loan and then doesn't play them? He did it with McGovern and now he's done it with Beck. I can't remember hearing of anyone else doing it. If you have only got a player for four games to start with and you are paying them Premiership wages, why on earth would you not play them in one of the four? I am changing my mind, maybe Gerry has suddenly gone completely off his trolley. At least that would explain why he signed Sammy Koejoe!

~ ~ ~

Lots of discussions amongst Rangers fans recently about the new contracts for Peacock, Wardley and Darlington. I'm pretty much in favour of all three getting new contracts, especially Wardley — I wouldn't want to lose him despite the criticism he gets for not getting involved in games too much. Dario I'm not so sure about, he can be a liability down the right and must be taught how to tackle. Still, his enthusiasm is catching and he lights up the crowd when he makes his runs forwards. Peacock is a different matter. I personally don't think he contributes so much to a game anymore and I cannot see the point of playing both him and Wardley at the same time. On the other hand, it is nice for a 'name' player to commit himself to the club long term and he will be bloody handy if we ever get another penalty. I do have trouble believing though that several clubs, including some in the Premiership, were ready to snap him up in the summer as was reported in a couple of papers.

~ ~ ~

Our Gerry must have been delighted deep down after the Barnsley game. What an excuse. Now lets see if I've got it right. The reason that Barnsley equalised was not that Hristov made a good run into the box, or that Ready may or may not have fouled him in the process or indeed that the referee, like so many before him this season, was

gagging to give the home team a penalty. No, the reason was purely and simply that Barnsley FC employs ball boys. Apparently ball boys did not exist in Gerry's day, especially ones that throw the ball back quicker when the home team is losing. Come on Gerry get real. When we are playing in our massive new 60,000 athletics stadium, we will need all the ball boys we can get hold of to throw the ball back, given that we will be playing in front of 50,000 empty seats every week.
(Paul Davidson – issue # 138)

Manchester City 1-3 QPR

I so much enjoyed the recent trip to Maine Road, it was almost a journey down memory lane back to the dark days of the late seventies/early eighties (except of course we won away up north!). We spent the game stuck in the corner out in the open perched atop a huge pile of scaffolding that posed as a 'temporary stand'. It wasn't too bad though considering a gale was blowing, but I'm sure it swayed about occasionally (mainly when we scored).

It was after the game that the feelings of the bad old days came back. The Greater Manchester Police, trying desperately to compete with the West Midlands force as Britains worst, insisted on us staying penned up in what resembled Stalag 17 for a quarter of an hour, for 'our own protection.' This was not because we had won. This had been decided before the game. Exactly whom we were being protected from wasn't very obvious, as by the final whistle, most of the City fans were well gone. Still it did give the local bobbies time to prance about whilst we huddled together in an open compound ringed by high brick walls with barbed wire on the top. And didn't our dear old boys in blue love it? Trying to look ferocious and talking secretly into their little radios, they were all stars.

By the time we got out, the only people left on the hospitable streets of Moss Side were the usual looters and urban terrorists. We couldn't care less though and the fact that my car (complete with non-removable QPR LSA sticker) had not been torched only added to the evening's enjoyment,
(Paul Davidson – issue # 139)

Cause for satisfaction

As I pointed out in my last piece (ITL # 137), this season has surpassed my expectations, and in many ways it is very comparable to Gerry's first season in his last spell as boss — plenty of draws, a few fine victories but above all, comfortably placed, difficult to beat and with some hope for the future. Being difficult to beat is so important, especially for a club that has been in free fall for the past few years. No longer do I necessarily expect us to concede late goals (even if we still do) and tactics such as these should always provide the sound platform that every club needs if they are to successfully rebuild.

This progress should not mask however, the fact that there is an urgent need to clear out this summer. But as I have said before some of the people on the 'dead wood' list have been there since Ali Osman sang on the 'Ferry Aid' album, and will not be easily disposed of. I also believe that we have adequate cover in midfield to dispense with Richard Langley, who whilst blessed with good ability, occasionally shows poor attitude, and to say we could use the money would not be overstating the case.

For the first time since Gerry was last here, I feel that there is genuine cause for optimism. One positive thing the financial crisis has done to QPR is force them back to what they always did best — a very simple economic principle — buy low, sell high. Successive managers contrived to reverse this uncomplicated theory by spending money on poor footballers.

Now any one of Langley, Wardley, Darlington or Baraclough would fetch decent fees — when combined they didn't even cost us a hundred grand. Gone are the days when we spent big on second rate players. Who have we ever bought for more than a million that can be considered a good quality long term signing? We are thinking in the realms of Hateley, Zelic, Osborn, Spencer and Sheron here, and the total paid for the first two in particular would have been better spent on a decent black cat.

This season has shown a major improvement and come May we can be very satisfied with, hopefully, a top ten finish and if Watford were to accept the £500,000 tabled for Darren Ward then this would be another master stroke by Gerry Francis. Ward has composure, height, discipline, strength and an excellent positional sense making him every inch the type of centre half we need on a long term basis.

(Aiden Magee – issue # 139)

A step too far

Well, the play-offs were always going to be a long shot, and our mini-revival at least kept the interest up for a little while longer. At last we've finally managed to field a team fit to wear the hoops. I doubt nobody quite expected the season to have gone the way it has, so it's big thanks to Gerry & Co for restoring some hope and pride. There's six games left and still a lot to play for, not least for the numerous players who are out of contract in the summer and want to stay. Once Beck and Taylor return to their clubs, it would be nice to see a bit of experimentation up front to see what we've got in reserve, and that includes Mr Koejoe — £250,000 is a lot of money to QPR these days and it's time to see if it really hasn't been wasted.

(Ed – issue # 139)

BARGAINS GALORE AT THE
QPR END OF SEASON SALE*

100 FREE AIR MILES

WE PAY YOU! **0% APR**

SAVE £££s **90% OFF 1995 VALUE!**

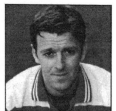

BUY 2 GET 1 FREE!
* But does anybody want them?

(Issue # 139)

Year 2000
'Nowadays everybody wants to talk like they've got something to say but nothing comes out'

Hands up who just knew that Palace were going to beat us back in March. Deep down I knew it but post euphoria from our day in Walsall had me almost believing that the unbeaten run would continue and a place in the play-offs booked. A painful evening saw our play-off hopes all but finished with the added rub of having our second nine match unbeaten run in the season ended once again by the most boring club in London, if not the world.

"There's always next season," is a not uncommon expression heard in my years of watching the R's. That was about the only grain of comfort following the entertaining draw against Norwich. With next season in mind I find it infuriating, given the fact there is nothing to play for but pride, that we haven't seen any new faces come into the team. The team was superb against Ipswich but to have deadwood like Kulcsar, Rowland and Scully on the bench instead of prospects from the youth side — such as Graham, Jeanne, Lusardi etc, makes absolutely no sense to me.

Jeanne started against Norwich and won the man of the match award even though he was substituted after 50 odd minutes. His reward was to be sent straight back to the reserves. We've only seen glimpses of him and as far as we know Gerry may have him playing at his true level in the reserves. However with no pressure on him and the team in a comfortable position and playing reasonably well it is now a golden opportunity to blood new talent such as Jeanne into the first team squad even if it means him starting on the bench.

The signing of Sammy Koejoe for a quarter of a million pounds has certainly raised a few eyebrows, especially when you consider that he was signed purely on the basis of a video recording of him in action. Gerry has certainly proven in the past that he is quite adept at discovering raw talent but paying £250,000 for Sammy Koejoe has seen him sadly fall foul to a quite elaborate hoax that gives a whole new meaning to buying dodgy Dutch videos.

Sammy, undoubtedly, is a raw talent and there is plenty there to work on but the player in the video that Gerry sat down to watch was Sammy cunningly superimposed, using state of the art computer technology, onto films of Pele at his peak. On viewing the video Gerry didn't think he was getting a future prospect but the finished article. Superlative skill and fantastic pace was all on show and all for £250,000. Must have seemed far too good to be true. There were, of course, aspects of Sammy's game that Gerry felt he could work on and improve. One particular clip saw Sammy shoot narrowly wide from the halfway line!

'The world we know is goin down'

Although Sammy's skills must have seemed too good to be true what has happened to Gerry could have happened to anyone and although we may not have Pele up front I think Sammy showed enough against Ipswich to suggest that the future may still be bright. However one would have expected Gerry to have been a little suspect — especially when one of Sammy's shots was saved by Gordon Banks.

'When they move their lips it's just a load of gibberish. But then again they forgot about Mat'

A quick point on Gerry's eye for a player. I'm not denying for one minute that he has had his moments — Jermaine Darlington and Stuart Wardley being recent examples but Gerry did not, I repeat DID NOT discover Les Ferdinand. Despite what the press, the programme and even Gerry himself says it was in fact Jim Smith who signed him from Hayes. It's fair to say that Les peaked under Gerry but then again he had started to show his full potential under Don Howe and only injuries impeded his progress — phew. I'm glad I've got that one of my chest.

'Cops try to search me but guns they'll never find. My lethal weapons' my mind'

I have been criticised in the past for my often-pessimistic attitude to life. It's true that with the correct mental attitude things do happen and often rub off on others around you. If I had bothered writing an article at the beginning of the season it would have been a reasonably optimistic one. I didn't think that we would struggle this season and whilst others including Gerry seem to be shocked I personally knew we'd be OK.

My reasons to name but a few were Matthew Rose and Richard Langley back in the side, Kiwomya and Steiner starting the season up front and the emergence of Darlington and Jeanne. I didn't even know about Wardley who while not being everybody's cup of tea has topped the goalscoring charts for most of the season.

Gerry may be being realistic when he has stated from day one that our aim is to get 50 points to avoid the drop but ever since it's been apparent that we were not going to struggle it wouldn't have hurt to have occasionally dropped some positive vibes. His constant negative attitude does little to inspire any excitement amongst the fans and we wonder why our gates are so low.

There are plenty of idiots out there who if Gerry said we're going to make the play-offs would believe him and therefore we may see some bigger gates or at least a little bit of expectation amongst our support. It's all about creating a buzzing environment, one that generates expectation and excitement. When Alan Sugar took over at Spurs and said they would win the title within five years, mark my words a lot of their fans believed him. OK his words have fallen flat but there's nothing wrong with the occasional bit of optimism even if at times you're speaking bullshit.

'It's a family affair'

Must admit I laughed when I heard that Gavin had done daddy a favour with his goal against Ipswich leading to the win that saw the Addicks finally promoted. Not losing the track here but I've been to the gym down the Valley on a couple of occasions. It's round the corner from me and that is quite honestly the only reason I would ever attend. It's a bit like a metaphor for Charlton's chances in the Premiership next season — ill equipped and not enough decent talent on view. Anyhow I digress — one aspect of going down there is that you get changed in the home teams' changing room and the blackboard is still up with a diagram of team formations and who should be marking who. I guess you'll be interested to know that I went down there the day after our 2-1 defeat and the message next to Gavin's name was — 'If he comes on just kick him!'

Oh yeah and just to show there are aspects to me that one would consider to be bad taste to Charlton fans, I have a AKUTR's 'We are QPR' sticker on my bedroom window. Following the Ipswich game did any of the locals come round and offer to buy me a drink? Did they fcuk.
(Matthew Holley – issue # 140)

Rambling on

Lots of speculation lately about Gerry signing Brian McGovern from Arsenal after his loan spell. Just to nip those ideas in the bud and also to give some insight into what actually happens in our dugout during a game, the following is part of an interview with Brian, who has just been made captain of Arsenal reserves. It was published in the Arsenal UEFA Cup programme against Lens a couple of weeks ago.

"I felt like I was flying whilst I was with QPR. I couldn't put a foot wrong(?) and playing in front of large crowds(?) where every kick counts was just amazing. When I was at QPR, if you made a mistake it was crucial and on Monday morning Gerry Francis would play a video of the weekend's game and whoever made the mistake had to re-live that moment and learn from it — there was no hiding."

The tall defender made his first team debut for Rangers coming off the bench against Crewe. That first game is one that fills him with pride and still raises a smile on his face; "I was sitting on the subs bench and Gerry Francis kept asking me if I could play in midfield and I replied yes. He asked the same question for practically every position on the park and I always replied yes because I was so keen to play. He then asked me if I could play wing-back on the right. I'd never played there in my life but of course, I said yes. I was still nodding my head when he barked "right, you're on.""

"I went on as right wing-back. The ball came right to me. I bolted down the right flank, skipped over the challenge from their left back and fired a shot that beat the 'keeper but cannoned back off the crossbar. It was like a dream and the crowd were going wild. From that game on I kept the right wing-back position and the crowd were really great to me. It was great and I want that again."

QPR are keen to sign the Dubliner, but the Gunners have offered him a fresh contract; "I've got a new one year contract with Arsenal and I hope it will give me a chance to break into the first team. I will give it my best shot and if I don't get picked for the first team squad, hopefully other teams will see what I can do. I've had a taste of what first team football can be like and I want more."

But not with us unfortunately!

~ ~ ~

I wonder if anyone actually sat and read the 'Head to Head' page in the Ipswich programme with Karl Ready. Now I must admit I have taken absolutely no interest in this page all season, but being the first of my crowd into the LSA that day, I gave it a cursory glance.

If the facts in it are true then it is absolutely staggering. It credits big Karl with just 70 tackles all season, of which he has won 33%. Given that he had played 28 league games up to that point, that makes it approximately two and a half tackles a match, of which he has won less than one a game! I don't know about you, but I really find that amazing. No wonder some of the fans around me give him so much stick. He might get over ten clearing headers in a match and almost three blocks, but less than one tackle a game is disgusting for a senior defender. No bloody wonder he can't get back in the Welsh Squad.

~ ~ ~

Whilst dipping into the programme, it is not too difficult to see why good old Stan has spent much of his life broke is it? Having got the first of his free bets stunningly right, he has not made one single correct prediction since. Let's face it, if you were in a betting shop and saw Stan putting some money on a horse you fancied, you would either pick another horse to bet on, pick another race to bet on, pick another sport to bet on, or just plain give up gambling altogether!

~ ~ ~

What on earth has happened to super Sammy Koejoe? From being an absolute joke, he has turned into quite a reasonable forward and he took his goal so well against Ipswich that I cannot wait to see what him and Steiner can do together next season. Perhaps

Gerry is not so mad after all, or perhaps he is a very lucky man. Either way, Koejoe will do for me, especially if the arrogant Kiwomya gets his wish to play in the Premiership next season (as if!).

(Paul Davidson – issue # 140)

Positives & negatives from the 1999/2000 season

Positives

No team has fully dominated us over 90 minutes.

The goalscoring exploits of Stuart Wardley and the midfield as a whole.

The season has gone far better than we honestly expected.

We were always in with a shout of the play-offs up until the closing matches.

Raising £8.5m from the sale of Wasps' training ground.

Having more away wins than the previous two seasons put together, including memorable ones at Ipswich, Blackburn and Manchester City.

Getting decent value out of Bosman-signing Chris Kiwomya.

Gavin Peacock agreeing to stay at QPR despite the lure of better things elsewhere, and his record breaking 5 goals in the opening 5 games.

Lee Harper finally proving to be a safe pair of hands between the posts.

A number of very good loan signings made by Gerry Francis.

The excellent comeback at Stockport County.

Not one team has given us a thrashing, and has never looked like doing so.

Not having to endure a third successive scrap against relegation.

Regaining the satisfaction that on our day, we can beat anyone.

Exuberance of fans in Q-block — half of it is now deemed unsafe for spectators!

Iain Dowie gaining an excellent reputation as first team coach – maybe our next manager when Gerry goes back to feeding his pigeons on a full-time basis.

Matthew rose (when fit) — a cultured figure in defence not seen since Glenn Roeder.

Superb away support at Fulham, West Brom, Norwich, Swindon, Charlton (cup) and Walsall.

Witnessing the Fulham team all pissed up in 'Bad Bobs' on a Tuesday night — and their fans really do believe they're bigger than us!

Negatives

The crippling injury list either side of Christmas.

Gerry Francis continually playing down our chances of success.

Losing to Cardiff City over two legs in the Worthington Cup.

The meningitis scare that ruined our early season momentum.

The fact we've failed to raise a single penny from outgoing transfers.

The state of the pitch in the second half of the season.

Lowly Crystal Palace ending both of our nine-game unbeaten runs.

Richard Langley not quite living up to expectations.

Rob Styles appalling manor in which he handled the matches at Fulham and Charlton.

Not enough home wins and a shortage of goals scored down the Loft end.

Too many sending-offs, mainly for the most innocuous of fouls or childish retaliation.

Ugly scenes at Fulham, Port Vale and, surprisingly, before the home game against Norwich on Shepherds Bush Green.

Our terrible record in London derbies.

All the ridiculous penalties awarded to opposing teams.

Home form during January, February and March — zzzzzzzzzz

Conceding late goals at Grimsby, Norwich, Barnsley and Charlton at the cost of 6 points.

Too many predictable team line-ups and lack of experimentation from Gerry Francis.

Kevin Gallen having another disappointing season — and probably his last.

Appalling treatment and conditions for QPR fans at Swindon Town and Manchester City.

Failing to capture Darren Ward on a permanent basis.

(Ed – issue # 140)

Rob Steiner receives commiserations from QPR fans after harshly being sent off at Fulham by 'referee' Rob Styles. A knee injury curtailed his career at just 26 years of age a year later

Gavin Peacock rejoined QPR in December 1996 and went on to make over 200 appearances for the club, scoring 39 goals. He was awarded a testimonial against Chelsea in May 2003

Kevin Gallen celebrates his goal at Portsmouth with Stuart Wardley on the final day of the season with just about his last kick of a ball during his first spell as a QPR player

1999/00 ~ Division 1

Date	Match	Comp	Scorers	Att	Issue
07/08/99	H Huddersfield W 3-1	League	Darlington, Kiwomya, Peacock	13,642	# 130
10/08/99	A Cardiff City W 2-1	Lgc Cup	Langley, Peaockc	5,702	
14/08/99	A Bolton Wndrs L 1-2	League	Peacock (p)	13,019	
21/08/99	H Wolves D 1-1	League	Peacock	13,239	
25/08/99	H Cardiff City L 1-2*	Lge Cup	Peacock (p)	6,185	# 131
28/08/99	A Notts Forest D 1-1	League	Ready	18,442	
31/08/99	H Port Vale W 3-2	League	Wardley (2), Kiwomya	9,502	
18/09/99	A Fulham L 0-1	League		19,623	
25/09/99	A Birmingham L 0-2	League		18,748	
02/10/99	H Blackburn D 0-0	League		14,002	# 132
09/10/99	H Tranmere W 2-1	League	Steiner, Peacock	9,357	
16/10/99	A Ipswich Town W 4-1	League	Peacock, Wardley, Steiner (2)	17,871	
19/10/99	A West Brom W 1-0	League	Wardley	9,874	
23/10/99	H Portsmouth D 0-0	League		13,303	# 133
27/10/99	H Birmingham D 2-2	League	Kiwomya, Steiner	11,196	
30/10/99	A Blackburn W 2-0	League	Wardley, Gallen	17,941	
02/11/99	A Stockport Cty D 3-3	League	Maddix, Gallen (2)	4,868	
06/11/99	H Man City D 1-1	League	Kiwomya	19,002	
14/11/99	A Crystal Palace L 0-3	League		15,861	
20/11/99	H Walsall W 2-1	League	Wardley, Kiwomya	10,058	# 134
23/11/99	A Grimsby Town L 1-2	League	Kiwomya	4,297	
27/11/99	H Barnsley D 2-2	League	Darlington, Steiner	11,054	
30/11/99	H Sheff Utd W 3-1	League	Steiner, Wardley, Breaker	9,922	
04/12/99	A Huddersfield L 0-1	League		13,027	
11/12/99	H Torquay Utd D 1-1	FA Cup	Wardley	8,843	# 135
18/12/99	H Charlton Ath D 0-0	League		14,709	
21/12/99	A Torquay Utd W 3-2	FA Cup R	Wardley (2), Kiwomya	5,232	
26/12/99	A Norwich City L 1-2	League	Wardley	17,800	
28/12/99	H Crewe W 1-0	League	Wardley	12,011	
03/01/00	A Swindon W 1-0	League	Langley	9,302	
08/01/00	A Charlton Ath L 0-1	FA Cup		16,798	
15/01/00	H Bolton Wndrs L 0-1	League		11,396	# 136
22/01/00	A Wolves L 2-3	League	Peacock, Slade	20,069	
29/01/00	H Notts Forest D 1-1	League	Kiwomya	12,297	
05/02/00	A Port Vale D 1-1	League	Wardley	5,493	
12/02/00	H Stockport Cty D 1-1	League	Kiwomya	10,531	# 137
19/02/00	A Barnsley D 1-1	League	Rose	14,212	
28/02/00	H Fulham D 0-0	League		16,308	
05/03/00	A Sheff Utd D 1-1	League	Beck	11,554	
08/03/00	A Man City W 3-1	League	Kiwomya, OG, Beck (p)	31,353	
11/03/00	H Grimsby W 1-0	League	Beck (p)	10,450	# 138
18/03/00	A Walsall W 3-2	League	OG, Wardley, Kiwomya	6,414	
22/03/00	H Crystal Palace L 0-1	League		12,842	
25/03/00	H Norwich City D 2-2	League	Kiwomya (2)	11,918	
31/03/00	A Charlton Ath L 1-2	League	Taylor	19,617	
08/04/00	H Swindon W 2-1	League	Ready, Beck (p)	12,633	# 139
15/04/00	A Crewe L 1-2	League	Langley	4,741	
22/04/00	H Ipswich Town W 3-1	League	Peacock, Koejoe, Kiwomya	14,920	
24/04/00	A Tranmere Rvs D 1-1	League	Peacock (p)	7,744	
29/04/00	H West Brom D 0-0	League		15,244	# 140
07/05/00	A Portsmouth W 3-1	League	Langley, Gallen, OG	16,301	

* Lost 2-3 on penalties

League Record - P46 W16 D18 L12 F62 A53 Pts 66. League position – 10th

In The Loft Player of the Season – Lee Harper

Chapter 5

2000/01

Five years of mis-management take their toll

Having written the review of the previous season before I started sifting through the ten editions of In The Loft from the 2000/01 campaign, perhaps the term 'under achieved' I used at the end wasn't the correct one to use for this campaign. Your memory can often blur things as time passes, but it's apparent that QPR finally succumbed to relegation because of the wrong tactics employed by Gerry Francis up until his departure in February. 3-5-2 or 5-3-2 (whichever way you saw it) worked during the 1999/00 season because we didn't have Peter Crouch up front. Once he arrived, the long-ball tactic was over-used and we paid the ultimate price.

Not that Peter Crouch could be held responsible. He had a fine season considering most of the time our only way to goal was through him, or quite often, above him. As we got to know then and as we all know now, Crouch is just as effective with the ball played to feet. Pity Gerry Francis failed to utilise this more. You only need to see how few goals Peacock, Wardley and Langley got between them compared to the previous season to provide further evidence; just 8 from 91 starts compared to 28 from 113 before. Each was under-used as the ball usually by-passed them, which in Wardley's case, made him look far worse than he actually was.

Looking at the stats, quite how Chris Kiwomya managed to get 10 goals from a season that saw a new striker arrive every other month with Chris demoted to the bench, is quite impressive. Paul Furlong, Paul Peschisolido, Kevin Lisbie, Michel Ngonge and Andy Thomson were all seen as the answer, but if the tactics don't change, it's not about personnel. Blaming injuries is also a bit of an excuse.

Mind you, when Ian Holloway took over he used the 4-4-2 system and won once in thirteen games. One less defender, same tactics = even fewer points. Seems to make sense. I guess it looks so straight forward from the stands, but Holloway should have made a better go at saving us than he did. He took over with the club fourth from bottom and a game in hand on the two sides above and below us. Just one win against an almost-relegated Tranmere was a poor effort, and to finish ten points from safety was some downfall. We'd have probably faired better had Crouch joined the list of absentees through broken legs – at least then both Francis and Holloway would have had to re-evaluate our approach to games.

'Holloway couldn't stop the rot,' some may say, though Gerry's last couple of months in charge were actually the best of the season points-wise, including two wins in his final three games when waiting for someone to come in and replace him. 5-0 defeats at Preston and Wimbledon had done him few favours though, and the time was right to move on. To Holloway's credit, it wasn't long before he got QPR heading back in the right direction.

Unlike relegation from the Premiership, dropping down to the third tier of English football proved not to be the catastrophe it seemed at the time. Financially, would the club have survived another season in Division 1? Division 2 was the start of a whole new era, the squad was finally obliterated, and somehow Holloway brought the good times back to Loftus Road on an ever-decreasing budget. ❏

High hopes

For the first time in four seasons we have genuine cause for optimism, with a place in the play-offs an achievable aim come May. The last time we felt the same was back in 1997/98, with talk of 100 goals and 100 points among the web communities, but you don't need reminding how the season turned out. It's hard to pinpoint exactly where we're capable of finishing this season, but I'd be surprised if we don't end up somewhere between 4th and 8th — but at 33/1 for the First Division title, that's got to be worth a fiver of anyone's money.

So why the optimism? Last season turned out better than anyone could have expected, and the play-offs were never that far off. A year on, the squad is stronger and many key players have gained valuable experience. The league is nowhere near as strong as last season, which should make for a tighter division. QPR are in a much better position than a year ago — on the pitch and off it — where others have faltered, so progression from last season should almost be expected. Gerry Francis is naturally playing his cards close to his chest, but even he must be feeling a tinge of expectancy. Pre-season has gone well, and although there are several injury problems, the strength in depth should see us through without too much fuss.

(Ed – issue # 141)

Rambling on

So the proposed clear out of players in the summer never happened then. Surprise, surprise. At the time of writing we have let go of Steve Slade, Michael Mahoney-Johnson, Rikki Lopez (possibly a big mistake) and a few other players I cannot remember. Not exactly a clear out do you think? I just cannot believe that certain players are still hanging around. It looks like we will have one of the biggest squads in the division at this rate and will struggle to put a decent team out. Ah well, some things never change.

~ ~ ~

How scary is it then that as soon as the Rangers players report back for pre-season training that all they and Gerry are on about is the 'Terrible Tuesday' run-arounds? Wouldn't it be nice if this season our players weren't, quote, "the fittest in the division" but could actually play a bit? Might get through the season with a few less injuries too!

~ ~ ~

I have to say that I fancy our chances of a decent mid-table finish this coming season. I like the look of the defence for the first time in ages (as long as big Karl isn't playing). I think that we should score more goals than of late and I think that we have two goalkeepers perfectly capable enough for this division. My only worry is midfield. I really don't think that Peacock cuts the mustard any more and I also think he is too similar to Wardley. I worry about who in there is going to win the ball for us although Langley is playing pre-season like a man possessed. I hope he can continue without getting sent off. He would have been sent off at least twice at Wycombe if it were a league match, not a friendly. All in all tenth would do nicely, but I suppose all we will hear is Francis saying that we haven't got enough points and the press suggesting that we are bound for the play-offs. Never mind, if we can finish above that heap of garbage down by the Thames it will do for me!

~ ~ ~

Hands up all those that are surprised that our new shirts will not be ready for the start of the new season. No hands going up? Oh well that really is a surprise. I had been wondering why we were playing all the pre-season games in the white and black kit. I don't know for sure but I am willing to bet that we are the only team in the top two divisions that cannot produce a new shirt in time for the new season. I wouldn't mind much, but this is the third time this has happened in the last few years and it really is just not good enough. If Le bloody Coq Sportif cannot come up with the goods then dump them for someone who can. Or is it of course not their fault but the hapless back-office staff at Loftus Road? That would be a surprise now wouldn't it?
(Paul Davidson – issue # 141)

Season ticket sales up

An impressive marketing campaign by QPR has seen a vast improvement in season ticket sales, with an estimated 5,000 to be sold by the start of the season. Personally, I've never really found the need to buy one, persisting with being a member only, but it was tempting to go it for purely on the basis that the club has made a real effort in this department and deserves to prosper from it. I was even sent a letter at the start of July, stating that the early bird deadline of June 30th has been extended until 17th July to tempt those that had yet to purchase a season ticket, but were still thinking of doing so. Pretty sure there's been a few hundred 'bonus' sales from this offer alone. Well done QPR...
(Ed – issue # 141)

The close season

The close season this summer has seemed particularly long, I suppose partly because of the awful failure of England at Euro 2000. But the other reason why the pre-season seems to have dragged is that, for once, QPR have been quick and decisive in the transfer market. With our comfortable place in the table assured about six games before the end of the season, Francis and Dowie were able to identify their targets and as soon as the season was finished, almost, we had a couple in the bag. Warren, Connolly and Carlisle — at least two of them seem very shrewd signings, were all signed before Euro 2000 even started, I think, and we've been waiting ever since then to see if they're any good.

After years and years of waiting for us to make pre-season signings and never seeing it happen, it finally did this year, and it's been very exciting, even if the fees have been low — as Wardley and Darlington proved last season (and Sheron before that) — price is no indication of quality. The other side-effect of these early pre-season transfers is that it strangulated most of the enjoyably frustrating transfer speculation we usually experience this time of year. All we've been treated to is constant reports that Jermaine is about to nip off to Wimbledon (a bigger sideways move I've rarely heard of) and that we're in for the highly erratic Dele Adebola. On top of this the much-anticipated clearout never really happened, with only Slade, Bankole and Gallen, of the first-teamers on their way accompanied by sundry ex-youths. Rowland, Morrow, Bruce and one or two others seem to have somehow made the cut.

The friendlies are under way and there was some excitement surrounding the lanky Peter Crouch who eventually signed for £60,000, while another midfielder who turned out to be Danny Grieves of Watford. The mystery surrounding him, though, is bizarre, with Francis seemingly happy to let people believe he was variously Mario Lusardi or Alex Dick. There was the idea that Francis was deliberately keeping his identity hidden so that no other clubs came in for him. It was an interesting idea which recalls those pro-wrestlers that fight with a mask on for months only to have it finally removed by his arch nemesis who then realises that the guy is his long lost brother who he had once double-crossed when they were tag-team partners. Except in this case he was eventually revealed as some midfielder no one had really heard of that Watford weren't too bothered about losing.

This kind of optimistic madness that has swept through the internet messageboards is occasionally tempered by those who are perennially talking down our chances, claiming we'll be lucky to even finish tenth again. At the forefront of these is Gerry Francis himself of course, but he has plenty of backers who can be found on at qpr.org, which can occasionally be a joy and where all kinds of pre-season madness has been developing over the last few weeks.

The pessimistic view is not one I subscribe to, incidentally. We've added some good players to an already fairly solid squad, and Gerry seems less pessimistic than usual, which is an excellent sign. I firmly believe that we have one of the best coaches in the league in Gerry and the play-offs won't be too far away. This season is probably still slightly too early for us, but next season may see us reap some real success.

Boredom struck with great ferocity almost as soon as the football season finished at qpr.org, which signalled the immediate start of the silly season. If you've never visited this site it is occasionally great fun. One issue that has gone on all summer regards Kevin Gallen — there are those who are still desperate to argue that him leaving is the worst thing that ever happened to us and he should be played in midfield as some kind of playmaker.

So there we have it. The pre-season. This could be a great season — and as countless managers will be saying in their programme notes on the first home game of the season — let's get behind the boys and hope we can make an improvement on last year's relative success.

(Dan Trelfer – issue # 141)

For sale or not for sale?

A reliable source (I know, aren't they all) from within the club tells me that most of the board believe Wright has a lot to learn as chairman of QPR, 'out of his depth' perhaps being the operative phrase. Wright has said on many occasions in the past he would sell his stake in the club if the right offer came along, which rather contradicts his ambitions to move QPR to the 35,000 seat-capacity 'Stadium of Wright' (sorry) in Feltham — forget all other rumours, this is where Wright wants to move QPR to. The cost? £30million — QPR can't raise the money, but Wright knows a man who can.

During the last twelve months, a rich Arab businessman, intent into buying into English football, offered to buy out Chris Wright and pump a guaranteed £20-25million into the club for new players. Absolutely true, but the offer was turned down by Wright, who it now seems wants to see his role through to the end — the end in this case overseeing a return to the Premiership for QPR, combined with a brand new home. Without outside financial help the latter really does seem an impossibility — the plans are in place, but where's the money going to come from?

(Ed – issue # 141)

I must confess, I still believe...

'The prophecy is an easy thing for rarely is the prophet brought to judgement'

So that's why, on that note, you won't get any sweeping predictions from me on the R's chances this season. Suffice to say that I don't think we'll struggle and if, and it's a big if, certain key men manage to stay fit — Matthew Rose being a good example here of someone who always seems to be unlucky in the injury department — then who knows?

Play-offs or maybe even more? Attitude, lack of faith and dare I say lack of ability may prove our downfall. Personally, though, I would struggle to see any real quality in that

Charlton side that won the title last year and with the likes of Langley, Darlington, Rose and a plethora of players you would always fancy to find the net, maybe this could be our season after all.

'I must confess'

So it was agreed. One Tuesday night near the end of May over a few (sic) drinks at that number one Tuesday night watering hole — 'Bad Bob's' — that come the new season, I would have composed an article by that name for the new look 'In The Loft'.

First, in case you don't know the reason for the title; Britney Spears' (a big favourite of the Ed's) popular number which goes a little something like this; 'My loneliness is killing me, I must confess I still Believe.' Personally I prefer the other version I've heard — 'My flat chest was killing me, I must confess, I paid for these.' But I digress...

Writing hasn't been easy lately. Last season I picked up my pen (outdated illustration) no more than twice. This was to give me time to get my brain back in gear and to find some inspiration from somewhere in time for the next edition. Two whole months to slowly compose notes in any spare seconds I get and hopefully end up with something resembling an article. Therefore I'm just starting to compose this on 31st July — deadline day, and realising with horror that the serious stuff starts again in two Saturday's time and wondering what happened to the summer break.

With horror — watching QPR isn't that bad is it? No, not at all, well last season was a big improvement on previous ones although that is not saying much. It's just that the summer has just disappeared and with it our break. As a football fan it has been said that we don't exist just in years but in seasons. Summer is our equivalent of Christmas, the day before the new season is our New Year. That's why all that Millennium nonsense just passed me by. Yes I went out on 31st December 1999 but only because I felt I had too.

New Year? How could it be? We still had over four months to go and Rangers at the time were 7th in the table! What a difference a year makes, or should that be a season.

I remember the first time Gerry was in charge and the amount of games we drew. A cover of ITL actually illustrated that had all those drawn games been wins we would have been top. Much the same last season really. Six straight draws starting the end of January were followed by three wins (our second nine match unbeaten run) leaving Rangers sitting in 10th place with realistic hopes of a play-off spot. Two games at home followed and saw Palace for the second time that season end our unbeaten spell and then of course a draw at home to Norwich. The season then just fizzled out as nothing was left to play for. Not even a relegation battle to give us some excitement at the end.

'If I was cloned never would I be alone'

So although not wanting to stick my neck out and foresee great times down the Bush the thought of going back to the Premiership is a little worrying. With the ridiculous prices being paid for players nowadays maybe human cloning is our best bet and the only way a club of our size will ever be able to compete at that level again. However, presuming that we won't get a mad scientist on our books to improve our chances this season what chance do the current squad have?

With Kiwomya signing a new contract, Crouch and Connolly signing, Steiner hopefully getting back to fitness and the emergence of Koejoe towards the end of last season we have a few players now bidding for the striker's slots.

A lot will depend on our midfield. Stuart Wardley scored 14 goals last season — all in open play from midfield, but amongst a lot of our support he generates no feelings of genuine excitement as to what a prospect he may be At times he can be an anonymous figure, disappearing for long periods only to emerge with a telling contribution often in the form of a breakthrough goal. He remains in many peoples' eyes a dilemma — split between those who see his goalscoring as invaluable and many who think he could be dropped because of his overall contribution to a game usually expected from a midfielder — winning tackles being an obvious weakness.

Take the draw at home to Nottingham Forest One would hardly have noticed him and then from the half-way line he brilliantly turned his marker and delivered a pinpoint cross, straight onto Kiwomya's grateful head. Then there are those games where he appears to do everything. Walsall away is a great example. Not only did he score but also brilliantly set up Kiwomya's equally brilliant finish for the winner. In between these two telling contributions he covered just about every blade of grass on the pitch — well that's how it seemed from the stands.

If at the start of the season us fans had been told that we would have a new midfield player who would weigh in with 14 goals, it's fair to say that we would probably be seeing him as our key player, the 'Mr Irreplaceable'. It is ironic therefore that despite his remarkable achievements in his first full season of pro football that the full weight of the fans expectations still does not fall onto his shoulders.

From a personal point of view, and I don't claim it be representative of a lot of my hopes for this season, are dependent on whether Richard Langley can continue as he finished the season. It's unfair maybe to expect so much of someone still in the early stages of his career and that is why maybe he disappointed and frustrated last season as much as he pleased. However a lot can be put down to the injury he suffered following his explosive introduction into the side the previous season.

However as the season progressed he slowly started to regain his confidence and the later stages of the season saw him boss the midfield in the way a lot had expected him to do on a more regular basis. His goalscoring has proved one disappointing aspect of his game but so far this year he has scored more than Wardley from midfield — the final one an absolute cracker at Pompey, illustrating the devastating skill he possesses.

A lot will depend on these two players but I believe the final piece of the midfield puzzle could be the re-introduction of Matthew Rose into a central midfield role — injuries permitting. This way we could also afford to play four at the back and also it will allow us to carry Wardley in the side, and by this no disrespect is intended. Tackling is not Stuart's strong point and we need someone in the midfield to win the ball, hence allowing Langley more space to strut his stuff. With Rose alongside Langley in the middle this would release Wardley to play just behind the front two, doing what he does best — making runs into the box from deep. In this formation we may even see another repeat of his heroics in front of goal last season.

When Gerry first took over Rose adopted the midfield role to good effect and he must be allowed the chance to make the position his own once again. As well as providing defensive cover in midfield he is also comfortable on the ball and could contribute at both ends of the field.

(Matthew Holley – issue # 141)

Moreno Bares All

I was quite happy for Kevin Gallen to go, partly because the club wouldn't have to surfer payment of his high wages and partly because he just hasn't turned into the player we all thought he would be. Gallen and Liverpool's Robbie Fowler were supposed great mates and I guess secretly I was hoping that Gallen would become as prolific a striker as Fowler, but unfortunately it was not to be. How times have changed, from being rated at £7m by Manchester United to a free transfer to Huddersfield Town, football really is a funny old game. Thankfully I don't have to hear any more of that stupid 'magic hat' song.

~ ~ ~

Farewell too to our beloved (sic) Bosman signing Ademole Bankole who has gone back to Crewe (thankfully shunted out of the way). We can thank Bruce Rioch for this particular transfer as I well remember eavesdropping on a conversation between them at a pre-season friendly at Millwall. Bankole told Rioch that Lincoln City had approached him and that they were guaranteeing him first team football to which Rioch replied, "you're a Rangers player and your staying a Rangers player." Ade at least did manage to get his boots sponsored on the kit sponsors page last season by 'Hopplos och Draplig, Sweden', which was a fantastic achievement untill Rob Steiner pointed out that it was Swedish for 'Hopeless and Rubbish'!

Goodbye also to Michael Mahoney-Johnson, who has now joined Sutton United. MM-J was actually at the club for ten years which means he could have been the only Rangers player to have played less than half a dozen games yet qualified for a testimonial game.

~ ~ ~

During the Summer I was dashing for my Metropolitan Line train at Wembley Park when I heard a commotion going on. A man with his back to the carriage I was in was voicing his disapproval of the late running of the train. The man, who had a Geordie accent, was having his name taken by the Transport Police and the station supervisor in a scene reminiscent of a footballer having his name taken by the referee for swearing at him. Imagine my shock and amusement when the man spun round to address the carriage and it turned out to be Terry Fenwick! Obviously our former player and skipper still likes to have a go at figures in authority.

~ ~ ~

(Issue # 142)

I really enjoyed Danny Maddix's testimonial against Spurs. Although the result didn't turn out the way we would have liked the day itself was entirely fitting to such a loyal servant of the club. I was really looking forward to the proposed cup final rematch between QPR and Spurs teams of 1982 which was to have taken place before the testimonial game, and also the reunion of the 1975-76 team at the open day. Unfortunately neither of these events happened.

According to the club, the majority of the personnel that were to take part in these events were still involved within the game and therefore would be heavily into pre-season training with their respective clubs (honestly). It would certainly have been interesting to see the old players again, especially as someone who knows Ian Gillard very well stated, "Gillard isn't a

259

stranger to a square meal, a good cigar and a nice pint (or three) so for him to run around for five minutes let alone a whole match would be entirely out of the question."
(Moreno Ferrari – issue # 142)

Rambling on

The Open Day at Greenford went well I thought. The current squad were great I have to admit. They all seemed genuinely happy mingling with the general public and all smiled and chatted and signed whatever was offered. I have heard various stories about Jermaine Darlington over the summer but he really seems happy at the Rangers and commented how much he loved the family atmosphere at the club. I spoke to Danny Grieves and Peter Crouch who both seemed a little bit overawed by it all, but the worrying aspect was Rob Steiner. Although a lovely man to chat to and is someone obviously very happy at the club, he told me that he had absolutely no idea at all as to when his knee would be up to scratch. He suggested it may be many months at least. Worrying that.

~ ~ ~

From the 'A star is born' department. What about Clarke Carlisle eh? What a prospect. Sure his distribution could be better but he looks every inch a star in the making to me. He looked good in the three pre-season games I saw but the way he 'looked after' that donkey Horsfield against Birmingham bodes extremely well for us for the next couple of years and even better news for our bank balance after that (if money related transfers are still happening that is).

I think the old boy sitting next to me at the Birmingham game summed up the situation in the game very nicely. Ten minutes into it with Crouch heading up the middle to flick the ball on to nobody and Kiwomya trying to get as far away from him as he could, he said to me, "No bloody goals for us today then. Same as last year. When's he going to be a bit more adventurous at home?" Couldn't agree more mate.

On the same subject Francis insists that we need a powerful centre forward as we are "not the greatest side in the world, so we need to get the ball into the box and hold it there." Fair enough I suppose given our defensive tactics (and I still refuse to believe we use 'wing-backs' and not a back five). He also admits that Peter Crouch is not the finished article and needs to build himself up like Sammy Koejoe did last season. Again fair enough. Can anyone then please explain to me why he didn't bring on Koejoe to replace Crouch against Birmingham? Or at the very least bring on Leon Jeanne (who Francis still thinks is a winger) to give us some width. Or maybe bring Connolly (who Francis 'likes very much') on to replace Kiwomya who was not going to score if the game had gone on until Monday week!

In the LSA at the West Brom game at the end of last season a bloke I have known for many years who always seems to know what is going on at the club tells me this story that a rich Arab (who incidentally hates Al Fayed's guts) is going to buy the Rangers from Wright. He will then flog Loftus Road for £25million and build some new ground in Abu Dhabi or Southall or somewhere where he can throw potfulls of money at the club to bring back our past glories (sic!). The boys and me laughed and laughed and laughed. We nearly laughed enough to forget how awful the beer was in the Smuts. Now I read in this very mag that there is some truth to this rumour after all, but Wright will not sell. This all makes me extremely confused. One minute Wright says he wants the best for the club, then the next he won't sell out to someone willing to invest huge amounts of dosh into it. Makes me wonder several things.

Firstly, if Wright is in it for the money as a lot of people believe, then surely he would have sold out? Secondly, if he isn't going to sell out, where on earth would the money for a new ground come from? And finally, is it not all a trick by Al Fayed to buy our club, close QPR down and use Loftus Road for Fulham until they get a new ground?

~ ~ ~

Watched the Palace game on 'Sky Sports' Active. Once you get used to all the graphics on the screen it's actually pretty good I thought. I spent a good deal of the game listening to the new Fan-Zone option, where instead of match commentary by a professional commentator, you get two fans, one from each club chatting meaningfully about the game. Our one was called Wheeler and I thought he did a pretty good job, although being a QPR fan his favourite QPR highlight was a defeat by Manchester United in the FA Cup Quarter final the other year. I wonder how many fans of other clubs would list a defeat as their favourite moment?

When I wasn't tuned into Fan-Zone, I watched the Player-Cam option, which proved a few things to me. Firstly, critics of Stuart Wardley are right when they say he doesn't contribute enough. The camera followed him around for twenty minutes and there was hardly ever another player in the shot with him. He really does have to get more involved if he is to make it in professional football. Come to that Gavin Peacock could be doing more as well as could plainly be seen when the camera focused on him. Our third and last choice on Player-Cam was Richard Langley who didn't ever seem to stop moving and getting involved. It would appear that the other two could learn a lot from young Richard about effort and that makes a very welcome change from last season. The only other conclusion I got from the game were that at £125,000 for three months, Paul Furlong might be a teeny-weeny bit expensive.

~ ~ ~

I was very surprised that Brian McGovern joined Norwich for £50,000 recently. He had made it pretty clear apparently that he would have loved to have joined the Rangers and Francis was certainly keen on him, having made several attempts to sign him full time (offering considerably more than £50,000 by all accounts). Then all of a sudden he joins Norwich for not very much at all. Strange!
(Paul Davidson – issue # 142)

Everyone loves us but we don't care

It seems there's just no getting away from the beautiful game. Or, for that matter, the beautiful Superhoops. During my close-season hibernation period in sunny Scotland, I settled down with a copy of the excellent 'White City Blue' by Tim Lott. Not only is the book set in my beloved Bush, but our beloved R's get more mentions than they do in a year's worth of newsprint, unlikely as that may seem. Above all however, it contains the immortal lines; 'Hopeless. Gallen. Hopeless. Gallen,' and "Who's going to buy Gallen?" Step forward Steve Bruce.

I was 100% behind our esteemed board all the way on the Gallen issue — why should we be held to ransom by the man who listed his hobbies on his Lilleshall application as 'football and maybe a hairdresser'? Let's face it, the boy's not Maradona, and as he was told, if someone else was foolish enough to meet his wage demands, then fair play to him. I'm just surprised that Huddersfield pre-empted Fulham's multi-million pound swoop.

Gallen's departure signals the end of the carefree spendthrift era that brought our club to its knees and we should all breathe a huge sigh of relief that we're now a long way away from matching the spending exploits of our bigger (and more foolish) rivals.

Unfortunately, big Peter Crouch did little against Spurs to convince us that he's the man to replace Gallen alongside Kiwomya, winning very few fifty-fifty challenges and never really threatening. Hopefully this can be attributed to a lack of match practice and the fact that we were generally outclassed by a team even of Spurs' mediocrity. I do worry that it was more a case of his doctor warning him not to get stuck-in in case his Bambi-like legs got snapped. After all, he does make Muzzy Izzett look like Mile End's answer to Linford Christie.

A very brief conversation I had during that Spurs friendly match with my good friend 'Honest Dave' sums it up; Honest Dave — "Have your boys had a shot on target yet?" Me — "Give us a chance, it's only August."
(Mark Poole – issue # 142)

Points but few plusses

Two wins, two draws, one defeat — not a bad start by any stretch of the imagination, but are we happy? Not really. Team performances so far have hardly given cause for inspiration — an acceptable situation two or three years ago, but not at the present. We know we can play better, but more importantly a reluctance by Gerry Francis to change things around is becoming irritating. The squad is bigger than ever before and it needs to be utilised to a greater extent.

Just what does Karl Connolly need to do to get a decent slice of the action? Is Peter Crouch really a better bet just because he's more likely to win a header? I know very little about Connolly except he was a bit of a star with Wrexham supporters, with no shortage of skill and bags of experience. At the moment, Crouch is only good for giving opposing supporters something to laugh at.

If Connolly isn't seen as an out-and-out striker by Francis, then will there ever be a place for him in the team? It sounds as if he could play the Wardley role, but I think we should stick with him for a few more games yet. Or perhaps, with Jeanne down the right and Connolly down the left, we could give the 4-4-2 formation a go. It's a formation Francis always used in his first spell as manager, and must be worth another shot at soon, especially if we continue to run out of central defenders rendering the 'sweeper system' impractical to continue with.

I was hoping to arrange an interview with Francis, but it seems being a football manager these days makes it impossible to spare some time for causes such as this. Perhaps a good job too, as I get the feeling I would end up asking questions Francis would not find too comfortable in answering.

By the time you've read this, perhaps a change in tactics and/or formation from Francis will have seen off the challenge of Colchester and seen us pick up three points against Preston, with a touch a style and swagger along the way, making us all a lot happier. Anymore performances along the lines of what we've witnessed so far, and I think we'll all be pulling our hair out.

Last season's injury crisis looks set to continue into this one, with casualty figures quickly mounting up. We won't be seeing Danny Maddix and Rob Steiner until next year, whilst news on Karl Ready's injury has yet to emerge — but it does seem we're looking at months rather than weeks. Baraclough's twisted his knee, Peacock's hamstring has gone again, Darlington's still limping around with cramp at the end of games (when his dodgy ankle allows him to play), Rose seems intent on picking up every injury in the book before he can concentrate his sights on the first team again whilst Plummer and Breacker have only just started their return to full match fitness. That's a very large chunk of the squad, and we can forgive Francis his usual moans in

this direction, but such is the size of the squad, the impact is barely noticeable, and I don't think can be linked to the way we have played so far.
(Ed – issue # 142)

Strength in depth?

Goalkeepers: Harper, Miklosko. Defenders: Morrow, Rose, Carlisle. Full-backs/Wing-backs/wingers: Warren, Darlington, Breacker, Scully, Heinola, Jeanne, Perry, Bruce, Graham. Midfielders: Rowland, Langley, Kulcsar, Grieves, Wardley. Forwards: Kiwomya, Crouch, Connolly, Koejoe, Dowie, Weare.

By my reckoning, that's 25 fit professionals Francis currently has to work with. There are many more injured, but talk of 'depleted ranks' is going too far. Also, of the above 25, at least 7 could consider themselves first team regulars, so I don't think supporters or Francis himself can hide behind this excuse for the reason behind our poor start to the season.

Francis is talking about going into the transfer market — if he does, the emphasis has to be on quality rather than quantity — someone that would be an automatic first choice even if there were no injuries. Players of this nature won't come cheap, but the current squad is brimming over with 'stop gap' players — we don't need any more, as Paul Furlong proved.

But there's no point in having such a large pool of players if you don't use them, and in any case I always like it when you see players tried out in different positions — you never know what it could throw up. Still, I think even if we won the league Francis would still find something to moan about. Loved the quote after the Crewe game; "We lost 90% of our defence in the opening half," — make that 40%, and please don't play Heinola in central defence (of wherever he was meant to be playing) again.

So if we can't heap the blame on the injuries, where can we point the finger at? Chris Wright? Not really. Francis proved last season he can work well with a tight budget — but we can question his team selections so far, so really the buck stops with him. I'm not about to jump on any 'Francis out' bandwagon, let's just show a little patience — no other manager has the background or could fully comprehend the financial situation that exists at the club, so let's give him our support.

The trouble is that expectations are higher this season, patience is at a premium. We need to progress but the signs so far suggest this won't be the case. But seven league games is hardly a lot to make rash judgements — whilst the first half at Barnsley was utterly unacceptable, Francis isn't the kind of manager that readily accepts such displays. It was no surprise to see a totally different performance in the second half where we so nearly managed to pull off another of our famous comebacks, but the consistency needs to be found.

Too many people strike up a conclusion based purely on results without considering the whole picture. We could have easily won those three home games a couple of weeks back and everybody would be talking of making the play-offs again — but we didn't take our chances. It's a thin line between success and failure in football — a great save or two, the woodwork or inept refereeing all play their part.

Yet if the next 15 or 20 games show little or no improvement on what we've seen so far, then questions really will need to be asked. I hope Francis will get it right in the end though and Loftus Road will be a much happier place to watch games. I'd like to think the current situation with QPR will transform itself from a poor start to another decent season. Let's hope I'm proved right.

(Ed – issue # 143)

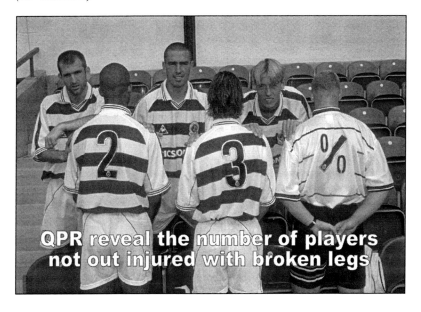

QPR reveal the number of players not out injured with broken legs

(Issue # 143)

Rambling on

Over a year ago now I wrote that the day would come when it would be time for Gerry Francis to step down as manager. I am 100% convinced that that time is now. If Kevin Keegan is tactically naive, then Gerry's team selection and tactics against Colchester were nothing short of idiotic. How an obviously unfit Matt Rose could be set the task of man-marking Lua-Lua I will never know. In the thirty-five years I have been going to the Bush I honestly believe that the Colchester game was the biggest embarrassment I have ever suffered there. Not the worst performance, it just adds to the ever-growing list, but definitely the most embarrassing.

There were just so many things wrong on the night that it would take up most of this mag to list them all. I suppose though that my biggest gripe is the total lack of our home-grown youngsters that didn't get the chance to play. If players like Leon Jeanne and Richard Graham are not even going to get the chance to sit on the bench for a League Cup tie against a lower division team when we have already won the away leg, then they might as well bog off and sign for someone that will give them a chance. And what has happened to Danny Grieves? Francis would apparently prefer to play a full-back in midfield than have a look at our new signing. And what was the point of getting Kulcsar to sign a contract extension? It looks as if the club would have to be struck down by a rabies epidemic before he got another game. Mind you I could be wrong. Maybe Bruce and Rowland will turn out to be good players after all. Yeah, right and maybe Francis will go back to a flat back four!

All of this though is not about one game. Possibly my biggest gripe about Francis is his almost unbelievable negativity. No matter how well we do or no matter what good things happen to the club, he is always so bloody negative about everything. He just has to be the most miserable man on the face of the planet. If Bill Gates bought the Rangers and gave him unlimited cash, Francis would still find something to moan about every single day. Last season with his farcical obsession with getting fifty points that lasted the entire season, which was bad enough, but this season he is breaking new ground. He still never shuts up about the injury crisis we permanently have even though he never seems to notice that with the far greater pace of the modern game everybody else has the same problems. Now he is convinced that our club, along with most others by all accounts, will be 'part-time' in a couple of years.

The top criticism I hear from people at Rangers matches is the fact that the players don't seem to give a toss about the club. With Given Francis' miserable negativity I do not find it surprising. It really must sink into the players and when things go wrong as they have of late, I just cannot see Francis being able to lift them. Francis has got to go now before this negative attitude sinks so far into the fabric of the club that it will never leave.

~ ~ ~

Rumour had it in the LSA before the Colchester game that Leon Jeanne was recently arrested in Cardiff for being drunk and disorderly in a night club. As usual we will probably never know the truth. Mind you if he suddenly signs for Arsenal then we will have a bit of a clue!

~ ~ ~

And then came Preston. What another piss poor game that was. Fifty-two minutes to get a proper shot on target. I know that their keeper played very well but for god's sake. And the answer? Bring on Peter Crouch again. Words absolutely fail me. Well they did for four days anyway.

What was Richard Langley thinking of at the end of the game? Deep into added time we get a free kick near their penalty area. What does Langley do? Bends down and reties his laces. Then what does he do? He moans about the distance the wall is away. Then what does he do? He messes around pointing at people and generally does not get on with taking the kick. The referee, quite rightly in my humble opinion, gets fed up waiting and blows the full time whistle. What does Langley do? His bloody nut!

~ ~ ~

No sooner do I thinking the programme is quite good this season when it starts printing crap again. Tony Incenzo writes that Rob Steiner is 'making steady progress'. Ten pages later Chris Wright says that 'there are certainly no signs as yet of him resuming training'. Now who are we going to believe? I think the most telling thing in the Preston programme was the terrible statistic that we had only 11 shots on target in the first four games this season. When you consider that in the same amount of games Fulham had 40 it really makes you think? Mind you the best fact in the same issue might be the odd answer to the question; 'At what stadium was the first ever FA Cup final replay played in 1970'. Somehow the answer was Chris Woods. Hmmm.

~ ~ ~

And so we come to Gillingham. How bad was the first eighty minutes of that game? Same players, same tactics, same old rubbish. Our first shot on goal came as early (?) as the 33rd minute, quickly followed by our second in the 59th. Crouch turned out to be a revelation, much to everyone's surprise. It would appear that someone has actually taught him how to jump. Now wouldn't it surprise some people (me included it has to be said) if he carries on in the same fashion for the rest of the season? The only other surprise was that we got a draw after being 2-0 down. Rowland apparently kept his place after 'impressing' against Preston. Who did he impress for Christ's sake? Not anybody I know that's for sure.

~ ~ ~

With the current farcical are they/aren't they opening of the LSA, I found myself in the 'new' 'Blue and White' club before the Gillingham game. £2.50 for a pint of flat lager in a floppy plastic cup. Now that's what I call a rip-off. They wont be getting any more of my money this season that's for sure.

Whilst in there I read the programme. That night's particular theme was 'don't boo the players as it upsets them'. What a load of crap. I realise that the 'to boo or not to boo' debate has raged on for many a year at the Rangers and I myself am firmly in the 'boo them if they don't even bother to try' camp. Mr Francis (or Mr Magoo as I have started to call him as he cannot see the obvious) says that the Colchester game was a one-off and that usually all his players give 110% to the cause all the time.

Now can someone explain to me how all these fragile little darlings can possibly get upset if someone boos them? Quite simply put, if they pulled their fingers out and put the required effort in, in the first place, no one would boo them. If they were halfway to being real men and not overly paid, over pampered little Prima Donnas then a good boo would spur them on to greater things. The only way that lot would get upset in the dressing room after the game would be if Chris Wright came in and announced that they would all in future be paid exactly what they had earned on the pitch. Half of the sods would struggle to rustle up the taxi fare home!
(Paul Davidson – issue # 143)

Here we go again...

How we laughed as Chelsea sacked Vialli after just five games of the season — would they, oh god, please yes, appoint super Ray Wilkins as his successor? Probably not, but it was worth the thought. How we laughed. Yet after just five, admittedly dull, league games, and one embarrassing home cup tie, many R's fans were themselves calling for this kind of dramatic change at an early juncture.

Some misguided souls were suggesting that it was time for Gerry Francis to move on. To be frank, this is barely worth a comment, except to say that Gerry has turned the club around in many ways and whilst I certainly don't agree with every decision he makes, it's totally implausible to suggest that we'll ever have a manager who does things exactly as everyone thinks he should. Simply, Gerry is a good manager and we're lucky to have him — without him we might be on the brink of extinction — or more probably a lot worse.

So Gerry's case is pretty much watertight then — he's never going to be the scapegoat. So if we can't, or don't want to, blame Gerry for our mediocre and poor performances, who can we blame? Some blame Richard Langley of course — the 'lazy bastard', others blame Peter Crouch who's been substitute most of the time, others blame Steve

Morrow, some even blame Iain Dowie, but increasingly fans are turning to the old chestnut of the chairman — Chris Wright.

The general gist of the argument against Wright is that he's taken more money out of the club than he put in because he leant the club money and then took it back with interest when the club sold Wasps' ground. Now, so they say, as the club struggles once more, he needs to flash the cash, wave the wad, get his chequebook out. Yet there are so many problems with these views.

QPR fans need to decide what it is they want — presumably that's promotion, and then, perhaps more importantly, how we're going to get it. Talksport's excellent 'Sunday Morning Kickabout' last week had a QPR fan on. He was asked whether if Wright was to allow £20m for transfers, would he be happy to have all that money spent on foreign players as long as QPR were successful. He didn't answer the question (I'm not sure why), but my view would have been that I'd rather we took the path forged by Charlton rather than that followed by Fulham. We dislike Fulham because their success has been manufactured almost by money alone (although only a fool would deny that Tigana is doing a superb job there), yet we simultaneously call for Wright to copy Fayed and buy us success. It simply isn't possible that QPR can go out and buy these players, and even if they did there's no guarantee that it would work.

The problem that seems to bypass all the people that want more money spent on players is the one that Gerry has repeatedly pointed out — and he's not doing it to fob us off for a bit of a lark — it's one of wages. I personally think Chris Wright would give Gerry between one and two million for a new player, but any player that commands that kind of fee is extremely unlikely to fit into the wage structure. Besides, why spend that kind of money when we can pick up players of the class of Clarke Carlisle for a fraction of the price?

Even with a more generous owner, buying new players for lots of money is a bad idea because the club has to get back on its feet before it can start running again. We are still paying players like Morrow, Scully, Ready, Rowland and Breacker far too much money when you consider they are basically squad players with the dubious exception of Ready. Only when we can have a more reasonable structure at the club in which every player fits can we afford to take some risks. This structure will not happen over night and did not immediately happen when the club announced it wouldn't pay signing-on fees and had put a new wage cap in place. It takes time, and people need to be less naive and remember that.

One thing I would never want is to be taken over by a sugar daddy and achieve immediate success through money alone. What QPR must do is build, and if it takes time then so be it. Sixteen years ago Charlton were just about extinct. But they survived, they rebuilt, they moved back to The Valley and look at them now! They don't pay and haven't paid ridiculous wages, they stick with their manager, they have huge gates most weeks. But to get to this stage has taken them sixteen years. We were close enough to extinction in the last two years to feel the breath of death on the back of our necks, yet we want what Charlton have got in a fraction of the time they achieved it. Yet consistently the only answer we come up with is to sack the board, get a new owner.

I believe Chris and Gerry now have a plan in place, and neither are willing to rush it through, which is only right. We shouldn't be castigating the chairman for QPR's failings as a football team. He threw money at the problem, and it failed. Now he's trying a long-term method. This group of players was good enough to finish tenth last season, not too far off the play-offs, and the fact remains we have a stronger squad than last year. Let's not panic, let's not needlessly cause the long term damage to the club that a concerted 'Wright Out' campaign would inevitably bring about. QPR need time, but we'll come again.
(Dan Trelfer – issue # 143)

Things could be worse...

Another team we now must all be feeling sorry for is Millwall who had joint managers Alan McLeary and Keith Stevens sacked after a couple of disappointing home losses. Why should we feel sorry for them? They have installed Ray Harford as their caretaker-manager ... and you think we've got problems.

At a recent Supporters Club meeting, Stevens and McLeary were asked what specifically does Ray Harford do. The reply was comical — "He comes in, shows us a few things, then goes home." Not much change there then!
(Moreno Ferrari – issue # 143)

Testing times

The arguments for and against Gerry Francis continue, and whilst I'm firmly in the 'for' camp for the time being, it's understandable for fans to get irate, if not at results then certainly for team selections — with so many injuries perhaps now is not the best time to experiment too much, but it would be nice to see a more positive approach to games, especially at home.

If people feel that just two years is the amount of time needed for Francis to have taken the club as far as he can, then I would like to see someone who could have done a better job in this period, and still have more to offer. After years of chop and change at management level, QPR need a period of stability — getting shot of Francis now would be a step back.

Hopes were high this season that a play-off place would be within our reach — it may yet be — but if we were to finish 'only' in mid-table, would it be such a disaster? The injury situation has been horrific for the best part of a year now and the fact remains that Francis has not been able to pick what he would consider to be his first choice eleven since the start of last season.

I often hear and read remarks along the lines of "this is the worst QPR side I've ever seen," — well I can only imagine such supporters haven't been around for very long. Such remarks during the 97/98 and 98/99 seasons were much more acceptable, and we're some distance off reaching those poor standards.

Ever get the feeling too many of our players are taking this quite literally?

Up until the Grimsby debacle, we were getting our act together slowly but surely — I took far more positives from the games at Sheffield United and Watford than against Crystal Palace and West Brom at the start of the season, and our last two home games yielded a good win against Wimbledon and a fine comeback against Gillingham. Things really aren't as bad as many people seem to think they are — our expectations simply aren't being fulfilled, but I guess 90% of fans from all other teams are feeling the same. Football is simply too complicated to make it predictable — ability, confidence, luck and officiating all play their part, game to game, in the final outcome.

I still believe that once a few more players return from injury that this season still has a lot to offer. There's over a hundred points to play for yet, and I'm sure we'll grab our fair share of them — depending of course on how badly Francis wants them.

So, no fresh activity in the transfer market, but not through lack of trying with a loan moves Darren Peacock falling through. I did believe we could make do with what we've got for the time being, but the need to bring in some cover at the back is now very apparent. Any hopes that Chris Wright might dip into his pocket for a spare million quid or two were well and truly quashed when Wright outlined the situation with himself and QPR in a recent webcast.

We should not forget the financial restraints imposed at the club, and we look no nearer to raising a penny in outgoing transfers. At times it's a minor miracle that QPR are still able to operate. We may not be pushing for promotion, but in many ways we should be happy enough to just see the club still in existence — the world of football is unfortunately too fickle for this to happen though.

Full credit to Peter Crouch who is adapting to life in the First Division far quicker than his early performances suggested. The more I see of Crouch the more I like him. His first touch is the best of all our forwards, he can hold the ball up as well as Gallen and as he proved against Gillingham, possesses a decent shot on him. His height is by no means his only strength (although it should be better considering his size), and we shouldn't necessarily see his inclusion in the team as an excuse to play the long ball — he offers far more than for this to be the case.

Similarities to Niall Quinn are spot on by Gerry — although it's taken a while for this to finally show through. Judging by the enormous strides (no pun intended) Crouch has made in recent games, at just £60,000 he looks set to turn out to be another fine bargain buy.

I feel almost apologetic for the lampooning of Crouch on the front cover of ITL # 142 — but he's answered his critics in the best possible way. If he can add a bit of meat to his bones, he could become a real star. The Peter Crouch success story I feel is only just beginning...

(Ed – issue # 144)

Tuesday 26th September

During a now less-than-frequent night out at the infamous 'Bad Bobs' in Covent Garden, several QPR players made an appearance towards the end of the night. Not being the kind to name names in case they were there against the best wishes of Gerry Francis, I can at least say that one cost the R's fuck all, one was a loan-Ranger, one made his debut for QPR at Swindon two years ago, one used to lug furniture around and the other is even taller than me. Before the beer took its toll, they all soon disappeared into the night in a couple if illegal cabs…

(Ed – issue # 144)

Players and managers in the news

As feared, Rob Steiner has been told his professional football career is over after the knee injury he suffered last season failed to respond to extensive surgery. It's a major blow for the club, and must be devastating news for someone that so obviously loved playing football for QPR.

There was cause for concern after the game at Sheffield United when Gerry Francis revealed, "We lost Keith Rowland on the way up here." Our sources can reveal he was last seen playing on the fruities at Watford Gap, apparently getting agitated when one machine refused to take his two pound coin...

Leon Jeanne failed to turn up for Wales' U-21 squad training, prompting renewed fears over his future with QPR and indeed football altogether. With the amount of injuries this season, to lose another player due to 'personal and social problems' would only be rubbing salt in the wounds. Seeing as the poor mixed-up kid can't read (allegedly), perhaps someone can pass on a special message for him — "Sort your fucking life out and come and play for the R's."

Paul Furlong has returned to Birmingham City halfway through his three-month loan spell after injuring his knee in training, ruling him out of action until the new year.

QPR have been linked with a loan move for the troublesome Stan Collymore — once rightly awarded the 'Wanker of the Week' award by that naughty northerner Sarah Cox on the long-forgotten 'Girly Show' on C4. Two years later, Cox and Collymore were going out with each other. All very strange.

After Kevin Keegan quits as England manager, Gerry Francis rules himself out of the job after revealing he wouldn't know what to say at press conferences compared to managing QPR. It is believed Francis would be lost for words without being able to mention any of the following — "50 points/tight wage structure/broken legs/small squad/loan players..."

Darren Peacock has turned down a loan move to QPR from Blackburn Rovers, much to the relief of the internet communities who's general opinion on the player was 'rubbish'. Funny that — when he was sold to Newcastle United for £2.75million it prompted protests and pitch invasions over 'asset stripping' by Richard Thompson.
(Ed – issue # 144)

Rambling on

I am absolutely fed up with the way that all I seem to do nowadays is moan about the Rangers. No, honestly, it really does upset me. I will seriously try this month to look at the positive things at the Bush rather than the negative. As I write this column throughout the month adding to it as I go, as it were, I have no idea at this time how it will turn out. Let's wait and see.

~ ~ ~

At last! A London derby win, against Wimbledon. For once and in the positive spirit I am trying to write this article, I must praise Mr Magoo, sorry, Gerry Francis. Having picked yet again the wrong players and using, yet again, the wrong tactics, he at least had the bottle to change things around. And well before half time too. The football didn't improve, but to be fair it wasn't likely to against a team like Wimbledon. But we scored a couple of good goals. And we won the game as well. Maybe things are starting to look up.

~ ~ ~

So Chris Wright is on his 'we're going broke and it's everyone else's fault except mine,' bike again. I for one will not disagree with him that we are in a financial mess. What makes me so angry is the way he tries to come out of it smelling of roses saying that it is only his generosity that is keeping us afloat when it was his bloody appalling business decisions that helped to get us in this mess in the first place. I used to have a lot of time for Mr Wright, against most of my friends judgement, but the longer it goes, the more I'm getting a bit fed up with him. Mind you, seeing as I am so behind the 'Gerry must go' movement, I think it in the best interests of the club that Wright stays at least for a little while longer.

~ ~ ~

And so on to Bramall Lane. Same standard QPR performance. If only we could play a bit in the first half we would be a more than half-decent team. This day was to be no exception. Abysmal first half (no shots on target other than super-Sammy's 45-yard power-drive) followed by a great battling display in the second half and a good point earned despite the referee giving us nothing all afternoon. I wonder why we are so much better after the interval than before it. Perhaps Francis gives the pre-match team talk that depresses the players so much they play poorly, but by half time he has gone somewhere to moan to someone else and Dowie perks the players up by telling them that things ain't quite so bad after all. Crazy idea, but no crazier than everything else that happens to our beloved Superhoops.

Much debate at Sheffield about Leon Jeanne. The general opinion seemed to be that although he was undoubtedly a silly little boy, he might not have been so daft if he had been involved in the first team more over the last twelve months as most people thought he should have been. And again the same questions were being asked e.g. why wont Francis ever pick home grown youngsters? Only he must know.

~ ~ ~

Shame about Rob Steiner having to quit. Never the best striker in the world but surely one of the most game. He would run all day for you and although he didn't score too many goals for us, he sure made a few for other people. Makes me wonder though exactly who the first alleged 'specialist' he saw after joining us was. If indeed it was a 'specialist' that said it was OK for him to carry on playing last season when obviously crocked, then why aren't we suing him to China and back?

~ ~ ~

Watched the Watford game from the rare treat of a sponsor's box. I do like to occasionally watch the Rangers in the company of fans of the other team to find out what other people think of us. On this occasion, once Francis made the necessary changes they were all very impressed. They especially liked the look of Peter Crouch who is rapidly becoming a real star, this had to be his best game yet. They also liked Carlisle and Koejoe, although I did think Carlisle showed his naivety letting Noel-Williams turn him for the third goal. I'll bet he won't do that again in a hurry. To a man the others in our box all thought that with a flat back four and three men up front we were as good as Watford. What a shame then that by the time Francis came to realise that we were as usual using the wrong tactics, the chances of a result had almost gone. We did play bloody well though for half an hour it has to be said. With a little luck we might just have snuck an equaliser and then I seriously reckon we could have nicked it with Watford starting to hit the panic button.

(Paul Davidson – issue # 144)

More losses

Loftus Road Plc has announced a loss of £4,735,000 for the year ending 31st May 2000, compared to £8,379,00 in the previous year. Player and management wages continue to be a major problem though — £8,421,000, seeing an increase of £85,000. All that effort by Gerry & Co to reduce it has yet to have the desired affect, and this coming in a period when high earners like Vinnie Jones and Mike Sheron had long since departed.

(Ed – issue # 144)

Best of luck, Rob

It's terrible news that Rob Steiner has had to retire, especially so young. It's a blow for QPR, and it must be devastating to him. Rob was a player who really wanted to play for QPR, and that is why I always liked him. He appreciated the fans, he played with fire, he took risks, he had a bloody personality in a game, and perhaps a club, devoid of them for the most part.

He was great for the youngsters — I remember him high-fiving Leon in one game for a run that earned a corner and then encouraging him to do more. Some, I think, care little that he is not going to play for us again — he's no Danny Maddix of course, but Rob Steiner was entertainment, he was incredibly determined, and he was willing to play through severe pain for us, for QPR. And how many of players are willing to do that nowadays? And how was Rob rewarded? With a career-ending injury. There's no justice, is there?

Steiner was a player with a lot of detractors and a lot of admirers — a player who split the fans last season — mostly between those who knew he was injured, and those who thought he was lazy. It's easier to think the latter and means you can slag off your own player for the ultimate football crime.

You could argue that Gerry should never have signed a player so patently injury prone as Rob — indeed, it seems that Gerry put off the transfer until there was really no other player who he could turn to, and had to take the risk on Rob. But it was a risk worth taking. For one thing, Steiner's partnership with Kiwomya was a good one — it had performed well against a poor Swindon side who we had trashed 4-0, and it would perform well again when he signed permanently.

Steiner was a nightmare to play against. He was quick — quicker man almost everyone gave him credit for — his strangely short strides certainly gave the impression he was slow, but he wasn't. Iain Dowie even said he was one of the fastest players at the club in training races. He was strong when he needed to be, but could go over when he had to — and sometimes when he didn't have to, and sometimes when he didn't need to, and sometimes when he blatantly shouldn't have done. But that was Rob. Good with his head, and, as I've said before, an amazing stumbling dribbling style that involved him playing the ball off the defenders knees, onto his own shins and past him — he did it so often it must have been deliberate, surely.

(Dan Trelfer – issue # 144)

No fun down at the Bush

Being a QPR supporter at the present time is not an enjoyable experience. After two years of rubbish, last year came as a welcome relief but now we've plummeted back to the dross witnessed during the 97/98 and 98/99 seasons. Back then there seemed no obvious answer to our problems on the pitch but presently it's all too clear where things are going wrong and how they can be corrected. Unfortunately, we don't pick the team.

Gerry Francis has the largest pool of players any manager of QPR has ever had to choose from. There's no doubting there is as much class in the squad as there is dross, but Francis seems intend on picking his team and tactics around one player — Peter Crouch. Crouch has done admiringly well considering his age and experience, indeed very few fans seem against his inclusion in the side, but we are playing to his aerial strengths and hardly anything else.

BORN-AGAIN Christian Dennis Bailey destroyed Manchester United with a New Year's Day hat-trick then declared: "God helped me to do this."

	P	W	D	L	F	A	Pts
Leeds	24	13	10	1	42	19	49
Man Utd	22	14	6	2	43	18	48
Sheff Wed	23	11	7	5	37	24	40
Man City	24	11	7	6	33	28	40
Liverpool	23	9	11	3	27	18	38
Aston Villa	23	11	3	9	34	29	36

By JOHN BEAN Man Utd 1 QPR 4

The striker QPR boss Gerry Francis prised from Third Division Birmingham for £175,000 in the summer is convinced his faith helped knock mighty United off the top of the First Divison.

"Make no mistake, God helped me today as he has always helped me in the past," declared Bailey after the first treble of his career sent United crashing in front of their stunned fans.

Convinced

"I pray before every game and I'll be offering prayers of thanks for what happened today, tomorrow and on Sunday," he revealed.

"I do that every weekend when I reflect on the week that has gone before. I'm convinced God gave me a helping hand today."

Bailey, 26, has graduated through the ranks from non-League Farnborough Town, and Francis had him on loan at Bristol Rovers before linking up again with the player this season.

The result made history. It was QPR's first win in Manchester and Bailey, a member of the Pentecostal Church in Brixton, admitted: "This has to be the greatest moment of my life.

"When I got that third goal in the second half I was in heaven. But there's no way I'm going to deride Manchester United."

By contrast United chief Alex Ferguson admitted his first day of 1992 had been hellish after his side conceded two goals in the first five minutes.

By the end of the day Leeds—kicking off two hours before United to chalk up an impressive 3-1 win at West Ham—had leap-frogged back on top of the First Division.

Leeds have also seen Manchester's goal difference edge drop to two.

Ferguson said: "It was a terrible start for us. Indecision, lack of determination in not defending properly and not clearing balls cost us the game.

"There is no excuse. We were totally outplayed but maybe this experience came at an appropriate time for us."

Rangers boss Gerry Francis, bubbling with excitement after seeing his side stretch their unbeaten run to seven games, said: "United must have wondered what had hit them.

"They caught us in great form.

"When I was at Bristol Rovers I played four at the back and I have reverted to this tactic at Rangers instead of using a sweeper and it's paid dividends.

Not that we're trying to live off past glories, but that final paragraph strikes a few chords...

Too many of our players are taking the easy way out when looking for an outlook by pumping aimless balls up to Crouch — instructed to by Francis or through their own choice we don't know — but I wouldn't like to put much money on it being the latter. Of course many players are under-performing, but this has come about largely due to the tactics employed that have been getting us nowhere all season, leading to ever decreasing levels of confidence.

If we are to persist with 3-5-2/5-3-2, play it the way it should be played — not only proper over-lapping full-backs, but also with a sweeper that likes to get over the half-way line occasionally, and most importantly, keeping the ball on the deck.

We can and should be doing better. It would be too simplistic to suggest Francis is losing the plot, but he's doing a great job in trying to get QPR out of this division. At least there is no apparent disharmony amongst the squad — always the first sign of major trouble, and wouldn't it be nice to play a side once in a while that had an off-day to help our cause? Maybe that game will come with the visit of Huddersfield Town, but what's the betting ... well I guess you know the rest.

For all our injury and financial problems, Francis cannot continue to use these as the reason behind our poor form — we coped well enough last season simply because our tactics weren't so one-dimensional.

We badly need to see some hope for the future, and the loan signing of Paul Peschisolido could well be it. If his signing were to become permanent, an outgoing transfer or two would be most welcome to help pay for him, but what chance of that happening? Doesn't anybody want any of our players?

Support for Francis is thin on the ground, but I still don't think his departure would be the correct solution — I just wish he took a long hard look at where his tactics are directing the club to. Twenty-five odd years as a player and manager will count for little if the unthinkable happens and QPR are relegated this season. It's a case of the blind leading the able, and all extremely disappointing after last season offered so much hope for the future.

(Ed – issue # 145)

Moreno Bares All

I guess the old joke why QPR players are not allowed any pets are about to resurface? Answer: Because they can't hold onto leads! It's happened on several occasions in the past month or so, away matches at WBA, Grimsby Town, Bolton Wanderers and Stockport County have seen us take the lead only to lose it, in most cases only a few minutes later. I think this is the difference between this season and last as last season the midfield would usually chip-in with the killer second goal, this season it just hasn't happened. Stuart Wardley is finding it hard to make any impact in the game whilst even crowd favourite Gavin Peacock is starting to get some abuse from the crowd with his distinct 'no-shows'.

We the supporters always talk about having a striker who can score 20+ goals a season but what we really require sometimes is a midfielder that can chip in a dozen goals himself. Last season Wardley was that player which went a long way into securing a decent finish for us, unfortunately this season nothing apart from the odd goal from 'one for the future' Richard Langley. I would feel far happier if Gerry Francis would try and bring in on loan a midfielder every now and then just for this purpose. Who knows we may just find that missing piece to the puzzle.

~ ~ ~

It was interesting to see how the 'little and large' combination of Peter Crouch and Paul Peschisolido would fair against Portsmouth. I thought that it worked quite well with the target man getting up well for Pesch to latch onto which is I guess how it's supposed to work! Pesch's all round play was a breath of fresh air and highlighted some of the basic problems we've been having this season — he was pacey, enthusiastic to the extreme chasing countless 'lost balls' and wanting to play rather than having to play. I hope that the £600,000 transfer of the wee man goes through as I think he will be an invaluable member of the team, we'll just have to wait and see.

~ ~ ~

I am just so glad that Darren Peacock did not come to Rangers on loan. Apparently just before he joined Newcastle, Richard Thompson and Gerry Francis were in fits of laughter at the amount the Geordies were willing to pay for the long haired central defender, so signing him would certainly have been a backward step. I understand though that former crowd favourite David Bardsley is training with the club on the understanding that if he gets himself fit then he would rejoin us to help out with our defensive problems. I don't know if this story is a leg-pull or not but I believe it speaks volumes for the state of the club at the moment.
(Moreno Ferrari – issue # 145)

Rambling on

So Paul Peschisolido eh, what a good signing — if it happens of course. In my humble opinion he is the first proper forward we have signed since John Spencer. Works his arse off, knows where the goal is and as long as he signs full time just could get us out of the mess we have got ourselves in. I honestly think that the signing or not of Pesch will not only decide the future of this season but possibly the future of the club itself. There was all sorts of publicity when Pesch signed on loan that a long term deal was almost a done thing. Then of course the harbinger of doom himself, Mr Gerry Magoo, chimes in with his usual happy thoughts. How did I guess that within two days of the loan signing, Francis would be giving it the, "of course he will have to take a big pay-cut to join us full time."?

Let's look at it rationally, despite the papers continually saying that we are 'one of the divisions highest payers', we are quite obviously not. However, if we cannot sign the likes of Peschisolido, then what hope is there for us? As much as I like Pesch, we are not talking David Beckham or Zinedine Zidane or even Mikkel Beck here. Mark my words, if this deal falls through, we can look forward to signing nothing more than non-league players and let's be fair, after a mass of early publicity, neither Darlington or Wardley have set the world alight.

We seem to have a straight choice here. We either start signing some players of half-decent quality, or we sink down into the mire. I have said before, that God knows what will happen if we get relegated and not signing players that fall into our lap like Peschisolido can only hasten our demise.

~ ~ ~

I'm not as sure about Marlon Broomes as I am about Pesch. Not a bad player Broomes, but a bit too similar to Carlisle for my liking. With the best will in the world, Clarke Carlisle can end up being a quality defender, but his ball skills leave a lot to be desired and Broomes looks the same sort of player. Mind you if Gerry is sticking with the back five idea, it looks like it will work with Matt Rose between them. I just think that if we go back to a flat back four as most people including myself want, we need a more skilful player than Broomes alongside Carlisle. Rumour has it that Blackburn want a million quid for Broomes, so it's probably not a matter for conjecture anyway. Time will tell.

~ ~ ~

The season is over a third complete and the league table has a dreadfully familiar and ominous took about it. It really looks like last season was a bit of a fluke and that we are in for another season of hard toil and another relegation battle. If you look at the table from last year and remove the stunning away wins we had at places like Ipswich, Blackburn and Man City etc, then there is very little, if any difference between what is happening now and what has been happening over the last few seasons — in fact ever since Francis came back over two years ago. I still think that Francis has to go, but maybe the signing of Peschisolido will save him.

Whilst on the same old boring subject of Mr Magoo, I notice that to raise the moral in the camp he has now started to slag the players off individually in public. First it was Clarke Carlisle then Lee Harper. Good move Gerry, just carry on and start slagging the supporters off next and then your job will be complete. You will have pissed off everyone available. I am beginning to wonder if Gerry Francis' body has been taken over by either Al Fayed or Ken Bates the way he seems to be almost single handedly driving the club towards the pit of despair.

Somebody, quite rightly, asked me the other day exactly why I hate Gerry Francis so much. The simple answer is that I don't. I just think that he is a very lousy manager. As a player I thought he was superb, very probably the best our club has ever had, Stan Bowles and Rodney Marsh included and definitely our best ever 'home grown' player. He was, after all, the only England captain we have ever produced and if it hadn't been for injuries, I am sure he had a very long and successful career in front of him as captain of his country.

As a manager though I think he is a disaster. Never the happiest of men, since he has come back for his second twirl at the helm, he seems to have turned into a suicidal maniac. I must admit I was all in favour when Gerry came back and for a time he did an excellent job in very trying circumstances. He appeared to turn the ship around for a while and we looked to be chugging back in the right direction.

The trouble is the ship never stopped turning and we are now almost pointing back in the direction we came from. I am just so afraid that disaster is looming unless we have a mutiny and change the ship's captain before we sink. As for Gerry himself, I am afraid that I just feel extremely sorry for him, I think that as a manager he is completely out of his depth. I don't want him to cut all his ties with the club, I just don't want him picking the team and tactics every week.

Several people have asked me if Francis is to go then who do we replace him with. A very good point. It is my own view that Dowie should be given a chance, as I understand he was originally supposed to have happened this season. I liked the teams he picked for the three games he was in charge waiting for Francis to take over and I just think he would be a bit more adventurous and be a bit more likely to pick our own kids. Plus of course he knows the players and naturally, the financial situation. I just say give the man a chance before we have to man the lifeboats!

~ ~ ~

A good goal from Richard Langley at Stockport, a very good goal. And the one from the free kick at Tranmere by Connolly wasn't half-bad either, but lets face it neither was exactly a thirty-yard screamer. We just don't seem to score real quality goals anymore.

For example, what exactly was our 'goal of the season' last season? I certainly cannot remember, I don't think that there was one. Up until Tranmere, I would assume that the best goal this season was the chest down and six-yard volley at Colchester by Kiwomya, and yet again that was in an away game.

I can only assume that the goal that Sinclair got against Barnsley in 1997 used up our entire allocation of great goals for the next millennium, cos' we ain't scored a real cracker since that I can remember and definitely not at home.
(Paul Davidson – issue # 145)

The calm before the storm?

Has anyone else noticed how surprisingly calm the majority of supporters seem to be with our current situation? If so, I think I have a simple explanation. It was probably around the time of the defeat at home to Sheffield Wednesday that supporters had given up hoping (or believing) we were good enough to challenge for a play-off place, and accepted we were in for a struggle this season. Attitudes change from anger and frustration to patience and understanding. If this season had followed 98/99 rather than 99/00, the anger and frustration wouldn't have existed in the first place, which makes everything all a bit confusing, but I hope you get my drift.

We are skint, we do have several players still injured, although we should be doing much better. Gerry doesn't appear to be going anywhere for the time being, so rather than berate him give him our support — something that appears to be happening. The football on offer recently has seen an improvement as we see the usual first team regulars return from injury, and despite our position, it's still too early to say we're doomed for Division 2. Keep the faith and rewards will follow (I hope).

More news on this mysterious Arab who reportedly put in a bid to buy the club off Chris Wright last season. At the AGM Wright denied such a person or offer has ever existed — but then he would — however I'm told the whole story is absolutely kosher, and the reason why nothing materialised was because the deal had been set up by Executive Director Simon Crane, who was in conflict with Wright at the time over the running of the club. After discovering the Youth Academy was going to be scrapped, Crane stepped up his efforts to bring new funding or ownership to QPR, and when rebuffed by Wright in his attempt to get him to sell his shares in the club to the Arab, parted company with QPR, and soon took up a new position as Marketing Director with Jaguar Racing in Milton Keynes.

More or less, that's the story — by no means 100% precise, but a long way there. It would seem Wright is doing things his own way and no one else's, but our trust in him is running thin.

At least things on the pitch are slowly picking up. The signing of Michel Ngonge from Watford is a strange one. He's 33, hardly a recognisable name but has scored goals in the Premiership for a struggling team. His debut against Nottingham Forest started well — he's not short of pace or skill, but tired towards the end. Whether he'll remain in the team when Kiwomya returns from injury, time will tell, but should hopefully prove to be a useful edition to the squad.

Also on his way back from injury is Danny Maddix, who is expected to make his comeback for the reserves in the new year. It's been a terrible time for Danny over the last 12 months, and if he can get back to anything near his best, his availability will be a huge bonus in the second half of the season. No such joy for Karl Ready though, who faces another two months on the sidelines having only just recovered from his broken leg.

(Ed – issue # 146)

Rambling on

Disaster. That is the only word for it. I know that all sorts of stories have since come out that the closing of the Youth Academy does not mean the end of the youth set-up, but just who exactly are we going to play? And when? Francis says that the old South-East Counties league was a good set-up. He is right, it was. But since then all the big teams in it, Arsenal, Spurs, Chelsea, West Ham etc have left to join the Academy set-up. Who the hell is it going to leave? We all know that our club is in the crap financially, we are not daft, whatever the directors think, but to close down the Academy?

In all my thirty-five years of supporting the club I have never heard of such a diabolical idea. We were told at some length when these Academies were being set up that this was going to be the future of youth football. The simple truth would appear to be that with this current board there is no bloody future to worry about. New ground my arse, we will be lucky to be playing on Shepherds Bush Green in five years if this board stay for much longer.

~ ~ ~

Huddersfield eh, what can anyone say? I have no idea what tactics we had on the day, but wasn't it pretty obvious with half an hour to go that they weren't working? Once again Francis seemed quite happy to settle for a point. If my eyes didn't deceive me I honestly thought that we started with a flat back four, before we panicked with Baraclough's injury and reverted to our usual five. Then when in doubt, lump the ball up to poor old Crouch and hope that for once he isn't being assaulted and can hold the ball up.

Then we came to Wolves and the usual pattern was broken for a change. We didn't actually win, god forbid, but for once we didn't half give it a go in the second half. With any luck at all we would have finally got three points, but as usual we came up short. But at least for once it wasn't for the lack of trying, in fact I actually thought that most of the players earned their money. Now let me see if I can work out why. Unless my eyes deceived me we played four at the back for the second half and actually had a different idea than just hump the ball up to Crouch. We appeared to be trying a brand new tactic that I believe is called WIDTH. A revolutionary concept and I'm not at all sure it will catch on but it is certainly worth another try. Now all we need is another revolutionary idea called PACE and we may be getting somewhere.

Gavin Peacock said afterwards that it had just sort of happened, the players all of a sudden had started to pass to each other rather than belt the ball up field at the first opportunity. For the life of me I cannot understand how it can just have happened. Does this mean then that Francis didn't change tactics at half time as I had assumed, but that it was all caused by some sort of divine intervention? If it was then long may it remain so; we could do with some divine help.

~ ~ ~

First win in 14 matches — famous groupies congratulate match-winning hero...

Just loved the Forest game. I really thought that we played very, very well although I cannot for the life of me see how Forest have been doing so well, they were rubbish. I know they had a few players out but then so did we. Still the highlight of the day just had to be Bob the Builder at half-time. In answer to his question 'Can we fix it? I think the answer now is definitely YES WE CAN!
(Paul Davidson – issue # 146)

A happy new year?

It was a massive bonus to draw Arsenal in the fourth round of the FA Cup, and whilst Luton would rightly argue we barely have the right to be here, we still might as well relish the occasion.

The scramble for tickets started as soon as the final whistle blew against Luton. The club have been criticised for the distribution method, with season ticket holders being allowed to purchase up to four guest tickets each. Too many maybe, but as long as they end up in the hands of QPR fans, that's the important thing. There may be many 'woodwork' fans in the ground, but they're all fans, and provides a taster of what the demand would be like for tickets if we were to once again rub shoulders with the best teams in the land on a permanent basis in the Premiership.

That seems a long way away at the moment, but as long as we can keep the divide by just one division come May, it's something we should all strive to aim for. Quite when we'll be good enough to challenge for promotion time will tell, but in the meantime all our efforts must stay focused on remaining in Division 1.

If we do go down, Francis will need to accept responsibility — something he shows little sign of acknowledging. Like him or loathe him, Ray Wilkins held his hands up and blamed himself for relegation from the Premiership, and Francis would need to do the same if the unthinkable happens this time around. He can blame injuries all he likes, but never once have we failed to field a recognisable team this season. He's amounted this massive squad, but has failed to use it to the best of its (limited) ability. As things stand, it's so tight at the bottom of the table that a couple of wins on the spin could almost haul us into a respectable mid-table position, but nothing should be taken for granted. *(Ed – issue # 147)*

Rambling on

Norwich, yuk! What the hell was going on in our penalty area? We play three centre backs and a defensive marking midfielder and not one off them bothers to mark the other team's only aerial threat. As for bloody Morrow, seems his only job of the afternoon for some reason was to look after their No.4, Lee Marshall, and the only time he had any work to do Marshall pissed past him like he was asleep and banged in the equaliser. Another good idea Gerry. And what was his response? Wait until there was five minutes left and bring on an attacking midfielder for Morrow. Yet another perfect example of Francis looking to get a draw out of a home game that we really had to win.

On the lines of defenders not bothering to mark people, I heard a very disturbing story from two separate sources before and after the Norwich game which if true, sum the Gerry Francis regime up perfectly I think.

Rather than say that Francis had dropped Harper a couple of weeks before-hand, it was given out officially that Harper had a stomach upset. The story doing the rounds was however that Harper had confronted Francis as to the vagaries of the marking of the three central defenders he insists on playing. Harper apparently saying something along the lines of, 'they are making me look bad as I never know which one, if any, is going to mark anyone, so I never know whether or not to come off of the line to try and look

285

after them myself.' Apparently rather than accept any criticism of his ridiculous defensive system, Francis decided to drop Harper. Now as I have said, I have no idea if there is any truth in this story, but it just sounds like there might be!

~ ~ ~

Then we had Crystal Palace. Two friends of mine that hadn't seen the Rangers for years were in the LSA before the game and asked me how the game would go. I said that we would start OK and probably go a goal up. The Palace manager at half time would then say to his players just to make sure that Crouch didn't see the ball in the second half and that Palace would go on to either get a draw or win because Rangers would not change their tactics. Now if a silly old sod like me can see that then why can't Francis?

Mind you what a fluke of a goal they did get. Talk of when you are down you are down. Still in the end I was happy to get a point. As was Francis obviously or he wouldn't have picked that team and as for the subs selection, words just fail me, no bloody wonder he didn't bother changing anyone. And then when he did, he brought on a defender for our only real goalscoring threat from midfield. I know Wardley has been poor but what are the chances of Perry scoring more than him? Or was it to make sure we got a point? As I said, sometimes words just fail me.

~ ~ ~

So we finally scored three times in the same game at Luton (in the FA Cup, at least, though I didn't go as I can't stand the place). I wonder if anyone can tell me when, if ever, we have gone over half a season before without scoring more than two goals in a match? And has anyone realised that we had not, up until the new year, gone more than one goal up in any game? I hadn't, until someone behind me pointed it out at the Palace game and is it true? I probably could look it up for myself but I am afraid that I am getting so fed up with this team that I couldn't really give a toss. Just thought it was interesting that's all.

~ ~ ~

So apparently we have no fewer than eighteen players out of contract at the end of the season so at last we can get rid of this rubbish that has been cluttering the club up for years. But maybe not! If you believe the reports that have been circulating the last few weeks we are desperate to re-sign 'several' of them and this leaves me a little baffled. Nobody, but nobody has tried to sign any of these deadbeats in the last year or so, so why on earth would we want to re-sign any of them. Surely it is the only chance we will get to have a good clearout and maybe start again. Now admittedly I am not sure exactly who all eighteen are, but apart from Carlisle, Rose and Crouch for definite and

Baraclough, Connolly, Harper, Plummer, Langley and Perry probably, I'm not bothered if they all go!

~ ~ ~

I did go to the Luton replay however. Got up off my sickbed and braved the freezing cold air. And for what? Yet another miserable performance from the most miserable QPR side in the history of football. Five defenders and a defensive midfield player and people wondered why we made so few chances. Barry Fry said on Sky Sports at the weekend that it was the most miserable QPR performance he had ever seen. Now we have Arsenal. Desperately looking for an opportunity to play a poor team to run back into a little bit of form, you can only guess how delighted they are that they have drawn us. Even if they put their bloody reserves out they should give us a good hiding. I'm beginning to wish I still had the flu!

(Paul Davidson – issue # 147)

You wait years for an exciting cup tie...

So, Rangers have finally managed to inject some kind of interest into this awful season with the two games against Luton. For the first time since, well, since that nervous fifth round tie at home to Millwall five years back when Willo converted a last minute penalty (caused by a handball not too dissimilar to the one at Luton, incidentally), we've actually got something to get excited about in the cup.

I'm writing this the day after our unbelievably lucky victory over Luton in the replay and I still can't believe how we managed it. Before the game everyone was talking about Arsenal. I think it's fair to say no one was sure we'd win, but most expected it. Deep down I thought we'd win too, but all I could think of was the amount of times Rangers have bottled the big games over the last few years — Palace being the important exception.

We've frozen so many times when we've really needed to win that I'm almost getting used to it. Time after time we fail to do ourselves justice. But it's not just the big games. We seem to reserve our very worst performances for games against teams we're expected to beat. I thought that some of this had been laid to rest last season when for the most part we beat the poorest teams in the league. But it's crept back again this season. We allowed Lua Lua the freedom of Loftus Road against Colchester, we've lost twice to a poor Sheffield Wednesday side, and drawn against many teams who we could have beaten with a little more adventure.

Some of this, for sure, is down to the manager. Gerry's plan early on this season seemed to be to keep things solid, not lose, get a couple of wins and build from there

— basically very unadventurous. The problem was that we never got the wins Gerry was looking for and he seemed to panic. While some managers might have thrown caution to the wind, Gerry continued to play it safe.

I would guess that 99% of supporters think that the reason for our current mess is our defensive outlook on games. I can see the argument of getting to half time without conceding, but too often we encourage away teams to attack us, and we end up playing like the away team on our own ground — all this after losing, what, only two games at home all of last season! For once Loftus Road was something approaching a fortress — a small castle, maybe, and it's taken us just half a season to lose that facade. Gerry just doesn't have enough faith in his own players. He thinks they have too many limitations to be able to play good football on the ground and so doesn't allow it to happen. Yet at times we played great football last season — Ipswich home and away are the classic examples — and arguably we have a stronger squad this year.

The last three games we have played — against Luton and West Brom — sum up our season perfectly. They expose our complete inability to dispose of inferior teams (and no matter how much Luton deserved to win the replay, they are an inferior side) and our marvellous ability to occasionally upset the odds by playing good football. WBA have been transformed under Megson and are a very good side — their front two are arguably the best in this division, yet we were in control for the whole game. Megson even admitted that he wasn't angry with his team — they'd played well and worked hard but Rangers were just better.

But the things we did well against West Brom, particularly in the first half, and against Luton at their place in the second half, are things we've been consistently failing to do all season for the most part. Most importantly, we stretched the opposition by using the wings. Meanwhile Gavin Peacock's mere presence in the second half against Luton and the WBA game made us a much more intelligent side. Whatever you say about Gav, and many people believe he is fading now, we are without doubt a better team when he's playing — we certainly seemed bereft of ideas without him in the replay. I have no doubt that the wings are the key both to more attractive and more successful football, yet Francis consistently ignores this.

In the middle up front we have Peter Crouch. Rarely have I seen a player improve in such a short space of time than Crouch. When I first saw him pre-season I thought he had potential but was largely ineffectual. But since he inspired our comeback against Gillingham he has improved every week, and is now averaging a goal every three games which is a decent record for someone in his first season of first team football. Yet it's not just his goals that are valuable. He saved us at Kenilworth Road with his double, but he also set up four good chances for Kiwomya in the replay, of which eventually Chris managed to stick away two. But there's no reason why we shouldn't congratulate players like Crouch for being a rare positive in a season of negatives. Apart from anything else his work-rate is absolutely superb, he's been very unlucky not to score more goals than he has, and his improving strength against some rough-house defending is particularly impressive. I suspect Iain Dowie may have had a little to do with that. And if anyone can find me a better striker for £60,000 then let's sign him now.

All of which, in my opinion, makes Francis' over-reliance on balls to Crouch's head even more mystifying. In games where we've solely relied on that tactic we've generally ended up with very little. The equaliser against Luton surely only came out of the law of averages — we'd bombed so many balls to him during the game that one had to end up in the net. Imagine, though, what we'd be like with a bit more variation in our attacks. Think how deadly Crouch might become if balls were whipped in from the byline rather than lumped in from the halfway line. Crouch is least effective when our attacks focus solely on the centre of their defence — the more players that mark him the more difficult it is for him to utilise his obvious advantage. In the Luton replay he was nullified for long periods because we were so poor at using the wings and stretching their defence. We allowed them to all bunch in on Crouch and collectively stop him from playing because there was no one else for them to mark.

Clarke Carlisle hasn't been in great form recently but I still believe that the time has come to switch to a back four. Last season I felt that our defence wasn't good enough to do this, but now I think we'd be a much better side playing in a similar fashion to Francis' first time in charge.

Back to the Luton games. Despite the fact we were absolutely dreadful in the first half up there, we still had enough chances to have gone in at the break at least on level terms. In the second half we dominated almost completely for long periods and the ease with which we prised open their defence was astounding at times. In the end we should have won about 6-3, although they had to gift us the equaliser before we could even claim a draw. That was the first game in such a long time where I'd been really excited — and the support in the second half was fantastic — how forgiving we all were after giving the players and the manager the booing they so thoroughly deserved at half time.

But, as usual with QPR, nothing is ever very easy. Gavin Peacock said in an interview that he thought we'd be 'too strong' for Luton at Loftus Road, and immediately I realised that we might just be a little complacent in the replay. What a surprise — we could have been watching the Worthington Cup matches of the last three years — against Walsall, Cardiff and Colchester, all were essentially similar performances. I felt very strange after the replay. I feared the worse after they went one up, and after twenty minutes I was convinced we weren't going to do it. I sulked for the whole second half and turned into one of those crap fans who criticises everything all the time and I didn't sing or anything. All I could think of was everyone I know taking the piss, all those non-regular fans who'd never come again, and how much the team had let us down. I just wanted to go home near the end. Luckily I didn't — although judging by the bundle in the Loft next to me after the equaliser a lot of people had. When Kiwomya scored that amazingly unjust goal — not only was it a foul (Langley even hugged the referee to say thanks for not giving it) but also seemed to be offside by a yard or two — I felt like a spoilt boy who'd sulked until he got what he'd wanted. I felt too guilty to even celebrate very much and as a bloke behind us said, absolutely brilliantly, "Well, you need a bit of luck to win the cup!" Bring on the Arsenal.

(Dan Trelfer – issue # 147)

Wright to leave, but what about Francis?

It is the correct decision for Chris Wright to leave. We are a club who needs someone who is prepared to spend a lot of money on the club, therefore has a lot of money to spend. I thought that after the Fulham game, Gerry would call it a day. I was hoping he would. I can't stand it when he keeps whingeing on about how many players are injured, he's got no money and that he is only here because it's QPR. OK Gerry, go, what's stopping you? A lot of people would like to see him leave, including me. Due to the injuries of Langley and Carlisle, against Bolton Gerry changed the formation at last. What happens? We out-play the second best team in the division for most of the game. Why didn't he play the 4-4-2 formation earlier in the season?

(David Jellis – issue # 148)

Moreno Bares All

So another month goes by and yet the embarrassing results still come. Actually the embarrassment has stopped now because I'm so used to it. Trudging away from Loftus Road (or any other away ground) has become the most excruciating journey that I seem to take these days.

I was not in the least surprised at the amount of verbal abuse that Chris Wright has supposedly received before he stepped down as chairman. Here is a man that was hailed as a saviour following the Thompson era yet made a very nice and tidy profit when he floated the club and Wasps on the AIM as 'Loftus Road Plc'. Whilst it's true that he is lending the club money he is also charging a sizeable interest rate on the loans, something that apparently Thompson never did. Wright was interviewed shortly after becoming chairman and was asked why he decided to take over the club. He said that, "The city was looking closely at the football industry as a future potential growth investment market," which basically means that he was in it for the money and hoping to make a quick buck and nothing else. We were all so keen on getting rid of

Thompson that anyone else apart from 'Tricky Dicky' would've done, we are now unfortunately paying for that blind optimism.

~ ~ ~

Some ex-players have been spotted at recent QPR matches; Ray Wilkins still manages to make it along to most games, allowing one irate fan to utter, "It's all your bloody fault Wilkins," at the Arsenal Cup tie. Terry Fenwick (Southall), Tommy Langley and Tony Roberts (Dagenham and Reclbridge) were all present for the visit of Fulham, Lee Charles (Nuneaton Borough) was at Loftus Road for the Crystal Palace game and Rufus Brevett cheered on the R's against Bolton. Apparently Rufus still talks very highly of his time at the dub and still has great affection for us although that didn't stop him crocking Clarke Carlisle a few days earlier.

~ ~ ~

The most satisfying (for me) incident of the season so far happened in the cup game against Arsenal. There's a flat capped gent and his son that have tended to stand up and sarcastically cheer the opposition's goals this season, must notably Gallen's goal for Huddersfield, much to the annoyance of everyone in the upper Loft. During the second half his son casually threw a plastic bottle of beer down about a dozen rows, striking a woman. Everyone seemed to witness this event except the stewards who seemed more interested in watching the match. A handful of QPR fans leapt over the seats in an attempt to eject this man, finally they were able to instruct the stewards as to what had happened but the stewards still didn't seem to want to get involved.

As the son was being lead away with his flat capped father in tow he started becoming abusive to everyone as if he was trying to justify his actions. The father then began to throw himself about and pushed quite forcibly a supporter, who took umbrage to this and thumped the old fellow, knocking him down a couple of rows! In a postscript to this story, the following game the son was missing — presumed to be in Shepherds Bush nick, whilst his father tried to sneak in but was forcibly ejected again.
(Moreno Ferrari – issue # 148)

2001 – A new era?
'As everything fell apart nobody paid any attention'
And so the rot at Loftus Road continues — a rot that dates back god knows how long. Where do you start? If I get a few spare months I may one day sit down and pen my personal opinions on where it has all gone wrong. I could highlight many turning points, many important events that in my opinion have so dramatically shaped this clubs' current desperate situation. Alas, no time though. Plus I find it increasing fruitful

nowadays going over old ground trying to make sense out of the madness. Hindsight is a wonderful thing they say. In the case of QPR though it merely leaves a bitter taste in the mouth and makes the current situation all the more painful to accept.

I could almost accept QPR going down to Division 2 if I thought we were going down with a semblance of pride or dignity. Also my own big fear, and I'm sure many others share this underlying fear, is that there won't be a QPR to support anymore. Not the end of the world but it would represent a massive chunk out of a lot of people's lives.

All those memories, too many too recall at one instant. As in the earlier scenario I may consider a book called 'A diary of an Obsessive' — people will be fascinated to know why? Why the obsession? Why the loyalty to such a total lost cause? Why do we still turn up every week? We all know the answers or do we? How many haven't questioned their sanity continuing to turn up watching this current side? Total blind devotion, that's what it is. I may have lost the faith a long time ago but still I remain faithful.

'Looking back it's so bizarre'
Some said at the time that there were six million good reasons to sell Les Ferdinand to Newcastle — I'm still trying to think of one. We don't get demonstrations anymore, all we can manage at QPR nowadays is a couple of drunken low-life's trying to break into the Director's Box. One can only hope that these morons are no longer allowed to set foot into this stadium again.

The same can also be said for the 'fans' that stood up throughout the majority of the Arsenal game in the upper Loft — watching not the game but a few idiots having a little tussle. OK, watching Rangers recently may be marginally less painful than having your cock cut off but why these individuals choose to come to football is beyond me. As a suggestion for alternative entertainment for these 'fans' may I recommend the all time classic movie 'Raging Bull' which has just been re-released on DVD and happens to contain fight scenes that are actually worth watching. An afternoon sitting in watching that will not only prove much cheaper but probably a lot less painful than this current shambles at QPR.

So the point of this article is that the club needs a good clearout. However getting rid of these so-called fans is the easy bit — most of them don't come here every week anyway. The big problem is that how do we get rid of a manger who clearly refuses to budge, is incapable of motivating a side and has shown this season all the tactical nouse of a gerbil?

I don't have the answers. In fact I don't have a clue. Should Francis go — probably yes but then who comes in? Wright out! Heard it all before with other chairman. Who is going to want to buy this club now? Thing is I'm still here every week and you may have guessed by my tone that I am a little disillusioned. Look at past years when the anger amongst fans was rife and demonstrations commonplace. What we have now is much more serious. We have at QPR a climate of total and utter dejection. It's almost like an acceptance of our current predicament and a helpless willingness to watch the side go further into oblivion by the week. This is not just something that exists amongst the fans either — the pathetic disintegration at Preston an example of how damaging this current climate is.

Does anyone at the club have a game plan for what happens when we get relegated? Is there a plan or are we once again going to stumble blindly into the wilderness thinking that we are too good to be here and that a triumphant return to the First Division is a mere formality. Sounds familiar doesn't it and that is what makes it all the more depressing.

(Matthew Holley – issue # 148)

Rambling on

Right let's start with the Arsenal game. Quite simply I just don't know what to say about it. I was going to say that as usual the ticket distribution was handled appallingly, but I have never seen such a high percentage of Rangers fans for a big game in my life. I was going to say how terrible I thought it was to charge £3 for a programme. But for once I thought it was an excellent edition. I was going to say that the Rangers had completely screwed up the replay tickets, but then we knocked in three quick goals for them and it didn't matter after all.

As for the game, again I just don't know what to say. We did play quite well for the first half-hour it has to be said, but was I alone in thinking that Arsenal just didn't look bothered? Until they got those two quick goals I just couldn't see us losing, but after that I thought that Arsenal could have scored ten if they had really wanted to (or alternatively if they had substituted that old tart Bergkamp). Again was it me alone that thought that Parlour and Vierra had probably the easiest afternoon of their careers in midfield?

And was it only me that nearly choked on my dinner as Francis said on TV that he brought on an extra striker as he always plays positively and tries to go for it? I nearly rang for a TV repair man to fix the bloody speakers. All I really know is that in 36 years of going I have never seen us get beat 6-0 at home before. Come to that I can never remember us getting beat by a team that seemed to give less than a toss about it before. I think that at the end of the day, the only word that sums it all up is 'embarrassing'. Oh well, roll on Fulham.

~ ~ ~

Did I say roll on Fulham? I must be mad. What another totally depressing evening that one was? You can just tell a Rangers fan walking to the ground nowadays by the haunted look on his face. And no wonder, this is just going on for far too long. Admittedly we played very well for about twenty minutes in the second half, but I don't think that anyone really thought we would turn it around and actually win If we are to go down then for God's sake lets go down fighting. I no longer come to Loftus Road to enjoy myself and watch the football. I come out of some blind loyalty and because I have always come. It will not last much longer!

A lot of fuss was made after the trouble in the Director's Box following the game, with Chris Wright eventually quitting. For the life of me I couldn't understand all the excitement it caused, after all hadn't he already announced that he was quitting as soon as some other mug could be found to take over? I still don't know what to think even now. A nice bloke with his heart in the right place, Wright just turned out to be a crap businessman, at least as chairman of a football club, which is strange given the amount of money he has made in his life, but there it is.

~ ~ ~

Missed Bolton, I was up to my neck in snow in Prague and quite simply couldn't be arsed to go to Preston. I don't think I would go all that way to watch this team any more if I'd won the lottery and had a chauffeur driven Roller.

All I know about the Preston game is that some of the goals looked ridiculous on the television and according to the four or five match reports I read, we mustered one shot on target all afternoon Francis has now seemingly changed tack and is saying that the injuries make no difference and that it is the attitude of the players that is wrong. Well at last we agree on something. Maybe if he had realised this before Christmas we would have half a shout of getting out of this mess. Now the Barnsley match could turn out to be the most important of the season. Win it and we are only two points behind them with a game in hand and the famous 'light at the end of the tunnel' will flicker on again. Another 'bore-draw' or defeat and I think that the time will have come to start wearing black armbands.

We must be very close to running out of last chances to get out of this mess. What really worries me is that if people like me that have been there when it mattered for over thirty-five years cannot be bothered to go and watch the away games, what chance do we have of the players giving a toss either? The teams we have to play in the next couple of months, like Barnsley, are not just going to roll over and die because they feel sorry for us but I just can't see the players putting the required effort in to win a bloody game or three. Mind you big Karl should be back in the starting line-up. Now all after me, whoopeeeeeeeeeeeeeeee!

Without Carlisle (and Langley to some extent) the battles on the pitch will be even harder. Great adversity though sometimes has a remarkable effect and I think this is our only hope now. Apparently the performance against Bolton showed exactly what can be done by these players, let's hope it continues and that lady luck will shine on us again — in league matches this time. Surely only fans of Crewe, Stockport, Sheffield Wednesday, Grimsby and Tranmere can begrudge us that?

(Paul 'more depressed by the hour' Davidson – issue # 148)

Will QPR ever be injury-free?

"That's six broken legs and two cruciate knee ligaments already this season," said Gerry after the Fulham match, well to be more precise, that's four broken ankles and two broken legs — not quite the same, but bad enough (if someone broke a finger, would Gerry class that as a broken arm?). Joking aside, the injury problems to have struck QPR over the last two seasons have been nothing short of horrific, and below are listed all the players that have been out of action during this time for at least two months, with—their respective injuries. It's not pleasant reading...

July 99, Chris Plummer - hernia, four months.
July 99, Antti Heinola - cruciate knee ligament, ten months.
July 99, Mark Perry - ruptured hamstring, seven months.
September 99, George Kulcsar - virus, two months.
September 99, Ludo Miklokso - shoulder injury, two months.
October 99, Gavin Peacock - hamstring, five months off and on up to present.
November 99, Danny Maddix - cruciate knee ligaments, fifteen months (and counting).
November 99, Karl Ready - sciateca, three months.
November 99, Steve Morrow - ruptured ligaments in shoulder, eight months.
December 99, Matthew Rose - strained calf, two months.
December 99, Tim Breacker - torn hamstring, eight months.
December 99, Ross Weare - varying back problems, fourteen months (and counting).
January 00, Rob Steiner - knee injury, retired.
March 00, Jermaine Darlington - ruptured ankle ligaments, six months.
July 00, Paul Murray - broken ankle, two months.
July 00, Chris Plummer - shoulder injury, two months.
August 00, Karl Ready - broken leg, two months.
August 00, Ian Baraclough - broken leg, three months.
August 00, Paul Furlong - hamstring, six months (and counting).
September 00, Chris Plummer - broken ankle, three months.
October 00, Paul Murray - broken ankle, four months (and counting).
November 00, Tim Breacker - hamstring, three months (and counting).
November 00, Chris Kiwomya - achilles tendon, two months.

November 00, Karl Ready - broken ankle, three months
January 01, Richard Langley - anterior cruciate ligament, one year.
January 01, Clarke Carlisle - cruciate knee ligaments, one year.
(Ed – issue # 148)

So now we know who to blame – ourselves

Tuh. There was me blithely going around thinking that QPR's mammoth, varied, and seemingly insurmountable problems were down to three things: 1. Poor management. 2. Poor player performances. 3. Poor management decisions at board level.

But, apparently, none of this really contributed to our spectacular downfall from being one of the Premier League's most attractive sides with a superb record in the early 90s, to being this poor excuse for a club that is about to be relegated to Division 2. No. Apparently, we all expected far too much and all our whinging and violence towards the chairman and chants for his head were the elements that caused the house of cards to collapse.

Really? Well, to read the papers following Wright's exit, that's exactly what you'd be led to believe. Forget 'New Labour', QPR span the press like a ten pence piece at the toss for ends. Not one of the reasons listed above was cited in the frankly lazy media reports that occurred in the aftermath of Wright's departure. All they said was that poor old Wrighty had 'Invested £20m in the club,' and all the thanks he received was abuse from disgruntled fans.

I don't particularly blame the newspapers, though. They all wrote their articles purely off the press release and statements coming from Wright and David Davies. You can't expect them to do any real research. But we're QPR and we have no right to expect success, so no one cared or bothered to find out what the fans thought or why the club is failing so badly. There was no counterpoint.

Wright was right and unlucky. We were wrong and, well, tough shit. We were proven guilty, but we had no defence counsel.

So just a few points. Firstly, the abuse at the Fulham game. According to the recent 'Fans Forum', just three people were involved, at least one of whom (and I believe all three) had consumed a pint or ten too many. An egg was thrown. There were some shouts and maybe a little chanting. Sitting in the Loft as I do, there are plenty of people around me who want Wright to go. Of course there are — after all, he's failed to deliver, no one can deny that. Is, then, such a wish so unreasonable? But at half time just one person stood up and shouted for him to go. And do you know why only one person shouted it? Because everyone else knew that if Wright could go, he would. But if there's no buyer there's not a lot he can do is there? He can't even take his loans back because there's no money there to take back. His eagerness to go was clear when he left two days later. Anyway, one of the abusers has been to visit David Davies and has apologised, and the other two are or were also due to go in for a chat. These serial, evil, abusers haven't even done enough to get themselves banned! So much for abuse.

Wright wanted an excuse, and he conveniently got it. What was despicable was the way that QPR supporters were pretty much branded as hooligans and thugs in his statement. Well, I'm sorry, Wright loved the adulation we gave him when he took over — indeed it was probably a factor in his decision to buy the club in the first place. But if you are happy to take the praise you have to be strong enough to take the flak when things go wrong. If you don't want that responsibility, if you're not prepared to face the consequences of failure, or you don't have the resolve to turn things around when they do, then, in short, don't do something as foolhardy as taking over a football club. This isn't a business, whatever people tell you nowadays.

I'm not saying Wright doesn't care. I know he does. But I'm not convinced he cares about the fans. Within the stories about how much he's 'invested' in the club (a lot of that £20m, I strongly suspect, was double-counted), there was not a single mention of the fans who have paid for their tickets, the fans who bought worthless shares in the club they could ill-afford because of a love for QPR and a desire to have a say in its running. What about those investments that have lost Rangers fans so much money? Ignored. Totally.

What about the fact that we have been failing totally on the pitch ever since Wright took over (as well as the year before). Perhaps, just perhaps, that's a little frustrating. Just perhaps we're all a little bit embarrassed that we're scratching around at the bottom of Division 1 with Crewe, Grimsby and Stockport. I'm not going to say 'no disrespect to them,' because, really, we shouldn't even be in a position where we even care about what those clubs are doing. And yet, we are, and it's embarrassing and we hate it and we're fed up. We're fed up of lies, we're fed up of a whole season of sticking with a formation that isn't working and substitutions when it's too late and long ball football and getting turned over by crap teams like Burnley at home. We're fed up with fighting against bloody relegation for four years out of six. We're fed up of paying good money for dull matches and poor food and unimaginative matchday programmes.

Contrary to Wright's view, the fans are pretty much the only innocent party, because there's not a lot we can do wrong except not go to matches, and most of us still do. Clarke Carlisle said at the fans forum that he was amazed by our passion. Presumably he can't believe why we support a club that is so obviously and sadly in terminal decline.

Yet not all of it is Wright's fault. Not by a long chalk. If Thompson had acted properly when he had the chance Wright might never have appeared on the scene. And what the papers failed to point out was that nearly all fans appreciate the financial problems the club is in and why they're in them and that Wright has done his best. Even after the fans had been humiliated and slated in the press the day after his resignation, there still wasn't a chant against him worthy of any note at the Bolton game. To show how poor some of the articles were, at least one suggested mat the reason fans were more angry was because of the rumour that Lawrie Sanchez was being lined up to replace Francis. Yet while most people still like Gerry and are grateful for everything he's done for Rangers, I know of very few people, if any, who would be upset if he were sacked or walked away tomorrow, because this season has been diabolical despite an arguably stronger squad than last year.

Football fans, as I said, are a soft target, and once again the blame has been unfairly laid at our door. Well, thanks Chris, for your parting shot, but how about growing up and publicly taking some responsibility for YOUR mistakes? Don't fancy it? Didn't think so.

(Dan Trelfer – issue # 148)

Counting the days...

If you consider that 50 points should guarantee safety this season, then we need to find 18 points from our remaining 10 games — five wins and three draws — unfortunately, I think that will be way beyond us and our only hope is that perhaps 45 points or less may be enough to finish above the relegation zone. Whatever the eventual safety barrier may be, I fear the damage has already been done — even getting to 40 points will be a struggle. It's the first time I've said it, but I really think we are going down.

Desperate times call for desperate measures...

New chairman and manager introduced to Loftus Road crowd

(Issue # 149)

It's not so much that there isn't enough quality in the squad to keep us up, more that the players simply don't believe in themselves anymore, or even care as much as we really believe they do — half the squad will be on their way in the summer, so how can we expect them to raise their game at such a crucial stage of the season?

The departure of Gerry Francis was the last throw of the dice. Ian Holloway has not and will not have enough time to rescue us. A change of formation has perhaps raised expectations a little, but we still don't look nearer to upping our scoring rate, and defensively, we're still a mess — so just where are the points going to come from?

Our only saving grace may be the games against Grimsby, Tranmere, Huddersfield and Stockport — all six pointers, and none of which we can afford to lose. You could have also included the match against Crewe, but an excellent run of form from them has seen them pull well clear, and proves it can be done. But by the time Stockport visit Loftus Road for our final home game of the season, the need for those points may be irrelevant as our fate could already be sealed.

As much as I admire Ian Holloway's positive attitude (and it is a breath of fresh air), talk of ending 14th or 15th in the table is quite laughable. Only today, Holloway has been quoted as saying, "Last year we ended 10th without the injury problems." Good to see he's been doing his homework! This season's injury problems have only been marginally worse than last season's, which of course makes our efforts on the pitch all the more disappointing this season.

Relegation to Division Two will of course be a disaster whatever way you look it, not least the damage it will do for our pride. As Gerry so often reminded us, it was not so long ago we were London's top club. To see us now almost makes you want to cry. We're following in the paths of Luton, Oxford and Oldham, three teams that not so long ago brushed shoulders with the best teams in the land but may well end up facing each other in Division 3 next season.

So what of Holloway's appointment? You have to feel sorry for him in a way, taking over a club that is in such a mess. Reports from the training ground suggest Gerry Francis is still having a major say in things, which is one of many reasons why supporters believe Holloway is merely acting as Francis' puppet. Not everything you hear should be taken as a matter of fact though, and I'm pretty sure Holloway is in complete control. Let's give him our support — he's going to need it.

Before the awful 3-1 home defeat to Sheffield United, the PA announced, "Welcome Ian Holloway and the start of a brand new era." 90 minutes later, and I seriously contemplated the reality of this new era — life in the Second Division.

Just a week after being assured his position at QPR was safe until the end of the season at least, Iain Dowie has his contract paid up after Holloway decided he wants his own men beside him after all. It's a decision going against the wishes of most QPR fans, myself included, but in many ways an entire fresh start for the club may be beneficial in the long run. Also leaving the club are Antti Heinola and Leon Jeanne.
(Ed – issue # 149)

Rambling on

February, a very strange month to say the least. Was the chairman going or staying? Was the manager going and more to the point, when was the manager going? And who on earth was going to be dumb enough to want the job? And so it dragged on for weeks while the directors of this once good club got it wrong time after time after time. Let's be absolutely fair about this, instead of Nick Blackburn, Paul Hart, Chris Wright and David Davies we would be better off with Tony Blackburn, Jennifer Hart, Orville Wright and Bette Davies running the club. And Orville Wright and Bette Davies are dead!

~ ~ ~

Weren't the 'Are you watching Rodney Marsh,' chants against Barnsley magnificent? A little bit like Gerry Francis being a great player but lousy manager, poor old Rodney was a great player and is a totally crap TV 'pundit'. Still he has to say these things, as he is desperate for any sort of publicity, presumably as he tries to prove to someone that he is employable. It must be awful to know that your only real claim to fame is as George Best's sidekick. Let's face it he has as much chance of getting a real job in football as, say a club like ours has of being in the Conference in five years time!

~ ~ ~

How many people noticed that our Stan almost got it right in the Barnsley programme for once. He missed out on the correct score (he said 2-1 not 2-0) but he got Kiwomya right as the first goal scorer. About time too! Mind you he has to get it right sometimes as he has so many goes at it, and seemingly can never quite make up his mind. Apart from his column in the QPR programme, he is also employed, if that is the right word, by the Internet betting service 'Zoobet' for weekly tips on football matches. No problem with that, or there wouldn't be if he was even vaguely consistent. In the programme he had us down for a 2-1 win, but on Zoobet apparently he had Barnsley down as a certain away win!

I suppose that if you hunted around long enough you would find somewhere where he was tipping the game as a score draw. Seems like our Stan is getting this gambling lark right at last. If you back every horse in a race you are bound to get the winner!

~ ~ ~

I rather bravely praised the programme a couple of month's back and then as soon as I say something nice about it we get the interview from hell. Michel Ngonge, what a nice man he seems to be. Loves being here at the club, even though he has never been at a struggling club before. Excuse me, didn't Watford come stone bloody last in the

Premiership last season, or was it my imagination? Doesn't that count as struggling? Or maybe he had just forgotten. Wiped the entire season from his mind.

So what about the rest of the interview? Let me see, oh yes, 'Michel finds himself in a relegation battle that he didn't necessarily see coming.' Christ almighty, even our Stan would have had money on that. At the time of Ngonge's signing QPR were 23rd out of 24 teams. If he couldn't see a relegation battle coming then who the hell did he think he was signing for, West Ham? Maybe that was Francis' technique, tell these players that they were signing for somebody else. With the average intelligence of a footballer you can be pretty sure that until they pulled their shirt on for the first time they wouldn't have a due where the hell they were. Come to that, probably half of the professionals in this country wouldn't know what club they were playing for if they had it tattooed on their forearm!

~ ~ ~

As for the Barnsley game itself, I must admit that I was worried when I saw Ready and Wardley as the first two men out on the pitch, but it all turned out OK in the end. Ready I thought played very well against Shipperley, as he always does against big slow immobile strikers, and Wardley had one of his better days, even chasing after the odd loose ball. Amazing what playing a few players in midfield can do isn't it? Too little too late I'm afraid Mr Francis.

~ ~ ~

And then we finally got a new manager and you just have to feel sorry for him. Not only was he kept waiting for a couple of weeks whilst the 'brains-trust' of the boardroom from hell were turned down by all and sundry, but then he puts his foot in his mouth by saying that in his opinion Chris Wright had done nothing wrong.

I'm sorry mate but you are not going to get yourself in favour with the fans with that attitude. There was such a gloomy atmosphere in the LSA before the Sheffield United game that I just knew disaster was on the horizon. And what about when they played that tape of Holloway giving it the big 'the players will die for the club today,' speech. You could have heard a pin drop in the ground, instead of the obviously intended cheering. How bloody embarrassing — for Holloway and the fans. And then Nick Blackburn writes in the programme trying to kid us that Holloway was the first choice for the job. Doesn't he realise that if he tried treating us like adults instead of twelve-year-olds we might believe him once in a while? When push came to shove, only Holloway and Dowie wanted the bloody job and I personally feel that Dowie didn't get it because the board were frightened that he wouldn't do what they said. The one single word being banded about in the LSA before the game was 'puppet' and I find that very

worrying. I hope desperately that this is not the case, but either way we are in for a very rocky road this next couple of months.
(Paul Davidson – issue # 149)

Moreno Bares All

"And at the chequered flag it's Holloway by a short nose from Perryman." Yes the great 'who will be the next manager of Queens Park Rangers Football Club' saga is thankfully and finally over and Ian Holloway has taken up the poisoned chalice of office. I'm sure that most supporters felt that Holloway would one day take over the reigns at Loftus Road, however perhaps not as soon as this.

I'm sure that there are a great deal of fans that feel that the club have swapped like for like, I'm not so sure. Whilst it's true that Holloway has greatly admired Francis' work it's also plainly apparent that Holloway is his own man.

Until this season he had had a pretty sound record with Bristol Rovers with a team who have been there or thereabouts in the race to get out of the Second Division. An excellent scouting system, a good youth set-up which Holloway oversaw, coupled with £3-4m worth of players sold-on made the club financially solvent, although finally he may have succumbed to his board's insistence of having to sell one player too many.

There is a strong feeling from supporters and insiders at the club that the man that Rangers really wanted was missed out on. Had Gerry decided to quit a couple of months earlier then the name of Joe Kinnear would have adorned the manager's door. I asked Rangers vice chairman Nick Blackburn before the Sheffield United game which men had been seen by the club apart from Holloway. Graham Rix was not interviewed even though he had shown up at some of QPR's matches. Once it was announced in the 'News of the World' that Rix had the job in the bag then I knew I could stop worrying — since when have they ever got a story correct!

He told me that Steve Bruce, Dave Bassett and Steve Coppell had been turned down because they seemed to lack a little spirit and heart and they had seemingly turned up as if they were not really interested in the job in the first place. Iain Dowie was rejected as the club didn't want another go at the first-time-manager game and make the same mistakes as it had done in the past with Wilkins and Houston, although they felt that Dowie would make a very good manager one day. Steve Perryman was a late entrant, which was partly why the appointment had dragged on for longer than had been envisaged. Perryman is a local lad from Ealing with managerial experience with Brentford and also in Japan although the club felt that he might have lost touch with the English game having spent many years in the land of the rising sun.

In his first programme notes Holloway started off by welcoming everyone to "today's Second Division clash." Obviously he had forgotten about what division he's in or maybe it's a realisation about what division we will be in!

~ ~ ~

The clear out has begun in earnest with Iain Dowie, Antti Heinola and Leon Jeanne all biting the bullet. Vice chairman Nick Blackburn told Dowie that he still had a future with the club, possibly on the training side. However, as anyone knows when a new manager is appointed he tends to bring in his own backroom staff. I understand though that Dowie was extremely unpopular with the players, which may have had repercussions on his tenure.

Although no tears will be shed over perennial absentee-through-injury, Heinola, a departure that will have caused a gnashing of teeth is Leon Jeanne's. Much was expected of the youngster but unfortunately family problems and his mental state have cut short what might have been a promising and fruitful career with QPR.

~ ~ ~

I have noticed that there is a site on the web that deals with suicide prevention training and claims that it has saved the lives of thousands of Americans. The name of this site is www.qprinstitute.org and the group's slogan is 'QPR is growing fast and will be expanding rapidly'. I can't help feeling a certain sense of irony that a suicidal prevention group should be called QPR, especially in our particular predicament.

~ ~ ~

Ian Holloway's first signing for QPR, albeit a loan signing, came in the shape of Chelsea's 18-year-old reserve team striker Leon Knight. What baffles me is firstly, I thought we wanted to get hold of someone with first team experience not someone who hasn't even started a league match and secondly, what's wrong with our youngsters then? With players such as Oliver Burgess, Richard Brady, Richard Pacquette and Ben Walshe all doing so very well for the under 19s surely it would have been a smarter move to promote from within then giving money to a club that already has more than it needs.

(Moreno Ferrari – issue # 149)

All change or no change?

I'm the first to admit that I've written plenty of pro-Gerry Francis articles in the past. It hasn't always been easy, I always genuinely felt that Francis was one of the best coaches, best managers, in this division, and was certainly good enough to hold his own in the Premiership. But events of this season have forced me to alter that view.

I have no doubt that during his first spell with us, and while he was at Bristol Rovers and his during first season at Spurs, he was an excellent coach. The old line always comes out that he was twice interviewed for the England job. Whether he was ever seriously considered is another question. For example, the QPR board interviewed Iain Dowie for the manager's job without ever having any intention of giving it to him. But Francis was losing the plot severely at Spurs by the end, floundering around quoting statistics that allegedly showed how unlucky Spurs had been. And of course there were the injuries. Almost the same thing happened at QPR this time around. He started well, but lost the plot this season. And of course there were the injuries. Anyone who can see beyond their blinkers will realise that he left us in a pretty desperate state last time he left too — only a combination of the euphoria surrounding Wilkins' appointment and the brilliance of Les Ferdinand ensured a good year back then.

I hope Gerry stays on as a director, because he's done a lot for this club, and he truly cares about QPR — he's one of the few legends we have, and no one should ever lose sight of that.

After Francis resigned the other week we promptly won our next two games – ironically with Francis still in charge as we waited for his replacement. Chris Kiwomya said that the players had put in extra effort because they realised they'd let Francis down over the season. Well, thanks, Chris, but why did it take the players so long to realise that, and how much longer before they realise they've been letting the fans down — badly — for the entire season too? But in reality the reasons we won those games had little to do with extra effort.

Against Barnsley Francis finally did the right thing and played 4-4-2, allowing Connolly to play for almost the entire 90 minutes, which was quite astounding. We also won because Barnsley were one of the worst sides I have ever seen. The 2-0 win was played before two sets of supporters wallowing in self-pity and grasping for any positives they could eke out from a dreadful game of football.

Against Gillingham, let's be honest here, we were lucky. We defended very well, with Ready again playing well, but we stole the game. We almost deserved the win through our refusal to concede alone, but if the Wimbledon game taught us anything other than how gutless we can be, it was that had Gillingham scored first they might well have racked up a few as well.

But did Francis see anything other than the result at Priestfield? Apparently he didn't see the same woeful performance that I saw because he picked the same team in the same formation to play a Wimbledon side who were purely and simply there for the taking. They have one of the worst home records in the division, and were coming off the back of a debilitating loss to Wycombe on penalties in the FA Cup a few days earlier. If we had attacked them with purpose from the start we could have taken them to the cleaners. But no, we came with the same single idea as we did at Gillingham. Defend, defend, defend, and if we nick a late goal then all well and good. The problem with this is that if you do concede first your whole plan is up the creek without a paddle.

4-4-2 worked against Barnsley and Watford because the players are far more comfortable with it. Five at the back still isn't working for us this season, and hasn't done all season. It didn't work at Gillingham, and it positively blew up against Wimbledon and Sheffield United.

I have to believe that the time was right for Francis to go. Whether Holloway is the right choice is another question. Judging by his tactics and teamsheet from the Sheffield United game, it seems he's little more than a Francis clone, which I sincerely hope he's not. I can't see the logic behind not dropping a single player following the Wimbledon debacle. The players must just think they only have to turn up to keep their places. What Connolly must be thinking God only knows. It does seem Olly was just giving them all a chance to perform under him — and they failed.

So what of the Holloway appointment? The very fact that it took a week and a half to appoint someone who wanted the job and had no ties means that at least two people must have turned it down. All of which leaves Dowie in, at best, fourth place for the job. The argument that we needed a fresh face is certainly a strong one, but I believe Dowie had plenty of his own ideas and had the added bonus of knowing the players well. It also appears that he heavily favoured 4-4-2 if his comments at the recent meet-the-players evening are anything to go by. I think he deserved a crack at the job.

While I like and admire Olly greatly, I must admit it was one of the most under-whelming managerial appointments I can remember. I hope he turns it around, but if we continue for much longer in this kind of form it really isn't going to happen — even Millwall are going to be bigger than us next season. Frightening, isn't it?
(Dan Trelfer – issue # 149)

As good as down

This has got to be one of the hardest pieces I've had had to write. Our once great club has come full circle, with an imminent return to the division where our modern history kicked off. Every problem that exists in football, we've got, and now we're paying the ultimate price. Unfortunately, my prediction in the last issue that we are as good as down looks most certainly to be true, writing as I am before the Crewe game, eight points from safety. We've had a few weeks to get used to it, so the shock has had time to settle in compared to the absolute horror of losing our First Division status on the final day of the season, as so easily could have happened two years ago.

Coupled with the fact QPR are now in administration, pending new owners, there are no greater depths we could plummet to. Next season will herald a whole new era once (if) our new owners are in place. In many ways, we'll be starting all over again, which will be no bad thing considering the turmoil we've been through these past few years. Time to put it all behind us and hopefully start to make this club great again.

Being in administration should not necessarily be viewed as a bad thing. Our debts are finally out in the open, and being handled by people who know a great deal more about the situation than Messrs Wright, Blackburn and Davies. The club has too many saleable assets to completely fold, and it should provide us with an opportunity to clear our debts once and for all, providing if one of the many interested parties showing an interest to take the reigns at Loftus Road are willing to find funds to repay all our debtors — not sure if this is a compulsory clause issued by Wright to interested parties, although it would be foolish not to. Otherwise, Wright may as well stay in charge.

> WE'RE GOING DOWN WITH THE TRANMERE...

The fat lady sings, but there will always be a Queens Park Rangers...

It's hard to say exactly how we'll compete next season in Division 2. It will be a new look QPR— with so many players out of contract in the summer, the culling of the squad will be severe. Those players that are signed on with QPR for at least another season should automatically take a pay-cut — after all, they've helped take the club down, and should be paid accordingly in relation to the level of football they will be playing next season.

Division 2 is by no means the end of the world — providing we can stay in the top half of the league, interest and attendances should keep up, naturally though our average gate will drop as many visiting teams will barely bring enough fans to fill a block of seats, let alone a whole stand of them. If I had the choice of another season like this in

Division 1, or one in the upper reaches of Division 2, I know which I'd take. It doesn't matter what division you're in or who you're playing, if your team is playing well, scoring goals and winning matches, supporters will be happy, and should be viewed as our goal.

It's galling to think that only last season we were doing the double over Ipswich Town 4-1 and 3-1 — next season, Ipswich could well be competing in the Champions League whilst QPR slog it out in the LDV Trophy. Football fortunes can change so quickly, and this sums it all up perfectly. It's taken us only five years to go from Premiership solvency to the scary realisation of Second Division football. Chris Wright mixed business with pleasure, and got it all wrong.

Wright of course isn't solely to blame — I could write a novel into the many varied reasons why we find ourselves back in the old Third Division, but it's a subject I'm frankly sick of writing about or even think about. Right now, it's all about the future — our day will come again. Come on you R's.
(Ed – issue # 150)

If only we could turn back time...

I really don't know what to say. On the night of Monday the second of April, I was just having a quick look at teletext when I saw the headlines that QPR had called in the administrators. My immediate reaction was that the end had come and I almost burst into tears. I didn't have a clue what the difference between administrators and receivers was or if there even was any difference.

I went to bed that night convinced that we were seven games away from oblivion. I did not sleep well. Now, a week later, I still don't really know what to think. If I have got the situation right, which for me would be a bloody miracle, the deep shit we are in might not be quite as deep as it looked on the evening of Monday the second of April. At least for now. On the other hand the way these administrators are operating, it makes me wonder if things are as bright as they say.

From what I understand, the only thing that has really happened is that Chris Wright and his bunch of trained chimps have admitted that they couldn't run a chip shop let alone a football club and have called in someone who can. Hooray! Why the hell didn't they ask me three years ago, I could have told them then and saved us a bloody fortune! Now it's a question of who is going to buy the club. The words 'property developer' keep getting mentioned and it's two words that I just don't like.

Now despite the administrators saying that they would wait and get all the offers for the various parts of Loftus Road Plc in before making any decisions, we hear that Wright has bought the Wasps part of it for £5million. Now personally I think that £5million quid for that pile of crap is fantastic, but it doesn't alter the fact that apparently the owner of Worcester Rugby Club was thinking of paying up to £7million! You don't by any chance think that this administrator lark is a bit of a stitch-up do you?

Chris Wright is now charging around on his big white horse saying that he doesn't really want all his money back and trying to look like a bloody hero. It just doesn't wash with me. We are losing over half a million pounds a month and yet we have recently brought in no less than four new players.

The administrators apparently think that the club has recently been run like a madhouse. I've got news for them. This club has been run like a madhouse for at least thirty-five years! But we are reaching new heights (or rather depths) each and every week.

We're getting relegated back to the old Third Division and the latest excuse is that we are paying for mistakes made five years ago, by a sheer co-incidence before this lot turned up. And they think we are so stupid that we believe them. It just makes my blood boil and I can't take much more.

Let's face a few facts. We are going to be relegated back to where we came from and whatever anyone thinks we fully and completely deserve it, both on and off the pitch. On the pitch the old boy that sits next to me is convinced that it all began with signing Crouch. Although he has been possibly our best player this season, the theory goes that as every attacking move goes through him once the other teams figure him out as they did around December, that's the end of us as an attacking threat. The old boy could very well be right.

Off the pitch, I think one of the most depressing things about these last few seasons has been looking at the average attendances for the First Division. I know full well that in the Premiership we were always in the bottom three or four, but we have spent the years since that relegation in 1996 in the bottom third of the First Division, attendance wise at least. It was alright for Chris Wright and now one of the potential new owners to bang on about us needing a new larger stadium to be a success in the Premiership, but no one ever explained to me exactly where the extra 20,000 fans we needed were or are going to come from. Or were we supposed to get promoted first and then build the new stadium? So how were we supposed to stay up whilst the new stadium was being built exactly? It just never added up to me.

By this time next year we might not exist at all and if we do it's going to be with a team of young cheap players that are going to struggle like hell next season to get anywhere near a promotion place. It may take years to get back to even where we are now, but by then we might have the consolation of playing in a brand new state of the art super-stadium. That'll look good with six thousand people in it! Handy having it down by the M4 though, easy for the tens of thousands of Brentford fans to flock to our big new 'derby' game.

I don't know exactly who is to blame for all this, or when it all started to go so hideously wrong, I wish I did. The one thing for certain is that even if it were all down to one single person, which I don't believe it can be, they wouldn't admit it. I don't even know exactly when it started to go so wrong. I suspect it may have been with the Roy Wegerle memorial staircase, but as usual I could be wrong.

So stand up and take a bow please Messrs Thompson, Wright, Wilkins, Houston, Rioch, Harford, Francis et al. You and no doubt countless others have managed between you to bring a once proud and even modestly famous football club not so much to its knees, but onto its belly in the gutter. And I'm willing to bet that every single sodding one of you is sleeping better at the moment than I am. I'm not sure I will ever sleep well again!

(Paul Davidson – issue # 150)

QPR 0-1 Grimsby Town

A game we simply had to win, and whilst it was a 3-0 or 4-0 type of performance, nothing is guaranteed in football and Grimsby duly stole the points with their only attack of the second half. Sadly now, we are as good as relegated — that's not being defeatist, but being realistic.

Can QPR get anything right these days? Even the supposed 'sell out' crowd on £5 tickets, printed as 17,608, looked more along the lines of 14,000 - 15,000 to me. How can the club explain this one? OK, so perhaps the weather put a few punters off, willing to sacrifice their meagre expenditure — but certainly not 2,000+ of them. The extra's that did find their way to Loftus Road mainly consisted of juveniles — where I was sitting it was almost like a crèche, never seen so many lunch boxes at QPR. Nothing wrong with kids of course, but I did feel like I was at a pantomime.

Cue nice little link — unfortunately, there was nothing pantomime about Danny Coyne's performance in goal for Grimsby. On six or seven occasions he kept his side in the match, meaning our most attack-wise performance of the season left us with nothing once Groves fraudulently grabbed the only goal of the game with ten minutes remaining.

It was the biggest kick in the teeth we'd had all season. Losing this game simply wasn't an option. The press rightly gave the reason why we did was down to Coyne — in truth any side with strikers far more potent than our own would have given Coyne no chance with many of the opportunities created.

(Ed – issue # 150)

Standing on the corner of the street

Recent events have rather overtaken the original point of this article and now that relegation is inevitable I thought I'd focus on next season. I'm actually writing this before both the Crewe and Portsmouth games but for once I'm not expecting events to overtake.

I essentially missed the last relegation season as I was at university, but I did manage to watch a significant number of Sunderland games that year as they stormed to the First Division championship. I thought it was bad enough standing on the Sunderland terrace watching them parade the championship trophy whilst the news came over the radio that we'd been relegated. The game at Forest was hardly a wake either. So this year really has been an experience. Not one I wish to repeat.

So, what of next year. I'm not going to go into the finances. It is all fairly well documented and by people more able than me. The only thing that I feel seems certain is that we will at least start next season. Despite everything that has happened over the last few months I actually think we are in a much better position to face next season than we were in our first year down from the Premiership. For a start the utter arrogance displayed by everyone associated with the club that year has long gone. Quite why there was such a strong feeling that we'd walk the First Division and that many of the teams weren't fit to tie the boots of our collection of Premiership 'stars' I don't know, but I think the lesson should have been well and truly learnt by now. Down in the depths of hell (a.k.a. Division 2) you need passion, fire, belief in yourselves and utter respect for your opponents.

If there is one person that realises this then I think that person is Ian Holloway. Midfield has been our weakest link all season and Olly has already moved to strengthen that area with the purchase of Marcus Bignot. At last a QPR player who looks like he 'gets off' on just playing football (if you'll excuse the expression). I'm expecting a few more acquisitions along those lines. It will be interesting to see which of the current crop Olly feels has the stomach for the fight next season. I'm betting not many of them. I think the defence is adequate for the Second Division but there isn't much beyond that (and I suspect Crouch will be sold to pay off the suddenly oval ball-loving chairman).

The first game of next season is going to require a lot of quick revising as we learn the names and faces of the new crop. Better dig out those sixth form notebooks and pens, they are going to be needed. It is going to be a test for us in the stands too, and I don't just mean the strain of watching Second Division football at £15 a throw. There is going to be no away support to speak of at the majority of games, in fact nothing to wind us up. We're going to have to do that ourselves.

So any huge reasons for optimism? Well not really I suppose, but at least this time we are heading into the fight with our eyes open (perhaps wide open in utter terror, but it's a start). We all know what we have to do, let's just make sure we aren't found wanting.

Right, I'm off to locate a lorry to transport all of QPR's dead sheep to the nearest foot 'n mouth cull. I hope they've still got some ammunition left. I may bring back a gun though and if anyone boos when it is nil-nil at half time in the first match of next season, so help me but I won't be responsible for my actions.
(Matthew Mannion – issue # 150)

Division 2 here we come

Throughout the history of football struggling teams have dumped their manager towards the end of the season to try to get a bit of a lift and pull themselves out of relegation trouble. We of course did the same thing with Gerry Francis jumping before he was pushed. And what sort of a lift did we get? We won one out of thirteen games! Just one. I wonder if any team in the history of football has won only one of its last thirteen games after replacing its manager. If anyone has, I'll bet it's not very many.

Now any of you that read this magazine regularly will know that I wanted Francis replacing a lot earlier than he was, but with hindsight it's probably just as well he wasn't. If he had been we could have broken every sort of low points scoring record going, including our infamous eighteen points of 1968-69.

So what can we conclude from this? Myself I'm not sure, but I'm willing to give it a go.

Does it mean that Holloway is a crap manager? Who knows, and after all, other than Dowie nobody else would have taken the job? Does it mean that Francis was still behind team tactics and selection even after he stepped down? I don't think so, maybe for a game or so, but not very long. Does it mean that the players just couldn't really give a toss? Now maybe we are starting to get somewhere. For the last few weeks of the season wherever I went I listened to radio phone-in shows about football and almost without exception they were bombarded by callers of clubs up and down the country all complaining about their teams players not giving a toss. From Luton to Everton and from Plymouth to Bradford there were fans on moaning that the players just couldn't care less about their club, only their wallets.

So maybe that was the problem. But even that doesn't really make sense. I could understand it if the team had continually been made up of players whose contracts were running out at the end of the season and knew they were not getting new ones. The fact of the matter is that the team against Stockport was made up almost entirely of players who will be here this coming season and yet they put in the what was probably the worst performance in the club's one hundred and god knows how many years of history! So who the hell knows, probably no one.

Rodney Marsh was quite rightly vilified back in March when he said that QPR would probably be in the Conference within five years. Given the results since he said it, he could very well be right after all!
(Paul Davidson – issue # 151)

Farewell my R's...
Taken from 'The Cure's' official website, penned by Robert Smith.
Queens Park Rangers were yesterday relegated to the 'third flight' of English football — Division 2 — for the first time in 34 years. They are also in administration with so-called 'crippling debts'...

In at number 14 on today's Sunday Times 'richest men in football' list.... Chris Wright, QPR owner, worth an estimated £190,000,000 (one hundred and ninety million pounds). Aaaah! The modern world.

I've been a QPR fan (and a football lover — the two go hand in hand — really!) since I was about eight years old, but this season I've accepted an awful truth... I DON'T LOVE EITHER OF THEM ANYMORE! In fact I've grown heartily sick of all the totally wank 'culture' that now surrounds a game that used to be, for me, mostly about playing with a ball in the most entertaining way possible (and maybe a few drinks thrown in later). But with the interminable vacuous speculation and prurient inane gossip and endless fake emotion and dreary face painting and continuous absurd hyperbole and useless spoilt 'superstars' and third away strips and fucking sound-fx noises and "football's coming home" and "vindaloo" and money money money money money... AAAAGH! I'VE HAD ENOUGH!

So, goodbye Sky shite. Goodbye tabloid toss. Goodbye C5 challiteration. Goodbye football. But these are still my favourite all-time QPR 'greats' — happier times!; 1) Stan Bowles/Rodney Marsh, 3) Don Givens , 4) Les Ferdinand, 5) Gerry Francis, 6) Trevor Sinclair, 7) Terry Venables, 8) Terry 'Henry' Mancini, 9) Dave Thomas, 10) Roy Wegerle, 11) Phil Parkes. Subs: Tony Currie, Tony Hazell, the Morgan twins (Ian & Roger), David Bardsley, David Seaman, Nigel Quashie, Kevin Gallen. ❑

End game. Gerry Francis and Iain Dowie's final stand during the 5-0 defeat at Wimbledon

League Division One 2000/2001	Pld	Home					Away					Overall					Pts	GD
		W	D	L	F	A	W	D	L	F	A	W	D	L	F	A		
Bottom of the table before Ian Holloway's first game																		
18 Grimsby Town	32	7	2	5	17	14	2	5	11	14	32	9	7	16	31	46	34	-15
19 Crewe Alexandra	32	6	4	5	17	16	3	2	12	14	29	9	6	17	31	45	33	-14
20 Stockport County	34	3	8	5	20	22	3	6	9	22	35	6	14	14	42	57	32	-15
21 Queens Park Rangers	33	5	8	4	19	17	1	6	9	14	36	6	14	13	33	53	32	-20
22 Sheffield Wednesday	34	5	2	9	23	33	4	3	11	12	27	9	5	20	35	60	32	-25
23 Huddersfield Town	31	3	5	8	17	19	3	5	7	15	22	6	10	15	32	41	28	-9
24 Tranmere Rovers	30	6	3	5	19	20	1	3	12	10	29	7	6	17	29	49	27	-20
Bottom of the table at the end of the season																		
18 Grimsby Town	46	10	4	9	26	27	4	6	13	17	35	14	10	22	43	62	52	-19
19 Stockport County	46	6	11	6	29	26	5	7	11	29	39	11	18	17	58	65	51	-7
20 Portsmouth	46	9	8	6	31	25	1	11	11	16	34	10	19	17	47	59	49	-12
21 Crystal Palace	46	6	6	11	28	34	6	7	10	29	36	12	13	21	57	70	49	-13
22 Huddersfield Town	46	7	6	10	29	26	4	9	10	19	31	11	15	20	48	57	48	-9
23 Queens Park Rangers	46	6	9	8	24	28	1	10	12	21	47	7	19	20	45	75	40	-30
24 Tranmere Rovers	46	8	7	8	30	33	1	4	18	16	44	9	11	26	46	77	38	-31

Ian Holloway had 13 games to save QPR but managed just one win

Danny Maddix pictured during his last game for QPR. Maddix made 348 appearances for QPR but injuries restricted him to just two appearances during the 2000/01 campaign

The only success story from the 2000/01 season – Peter Crouch

2000/01 ~ Division 1

Date	Match	Comp	Scorers	Att	Issue
12/08/00	H Birmingham D 0-0	League		13,926	# 141
20/08/00	A Crystal Palace D 1-1	League	Carlisle	19,020	
23/08/00	A Colchester W 1-0	Lge Cup	Kiwomya	3,900	
26/08/00	H Crewe W 1-0	League	Furlong	9,415	
28/08/00	A WBA L 1-2	League	Kiwomya	14,831	
06/09/00	H Colchester L 4-1	Lge Cup	Kiwomya	4,042	
09/09/00	H Preston D 0-0	League		11,092	# 142
13/09/00	H Gillingham D 2-2	League	Crouch, Kiwomya	10,655	
16/09/00	A Barnsley L 2-4	League	Kiwomya (2)	12,763	
23/09/00	H Wimbledon W 2-1	League	Wardley, Crouch	11,720	# 143
30/09/00	A Sheffield utd D 1-1	League	Koejoe	13,803	
14/10/00	A Watford L 1-3	League	Connolly	17,488	
17/10/00	A Grimsby Town L 1-3	League	Connolly	4,428	
21/10/00	H Burnley L 0-1	League		11,427	# 144
25/10/00	H Sheff Weds L 1-2	League	Peacock (p)	10,337	
28/10/00	A Tranmere D 1-1	League	Connolly	7,263	
31/10/00	A Bolton L 1-3	League	Crouch	10,180	
04/11/00	H Portsmouth D 1-1	League	Peschisolido	12,036	
11/11/00	A Stockport Cty D 2-2	League	Carlisle, Langley	6,356	
18/11/00	H Huddersfield D 1-1	League	Connolly	11,543	# 145
25/11/00	H Wolves D 2-2	League	Peacock (2)	11,156	
02/12/00	A Sheff Weds L 2-5	League	Crouch (2)	21,782	
09/12/00	A Blackburn D 0-0	League		16,886	
16/12/00	H Notts Forest W 1-0	League	Crouch	14,409	
23/12/00	A Birmingham D 0-0	League		24,311	
26/12/00	H Norwich City L 2-3	League	Carlisle, Wardley	12,338	# 146
30/12/00	H Crystal Palace D 1-1	League	Crouch	14,439	
06/01/01	A Luton Town D 3-3	FA Cup	Crouch (2), Peacock (p)	8,677	
13/01/01	H WBA W 2-0	League	Plummer, Koejoe	11,881	
17/01/01	H Luton Town W 2-1*	FA Cup	Kiwomya (2)	14,395	
20/01/01	A Norwich City L 0-1	League		16,472	
27/01/01	H Arsenal L 0-6	FA Cup		19,003	# 147
03/02/01	H Bolton D 1-1	League	Ngonge	10,293	
10/02/01	A Preston L 0-5	League		9,446	
17/02/01	H Barnsley W 2-0	League	Kiwomya, Crouch	9,388	# 148
20/02/01	A Gillingham W 1-0	League	Kiwomya	10,432	
24/02/01	A Wimbledon L 0-5	League		9,446	
03/03/01	H Sheffield Utd L 1-3	League	Ngonge	11,024	
07/03/01	H Watford D 1-1	League	Ngonge (p)	12,436	
10/03/01	A Fulham L 0-2	League		16,021	
17/03/01	H Grimsby Town L 0-1	League		17,608	# 149
24/03/01	A Burnley L 1-2	League	Bignot	14,018	
31/03/01	A Notts Forest D 1-1	League	Wardley	22,208	
07/04/01	H Blackburn L 1-3	League	Plummer	12,449	
10/04/01	A Crewe D 2-2	League	Crouch, Thomson	6,354	
14/04/01	A Portsmoouth D 1-1	League	Thomson	13,426	
16/04/01	H Tranmere W 2-0	League	Thomson, Crouch	9,696	# 150
21/04/01	A Huddersfield L 1-2	League	Thomson	12,846	
28/04/01	H Stockport Cty L 0-3	League		10,608	
06/05/01	A Wolves D 1-1	League	Bruce	17,447	

* AET

League Record - P46 W7 D19 L20 F45 A75 Pts 40. League position – 23rd

In The Loft Player of the Season – Peter Crouch

Facts and figures

Such were the quality of some of the goals scored by QPR during the 1996/97 season, Sky's 'Soccer AM' broadcast a '20 best QPR goals of the season' feature. Daniele Dichio's goal at Wolves won Sky Sports goal of the season, whilst Trevor Sinclair's overhead kick won the BBC goal of the season.

QPR found the net in 21 consecutive away games starting with the 2-1 defeat at Norwich City on 26th December 1999. The run came to an end after the 0-0 draw at Blackburn Rovers on 9th December 2000.

After making his debut against San Marino in 1993, Les Ferdinand went on to make 17 appearance for England, scoring 5 goals. Though he never took a penalty during his club career, his very last kick of a ball in an England shirt was in a penalty shoot-out after a 1-1 draw against Belgium in the King Hassan II International Cup tournament in Morocco, prior to the 1998 World Cup. Ferdinand's shot was saved by goalkeeper Philippe Van der Walle.

The crowd of 62,539 for the League Cup fourth round tie at Old Trafford on 11th November 2008 was the biggest ever to witness a QPR game that did not involve a major final.

The 0-0 draw at Selhurst Park on 29th November 2008 saw Crystal Palace line up in all-white, and QPR in all-black – a rarity in football and a first for QPR.

Carl Leaburn boasts the shortest ever career in a QPR shirt – precisely three minutes as a substitute in the 1-0 defeat at Reading on 5th January 2002.

The Football League deemed it fit for clubs to play games on consecutive days during the 1987/88 season. On January 1st QPR beat Southampton 3-0 at Loftus Road, then on January 2nd drew 0-0 at Arsenal. 10 of the 11 players started both games – an unthinkable situation on both counts in this day and age.

Shabazz Baidoo, currently with Croydon Athletic, is also a wannabe hip-hop artist, calling himself Grime MC; Terminator. Well known for his creative lyrics and sluggish flow (so says Wikipedia), one particular ditty glorifying knife crime is in particular bad taste. Most of his material seems to involve stuff he'd like to do to other people's mums.

Nigel Quashie made his first debut for QPR on 30th December 1995, and his second debut after re-joining the club from West Ham, on 26th January 2010 – a gap of over 14 years, the longest by some considerable distance for players who have had more than one spell with QPR. Quashie made his international debut for Scotland in 2004 –

only the second black player to represent the country (the other was in 1881). Berti Vogts said of him at the time, "Nigel is a fantastic player and a real leader on the pitch. He feels so Scottish and that's great."

Tony Roberts made his professional debut for QPR in 1987. 23 years later he is still going strong at Dagenham & Redbridge, for whom he has made over 400 appearances. Roberts played for Dagenham & Redbridge in an LDV Trophy 2nd round game at QPR in 2003 – when he was goalkeeping coach at QPR. He holds the record for the only goalkeeper ever to be sent off in the FA Cup in the opposing area when he was red carded late on after a clash with Peter Clarke during a 5–2 defeat to Southend United in the 3rd round of the FA Cup on 5th January 2008.

Lakshmi Mittal, now the largest shareholder at QPR, is reportedly worth £19.3bn – the richest man in football, the richest man in Europe and the fifth richest man in the world. He lives in Kensington Palace Gardens in what was once the world's most expensive house, next door to the Sultan of Brunei. Having allegedly spent £30m on his daughter's wedding in 2004, and £16m of the £19.1m cost towards the 'ArcelorMittal Orbit' observation tower being built at the Olympic Park in Stratford, would it be too much to ask for new toilets in the Ellerslie Road stand?

Gavin Peacock spent five years as a BBC football pundit after retiring in 2003, before relocating to Canada to study Theology with a view to becoming a Christian minister. "When you score a goal you never feel more alive," he says. "But that's just a momentary high, it's not reality. It's not the truth, it's just a glimpse of something. In the big picture my reality is my walk with God and it's eternal and everlasting."

They came back to haunt us…
Something of a trend started in the 1990s – former players always seemed to score on their return to Loftus Road. Not just a few, but just about all of them…

1996/97 – QPR 1-2 Charlton Athletic – Bradley Allen
1998/99 – QPR 3-2 Port Vale – Simon Barker
1998/99 – QPR 1-2 Swindon Town – Alan McDonald (well, as good as!)
1999/00 – QPR 1-2 Cardiff City (LC) – Matthew Brazier
1999/00 – QPR 1-1 Nottingham Forest – Nigel Quashie
2000/01 – QPR 1-1 Huddersfield Town – Kevin Gallen
2003/04 – QPR 2-1 Daggenham & Redbridge (LDV) – Tony Scully
2003/04 – QPR 1-1 Oldham Athletic – Paul Murray

Picture credits

Pages 56, 57, 175, 246, 313 – © Getty Images

Pages 116, 248 & front cover – © Action Images

Pages 177, 247, 314, 315 – © Associated Sports Photography

Pages 174 – © In The Loft